Scripts and Communication for Relationships

This book is part of the Peter Lang Media and Communication list.
Every volume is peer reviewed and meets
the highest quality standards for content and production.

PETER LANG
New York • Bern • Frankfurt • Berlin
Brussels • Vienna • Oxford • Warsaw

James M. Honeycutt and Pavica Sheldon

Scripts and Communication
for Relationships

SECOND EDITION

PETER LANG
New York • Bern • Frankfurt • Berlin
Brussels • Vienna • Oxford • Warsaw

Library of Congress Cataloging-in-Publication Data

Names: Honeycutt, James M., author. | Sheldon, Pavica, author.
Honeycutt, James M. Scripts and communication for relationships.
Title: Scripts and communication for relationships /
James M. Honeycutt and Pavica Sheldon.
Description: 2nd edition | New York: Peter Lang
Revised edition of Scripts and communication for relationships, c2011.
Includes bibliographical references and index.
Identifiers: LCCN 2017019787 | ISBN 978-1-4331-4217-8 (paperback: alk. paper)
ISBN 978-1-4331-4263-5 (ebook pdf)
ISBN 978-1-4331-4264-2 (epub) | ISBN 978-1-4331-4265-9 (mobi)
Subjects: LCSH: Interpersonal relations.
Couples.
Interpersonal communication.
Intimacy (Psychology).
Interpersonal conflict.
Classification: LCC HM1166 .H66 | DDC 302—dc23
LC record available at https://lccn.loc.gov/2017019787
DOI 10.3726/b11028

Bibliographic information published by **Die Deutsche Nationalbibliothek.**
Die Deutsche Nationalbibliothek lists this publication in the "Deutsche
Nationalbibliografie"; detailed bibliographic data are available
on the Internet at http://dnb.d-nb.de/.

This book is dedicated to the love of my life, my wife, Elizabeth and Abby. We have similar scripts for the development and maintenance of relationships including the soulmate and work-it-out theories which are not mutually exclusive. Communication, humor, and spirit in relationships are a wise investment; not taken for granted.

JMH

This book is dedicated to my husband and best friend, Luke. He has provided continued support and love throughout the writing of the book. Our marriage reflects the "matching hypothesis," as we have similar values and interests.

PS

Table of Contents

Acknowledgments   xiii

Chapter One: The Pursuit of Intimacy and Relational Scripts   1
    Fatal Attraction   6
    Symbolic Interdependence in Relationships   9
    Matching Hypothesis: Birds of a Feather Flock Together   11
    Interpersonal Attraction   11
        Ratings of Physical Attractiveness   14
    A Brief Introduction to Relational Scripts   15
    Summary   17
    Discussion Questions   17
    Applications   18
    References   18

Part One: Emotions, Imagination, and Physiology of Relationships   23
Chapter Two: Emotion and Cognition About Relationships   25
    Characteristics of Happiness   26
    Representation of Affect According to Cognitive Theories of Emotion   27
    Differences Among Emotions, Moods, and Affect   29
    Similarities and Differences Among Love, Hate, Anger, and Jealousy   32

Prototypes of Anger in Relationships   35
Types of Anger   36
Scripts for Anger   37
Emotional Scripts for Relationships   38
Communication and the Sentiment-Override Hypothesis   39
Emotions and Social Media Relationships   43
Summary   45
Discussion Questions   46
Applications   46
References   47

Chapter Three: Generating and Maintaining Relationships Through
Imagined Interactions   52
Creating Relationship Scripts Through
Imagined Interactions   52
Main Features of Imagined Interaction Theory   53
Third-Party IIs   56
Relational Maintenance Function of Imagined Interactions   57
Imagined Interactions with Ex-partners   60
Comparisons Between Friends and Friends with Benefits   61
Imagined Interactions and Social Isolation: Parasocial Relationships   61
Affect and Imagined Interactions   63
Use of Imagined Interactions in Linking Together Prior Conversations   64
Gender Differences in Imagined Interactions and Memory   67
Imagined Interactions in Marriage   69
Imagined Interactions Among Engaged and
Married Couples   70
Imagined Interactions in Virtual Relationships   72
Summary   73
Discussion Questions   74
Applications   74
References   75

Chapter Four: Physiology and Relationships   79
Communibiology Assumptions   79
Imagined Interactions (IIs) Conflict-Linkage Theory   80
Why Study Physiology in Relationships?   82
Common Physiological Measures of Arousal   83
Oxytocin and the Physiological Development of Love   85
Cortisol and Stress in Relationships   86
Diffuse Physiological Arousal in Couples   89
A Physiological Script for Relational Deterioration   93

Study of the Impact of Imagined Interactions and Arguing Among
Couples on Heart Rate   99
   Procedure   99
Case Study of a Couple Discussing Pleasing and Displeasing Topics   102
   Agenda Initiation   102
Summary   106
Discussion Questions   107
Applications   107
Notes   108
References   108

Part Two: Bases of Relational Scripts   113
Chapter Five: Schemata, Scenes, and Scripts for Relationships   115
   Sex Differences in Interpreting Flirtatious Signs   116
   A Comparison of Memory with the
   Organization of a Computer   117
   Schemata   118
      Relational Schemata   118
   Scenes   121
   Scripts   122
      Mindlessness Versus Mindfulness   124
      Initial Interaction Scripts   126
      Scripts for Dating   128
      Sequences of Dating Behavior   129
      Sequence-Grouping in Dating Behavior   130
      Sexual Scripts   131
      Sex with Androids   134
      Hooking Up   134
      Friends with Benefits   136
      Online Relationship Scripts   136
      Cultural Scripts and Performances for Sex   137
      Changes in Interactive Scripts   138
   Summary   141
   Discussion Questions   141
   Applications   142
   References   142
Chapter Six: Development of Relationships: Stage Theories and
Relational Script Theory   147
   Developmental Models of Relationships   148
   Criticisms of Developmental Models   153

Relational Dialectic Models   157
Criticisms of Relational Dialectic Models   160
Social Cognition: The Script Approach   161
Gender Differences in Intimate-Relationship Scripts   162
Summary   166
Discussion Questions   167
Applications   167
References   167

Part Three: Relational Escalation and Deescalation   173
Chapter Seven: Scripts for Romantic Development and Decline   175
Redundancy and the Complexity of Romantic Scripts   176
Content of Romantic Scripts   179
Deescalating Script   183
Inferences Associated with Relationship Decay   185
Typicality Versus Necessity in Predicting Beliefs About Relational
Development   186
Predicting Beliefs About Relational Decay   189
Underlying Dimensions of Relational Development and Decline   191
Card-Sorting Experiment for Escalating and Deescalating Actions   192
Story-Segmentation Analysis   195
Gender Differences in Generating and Processing Scripts   200
Scripts for Friendships Compared with FWBs   204
Summary   205
Discussion Questions   206
Applications   206
References   207
Chapter Eight: Semantics of Break-ups   211
Linguistic Codes of Omissions and Commissions   212
Semantic Codes of Action   212
An Attributional Explanation   212
An Implicit Benefit-of-the-Doubt Explanation   214
A Rules-Based Explanation   216
Gender Differences in Omissions and Commissions   219
Summary   220
Discussion Questions   220
Applications   221
Note   221
References   221

Part Four: Relationship Scripts in Context   223

Chapter Nine: Online Communication and Relational Scripts   225
    Cues-Filtered Out Theories and Computer-Mediated
    Communication   225
    Online Relationships Development   226
        Uncertainty Reduction Theory   227
        Social Penetration Theory   228
        Hyperpersonal Perspective   229
    Changing Nature of Friendships   230
    Romantic Relationships Online   232
        Tinder   233
    Who Forms Online Relationships?   234
    Attitudes Toward Online Relationships   237
    Summary   238
    Discussion Questions   238
    Applications   239
    References   239

Chapter Ten: Scripts for Office Romance: Approved or Forbidden?   245
    Proximity Theory and the Formation of Relationships   248
    When Mentoring Scripts Include Romance   249
    Gender Scripts in Office Romances   251
    Hierarchy Differences   252
    Sexual Harassment Scripts   254
    Same-Sex Sexual Harassment   258
    Intercultural Differences   259
    Summary   260
    Discussion Questions   261
    Application   261
    References   262

Part Five: Cautions and Recommendations   267

Chapter Eleven: Dysfunctional Scripts for Abusive Relationships   269
    Conflict Tactics and Types of Abuse   270
    Cycle of Abuse   273
    Stalking   274
    Gender Differences in Relational Abuse   276
    Signal Detection Theory and the Ability to Notice Escalating
    Conflict   278
    Verbal Aggression, Arguing, and Physical Coercion   281

Imagined Interactions and Verbal Aggression in
Predicting Physical Coercion 283
Pit-Bull and Cobra Batterers 288
Summary 290
Discussion Questions 291
Applications 291
References 291
Chapter Twelve: The Dark Side of Social Media Communication 298
Mechanization, Attention Deficit, and Addiction 298
Selective Self-Presentation and Narcissism 302
Declining Quality of Interpersonal Relationships 304
Privacy and Security 306
Cyberbullying 307
Cyberstalking 310
Misinformation and Deception on Social Media 311
Summary 312
Discussion Questions 313
Applications 313
References 313
Chapter Thirteen: Scripts for Constructive Communication 323
Communication Competence 324
Communication Behaviors Leading to Breakup or Divorce 325
Conflict Tactics 327
Rules for Arguing 328
An Acronym for Effective Communication Tips: Listen
Observe (or Oxytocin) Verify (or Validate) Express 330
Biofeedback to Reduce Stress 333
Linguistic Cues Signifying a Happy Relationship 335
Tests of Grievances and Arguing Behaviors 336
Summary 339
Discussion Questions 340
Application 340
References 340

Author Index 345
Subject Index 363

Acknowledgments

We wish to acknowledge our motivated students in our relational communication classes for their vibrant and energetic opinions on relationship development. We continue to have inspiring and lively discussions over gender similarities and diversity in attending to relationship processes. Human beings including hermits to a degree are social creatures. General systems theory has always indicated through the concept of "holism" how collaboration and strength in numbers overcome isolationism. Couples live longer than single people and insurance companies know this by the amount that you pay for your insurance policy as a single or a couple. We would also like to thank the couples over the years who have participated in various interaction, physiological, and psychological studies at LSU. We also thank Jonathan Frost for providing valuable research assistance in the MatchBox Interaction Lab at LSU.

CHAPTER ONE

The Pursuit of Intimacy and Relational Scripts

Relationship diversity is a popular term that captures the wide array of relationships that exist. Relationships can be characterized among multiple dimensions including intimacy which is a basic human need just as we have physiological needs (e.g., food). Indeed, feeling connected to others along with a sense of autonomy and competence has been identified as a basic human psychological need (Deci & Ryan, 2012). A simple continuum of intimacy ranging from superficial to intense intimacy could be strangers, acquaintances, casual friendships, close friendships, best friends, and intimates. Other relationships that can fall anywhere on the intimacy continuum are online and social media liaisons, relations with pets (e.g., some people are afraid of certain pets due to their experiences), your relationships with characters in various forms of multiplayer online games (e.g., World of Warcraft, League of Legends), imaginary companions or parasocial relationships, supervisor–subordinate, mentor–mentee, coach–player, teacher–student, business provider–client, etc.

Classic pioneering research indicates that all human relationships can be classified among four bipolar dimensions: cooperative/friendly versus competitive/hostile, equal versus unequal, intense versus superficial, and socioemotional/informal versus task-oriented/formal (Wish, Deutsch, & Kaplan, 1976). Hence, your relationship with a given coworker may be formal, superficial, unequal (e.g., he or she gives orders), and hostile; you can easily think of someone in your social network where the relationship is cooperative, equal, intense, and informal (e.g., a romantic romantic).

Over 200 years ago, Jane Austen, an astute observer of the rituals of late 18th-century courtship, wrote rather pragmatically that a happy marriage was the result of chance (Austen & Shapard, 2012). With due respect to Miss Austen, modern relationship researchers have revealed that scripts concerning pair bonding rituals are constituted in a manner so as to leave *little* to chance when romantic attachments are formed, intensify, and sometimes dissolve. According to Consumer Rankings, the five highest ranked web sites for meeting people were Zoosk, Match.com, Our Time, e-harmony, and Elite Single (consumer-rankings. com, 2016). Other popular sites are kindle and a host of specialized sites for various groups including seniors, gay, lesbian, and Christians.

This sorting process is exemplified by the classic stimulus-value-role (SVR) theory of Murstein (1987) who suggested that courtship begins as a simple exchange of information involving initial impressions of physical attributes followed by an interpretation of values, attitudes, and beliefs about a variety of topics that are of interest to each potential partner (*cf.*, Reis & Sprecher, 2009). Recall the cliché that you cannot judge a book by its cover. However, you can often tell if the book is an encyclopedia, comic, or novel. People tend to be right two-thirds of the time in judging personality impressions of strangers based on appearance.

Indeed, this is referred to as "thin slices" which refers to a brief observation that leads to accurate judgments about others (Lambert, Mulder, & Fincham, 2014). Indeed, people watching short clips of others who were simply giving instructions on how to draw an object were able to accurately judge which persons had engaged in infidelity in the past. The researcher asked each participant to describe their current romantic relationship and if they had been intimate with another person outside of that relationship. Voice pitch may have influenced infidelity perceptions since O'Connor, Re, and Feinberg (2011) found that voice pitch influences perceptions of infidelity.

Research reveals that the sound of a person's voice communicates a great deal of biologically and socially important information to potential mates (Hughes, Farley, & Rhodes, 2010). Voices of those with greater bilateral body symmetry which past Miss America contestants have had are rated as sounding more attractive than those with less symmetrical features and body symmetry has been shown to be a marker of developmental fitness (Baumeister, 2005; Hughes et al., 2010). More attractive voices are associated with positive personality traits including warmth, likability, honesty, and achievement while both sexes lower the pitch of their voices when communicating with more attractive people (Hughes et al., 2010).

Once a similarity is noted, the individuals are categorized and assigned to possible roles such as business acquaintance, tennis partner, best friend, potential lover. While this simple model has been criticized, it is noted that the typical sequence is SVR. However, a person could begin a relationship with another in the role stage such as mother–infant which is designated at birth or adoption. Further communication and ritualized behavior provide additional information about the partners' abilities to function in additional roles in preparation for potential roles as mates or parents. This chapter introduces the concepts of relational schemata and the scripts that evolve from them including the changes that have occurred in the manner in which relationships are perceived and enacted.

The concept of interpersonal intimacy in its current form began evolving in 19th-century America and Europe, with the development of industrial society. More recently, in the computerized information society, the emphasis has shifted more to the individual as a reaction to the impersonalization of factory and business life. This trend continued and accelerated as the world approached the 21st century because of the migration to urban environments: in 1905 the percentage of the world's population living in cities was 15%; a hundred years later, almost 50% of the citizens of our planet live in urban environments (Acedevo, 2005). In urban society, individuals often gain their primary identity and psychosocial support from personal relationships rather than from their roles in the community since these roles may be unknown or more fluid. The change in scripts for relationships has extended beyond the United States and western society. For example, research in India reveals that while arranged marriages are still relatively common, the prospective bride's preferences guide the process in a much more definitive manner than her mother or grandmothers did when partners were selected for them with idea of marrying up in terms of status and economic resources (Banerjee, Duflo, Ghatak, & Lafortune, 2013). Interestingly, marital satisfaction expressed by partners in arranged marriages appears to be very similar to the level of satisfaction expressed in western cultures where individuals select their own partners. However, couples from India in arranged marriages scored higher on spirituality, nutrition, and cultural identity while Americans scored higher on realistic beliefs and work, sense of humor, and self-care (Myers, Madathil, & Tingle, 2005). In terms of the last factor on self-care, the American cultural script stresses individuality, competition, and self-reliance.

Individuals now develop relationships in cyberspace through the use of dating web sites for singles and divorcees, and correspondence with others through social networking sites. Individuals increasingly work at home due to satellite technology on their smartphones, tablets, and computers which actually parallels working out of the home in the 19th century before the Industrial Revolution, which preceded the information revolution in the late 20th and this century. Indeed, the Industrial Revolution, which took place from the 18th to 19th centuries, was a period during which predominantly agrarian, rural societies in Europe and America became industrial and moved from isolated rural areas to metropolitan cities. Prior to the Industrial Revolution, which began in Britain in the late 1700s, manufacturing was often done in people's homes, using hand tools or basic machines.

Working out of the home is a return to the pattern in colonial times when the business was the home, in the form of farms and shops attached to living quarters. Yet, the proliferation of computers decreases face-to-face interaction as web sites are accessed to find and track individuals with similar interests so they can be harnessed as consumers of goods. For example, have you noticed how Facebook tracks where you visit and then transmits advertisements to you when you log on. Relatedly, online dating services such as Tinder and match.com report a thriving business and suggest that couples matched through their services enjoy better quality relationships than individuals who select their own partners in more conventional ways. Facebook and Instagram exist as virtual networking sites allowing users to "friend" someone with whom they have never had any face-to-face interaction while easily allowing the use of ghosting and unfriending people with no explanation required. Yet as Bruno (2007) described a number of years ago, "Facebook might well be changing the nature of relationships, making them both more intrusive and yet somehow less intimate at the same time" (p. 9).

Only time will tell if courtships will develop through computer contact, as they have evolved in face-to-face communication. According to evolutionary psychologists, these rituals of courtship are learned, defined, and expressed in the context of society and culture because of biological drives for procreation. For example, Fisher (1994) discussed how biochemical processes contribute to the development of romance. Human brain chemistry creates a heightened sense of excitement that people often describe as falling in love or infatuation. Fisher further suggested that the brain physiology and chemistry associated with bonding evolved as part of the human primordial mating system.

According to the self-expansion model, people have a fundamental motive to expand their sense of self that is primarily achieved through the formation of close relationships. Hence, research has revealed that romantic love remains steady and that obsessive love shows a steady decrease as a function of aging rather than time spent in the relationship (Sheets, 2014). Additionally, Fisher's cross-cultural research reveals that in societies allowing divorce the most common length of marriage is 4 years. This length of time conforms to the traditional period between successive human births. Fisher proposed that this 4-year cycle is a pattern that evolved as a reproductive strategy to successfully raise a helpless infant. That is, she believes that couples remain partners for the length of time it took for an infant to become somewhat able to fend for himself. When our distant ancestors began to walk upright, infants had to be carried, thus precluding the caretaker from effectively foraging or defending herself. In order for the infant to survive and the genetic material inherited from its parents to be transmitted to future generations, it had to be protected, a task that took two individuals; however, when the infant became able to forage and walk herself (approximately four years), the necessity of having a pair bond dissolved.

In addition to human brain physiology, part of the reason for failed relationships is that the stability of contemporary relationships is contingent on positive emotions as the glue for relationship bonding and the reason for a relationship to continue. Commitment to a relationship depends on the ebb and flow of levels of intimacy. However, such has not always been the case in most of the western world. In earlier agrarian societies, a large family was essential to provide farm labor. Infant mortality was high, so women were encouraged to have many children with the hope that some offspring would survive past infancy. Consequently, mates were chosen with great care for their potential as partners and parents, and were assessed and tested for their compatibility through the ritualized stages of courtship. During the colonial period in the 18th century, intimacy was, at best, the result of the formal relationship rather than the cause of the romantic bond or marriage (Gadlin, 1977). Individuals were admonished to be faithful partners even though physical assaults were common. Only later did affection become both the cause and cement of marriage.

For most of the 20th century, cultural scripts included the idea of women marrying up. That means marrying a man who was 2–3 years older and who had a higher income level in order to provide a secure base for offspring. Additionally, there is the earlier sexual maturation of females as well as male delay in achieving stable levels of emotional maturity. Yet, this has changed since 2007 with men marrying up. According to the Pew Research Center, economic gains from marriage have been greater for men than for women in recent years (Fry & Cohn, 2010). With more women attending college and entering the workforce, they are more likely to marry men who have less education and earn less money, showing a reversal from times when fewer women worked outside the home. Only 4% of husbands had wives who brought home more income than they did in 1970, a share that rose to 38% in 2015.

Marriage rates have declined for all adults since 1970 and gone down most sharply for the least educated men and women (Fry & Cohn, 2010). As a result, those with more education are far more likely than those with less education to be married, a gap that has widened since 1970. Because higher education tends to lead to higher earnings, these compositional changes have bolstered the economic gains from being married for both men and women.

In the 20th century, affection was eroticized, although seen as fleeting and unstable. Stephen (1994) discussed how people think of marriage as a status that symbolizes mutual affection. Affection is necessary for marriage, whereas its erosion is a sufficient reason for divorce. However, Lewis and Spanier (1982) explored temporary high-quality (i.e., high-affection), low-stability marriages that ended in divorce and cited examples of dual-career couples who, after having to relocate in different cities in order to pursue each partner's career, eventually terminated their relationships. Is something more than simple affection necessary here?

According to Stephen (1994), some other possible causes of divorce are living in a pluralistic society that is saturated with diverse information, lifestyle choices, political interests, and religious values. For example, Cameron and Quinn (2006) note that one week-day edition of any major newspaper contains more information than an individual in the 18th century was exposed to in his/her entire lifetime. This plethora of information extends to relationships as well, providing a variety of possible scripts for initiating, maintaining, and dissolving relationships. People *construct* their realities from diverse sets of resources.

Fatal Attraction

Some people have a relationship script that involves being drawn to a quality or behavior that while initially attractive, ultimately proves dissatisfying. Fatal attraction occurs when two people drawn to each other romantically become involved in a relationship, but over time discover annoying or disturbing aspects of the other's behavior or personality (Felmlee, 1995). There is a link between the seemingly disparate processes of romantic attraction and disenchantment. Consider a moth attracted to a flame. This research indicates that the sequence begins with attraction to a quality exhibited by a partner and ends in disillusionment with that quality.

In previous work on fatal attraction, individuals recalled their most recent romantic relationships that had ended and described qualities that initially attracted them to their former partners and the characteristics they later disliked (Felmlee, 1995). Specifically, this research shows 33% of the participants themselves identify similarities between attracting and disliked partner characteristics. The three most common types of attractors were physicality, fun, and caring; qualities they didn't like were selfishness, insecurity, and undependability.

The qualities that attract two individuals sometimes become complaints if the relationship starts to sour (Felmlee, 1995). "At first, I thought he was carefree and laid-back. Now, he is indecisive and irresponsible." This process in which individuals change their evaluations of each other after a time, as opposed to persevering in their initial impressions, is known as cognitive accommodation. Box 1.1 contains sample cognitive beliefs about the qualities that first attract couples to each other that could be restructured later into negative attributes.

Box 1.1. Cognitive Reframing: Sample Attractions in Couples That Later Evolved into Relationship Complaints

Initial Attribute of Attraction	Evolved Complaint
1. Direct; intelligent	Unfairly critical; given to outbursts
2. Easygoing; laid-back	Self-absorbed and indulgent
3. Independent; strong	Has to have own way; selfish
4. Self-confident	Doesn't respect my wishes and withholds
5. Prudent, wise, and practical	Calm demeanor drives me nuts
6. Masculine; strong	Abusive; we fight
7. Feminine; warm	Hysterical; we fight
8. Good listener	Doesn't have own opinion
9. Exciting and likes to talk	Restless and doesn't let me relax
10. I am the center of his world	Despicably insecure
11. Open-minded and accepting	Doesn't give without being asked; no initiation
12. There's a mystery about her/him	No true intimacy; not completely there
13. Very smart and capable	Makes me feel stupid and incompetent

Another study by Felmlee (2001) found that 44% of the participants who were surveyed reported a fatal attraction in a prior or current relationship. Felmlee (1998) also has found that individuals who stated that the quality that attracted them to their partner was "dissimilarity" were more likely than those with other types of attractions to really dismiss that particular attracting characteristic.

Three possible explanations accounting for fatal attraction are given. (1) People's virtues and vices are one and the same (Goldberg, 1993). (2) Some individuals are drawn to characteristics in another that exemplify one dimension of these opposing forces, but they find the relationship lacks the corresponding dimension. (3) The individuals need to sustain confidence in the belief that they are in the right relationship with the right person and that they will use various cognitive tactics to maintain satisfaction and commitment. However, presumably once a relationship has ended, the motivation of weakness is removed and the faults once transformed into virtues are now seen as vices.

Today, each individual's sense of uniqueness permeates his or her views of the characteristics of an ideal relationship. This is especially true in our individualistic Western society. Research by Wish et al. (1976) revealed that individuals distinguish communication behaviors (e. g., cooperative versus competitive) among relatively few dimensions that are used to distinguish almost all types of relationships (e.g., personal enemies, husband/wife). In addition, people make different distinctions in their own relationships than in typical or other people's relationships. For example, cooperation is more important for evaluating typical relationships than for evaluating their own relationships. In evaluating their own relationships, individuals mention fewer hostile relations (e.g., one's relationship with a lover is mentioned more often than one's relationship with a bitter enemy). Hostile relations (e.g., business rivals, political opponents, guard/prisoner, supervisor/employee, and interviewer/applicant) are perceived as characterizing other people's relationships. In essence, people select highly positive relational attributes to construct seemingly ideal life spaces in which they live, learn, and love.

Another relatively recent evolution in romantic relationships is the tendency to distinguish between long-term and short-term relationships, each having a distinct set of scripts. While at one time, courting was considered a prelude to the formation of a relationship for life, at present, there appear to be criteria and scripts for two distinct types of relationships: those that may evolve into a long-term commitment and those considered short term only. Stewart, Stinnett, and Rosenfeld (2000) suggest that while there may be gender differences in heterosexual couple's expectations regarding partner selection, both men and women listed different attributes for long-term versus short-term romantic partners. In regard to short-term relational partners, women rated good earning capacity, dependability, sense of humor, and ambition most important; men rated physical attractiveness and good heredity most important. In long-term relationships, women rated kindness/understanding and ambition as important; men rated physical attractiveness and adaptability as more important for long-term relationships. Buunk, Dijkstra, Fetchenhaur, and Kenrick (2002) reported that men valued intelligence in a longer term relationship and physical attractiveness in the short term, while women valued education more in long-term relationships.

Each individual's construction of reality is based on experiences which also affect beliefs about the development and decline of romantic relationships. Individuals vary in their expectations of how relationships should develop due to the variety of informational sources that form the foundation for their expectations. In this regard, Staines and Libby (1986) discussed predictive romantic expectations, which are beliefs about behaviors that are expected to occur in a romantic role regardless of one's desires. Thus, a person who has been spurned before may be more likely to expect this to happen in future relationships than is someone who has not been rejected.

Staines and Libby (1986) have investigated these idealistic romantic expectations or beliefs reflecting an individual's desires of what should ideally happen in the role of a lover or spouse. Perhaps not surprisingly, women report more discrepancies between prescriptive and predictive expectations than men do. A common complaint is that wives prefer their husbands to do more household cleaning even though they don't expect that it will happen. Consequently, women often report lower levels of marital happiness than their husbands (Gottman, 2011). Broughton and Van Acker (2007) discovered romantic expectations of marriage and motherhood can have deleterious consequences for low-income women whose early life choices preclude furthering their education. That is, the discourse of romance was a significant factor that influenced their early life choices. Expectations not met resulted in failed marriages requiring these women to reevaluate their aspirations.

Nonetheless, even in an age of too-often-failed expectations, women and men meet, fall in love, and some even live happily ever after. Why? Symbolic interdependence provides an answer to this question.

Symbolic Interdependence in Relationships

Long-term relationships provide continuity and confirmation for idiosyncratic beliefs and protection from doubt, loneliness, and ambiguity. We tend to be attracted to those who reinforce our attitudes and beliefs. Hence, we are more attracted to those who agree with us rather than constantly challenging our views. Social homogamy refers to "passive, indirect effects on spousal similarity" (Watson et al., 2004, p. 1034). The result showed that age and education level are crucial in affecting the mate preference. While there are exceptions expressed in slang language, that is, "cougar," or "gold-digger," many people are attracted to someone with similar ages who go to their school because of the frequency of face-to-face communication beyond text messaging and Facebook interactions.

Stephen (1994) discussed the idea of individuals sharing conceptions of relationships in terms of symbolic interdependence. This is a type of mental sharing in which individuals share similar beliefs about the world: relational partners react to events in similar ways and derive similar conclusions from information. Furthermore, Honeycutt (2009) has found that symbolic interdependence predicts a quality relationship. He tested this among randomly paired strangers, casual dating, engaged, and married couples. He correlated the scores on the Relationship Worldview Inventory from Stephen and Markman (1983), which is a survey asking individuals what they value in a relationship. Sample items include "Being in a relationship can provide purpose for one's own life. One has to make great efforts to get the most from a relationship." The higher the correlation, the more individuals agree on underlying relational values. The idea is that individuals may bring these values into the relationship or actively communicate about them as a joint couple's identity is created. Engaged couples had the highest level of symbolic interdependence ($r = .50$) followed by married and dating couples, with random couples demonstrating the least interdependence ($r < .18$). There were significant differences between engaged couples and the others. Part of this explanation has to do with the fact that engaged couples are in a "honeymoon" phase (pun intended) where assumed agreement is higher and individual differences of opinion are ignored or glossed over. Married couples show slightly lower agreement.

Stephen (1994) found that it is not that the self has found another who can penetrate the self, but that both self and another have refashioned themselves (and indeed the rest of their world) through the dialogue of their relationship until they are possessed of a type of self consistent with the relationship worldview. The couple creates an interpretive framework and at the same time reinterprets themselves within it. Needless to say, persistently deviant interpretations will be regarded as problematic and effort is likely to be expended in smoothing discrepancies.

These discrepancies can be seen as relational conflicts about behaviors, attitudes, and appropriate performance of romantic roles. If the smoothing does not resolve the discrepancies, the relationship may dissolve. More importantly, the smoothing strategies go into memory and act as a repository of information that may be opened for subsequent relationships. Thus, happy long-term relationships are enhanced when individuals have a shared social reality and relationship worldview. The partners share similar expectations about what constitutes relationship development and those qualities that characterize a satisfying relationship. The sharing of expectations reflects evolving stories that individuals construct as they communicate with each other. Yet the mere sharing of expectations and predictions is not enough; the intimate conversations between romantic partners do not get lodged in memory in some pure form. Rather the discourse becomes embedded in some form of preexisting mental script that can allow prospective partners to separate out irrelevant data, mill the appropriate associations between actions and intents, and forge a stable, shared relational worldview. Thus, relational schemata serve as scripts that organize relevant information and, ultimately, test the tensile strength of any romance.

Symbolic interdependence is based on the idea that individuals share a similarity of beliefs and views. However, the initial stimulus resides in a classic concept of "birds of a feather flocking together" rather than "opposites attracting." Indeed, research on the "matching hypothesis" is vast and reveals the power of individuals initially seeking out others that physically resemble themselves.

Matching Hypothesis: Birds of a Feather Flock Together

The matching hypothesis claims that people are more likely to form long-standing relationships with those who are equally physically attractive. They also look for similarity in hobbies, interests, and values over time. People with dissimilar looks do form and sustain relationships, but it takes longer because the communication about personality traits and motivation takes longer (Lewandowski, Aron, & Gee, 2007). The notion of "birds of a feather flock together" points out that similarity is a crucial determinant of interpersonal attraction. Similarity seems to carry considerable weight in initial attraction, while complementarity assumes importance as the relationship develops over time (Vinacke, Shannon, Palazzo, Balsavage, & Cooney, 1988). Furthermore, the idea of "opposites attract" appears more plausible if the areas of dissimilarity are not critical underlying values that are important to the relational partners. Hence, Gottman and Silver (2015) report how conflict-engagers, or those who like to argue, paired with conflict-avoiders have more relational problems and long-term incompatibility than symmetrical pairings of avoiders with avoiders and engagers with engagers. Similarly, couples who reported the highest level of loving and harmonious relationship were more dissimilar in dominance than couples who scored lower in relationship quality (Markey & Markey, 2007).

Interpersonal Attraction

Research on attraction has found that physical attractiveness and indicators of attachment anxiety and avoidance were related to the number of first dates, and the probability of entering into an exclusive relationship in an eight-month period (Poulsen, Holman, Busby, & Carroll, 2013). Moreover, people with similar levels of perceived attractiveness form relationships quicker while persons with dissimilar levels take longer to form sustained relationships. McCroskey and McCain (1974) initially conceptualized interpersonal attraction as a multidimensional construct. Prior research in this area suggested that interpersonal attraction was characterized by three distinct dimensions: (a) a liking or social dimension; (b) a task or respect dimension; and (c) a physical dimension. They concluded that perceptions of attraction were responsible for increased communication and interpersonal influence.

Each complete dimension offers unique characteristics that incorporate many other known types of attraction. Social attraction, or the liking dimension, is influenced by how much time we want to spend with another person. The second dimension, or task attraction, is known for the desire to want to work toward objectives with the other person, which is quite common in workplaces since socializing is usually required in order to work with others toward a goal. Finally, the last type of attraction or dimension is physical attraction. This is attraction based on the physical characteristics of the other person. Overall, the three dimensions are also known as the "Big 3" due to the ability for other types of attraction to be subsumed within them, therefore making it unlikely for any other type of attraction to occur without these three having an influence. Heterosexual, cross-cultural research indicates that men are subliminally looking for fertility cues in women and have a desire for women with a low waist-to-hip ratio, while women prefer men with a similar wait and hip size (Donohoe, von Hippel, & Brooks, 2009; Swami & Furnham, 2008).

A study of online dating involved the matching hypothesis (Shaw, Fiore, Mendelsohn, & Cheshire, 2011). The attractiveness of 60 males and 60 females was measured and their communication was monitored. The people with whom they interacted were then monitored to see who they interacted with, and returned messages to. They found that people contacted others who were significantly more attractive than they were; however, it was found that the person was more likely to reply if they were closer to the same level of attractiveness.

Studies have revealed that very attractive people flock together, while individuals lacking the perfect face and body also stick together. According to Morry's |attraction-similarity model (2007), there is a common belief that people with actual similarity produce initial attraction. People who lack looks place more stock in nonphysical features, such as sense of humor, than in physical beauty (Lee, Loewenstein, Ariely, Hong, & Young, 2007). However, the data also reveal that guys are less concerned with their own looks when deciding whom to date. So while a man might have no qualms about going after someone much better looking than he is, a woman will tend more to choose partners with compatible looks. Yet, for both men and women, physical attractiveness guides Cupid's arrow.

Lee and his colleagues (2007) analyzed an online dating web site called HOTorNOT.com, which was an influence on the founding of Facebook and YouTube. This site allowed members to rate others on their physical attractiveness. They analyzed how an individual's attractiveness rating affected how that person rated others' physical attractiveness on a scale from 1 to the hottest value of 10. Then, the researchers compared the average hot-or-not ratings for each person with the number of dating requests. On average, participants paired up with others having compatible attractiveness. Compared with the women, men were most influenced by physical attractiveness when requesting dates, but their own appearance ratings had less effect on their date choices. The study concluded that males were less affected by how attractive they themselves are compared to females. Men were more likely than women to request dates out of their league. Individuals who slid furthest down the hot-or-not scale seemed more desperate, as they were the most likely to respond "yes" to any date requests. For every unit decrease on the 10-point scale of the member's own attractiveness the member was 25% more likely to say "yes" to a potential date. The hot-rated members tended to accept only dates from others in their attractiveness neighborhood.

To understand how the physically lacking individuals cope with the cards they were dealt, Lee et al. (2007) conducted a follow-up speed-dating study. At an event sponsored by a Boston-based online dating company, 24 participants indicated how high they rated the relative importance of six criteria—physical attractiveness, intelligence, sense of humor, kindness, confidence, and extroversion—for selecting dates. The participants then chatted for four minutes with each potential date, after which they rated each other on physical attractiveness and decided whether to meet up again with that person. The data revealed that more attractive people placed more importance on physical attractiveness than other qualities in selecting their dates. Less attractive people placed more weight on other qualities, including sense of humor. Hence, it appears that people who are less attractive change their scripts for initial attraction by caring less about beauty and more about sense of humor.

A "hot" or "not" type of study, involving men and women who were exposed to pictures, revealed that the human brain determines whether an image is erotic long before the viewer is even aware they are seeing the picture (Anokhin et al., 2006). Moreover, the brain quickly classifies images into a hot or not type categorization. The study's researchers also discovered that sexy shots induce a uniquely powerful reaction in the brain, equal in effect for both men and women, and those erotic images produced a strong reaction in the hypothalamus.

Not only does the matching hypothesis explain desire in initial attraction, but it has been supported in studies of couples who have celebrated their silver anniversaries (25 years of marriage). Zajonc, Adelman, Murphy, and Niedenthal (1987) found that people who live with each other for a long period of time grow physically similar in their facial features. They had photographs of couples when they were first married and 25 years later. The photos were judged for physical similarity and for the likelihood that they were married. The results showed that there was indeed an increase in apparent similarity after 25 years of living together. In addition, an increase in resemblance was associated with greater reported marital happiness.

Possible explanations for this involve facial mimicry in which partners subliminally imitate the facial expressions of each other. Hence, if you live with a happy person, you are more likely to smile compared to living with a gloomy person. Emotional processes produce vascular changes that are, in part, regulated by facial muscles. The facial muscles act as ligatures on veins and arteries, and are able to divert blood from, or direct blood to, the brain. An implication of this process is that habitual use of facial musculature may permanently affect the physical features of the face. The implication holds further that two people who live with each other for a longer period of time, by virtue of repeated empathic mimicry, would grow physically similar in their facial features. Kin resemblance, therefore, may not be simply a matter of common genes but also a matter of prolonged social contact. Finally, research among women has revealed that women who enjoy good childhood relationships with their fathers were more likely to select partners who resemble their fathers, while women who had negative or less positive relationships were not attracted to men who looked like their fathers (Wiszewska, Pawlowski, & Boothroyd, 2007).

Ratings of Physical Attractiveness

Even as people age, they may hold positive illusions about a partner's physical attractiveness. Research reveals that the more newlyweds idealized each other, the less they reported decline of love over a thirteen-year period (Miller, Niehuis, & Huston, 2006). Individuals tend to rate their partner as more physically attractive than they rate themselves, which is referred to as "the love is blind bias" (Swami, Stieger, Haubner, Voracek, & Furnham, 2009). Other studies reveal that observer ratings of partners' physical attractiveness are associated with the couple's relational satisfaction (McNulty, Neff, & Karney, 2008) and dealing more constructively with relationship problems (Barelds & Dijkstra, 2009). However, it is interesting to note that both spouses behaved more positively if the wife was more attractive than the husband. Additionally, it has been reported that younger and older couples do not differ in the association between positive bodily attractiveness and relationship quality. There is the stereotype that physical attraction declines as the body ages. Barelds and Dijkstra (2009) found in a sample of Dutch married and cohabiting, heterosexual couples that with aging, positive facial attractiveness illusions were associated with self-reported relationship quality. They surmise that while young people may emphasize the beauty side of bodily attractiveness such as having a tight waist or large breasts, older people may define bodily attractiveness in terms of health or physical condition. As people age, facial attractiveness may be a more important characteristic in a mate because it reflects overall physical health.

In conclusion, the matching hypothesis studies have revealed that physical attraction is an initial filter cue by which undesirable people are quickly filtered.

Indeed, research reveals that initial impressions are formed within milliseconds of seeing someone, such that persons in speed dating or any social gathering quickly decide if they want to meet the person or continue talking. Hence, during social encounters, it is common for some people to quickly exit conversations while looking at other people across the way as they seek means of escape (Todorov, Fiske, & Prentice, 2008). Persons with similar levels of looks, attitudes, hobbies, values, and personality form relationships more quickly than persons with dissimilar qualities (Watson et al., 2004).

A Brief Introduction to Relational Scripts

Duck (1986) suggested that relationships should be regarded as changing mental and behavioral creations of individuals. The time spent alone analyzing future encounters reflects an individual's use of relational schemata to understand and differentiate among different types of relationships, such as distinguishing a casual dating relationship from an exclusive romance. Baldwin (1992) reviewed studies indicating that people develop cognitive structures representing regular patterns of interaction, scripts for behaviors associated with the formation of relationships. A relational schema includes an image in which people imagine seeing themselves with someone else.

Individuals have scripts based on memory and experiences that create expectations about what is likely to occur during the course of their lives in different types of relationships. These scripts emanating from relationship scripts are hierarchically ordered on the basis of recall of particular scenes (e.g., meeting an individual for the first time at a specific place) and scripts for behavior embedded within various scenes. Even though relationships are in constant motion, these scripts provide a perceptual anchor with which individuals can determine where they are in a relationship. These scripts are similar to mental file folders into which information is placed, retrieved, and often revised.

Scripts about relationships may be functional or dysfunctional. For example, Swann (1987) reviewed research indicating that individuals chose relational partners who verified their self-concepts even if their self-concept at the time was negative. Individuals who had high self-esteem preferred their relational partners to view them favorably, whereas individuals with low self-esteem preferred their relational partners to view them in relatively unfavorable terms. An individual's preference for relational partners with either positive or negative views of the individual was associated with the actual appraisal of their friends. Hence, if an individual viewed him or herself somewhat negatively, a relational partner who perceived the individual similarly was liked more than a relational partner who did not. Swann (1987) suggested "that people translate their desire for congruent relationship partners into actual selection of partners" (p. 1040). He further suggests (Swann, 2005) that if this initial strategy does not work (seeking self-verifying partners), individuals will act in certain ways to bring their partners' view of themselves in line with their own self-perceptions.

Relationships are constantly moving entities rather than static events. People tell stories or give accounts about their relationships that help provide order to events. Understanding is the result of an active, cooperative enterprise of the people in relationships. Problems in a relationship are understood as stories that individuals have agreed to tell.

Relationships represent the juxtaposition between individual needs and dyadic goals. A cognitive approach to the study of relationships examines how individuals mentally create their relationships. The behavioral study of relationships has a long, rich legacy. For example, communication patterns between happy and unhappy couples have been examined. However, an exclusive focus on the behavioral patterns of couples ignores the fusion between the individual and the relationship. The mental creation of a relationship may sustain or constrain individuals in everyday mundane living, depending on the content of relational expectations.

Relational expectations reflect past experiences in relationships. Cognitive researchers refer to expectations as knowledge structures. Various types of scripts emanating from knowledge structures are discussed in the next chapter. For example, if an individual has experienced a lot of deception in prior relationships, he or she may believe that his or her partner's words may not be taken at face value and that caution is wise before venturing far into self-disclosure. The individual may even be wary of people who seem gregarious.

Cognitive researchers believe that people's complex personal memories (scripts) create the bias they read into one another's signals. Research indicates that the most influential scripts are those initially developed in early childhood through interaction with parents, particularly with the primary caregiver, which traditionally has been the mother (Ainsworth, 1989; Bowlby, 1982; Carnelley & Janoff-Bulman, 1992). Additional influences on people's relationship scripts develop from other life experiences and the media. And the role and influence of scripts plays out in everyday interaction in a relationship. For example, when partners interact, they often think about what they are going to say in the form of imagined interactions (IIs), mentally processing what has been said, and sorting through memory to compare and contrast new information with earlier experience (Honeycutt, 1995, 2010). As relationships develop, people's internal responses create not only their views of themselves, but their views of their partner and the ways in which they think about themselves in relation to the other person. In short, relationships are the combined products and producers of both cognitive activity and behavior. They are both the input and outcome of one's perceptions and experiences.

Summary

Individuals think about relationships based on experiences, observations, and cultural images. People experience relationships through personal experience, vicarious experience, or a combination of direct and indirect encounters, and includes virtual encounters via online networking sites. As a consequence of these experiences, many people feel that they are experts on relationships. Yet, it can be argued that many people are experts at failed relationships.

Memories of relational events create expectations for relationships that are hierarchically organized on the basis of scenes and recalled messages within those scenes emanating in scripts that are pervasive yet malleable. Thus, relationships exist in people's minds, as well as in the observable communication between any two individuals. The role of cognition in categorizing romantic relationships has been ignored in the scholarly literature, not receiving much empirical research attention, whereas behavioral studies for classifying relationships are more popular. The cognition of romance is examined in this book in terms of relational scripts derived from experience and the scripts formed from these memory structures.

Discussion Questions

1.1. Discuss the idea of individuals as experts at failed relationships. Define what is meant by a failed relationship. Do people learn from failed relationships? One hears stories about individuals being in serial, unhealthy relationships. How many individuals do you know who have gone through a series of failed relationships? How many of these seem to have similar characteristics? Did their expectations change after each relationship ended? Why do individuals persist in utilizing scripts for relationship formation that generate unsuccessful partnering?

1.2. Discuss the proposition that successful relationships are more likely when individuals have a joint relationship worldview and shared conceptions of relationships. Do internet web sites foster the probability of selecting someone who is more similar in your values and temperament? How similar must the individuals' expectations for the development of relationships be in order to enhance the quality of the relationship?

Applications

1.1. Think of couples you know who seem to be well matched and those who are not well matched at all. Interview the partners in these couples about how they met, what made the other person stand out, what hobbies or interests they share, the problems they deal with in the relationship, how they communicate, and what they expected from the relationship. Have them complete the survey individually. Ask them their views about what characterizes a romantic relationship. You may interview them individually and contrast the partners' reports. Write a brief report in which you contrast the couples in terms of relationship happiness, compatibility of beliefs about relationship values, and anything that is especially memorable about these couples.

1.2. With a close friend, try an experiment in which each of you individually thinks of two couples whom you both know. One couple should be very happy and compatible; the other couple should be the opposite. Decide which couple is in each category individually; do both of you agree on the classifications? What made you classify the couples in the way you did? How similar or different are your perceptions of these couples compared to your friend's?

References

Acedevo, W. (2005). *Analyzing land use change in urban environments.* USGS Science for a Changing World. Accessed 2008, May 17. Retrieved from http://landcover.usgs.gov/urban/info/factsht.pdf

Ainsworth, M. D. S. (1989). Attachments beyond intimacy. *American Psychologist, 44,* 709–716.

Anokhin, A. P., Golosheykin, S., Sirevaag, E., Kristjansson, S., Rohrbaugh, J. W., & Heath, A. C. (2006). Rapid discrimination of visual scene content in the human brain. *Brain Research, 1093,* 167–177. doi:10.1016/j.brainres.2006.03

Austen, J., & Shapard, D. M. (20107). *The annotated pride and prejudice.* New York, NY: Anchor Books.

Baldwin, M. W. (1992). Relational schemas and the processing of social information. *Psychological Bulletin, 112,* 461–484. doi:10.1037/0033-2909.112.3.461

Banerjee, A., Duflo, E., Ghatak, M., & Lafortune, J. (2013). Marry for what? Caste and mate selection in modern India. *American Economic Journal: Microeconomics, 5,* 33–72.

Barelds, D. P. H., & Dijkstra, P. (2009). Positive illusions about a partner's physical attractiveness and relationship quality. *Personal Relationships, 16,* 239–261. doi:10.1111/j.1475-6811.2009.01222.x

Baumeister, R. F. (2005). *The cultural animal: Human nature, meaning, and social life.* New York, NY: Oxford University Press.

Bowlby, J. (1982). *Attachment and loss: Vol. 1. Attachment* (2nd ed.). New York, NY: Basic Books.

Broughton, S., & Van Acker, E. (2007). *Romantic expectations* and harsh realities: Tertiary access to the rescue. *International Journal of Lifelong Education, 26,* 279–293. doi:10.1080/02601370701362226

Bruno, D. (2007). A mother and daughter face up to Facebook. *Christian Science Monitor, 99*(36), 809.

Buunk, B. P., Dijkstra, P., Fetchenhaur, D., & Kenrick, D. T. (2002). Age and gender differences in mate selection criteria for various involvement levels. *Personal Relationships, 9,* 217–278. doi:10.1111/1475-6811.00018

Cameron, K. S., & Quinn, R. E. (2006). *Diagnosing and changing organizational culture* (2nd ed.). San Francisco, CA: Jossey-Bass.

Carnelley, K. B., & Janoff-Bulman, R. (1992). Optimism about love relationships: General vs. specific lessons from one's personal experiences. *Journal of Social and Personal Relationships, 9,* 5–20. doi:10.1177/0265407592091001

Consumer-rankings.com. (2017). Our 5 best online dating sites of 2017. Retrieved from http://www.consumer-rankings.com/dating/?vn=cl2-ph1-h2-dn-elitepone-sb2&a=144&c=101560&s1=742779039.731032215&agid=9116134150&g=1&s4=c&s3=b.g.168235669573&s6=9025395&ls=g

Deci, E. L., & Ryan, R. M. (2012). Motivation, personality, and development within embedded social contexts: An overview of self-determination theory. In R. M. Ryan (Ed.), *The Oxford handbook of human motivation* (pp. 85–107). Oxford: Oxford University Press.

Donohoe, M. L., von Hippel, W., & Brooks, R. C. (2009). Beyond waist-hip ratio: Experimental multivariate evidence that average women's torsos are most attractive. *Behavioral Ecology, 20,* 716–721. doi:10.1093/beheco/arp051

Duck, S. (1986). *Human relationships: An introduction to social psychology.* London: Sage.

Felmlee, D. H. (1995). Fatal attractions: Affection and disaffection in intimate relationships. *Journal of Social and Personal Relationships, 12,* 295–311. doi:10.1177/0265407595122009

Felmlee, D. H. (1998). Fatal attraction. In B. H. Spitzberg & W. R. Cupach (Eds.), *The dark side of close relationships* (pp. 3–32). Mahwah, NJ: Erlbaum.

Felmlee, D. H. (2001). From appealing to appalling: Disenchantment with a romantic partner. *Sociological Perspectives, 44,* 263–280. doi:10.1525/sop.2001.44.3.263

Fisher, H. (1994). *The natural history of monogamy, adultery and divorce.* New York, NY: Fawcett.

Fry, R., & Cohn, D. (2010). *New economics of marriage: The rise of wives.* Pew Research Center Publications. Retrieved from http://pewresearch.org/pubs/1466/economics-marriage-rise-of-wives

Gadlin, H. (1977). Private lives and public order: A critical view of the history of intimate relations in the United States. In G. Levinger & H. L. Raush (Eds.), *Close relationships: Perspectives on the meaning of intimacy* (pp. 33–72). Amherst, MA: University of Massachusetts Press.

Goldberg, J. G. (1993). *The dark side of love.* New York, NY: Putnam.

Gottman, J. M. (2011). *The science of trust: Emotional attunement for couples.* New York, NY: W. W. Norton.

Gottman, J. M., & Silver, N. (2015). *The seven principles for making marriage work.* New York, NY: Harmony.

Honeycutt, J. M. (1995). Predicting beliefs about relational trajectories as a consequence of typicality and necessity ratings of relationship behaviors. *Communication Research Reports, 12,* 3–14. doi:10.1080/08824099509362033

Honeycutt, J. M. (2009). Symbolic interdependence, imagined interaction, and relationship quality. *Imagination, Cognition, and Personality, 28,* 303–320.

Honeycutt, J. M. (2010). Introduction to imagined interactions. In J. M. Honeycutt (Ed.), *Imagine that: Studies in imagined interaction* (pp. 1–14). Cresskill, NJ: Hampton.

Hughes, S., Farley, S., & Rhodes, B. (2010). Vocal and physiological changes in response to the physical attractiveness of conversational partners. *Journal of Nonverbal Behavior, 34,* 155–167. doi:10.1007/s10919-010-0087-9

Lambert, N. M., Mulder, S., & Fincham, F. (2014). Thin slices of infidelity: Determining whether observes can pick cheater from a video clip interaction and what tips them off. *Personal Relationships, 21,* 612–619. doi:10.1111/pere.12052

Lee, L., Loewenstein, G. F., Ariely, D., Hong, J., & Young, J. (2007). *If I'm not hot, are you hot or not? Physical attractiveness evaluations and dating preferences as a function of own attractiveness.* Retrieved from http://ssrn.com/abstract=950782

Lewandowski, G. W., Jr., Aron, A., & Gee, J. (2007). Personality goes a long way: The malleability of opposite-sex physical attractiveness. *Personal Relationships, 14,* 571–585. doi:10.1111/j.1475-6811.2007.00172.x

Lewis, R. A., & Spanier, G. B. (1982). Marital quality, marital stability and social exchange. In F. I. Nye (Ed.), *Family relationships: Rewards & costs* (pp. 49–65). Beverly Hills, CA: Sage.

Markey, P. M., & Markey, C. N. (2007). Romantic ideals, romantic obtainment, and relationship experiences: The complementarity of interpersonal traits among romantic partners. *Journal of Social and Personal Relationships, 24,* 517–533. doi:10.1177/0265407507079241

McCroskey, J. C., & McCain, T. A. (1974). The measurement of interpersonal attraction. *Speech Monographs, 41,* 261–266. doi:10.1080/03637757409375845

McNulty, J. K., Neff, L. A., & Karnery, B. R. (2008). Beyond initial attraction: Physical attractiveness in newlywed marriage. *Journal of Family Psychology, 22,* 135–143. doi:10.1037/0893-3200.22.1.13

Miller, P. J. E., Niehuis, S., & Huston, T. L. (2006). Positive illusions in marital relationships: A 13-year longitudinal study. *Personality and Social Psychology Bulletin, 32,* 1579–1594. doi:10.1177/0146167206292691

Morry, M. M. (2007). The attraction-similarity hypothesis among cross-sex friends: Relationship satisfaction, perceived similarities, and self-serving perceptions. *Journal of Social and Personal Relationships, 24,* 117–138. doi:10.1177/0265407507072615

Murstein, B. I. (1987). A clarification and extension of the SVR theory of dyadic pairing. *Journal of Marriage and the Family, 49,* 929–933. doi:10.2307/351985

Myers, J. E., Madathil, J., & Tingle, L. R. (2005). Marriage satisfaction and wellness in India and the United States: A preliminary comparison of arranged marriages and marriages of choice. *Journal of Counseling and Development, 83*(2), 183.

O'Connor, J. M., Re, D. E., & Feinberg, D. R. (2011). Voice pitch influences perceptions of sexual infidelity. *Evolutionary Psychology, 9*(1), 64–78.doi:10.1177/147470491100900109

Poulsen, F. O., Holman, T. B., Busby, D. M., & Carroll, J. S. (2013). Physical attraction, attachment styles, and dating development. *Journal of Social & Personal Relationships, 30*, 301–319. doi:10.1177/0265407512456673

Reis, H. A., & Sprecher, S. (2009). *Encyclopedia of human relationships, Vol 1.* Thousand Oaks, CA: Sage.

Shaw, T. L., Fiore, A. T., Mendelsohn, G. A., & Cheshire, C. (2011). 'Out of my league': A real-world test of the matching hypothesis. *Personality and Social Psychology Bulletin, 37*, 942–954. doi:10.1177/0146167211409947

Sheets, V. I. (2014). Passion for life self-expansion and passionate love across the life. *Journal of Social and Personal Relationships, 31*, 958–974, doi: 10.1177/0265407513515618

Staines, G. L., & Libby, P. L. (1986). Men and women in role relationships. In R. D. Ashmore & F. K. Del-Boca (Eds.), *The social psychology of female-male relations* (pp. 211–258). New York, NY: Academic Press.

Stephen, T. (1994). Communication in the shifting context of intimacy: Marriage, meaning, and modernity. *Communication Theory, 4*, 191–218. doi:10.1111/j.1468-2885.1994.tb00090.x

Stephen, T., & Markman, H. J. (1983). Assessing the development of relationships: A new measure. *Family Process, 22*, 15–25. doi:10.1111/j.1545-5300.1983.00015.x

Stewart, S., Stinnett, H., & Rosenfeld, L. (2000). Sex differences in desired characteristics of short-term and long-term relationship partners. *Journal of Social and Personal Relationships, 17*, 843–853. doi:10.1177/0265407500176008

Swami, V., & Furnham, A. (2008). *The psychology of physical attraction.* New York, NY: Routledge/Taylor & Francis Group.

Swami, V., Stieger, S., Haubner, T., Voracek, M., & Furnham, A. (2009). Evaluating the physical attractiveness of oneself and one's romantic partner: Individual and relationship correlates of the love-is-blind bias. *Journal of Individual Differences, 30*, 35–43. doi:10.1027/1614-0001.30.1.35

Swann, W. B., Jr. (1987). Identity negotiation: Where two roads meet. *Journal of Personality and Social Psychology, 53*, 1038–1051. doi:10.1037/0022-3514.53.6.1038

Swann, W. B., Jr. (2005). The self and identify negotiation. *Interaction Studies, 6*, 69–83.

Todorov, A., Fiske, S. T., & Prentice, D. (Eds.). (2008). *Social neuroscience: Toward understanding the underpinnings of the social mind.* Oxford: Oxford University Press.

Vinacke, W. E., Shannon, K., Palazzo, V., Balsavage, L., & Cooney, P. (1988). Similarity and complementarity in intimate couples. *Genetic, Social, and General Psychology Monographs, 114*, 51–76.

Watson, D., Klohnen, E. C., Casillas, A., Nus, S. E., Haig, J., & Berry, D. S. (2004). Match makers and deal breakers: Analyses of assortative mating in newlywed couples. *Journal of Personality, 72*, 1029–1068. doi:10.1111/j.0022-3506.2004.00289.x

Wish, M., Deutsch, M., & Kaplan, S. J. (1976). Perceived dimensions of interpersonal relations. *Journal of Personality and Social Psychology, 33*, 404–420. doi:10.1037/0022-3514.33.4.409. Retrieved from http://en.wikipedia.org/wiki/Interpersonal_attraction

Wiszewska, A., Pawlowski, B., & Boothroyd, L. G. (2007). Father–daughter relationship as a moderator of sexual imprinting: A facialmetric study. *Evolution and Human Behavior, 28*, 248–252. doi:10.1016/j.evolhumbehav.2007.02.006

Zajonc, R. B., Adelman, P. K., Murphy, S. T., & Niedenthal, P. M. (1987). Convergence in the physical appearance of spouses. *Motivation and Emotion, 11*, 335–346. doi:10.1007/BF00992848

Emotions, Imagination, and Physiology of Relationships

Chapter 2   Emotion and Cognition About Relationships
Chapter 3   Generating and Maintaining Relationships Through Imagined Interactions
Chapter 4   Physiology and Relationships

What emotions are associated with relationships? What is the underlying physiology that drives these emotions and how does imagery, specifically imagined interactions, influence both our emotions and our assessment of these emotions? The secrets of happiness are revealed in Chapter 2. In addition, this chapter includes material that assists us in distinguishing our emotions, moods, and effect the differences and similarities among love, anger, hate, and jealousy. The interconnectedness of emotions, mental imagery, and actions is explored in Chapter 3, an examination of imagined interactions, the mental images that influence our emotions and our assessments of those emotions. You'll discover how it is possible to imagine yourself into an angry or joyful state. Relationships can prolong our lives or shorten them as our emotions soothe or stimulate our bodies in ways we are just beginning to understand; Chapter 4 reveals the physiological pathways that regulate social attachments.

CHAPTER TWO

Emotion and Cognition About Relationships

When people are asked to describe the relationships that are the most meaningful in their lives, they often use emotional inferences to express how they feel about the relationship. Indeed, people find it difficult to be descriptive as opposed to being evaluative in describing their romantic partners. How they currently feel about a relational partner affects their recall about the events in the relationship. For example, a married couple who has just had a heated argument will view their wedding video with more cynicism as compared to how they felt on the day of the wedding. This chapter reviews research on the role of emotions in processing information about the development of relationships. People have emotion prototypes for anger and love that reveal an association with other types of emotion, such as despair or infatuation. Furthermore, during relationship conflict, there are three types of emotion referred to as hard, soft, and flat emotion (Sanford & Grace, 2011). "Hard" emotion is associated with hostility and asserting power (e.g., anger is a prototypical hard emotion), while "soft" emotion reflects vulnerability including sadness, hurt, concern, and disappointment. "Flat" emotions reflect withdrawal, boredom, indifference, and disinterest (Nichols, Backer-Fulghum, Boska, & Sanford, 2015). People in relationships feel a threat to their status when partners communicate hard emotions and feel neglect when they observe an increase in partner flat emotion or a decrease in partner's soft emotion.

The role of emotions in the development and maintenance of relationships is critical to understanding how people differentiate among different kinds of relationships. For example, friendships are distinguished from intimate relationships on the basis of arousal and feelings of passion. The role of emotions in interpersonal relationships is a frequent theme in popular music. Songs deal with love, finding the right partner, and how happiness is a consequence of being in a romantic bond.

Characteristics of Happiness

Research reviewed by Diener and Biswas-Diener (2008) suggests that there are various predictors of happiness which are listed in Box 2.1. The most important predictor is being in a quality relationship. This is supported by Issacowitz, Valliant, and Seligman (2003) who reported that among their middle-aged and older participants, a loving relationship was strongly predictive of life satisfaction. In fact, among middle-aged individuals it was the *only* predictor of being happy with one's life. Furthermore, married people of both sexes report more happiness than those who are never married, divorced, or separated (e.g., Lee, Seccombe, & Shehan, 1991). Interestingly, Diener and Suh (2003) report that life satisfaction is lower when one's parents had a highly conflictual marriage or when they were divorced, and that this pattern was true in both individualistic and collectivistic cultures. Perhaps growing up in a conflictual or distrusting environment interferes with one's later social relationships because of the cultural script it builds for relating to other people.

Box 2.1. Components of Happiness

1. Being in a quality relationship.
2. Genes—As much as 50% of a person's happiness is due to a genetic tendency. Like cholesterol and blood pressure levels, happiness is genetically influenced, yet amenable to volitional control.
3. Internal locus of control, as opposed to being a victim or feeling helpless.
4. Belief in God.
5. Optimism—Refusing to accept setbacks or hindrances. The glass is half full.
6. Flow—Feeling needed and use of one's training or experiences.
7. Extroversion—They are outgoing and draw their energy from people.
8. Self-esteem—They see themselves as emotionally and physically healthy while having ethics and intellect. They believe they are less prejudiced and better able to get along with people.

The genetic tendency for happiness has been demonstrated in cases of identical twins who were separated at birth and raised in different families in different states (Lykken & Tellegen, 1996). Later, the twins demonstrate similar levels of humor and reactions to events even though they have no shared family experiences. The genetic argument is strong in explaining happiness among individuals in countries where the standard of living is low and resources are scarce, and depression among individuals with more affluent lifestyles. Even having one's standard of living raised significantly does not appear to predict increased levels of happiness. For example, Brickman, Coates, and Janoff-Bulman (1978) found that former lottery winners were no happier than individuals who had not won the lottery and, in fact, took less pleasure from mundane events than those who were not lottery winners.

Predictors of happiness appear to be independent of cultural influences (Argyle, 2002). In a cross-cultural study of nearly 13,000 Swiss and American adults, Peterson, Ruch, Bermann, Park, and Seligman (2007) found that life satisfaction was most highly associated with being engaged, having pleasurable experiences, and having meaningful experiences. All of these arguably associated with quality relationships. This in turn led to individuals' reports of loving, fulfilling lives.

Representation of Affect According to Cognitive Theories of Emotion

The cognitive theories of emotion seek to explain how people experience emotion and the phenomenology of emotions (Zajonc & Markus, 1984). The cognitive theories of emotion assume that the representation of affect is imposed by individuals using contextual cues. According to Schacter and Singer (1962), individuals construe emotions by combining perceptions of their feelings with observations of external events. For example, individuals injected with adrenaline were friendly in a friendly context and hostile in a hostile environment. Yet, as Zajonc and Markus (1984) noted, the representation of people's internal feeling states, how they label their internal experiences as representing a given emotion, is rather abstract and is inferred by observing behavior and its antecedent conditions. By observing behavior and antecedent conditions, people often learn to habitually associate emotions with certain contexts. Emotion theorists have shown that by altering individuals' cognitive appraisals of a stimulus (e.g., viewing a disturbing movie of a surgical incision from the viewpoint of a surgeon or from the stance of an observer), it is possible to alter individuals' emotional responses (Mandler, 1975).

People's expectations from relationships affect their emotional responses to events in relationships. Mandler (1975) argued that past experiences provide expectations about relationships. He suggested that an interruption of the expectations may result in positive or negative emotion, depending on the degree and intensity of the interruption. Low-level interruptions occur when people's expectations are more closely met, whereas high-level interruptions produce more arousal and more intense emotional reactions. An example of a low-level interruption would be an individual asking someone out after he or she has spoken with the other person who is now involved in a conversation with others. Because it is now harder to isolate this person in order to pop the question, a low-level interruption in what was expected occurs.

Indeed, people have expectations for emotions in relationships and scripts for emotions in relationship. These expectations influence how emotions are displayed and interpreted. For example, individuals who have prior experience with meaningful relationships are more likely to express more emotions, suggesting that the working models formed through earlier relationships have significant influences on later relationships (Simpson, Collins, Tran, & Haydon, 2007). Planalp (1999) noted that many emotions are played out and negotiated through interpersonal scripts. Some emotions are only experienced internally and dissipate, whereas other emotions provoke a response from other people, such that there may be some mutual adjustment. A common example on a first date is avoiding any display of anger even if the dating partner has done something to offend. The motivation for the emotional control is to foster the best possible impression of oneself, yet, this may be part of individual's scripts for emotions in terms of appropriateness of display.

Gottman (2011) defined affect in terms of the nonverbal behaviors emitted by a speaker while delivering a message. Affect is the observable outcome of an emotion. For example, labeling a person angry is done by observing his or her facial expressions, tone of voice, or some combination of behaviors. Gottman coded affect on a continuum ranging from very negative to very positive. He found that nonverbal affect discriminates happily married couples from less happily married couples more than the content of their speech does. Unhappily married couples tend to match negative affect, whereas happily married couples tend to respond to negative affect with neutral or positive affect. Indeed, among less happily married couples, there is a vicious affective cycle in which the wife expresses negative feelings while the husband withdraws emotionally. She then responds with increasingly intense negative affect and the husband either withdraws or becomes exceedingly expressive as he loses control of his emotions (Fitness & Strongman, 1991; Gottman, 2011).

Differences Among Emotions, Moods, and Affect

Before discussing the affect of emotion on processing information about personal relationships, the terminology should be defined. *Emotion* is a loosely used, vacuous term because it has multiple meanings to different people. Furthermore, what is emotional to one person may be unemotional to someone else. Although some emotion theorists believe that emotions are hardwired biological processes, Planalp (1999) discussed how emotions evolved not only in response to the physical environment but to the social environment as well. This has been supported by Hastings and De (2008) who studied over 100 preschool children, examining both biological predispositions and parental socialization patterns. They discovered children who had less regulatory parasympathic capability were more susceptible to parental responses to their emotions.

Andersen and Guerrero (1998) reviewed studies indicating how emotions arise more in social situations than in nonsocial ones. Examples of social emotions are guilt, love, contempt, jealousy, and embarrassment (Planalp, 1999). These emotions are commonly elicited in romance. Some emotions are even defined as being ways an individual feels about other people.

Shields (1987) performed a classic, pioneering study in gender differences in emotions in which individuals were asked to think of the most emotional person they knew and explain why they chose the person. Emotional people were designated in terms of the magnitude of their responses such as the extremity of their reaction to an event. Negative emotions were cited more often than were positive ones. Participants were also asked to describe a particular situation in which the person that they were thinking about had been emotional. Sadness and depression were mentioned most (41%), followed by anger (37%). Shields reported that positive emotions such as love or happiness were mentioned in 13% of the cases. Interestingly, in retrospect, negative emotions are not always evaluated negatively. The participants in Saffrey, Summerville, and Roese's study (2008) who were asked to recall past negative emotions identified "regret" in a favorable manner. These individuals appeared to value their past regret experiences, which they attributed to themselves more often than others, reporting that regret assisted in self-understanding leading to preserving harmony in interactions with others.

In Shield's study, negative emotions appeared to be most associated with male participants. The only emotion that men felt they could express without being labeled as girlish was anger and for the most part they were judged to be hiding their emotions. Men also reported that the emotional women that they were thinking about expressed more healthy emotions than they did. The association between men and anger and between women and other common emotions such as sadness, fear, or happiness is learned by age 5 (Birnbaum, Nosanchuck, & Croll, 1980). Indeed, women experience just as much anger as men do, but that they may cry or feel hurt as a reaction to it.

Appraisal occurs when labeling the event. Appraisals are interpretations of the relationship between the individual and the environment in terms of how the individual's well-being is affected and his or her ability to cope with the event (Dillard, Kinney, & Cruz, 1996). Positive emotions emanate from a compatible fit between environmental events and an individual's motives, desires, or goals. Negative emotions occur when there is a mismatch between the environment and an individual's motives. Initial appraisals appear to influence later perceptions whether positive or negative. Halberstadt and Niedenthal (2001) reported that individuals who initially told angry stories they identified with a facial expression later recalled faces much angrier than were actually shown; individuals who told happy stories identified faces as being much happier than actually indicated.

Appraisal theories distinguish between positive and negative emotions based on the relationship between events in the environment and individual motivations, needs, or desires at given times. Appraisal theories of emotion posit that emotions unfold in a sequence in which an event occurs in the environment that may or may not be noticed (Dillard et al., 1996; Roseman, Spindel, & Jose, 1990; Smith & Lazarus, 1990). If the event is noticed, the individual appraises it by deciding if the event may harm or benefit him or herself. Depending on the magnitude of the appraisal, an emotion arises. Appraisal theorists claim that individuals compare what they observe in the environment to their goals, desires, or motives. When the observations are congruent with their desires, positive emotions follow. The perception of mismatch results in negative emotions. The intensity of emotion depends on the degree of congruence or mismatch.

Mandler (1975) also discussed how philosophers and psychologists argued that emotions follow an initial appraisal of an object as good or bad. It is important to note that there are instances in which an event generates some particular meaning regardless of whether arousal is associated with it and that the final emotional expression leads to a post hoc assessment of the event as bad or good (Mandler, 1975). In addition, behaviorists such as Bowlby (1999) argued that approach toward and avoidance of stimuli are not inherently positive or negative, respectively; rather, approach and withdrawal tendencies with respect to a potential emotional stimulus are independent of linguistic labels of "good" and "bad." People often approach bad stimuli, as well as the reverse. Indeed, Mandler (1975) argued that bad evaluations are often a consequence of invoking an expectation about some event and that the observed behavior cannot be assimilated into the expectation or the expectation cannot be accommodated to account for the unexpected behavior.

An example is someone expecting a partner to be supportive in times of need, only to find out that this partner is busy coping with his or her own problems and, consequently, is too busy to provide the expected support. Negative evaluations of the intimate partner are likely to result. A relational expectation of support or comfort is violated.

This is an example of the assimilation of the unsupportive behavior into the expectation that the intimate partner should be supportive in times of stress. On the other hand, accommodation occurs when the expectation is modified such that intimate partners are now conditionally expected to provide support only to the extent that intimate partners are not overwhelmed with stress.

A good working definition of *emotion* is provided by Clore, Schwartz, and Conway (1994). According to these researchers, emotions are defined as "internal mental states that are focused primarily on affect (where affect simply refers to the perceived goodness or badness of something)" (p. 325). Examples of emotion terms are "adore," "aggravated," "anguished," "apprehensive," and "awestruck." These terms do not refer directly to events or to bodily reactions or behavior. Instead, they refer to mental events that integrate feelings. That is, we note our mental state and physiological reactions and provide terms to assist us in understanding these feelings and communicating them to others. Common terms that do not constitute emotions refer to external events (e.g., abandoned) or bodily states (e.g., tired).

Clore et al. (1994) defined *affect* in terms of valence or the positive and negative aspects of things. Affect reflects the evaluative component of emotions. Indeed, Clore et al. (1994) stated that all emotions are affective, but that not all affective terms are emotions. They indicated that attitudes and preferences are affective, but are not emotions. Emotions are also seen as states, whereas preferences and attitudes are personality dispositions.

The distinction between moods and emotion is clear. Batson, Shaw, and Oleson (1992) indicated that emotions are concerned with the present, whereas moods concern anticipation of the future. Furthermore, Schwartz and Clore (1988) argued that emotions have a specific focus, whereas moods are nonspecific. Emotions have an object that moods may not have. Moods do not have to be caused by emotion. In essence, a working definition of *mood* is a feeling state, "which need not be about anything, whereas emotion refers to how one feels in combination with what the feeling is about" (Clore et al., 1994, p. 326).

An implication of these definitions is that cognition is essential for emotion, but not for mood (Clore, Ortony, Dienes, & Fujita, 1993). Hence, a person may be in a depressed mood on dreary morning because the absence of sunlight inhibits the release of a hormone as opposed to simply appraising the day's opportunities as futile. In addition, Clore et al. (1994) argued that such changes may alter moods rather than emotions. In essence, emotions result from ongoing appraisals of situations regarding whether they are negative or positive for one's goals. Emotions serve as intrapersonal communication concerning the nature and urgency of the situation. Emotions appear to have biological correlates that set up cycles of behaviors. Boyatzis and McKee (2005) write that situations that are interpreted as emotionally threatening cause stress arousing the sympathetic nervous system which in turn releases the hormones epinephrine and norepinephrine, elevating blood pressure. Concurrently the brain becomes focused on the stressor, inhibiting creativity and flexibility.

Indeed, the people at HeartMath LLC are dedicated to improving health, performance, and well-being at home and in the workplace (www.heartmath. com). They provide products and services that enable people to transform stress, better regulate emotional responses, and harness the power of heart/brain communication. Stress is almost an emotional reaction to a situation. The brain has emotional memories that activate the autonomic nervous system through the amygdala (LeDoux, 1996). Imagine an argument between two partners in which one partner has said something that got under the skin of the other partner. The heart rate remains elevated after the argument ends. This will be discussed further in the chapter on physiology and relationships.

Given that emotion is concerned with feedback or information about the nature of a stimulus (Clore et al., 1994), the question arises about the characteristics that provide the prototypes for many human emotions such as love, hate, anger, and jealousy. Holmes (1991) noted that couples often have distinct and specific memories of past hurts. Furthermore, spouses may misremember or not remember specific emotions that are incongruent with their beliefs about the types of emotions that are commonly expected in marriage (Fitness, 1996).

Similarities and Differences Among Love, Hate, Anger, and Jealousy

Fitness and Fletcher (1993) examined the emotions of love, hate, anger, and jealousy in marriage. Both love and anger events, as opposed to hate or jealousy, had occurred the preceding month. In addition, both anger and love scripts reflected the desire to communicate with the partner, whereas hate or jealousy scripts reflected the desire to withdraw from the partner (cf., Gottman, 1994).

A love, hate, anger, or jealousy survey was randomly assigned to 160 married individuals who were asked to remember the most recent time they had felt their assigned emotion in relation to their spouses. They answered a series of open-ended questions dealing with their mood before the events; details of the actual events including what they remembered thinking, saying, or feeling; whether they had any urges to do something; and how they actually behaved during the incident. They also reported about controlling their emotions, the duration of the emotion, their mood after the event, and their partners' reactions. Both love and anger events had occurred recently, whereas hate or jealousy events had occurred earlier.

As expected, love-eliciting events were evaluated as pleasant, involving little effort and few perceived obstacles. The cause of love was global ("She's such a beautiful woman") rather than being isolated to a context. Love was also associated with a feeling of security for some individuals. Prototypes for both romantic and companionate love include trust, caring, and respect. Characteristics of romantic love were contentment, euphoria, smiling, gazing, butterflies in one's stomach, and periods of uncertainty. Passionate attributes such as "thinking about the partner all the time" were only secondary in describing love; however, they were primary qualities in describing emotions like hate. Indeed, people sometimes talk about the fine line between *love* and *hate* in a variety of codependent relationships involving chemical dependency, battery, or jealousy.

Not surprisingly, hate-eliciting events were seen as unpleasant and the opposite of love-eliciting events. Participants feeling hate reported lack of support by the partner and less control of the situation. Hate was elicited by being humiliated by the spouse in public. For wives, this often involved the husbands drinking too much at a social gathering and becoming aggressive. Husbands reported feeling humiliated and hating their wives when they made angry or jealous scenes in public. Both spouses reported wanting to withdraw and escape from the situation. There were feelings of being powerless and trapped.

Regarding jealousy-eliciting events, few of the spouses reported infidelity. The most intense jealousy occurred when the third party was the partner's ex-spouse. Jealousy was characterized by worrying, brooding, and less self-esteem. A common jealousy theme was that the partner was not necessarily responsible for the third party's overtures, but that the partner could have reacted more distantly. Interestingly, self-reported lonely individuals report experiencing heightened levels of jealously more frequently that nonlonely people (Rotenberg, Shewchuk, & Kimberley, 2001). It should be noted that infidelity occurs in two forms: sexual and emotional infidelity. Emotional infidelity develops after one self-discloses with another that result in an emotional bond characterized by trust, while sexual infidelity obviously involves sexual experiences (Barta, 2005).

These results reveal that people share socially constructed scripts or knowledge structures for basic emotions in close relationships like marriage. Furthermore, there are facial scripts for communicating emotion such as using the facial zygomatic muscles to smile, while disgusted and mixed-emotion people use their corrugator muscles between the eyebrows to frown (Kreibig, Samson, & Gross, 2013). Additionally, heart rate decreases while respiration increases, while heart rate does not increase as much with disgust. Physiological arousal is discussed in Chapter 4.

Fitness (1996) discussed how individuals share knowledge about emotions in general, as well as having more specific knowledge structures about the display of emotions in their own personal relationships. She provided an example of jealousy in which a spouse expressed jealousy to his or her partner because the expression of jealousy has positive outcomes such as loving reassurances from the partner who perceives the jealousy as flattery. Guerrero and Andersen (1998) also reported that relational partners may respond to jealousy in order to maintain the existing relationship. However, in other instances, the negative sentiment endures and neutral or positive emotions are labeled as cynically motivated by a partner. Moreover, jealousy shows no limitations as to age as revealed in Picture 2.1. Prior studies have revealed that younger women in their twenties are more affected by emotional infidelity while men are distressed by sexual infidelity. Research contrasting older adults in their sixties (mean age = 67 years) with younger people (mean age = 20) found similar results. Moreover, older women were less likely than younger women to select a partner's emotional infidelity as more distressing than a partner's sexual infidelity (Shackelford et al., 2004).

Picture 2.1. Jealousy knows no age.

Finally, the research by Fitness (1996) revealed that in contrasting anger with hate-eliciting events, anger was reported to be less demeaning and associated with less loss of self-esteem. The common elicitor of anger was the perception of having been treated unfairly, whereas hate was associated with humiliation and neglect. Anger events were viewed as more controllable and predictable than hate or jealousy events. Fitness (1996) and Fehr and Baldwin (1996) reported that the anger script is very common in and outside of close relationships.

The role of communication in eliciting emotion is critical. Planalp (1999) and Andersen and Guerrero (1998) discussed that emotions are elicited by communication, manifested in communication, and socialized through interaction. For example, emotions in romance often serve interaction goals such as embarrassing others to discredit or help them. An individual's inability to communicate effectively with partners can lead to anger, depression, and loneliness, just as effective communication may lead to happiness, joy, and contentment.

Prototypes of Anger in Relationships

There has been intriguing research on emotion prototypes of anger in personal relationships. Indeed, American culture has idioms indicating the prevalence of anger in people's closest relationships, such as "knowing which buttons to push." When individuals are asked to describe anger, 90% of the descriptions mostly involve another person as the target of anger (Fehr & Baldwin, 1992). Anger can be defined as a type of social relationship because the emotion so often emanates from frustration with another person.

Fehr and Baldwin (1996) described a series of studies of the conditions leading to anger and the reaction to it. Fehr and Baldwin's research indicated that there are different types of anger, including hurt, rage, and contempt. There is a temporal sequencing of events for anger. Rage and hatred tend to precede feelings of contempt. Some individuals attempt to control the expression of anger until a saturation point is reached. There is a loss of control followed by verbal aggression, physical aggression, and leaving the scene.

Box 2.2 contains a script reflecting the escalation of anger that results in physical aggression. Violations that occur in the culturally endorsed rituals for compliments indicate that the rules for conflict resolution are not endorsed by both partners in a given interaction. Hence, individuals over time increasingly condone higher levels of coercive responses in the belief that the other person is being irrational and is unwilling to use constructive communication to reduce conflict.

Box 2.2. Scripts for the Escalation of Anger Leading to Aggression

Honeycutt, Sheldon, Pence, and Hatcher (2015) discuss how anger and aggression may be sanctioned or even advisable after time has elapsed and the parties have not resolved the conflict. Aggression may be seen as a culturally sanctioned form of relationship governed by rules. Individuals were asked to predict, advise, and evaluate two scenarios in which two roommates came to blows and another scenario in which a husband criticized his wife's cooking after she had spent hours preparing the meal. Over time, as conflict escalates, individuals judge that the probability of aggressive actions increase, whereas the probability of conciliatory actions decreases. Individuals judge aggressive actions to be increasingly desirable, whereas conciliation becomes less desirable. Here is one:

1. Lee criticized Lisa's cooking. 2. Her response could be any of the following: embrace or kiss Lee, apologize for the meal, laugh about the remark, defend her cooking, criticize Lee, curse sarcastically at Lee, throw the dinner on the floor, or slap Lee. How probable, advisable, and desirable is it that each of these responses be used at this time? 3. Lee's reaction to Lisa's response was to defend his criticism. How probable, advisable, and desirable is this reaction? 4. Lisa's reaction was to curse Lee. 5. The conflict escalated until Lisa slapped Lee. The study participants tended to increasingly recommend aggression as the scenario proceeded. With increasing amounts of aggressive interchange over time, they recommended conciliation less and less. They realize the name of the game and play accordingly. But how often does conflict escalate in an argument with a relational partner? What does it take to stop the argument from increasing in hostility?

Types of Anger

Fehr and Baldwin (1996) asked 317 individuals to list all the terms they believed to be synonymous with anger. A total of 635 terms were generated. Over one-third of the participants listed terms such as "mad," "frustration," or "hate"; only 1% or 2% listed "exasperation" and "contempt." A subset of the terms was rated by a different group of participants on how representative the terms were of anger. The highest ratings were "fury," "rage," and "mad." The lowest ratings were for "depression," "fear," and "sorrow." Intermediate ratings were given to "irritation," "bitterness," and "spite."

Anger often takes over in other thoughts, so that when angered, individuals often have difficulty focusing on anything else. Fehr and Baldwin (1996) reported that brooding and dwelling on the event are prototypical thoughts and that individuals formulate plans for revenge or imagine attacking the cause of their anger. In essence, anger results in intrusive thinking so that individuals often are obsessed with the emotion until it is lessened in intensity by time passage or other events.

A number of physiological reactions are associated with anger. Common features are headaches, increased heart rate, shaking hands or knees, tense muscles, and a tight or knotted stomach. The anger prototypes also reflect behaviors such as using profanity, attacking something other than the cause, for example, slamming doors, leaving the scene, crying, and attempting to resolve the situation. Fitness and Fletcher (1993) found that 75% of survey participants reported that they tried to control their anger, whereas over 25% did not. Individuals who did not want to control their anger also reported that they wanted their partner to know they were angry or that the emotion was too intense to control. A minority (10%) of the participants reported that they believed it was healthier to express anger rather than keep it bottled inside themselves.

How individuals choose to display felt emotions are associated with mood, self-esteem, and affect. Nezlek and Kuppens (2008) asked participants to log the manner in which they attempted to regulate their emotions in daily interactions. Those individuals who suppressed their emotions reported lower levels of positive emotions, a reduction in self-esteem, and poorer adjustment, whereas those who used a reappraisal strategy reported increases in positive affect, better psychological adjustment, and enhanced self-esteem. Suppressing emotions may have serious consequences for physical as well as psychological well-being. Harburg, Kaciroti, Gleiberman, Julius, and Schork (2008) reviewed records of couples enrolled in a longitudinal analysis from 1971 to 1988 in terms of anger-coping mechanisms. Increased mortality was associated with couples where both partners were coded as "anger in" or "anger suppressive."

Fehr and Baldwin (1996) indicated that the agreement about the anger prototype is widespread as shown by data gathered in different countries. People perceive different causes for anger, react in a variety of ways, and often think that their reactions will elicit a response by the target of their anger.

Scripts for Anger

Fehr and Baldwin (1996) examined gender differences in how an unfolding sequence of anger was interpreted. In one study, men and women rated how they would feel if their partner engaged in a number of anger-provoking behaviors. A second study was conducted to examine people's responses when feeling angry, and a third study determined the reactions that individuals expected from their relationship partners in response to their expressions of anger.

The first study examined the causes of anger derived from earlier research. The causes of anger were being criticized, having one's trust betrayed by a partner disclosing confidential information about one to outsiders, and being rebuffed where one's partner repels plans for an evening together. Additional causes were negligence such as forgetting one's birthday and cumulative annoyance when an irritating habit keeps reoccurring. Women were more angered by all of the events, especially by a betrayal of trust. Other research has revealed that men were more likely to report feeling angered by their partner's moodiness, physical self-absorption, and the withholding of sex, whereas women reported feeling angered by their partner's neglect and remarks about their appearance (Buss, 1989).

The second study by Fehr and Baldwin (1992) revealed gender differences in responses to being angered. Women reported being more likely than men to express hurt feelings, using indirect aggression such as complaining to someone else or getting angry at someone else, and using direct aggression such as trying to hurt the partner either verbally or physically. This flies in the face of long-standing evidence that men are more likely to behave with physical aggression (Stets & Straus, 1990). Several studies found that men would rather express anger to another man, whereas women were more comfortable expressing anger directly to their partners. In addition, when men used physical aggression, they were more likely to use intense forms such as hitting, whereas women used less intense forms such as slapping (Stets & Henderson, 1991).

A third study examined individuals' beliefs about their partners' reactions to the individuals' expressions of being angry. The reactions considered were avoidance, responding with aggression, talking it over, responding with indirect aggressions, being conciliatory, expressing hurt feelings, denying responsibility, rejecting the partner, and mocking the partner. Participants expected more positive reactions to positive expressions on their part and more negative reactions to negative expressions. In reaction to avoidance or withdrawal, men were more likely to talk and to express hurt feelings. In reaction to indirect aggression, men were more likely to reject women and to express hurt feelings. When the men engaged in direct rather than indirect aggression, they expected their partners to avoid them, reject them, or express their hurt feelings. Women were more likely to expect their partners to ridicule them or to deny responsibility. Individuals of both genders agreed that their partners would react positively if the individuals were to conciliate, talk without hostility, or express hurt feelings.

Emotional Scripts for Relationships

Forgas (1991, 1996) examined the scripts for romantic heterosexual relationships and found that the scripts were based on affective and connotative characteristics rather than on objective and denotative features. Three dimensions characterize romance: love and commitment versus unlove and instability, mutual versus one-sided, and sexual or physical versus nonsexual or emotional. Having an affair with a married person was associated most with the sexuality dimension. This relationship was viewed as one-sided and reflected more of a transient, uncommitted, superficial, and unloving relationship. The most prototypical instance of commitment and mutuality was a marriage of 25 years. This marriage was modestly related to sexuality.

These dimensions are mostly affective and evaluative in nature, indicating the critical role of emotion in the cognitive representations of relationships. Conversely, cognition has a critical role in emotion. Often it is not the partner's behavior, but rather the attributions or the manner in which the behavior is evaluated that predicts conflict in the relationship (Epstein & Baucom, 1993). Forgas (1991) indicated that mutuality and love are more evaluative because they reflect how individuals feel about some relationships (e.g., a long-lasting platonic relationship) rather than the objective characteristics of the relationships themselves. Only the sexuality dimension is descriptive.

Individual differences were found among the relationship dimensions. Women tended to represent heterosexual relationships more in terms of their mutuality than did men. In addition, love and commitment were more important characteristics for those who were currently in a romance and who had idealistic attitudes about love in general. Individuals who were more extroverted tended to view relationships according to sexual appeal as opposed to the mutuality (Forgas & Dobosz, 1980). These findings indicate that cognition about relationships is not based only on affect, but is related to an individual's personality, attitudes, and previous dating history.

Communication and the Sentiment-Override Hypothesis

An important relationship attitude that has received considerable examination is the general sentiment that partners feel toward each other when they are asked to interpret the intentions behind their partner's statements. Weiss (1984) proposed the sentiment-override hypothesis that links cognition in terms of the processing of current information with the history of interaction in long-term relationships such as marriage. The sentiment-override hypothesis proposes that the history of interaction with another person affects the interpretation of current behavior by the other person. For example, an unhappily married wife could interpret her husband's statements about being late for dinner as an irresponsible excuse indicating his lack of concern about her. This reflects the assimilation of his tardiness into the wife's overall sentiment that her husband is irresponsible. According to

Piaget (2001), assimilation occurs when new information is made compatible with existing expectations or cognitive structures.

Accommodation occurs when the expectation is changed or modified so that new events become part of the expectation. As Mandler (1975) noted, an individual's view of the world is changed by including the new event as a legitimate part of some new conceptual structure in terms of simply modifying the original expectation. Weiss (1984) suggested that many spouses are insensitive to the nonverbal intent behind partner's behaviors. Instead, their reactions to their partners' behaviors are determined by the general sentiments about the partner at a given time. Hence, assimilation is taking place as spouses with positive sentiments interpret their partners' behaviors in a positive light and respond positively toward their partners. Spouses with negative sentiments view their partners' intentions negatively and respond negatively. Indeed, in a study of clinical couples Cornelius, Alessi, and Shorey (2007) write of the importance of sentiment-override: "Positive sentiment override, or the degree to which a partner makes 'trait' attributions for positive partner behaviors and 'state' interpretations for negative partner behaviors, may be a fundamental foundation of the marital relationship that is more important than the specific behaviors" (p. 129). Still, the question persists as to why memories of past events are so powerful in biasing the cognition of current behaviors. In the following, some studies are reviewed that provide partial answers to this question.

Fitness (1996) cited examples of clinicians who comment that couples often have memories like elephants for past hurts. The gap-filling function of scripts indicates that using a script to process information is biased with the perception and recall of script-consistent features that, in fact, may not have occurred. Spouses may recall inaccurately emotions that are incongruent with their beliefs about the kinds of emotions that are permissible in marriage. Fitness cited the example of jealousy in a marriage in which jealousy is considered an unacceptable marital emotion. Therefore, the wife recalls her feelings about her husband's paying close attention to an attractive young woman as worry that he not look foolish or be exploited by another woman's flirtatious interests.

Forgas (1991) discussed how emotion affects the organization and storage of information events in the past. Emotions affect the recall of events from the immediate past as well as events in early childhood. Individuals who are feeling happy are more likely to remember interactions that are pleasant, whereas those who are in a bad mood are more likely to recall events that are sad or depressing.

Forgas, Bower, and Krantz (1984) examined the effect of emotion on how individuals interpret the behavior of others and their own behavior. Participants who were induced to feel sad or happy through hypnosis were asked to look at a video of a conversation they had had the previous day with a stranger. They were asked to identify positive and negative behaviors on the tape for themselves and for the interaction partner on the tape. Forgas et al. (1984) found a strong bias for interpreting the behaviors on the tape according to the temporary mood of the participants. Happy participants identified more positive behaviors than negative behavior, both in their partners and in themselves. Sad participants tended to be more critical of themselves than their partners. Forgas (1991) attributed this to social norms that constrain negative evaluations of superficially known others such as the Pollyanna Principle, the belief that we expect initial encounters should be warm, polite, and cooperative as opposed to being unfriendly or competitive.

Forgas reviewed additional research supporting the sentiment-override hypothesis. Individuals were led to form impressions of others by reading about a variety of people on a computer screen and to evaluate the people along a number of social dimensions. The computer was programmed to record how long each individual took to read each piece of information and to evaluate the person. More time was spent reading and learning about information that matched the current mood of the individuals.

Sometimes positive thoughts generate other positive thoughts regardless of any logical connections between the thoughts. This is observed in conversations in which individuals engage in a series of positive or negative statements during which they seem to be caught in a repetitive loop. Planalp (1999) argued that cognition and emotion often work hand in hand in conversations. She cited examples of talking to people about their fear or sadness and providing reasons for why they should feel differently. She speculated that communication is the principal mechanism for changing emotions. This has been supported by Shapiro and Gottman (2005) who developed a training program for new parents incorporating information regarding the sentiment-override hypothesis into a comprehensive series focusing on developing communication strategies. The sentiment-override discussions specifically emphasized positive rather than negative sentiment override. Both self-report measures and observations of actual interactions revealed enhanced marital quality, lower levels of postpartum depression, and less observed marital hostility in the treatment couples.

In the absence of communication, individuals pay selective attention to mood-consistent rather than mood-inconsistent information. For example, happy participants spent more time focusing on the positive characteristics of another person, whereas sad participants noticed negative behaviors more. In addition, these studies support the concept of spreading activation in which a dominant emotion (e.g., happy) enhances the availability of emotion-congruent perception. Noticing behaviors that are congruent with one's existing mood may enhance the intensity of the existing moods, motivating the individual to give such information more attention. Indeed, a number of studies in communication and psychology reveal that happy people make positive and lenient judgments of others' behavioral intentions, whereas sad people are more likely to be critical in their interpretation of others' behavioral intentions.

Forgas (1991) summarized the studies on the sentiment-override hypothesis in terms of adaptability: when a person is in a positive mood, he or she is open, constructive, and relatively mindless about the careful processing of information that is incongruent with positive feelings. In close relationships, a positive mood corresponds with easy-going and uncritical judgments that are associated with lenient and generous interpersonal evaluations. Being in a negative mood results in slow, detailed, and analytic processing of more available information and a focus on oneself. This reaction may result in conscious information-processing strategies that offset the greater availability of affect-consistent cognition and may lead to negative assessments of oneself without negative evaluations of others. Yet, in close relationships, the judgments of oneself and the judgments of one's partner are interdependent.

Floyd (1988) provided qualified support for the sentiment-override hypothesis in which males in close relationships made judgments about their partners' communication behaviors that were affected by their previous sentiment. The women made judgments in accordance with their partners' current intent. Floyd had 40 dating couples discuss problems in their relationships for 10 to 15 minutes while being videotaped. Initially, the men and women individually completed surveys asking how satisfied or distressed they were with the relationship. During the discussion, couples used the communication box procedure developed by Markman and Floyd (1980) to evaluate the immediate impact of their partners' statements. The relational partners spoke one at a time and rated one another's statements after they finished on a 5-point scale ranging from "very negative" to "very positive."

Half of the couples completed a communication skills intervention program after the videotaping. The program consisted of lectures in small groups, homework assignments to practice the skills, feedback about their videotape, and individual practice sessions with a paraprofessional consultant. The intervention was designed to have couples focus on their expectations about marriage in general and their specific relationships in order to challenge any irrational beliefs or unrealistic expectations. Couples were encouraged to focus on specific communication behaviors (e.g., "He/she interrupts me when I state a problem.") rather than abstract negative personality traits (e.g., "He/she is a jerk.").

Two months after the videotaping, a second videotaping session was conducted for all the couples. The videotapes of the couples' pre- and postinterventions were rated by trained observers in terms of communication proficiency using a 5-point positive to negative scale.

The results revealed that the intervention did not improve communication proficiency. The men's ratings of the impact of the women's statements were consistent with the sentiment-override hypothesis in that their ratings at the second session were affected by their general satisfaction with the relationship. On the other hand, the women's ratings of the men's statements were not associated with the women's overall sentiment about the relationship. These results are consistent with the findings of other studies reviewed by Noller (1984), suggesting that men are inaccurate decoders of their partners' nonverbal affect. In the course of an interaction, men's interpretations of their partners' behaviors appear to be distorted by their own cognitive evaluations which are incongruent with the communication quality of the behaviors. Men misinterpret their partners' communication behaviors and their own behavioral responses are a result of these misinterpretations (Floyd, 1988).

Despite relationship, partners' shared knowledge of one another's experiences, similar behaviors, or activities are understood and interpreted by the partners differently. In marriage counseling, there is often a situation in which partners have different feelings about the same conditions eliciting the underlying problems in the relationship. Forgas (1991) indicated that the effect of mood, cognition, and judgment is intensified in close relationships because close relationships provide a context where the information base is elaborate such that selective processing is required.

Emotions and Social Media Relationships

Several studies have examined the relationship between emotions, such as sadness and loneliness, and social media use. To this date, however, research has produced contradictory findings regarding the relationship between social network site use and loneliness. While some studies found that technology serves as an outlet that helps users to buffer their social separation (Deters & Mehl, 2013), others have shown that social network site use increases loneliness (Krasnova, Wenninger, Widjaja, & Buxmann, 2013). The relationship between social network sites and loneliness depends how social network sites are used. Matook, Cummings, and Bala (2015) developed a model to explain the effects of relationship characteristics and social network sites features (i.e., active or passive) on perceived loneliness. The results of their study conducted with college students revealed that loneliness increased for individuals who were involved in passive features use (e.g., reading postings). However, loneliness was reduced when a user used active SNS features for broadcasting (e.g., sharing information).

Sheldon (2013) conducted a survey of 150 students to determine the relationship between social loneliness and self-disclosure on Facebook. Sheldon's (2013) results showed that, overall, socially lonely students disclose on Facebook less frequently than students who are not lonely. Socially lonely individuals in particular self-disclose fewer topics to their Facebook friends than individuals who feel "in tune" with others.

Cotten, Anderson, and McCullough (2013) studied how Internet use affects perceived social isolation and loneliness of older adults in assisted and independent living communities in Alabama. They found that going online was not associated with perceived social isolation. In fact, the frequency of going online was associated with an increase in agreement that using the Internet had: (1) made it easier to reach people, (2) contributed to the ability to stay in touch, (3) made it easier to meet new people, (4) increased the quantity of communication with others, (5) made the respondent feel less isolated, (6) helped the respondent feel more connected to friends and family, and (7) increased the quality of communication with others. Cotten et al. (2013) concluded that using the Internet may be beneficial for decreasing loneliness and increasing social contact among older adults in assisted and independent living communities.

Volkova and Bachrach (2015) analyzed a sample of 123,000 Twitter users and 25 million of their tweets to investigate the relation between the emotions that users express and their predicted psychodemographic traits (gender, income, political views, age, education, optimism, and life satisfaction). They found that users with high income produce significantly less sad tweets and users with lower income express more negative emotions. Female users are more emotional than male users. Older users expressed more joy and less sadness than younger users. Optimism and life satisfaction correlate with positive emotions, as well as being in a relationship and having children.

Blomfield Neira and Barber (2014) surveyed 1,819 Australian teenagers to find out if there is a relationship between their use of social networking sites and depression. Results revealed that having a profile and using social networks frequently was correlated with depressed mood. Blease (2015) argued that Facebook has a lot of features that are possible triggers for mild depression (more online "friends," a content of bragging nature). In other words, Facebook presents more opportunities to feel like a loser.

Depressed individuals might also be more attracted to social media where they feel safe posting about depression or seeking support from others. Moreno et al. (2011) evaluated college students' Facebook disclosures that met the Diagnostic and Statistical Manual (DSM) criteria for a depression symptom. They found that overall, 25% of profiles displayed depressive symptoms. For example, a status update stating "I feel hopeless" was coded as a reference to depression. The most common type of depression symptom reference was to depressed mood, followed by feelings of guilt or worthlessness. Other symptoms included indecisiveness, loss of energy, change in appetite, and decreased interest or pleasure. In addition, those students who received online reinforcement from their friends were more likely to discuss their depressive symptoms publicly on Facebook.

Social media depression is a new concern as adolescents struggle with peer pressure. Sheldon and Newman (2016) surveyed 181 preteens and teens (99 boys, 82 girls), ages 12 to 17 years, to find out how depression relates to their use of Instagram. They studied two aspects of depression: excessive reassurance-seeking and interpersonal rejection. Sheldon and Newman (2016) discovered that excessive reassurance-seeking could explain why teens use Instagram to become popular, to escape from reality, and for creative purposes. They use Instagram to get positive feedback (in the forms of "likes") and to validate their sense of self. Barker (2009) and Bonetti, Campbell, and Gilmore (2010) found that social network sites may be utilized as a form of social compensation for those youth who are feeling disconnected from their peer group. Sheldon and Newman's (2016) study also revealed that teens who perceive that nobody loves them and that they cannot be as good as other kids use Instagram to escape from reality and to avoid loneliness. Those teens use social media to compensate for the lack of social contacts that they have with others face-to-face.

Despite some studies suggesting that Facebook use negatively influences subjective well-being (Krasnova et al., 2013). Verduyn et al. (2015) found that people do themselves the most harm when they're not posting. Their study with 84 undergraduate students demonstrated that passive Facebook usage decreased affective well-being, but not life satisfaction. Passive Facebook use involved browsing Facebook—for example, scrolling through news feeds, looking at friends' pages and pictures. Active Facebook use involved communicating with others on Facebook—posting status updates, sharing links, reacting on friends' posts or private messages. Verduyn et al. (2015) concluded that interacting with Facebook helps people connect with others.

Summary

Cognition affects emotion and vice versa. Even though people's expectations about romance reflect emotions, the inferences represent the outcome of behaviors that occur in relationships. For example, if someone describes his or her best friend as caring, then the underlying behaviors may represent a script in which the friend is available in times of a crisis, the friend listens sensitively to the individual's concerns, the friend laughs at his or her jokes, or the friend calls at the right times. Caring is a constellation of many behaviors. Yet, what is considered caring for an individual in a given context or time period may be labeled as "intrusive" or "not minding one's own business" at a different time.

People have scripts for anger that reflect the intensity of the emotion. The sentiment-override hypothesis states that current emotions override objective judgments of a partner's behavior. If an individual is feeling comfortable and a partner interrupts him or her, the individual may overlook the interruption without comment. On the other hand, if the individual is feeling tense or agitated, then the interruption by his or her partner may be seized as an opportunity to escalate conflict.

Discussion Questions

2.1. Discuss the sentiment-override hypothesis and think of two recent events involving yourself and a close friend in which you went into the interaction feeling
   a) very elated about an event and wished to tell your partner
   b) angry toward your partner for something he or she recently did that affected you
   What happened in both scenarios? Did conflict escalate or did you both calmly resolve the issue in the second scenario?
2.2. Discuss how you often express anger. Does your expression of anger reflect the research findings on anger expression discussed in this chapter? How are your experiences similar to or different from the research findings presented here?
2.3. What are your experiences with the similarities and differences among love, hate, anger, and jealousy?

Applications

2.1. Interview two people about the following situation and apply the sentiment-override hypothesis to their statements: Think about someone with whom you have been in an intimate relationship. It is a weekend and you want to go to a movie matinee to see a popular show that has received good reviews.

You and your partner have not done anything together for a while because of jobs and schoolwork. After asking your partner about going to the movie, you are told that he or she desires to read a novel at home for a few hours and then study some more. What is your reaction? Do you communicate your response to your partner or keep your feelings to yourself?

2.2. Think of the most emotional person you know. Describe him or her. What makes this individual emotional? Think of the frequency and amount of emotional displays. Are this person's emotions primarily positive, negative, or a combination?

2.3. Think of the most emotionless person you know. What makes him or her unemotional? What would make this individual more emotional? If possible, also interview this person and ask if he or she has ever had any difficulty expressing emotions.

References

Andersen, P. A., & Guerrero, L. (1998). *The handbook of communication and emotion*. San Diego, CA: Academic Press.

Argyle, M. (2002). *The psychology of happiness* (2nd ed.). London: Routledge.

Barker, V. (2009). Older adolescents' motivations for social network site use: The influence of gender, group identity, and collective self-esteem. *Cyberpsychology & Behavior, 12*, 209–213. doi:10.1089/cpb.2008.0228

Barta, W. (2005). Motivations for infidelity in heterosexual dating couples: The roles of gender, personality differences, and sociosexual orientation. *Journal of Social and Personal Relationships, 22*, 339–360. doi:10.1177/0265407505052440

Batson, C. D., Shaw, L. L., & Oleson, K. C. (1992). Differentiating affect, mood, and emotion. In M. S. Clark (Ed.), *Review of personality and social psychology* (Vol. 11, pp. 294–326). Beverly Hills, CA: Sage.

Birnbaum, D. A., Nosanchuck, T. A., & Croll, W. L. (1980). Children's stereotypes about sex differences in emotionality. *Sex Roles, 6*, 435–443. doi:10.1007/BF00287363

Blease, C. R. (2015). Too many 'friends,' too few 'likes'? Evolutionary psychology and 'Facebook depression'. *Review of General Psychology, 19*(1), 1–13. doi:10.1037/gpr0000030

Blomfield Neira, C. J., & Barber, B. L. (2014). Social networking site use: Linked to adolescents' social self-concept, self-esteem, and depressed mood. *Australian Journal of Psychology, 66*(1), 56–64. doi:10.1111/ajpy.12034

Bonetti, L., Campbell, M. A., & Gilmore, L. (2010). The relationship of loneliness and social anxiety with children's and adolescents' online communication. *Cyberpsychology, Behavior, and Social Networking, 13*, 279–285. doi:10.1089/cyber.2009.0215

Bowlby, J. (1999). *Attachment and loss: Vol. 1. Attachment* (2nd ed.). New York, NY: Basic Books.

Boyatzis, R., & McKee, A. (2005). *Resonant leadership*. Boston, MA: Harvard Business School Publishing.

Brickman, P., Coates, D., & Janoff-Bulman, R. J. (1978). Lottery winners and accident victims: Is happiness relative? *Journal of Personality and Social Psychology, 36*, 917–927. doi:10.1037/0022-3514.36.8.917

Buss, D. M. (1989). Conflict between the sexes: Strategic interference and the evocation of anger and upset. *Journal of Personality and Social Psychology, 56*, 735–747.

Clore, G. L., Ortony, A., Dienes, B., & Fujita, F. (1993). Where does anger dwell? In T. K. Srulla & R. S. Wyer (Eds.), *Advances in social cognition* (pp. 57–87). Hillsdale, NJ: Lawrence Erlbaum.

Clore, G. L., Schwartz, N., & Conway, M. (1994). Affective causes and consequences of social information processing. In R. S. Wyer Jr. & T. K. Srull (Eds.), *Handbook of social cognition* (pp. 323–417). Hillsdale, NJ: Lawrence Erlbaum.

Cornelius, T. L., Alessi, G., & Shorey, R. C. (2007). The effectiveness of communication skills training with married couples: Does the issue discussed matter? *Family Journal, 15*, 124–132. doi:10.1177/1066480706297971

Cotten, S. R., Anderson, W. A., & McCullough, B. M. (2013). Impact of Internet use on loneliness and contact with others among older adults: Cross-sectional analysis. *Journal of Medical Internet Research, 15*(2), 215–227. doi:10.2196/jmir.2306

Deters, F. G., & Mehl, M. R. (2013). Does posting Facebook status updates increase or decrease loneliness? An online social networking experiment. *Social Psychological and Personality Science, 4*, 579–586. doi:10.1177/1948550612469233

Diener, E., & Biswas-Diener, R. (2008) *Happiness: Unlocking the mysteries of psychological wealth*. Malden, MA: Wiley-Blackwell.

Diener, E., Suh, E. M. (2003). *Culture and subjective well-being (Well Being and Quality of Life)*. A Bradford Book.

Dillard, J. P., Kinney, T. A., & Cruz, M. A. (1996). Influence, appraisals, and emotions in close relationships. *Communication Monographs, 63*, 105–130. doi:10.1080/03637759609376382

Epstein, N., & Baucom, D. H. (1993). Cognitive factors in marital disturbance. In K. S. Dobson & P. C. Kendall (Eds.), *Psychopathology and cognition* (pp. 351–385). San Diego, CA: Academic.

Fehr, B., & Baldwin, M. W. (1992, June). *Gender differences in anger scripts*. Presentation at the Sixth International Conference on Personal Relationships, Orono, Maine.

Fehr, B., & Baldwin, M. W. (1996). Prototype and script analyses of laypeople's knowledge of anger. In G. J. O. Fletcher & J. Fitness (Eds.), *Knowledge structures in close relationships: A social psychological approach* (pp. 219–245). Mahwah, NJ: Lawrence Erlbaum.

Fitness, J. (1996). Emotion knowledge structures in close relationships. In G. J. O. Fletcher & J. Fitness (Eds.), *Knowledge structures in close relationships: A social psychological approach* (pp. 195–217). Mahwah, NJ: Lawrence Erlbaum.

Fitness, J., & Fletcher, G. J. O. (1993). Love, hate, anger, and jealousy in close relationships. *Journal of Personality and Social Psychology, 65*, 942–958.

Fitness, J., & Strongman, K. T. (1991). Affect in close relationships. In G. J. O. Fletcher & F. D. Fincham (Eds.), *Cognition in close relationships* (pp. 175–202). Hillsdale, NJ: Lawrence Erlbaum.

Floyd, F. J. (1988). Couples' cognitive/affective reactions to communication behaviors. *Journal of Marriage and the Family, 50*, 523–532.

Forgas, J. P. (1991). Affect and cognition in close relationships. In G. J. O. Fletcher & F. D. Fincham (Eds.), *Cognition in close relationships* (pp. 151–174). Hillsdale, NJ: Lawrence Erlbaum.

Forgas, J. P. (1996). The role of emotion scripts and transient moods in relationships: Structural and functional perspectives. In G. J. O. Fletcher & J. Fitness (Eds.), *Knowledge structures in close relationships: A social psychological approach* (pp. 275–296). Mahwah, NJ: Lawrence Erlbaum.

Forgas, J. P., Bower, G. H., & Krantz, S. (1984). The influence of mood on perceptions of social interactions. *Journal of Experimental Social Psychology, 20*, 497–513. doi:10.1016/0022-1031(84)90040-4

Forgas, J. P., & Dobosz, B. (1980). Dimensions of romantic involvement: Towards a taxonomy of heterosexual relationships. *Social Psychology Quarterly, 43*, 290–300. doi:10.2307/3033731

Gottman, J. M. (1994). *What predicts divorce?* Hillsdale, NY: Lawrence Erlbaum.

Gottman, J. M. (2011). *The science of trust: Personal attunement for couples.* New York, NY: W. W. Norton.

Guerrero, L. K., & Andersen, P. A. (1998). Jealousy experience and expression of in romantic relationships. In P. A. Andersen & L. K. Guerrero (Eds.), *Handbook of communication and emotion* (pp. 156–188). San Diego, CA: Academic Press.

Halberstadt, J., & Niedenthal, P. (2001). Effects of emotion concepts on perceptual memory for emotional expressions. *Journal of Personality and Social Psychology, 81*, 587–598.

Harburg, E., Kaciroti, N., Gleiberman, L., Julius, M., & Schork, M. A. (2008). Marital pair anger-coping types may act as an entity to affect mortality: Preliminary findings from a perspective study (Tecumseh, Michigan, 1971–1988). *Journal of Family Communication, 8*, 44–61.

Hastings, P. D., & De, I. (2008). Parasympathic regulation and parental socialization of emotion: Biopsychosocial processes of adjustment in preschoolers. *Social Development, 17*, 211–238. doi:10.1111/j.1467-9507.2007.00422.x

Holmes, J. (1991). Trust and the appraisal process in close relationships. In W. H. Jones & D. Perlman (Eds.), *Advances in personal relationships* (pp. 57–106). London: Jessica Kingsley.

Honeycutt, J. M., Sheldon, P., Pence, M. E., & Hatcher, L. C. (2015). Predicting aggression, conciliation, and concurrent rumination in escalating conflict. *Journal of Interpersonal Violence, 30*, 133–151. doi:10.1177/0886260514532717

Issacowitz, D. M., Valliant, G. E., & Seligman, M. E. P. (2003). Strengths and satisfaction across the adult life span. *International Journal of Aging and Human Development, 57*, 181–201. doi:10.2190/61EJ-LDYR-Q55N-UT6E

Krasnova, H., Wenninger, H., Widjaja, T., & Buxmann, P. (2013). *Envy on Facebook: A hidden threat to users' life satisfaction?* Proceedings of 11th Annual Conference on Wirtschaftsinformatik (pp. 1477–1491), Leipzig, Germany.

Kreibig, S. D., Samson, A. C., & Gross, J. J. (2013). The psychophysiology of mixed emotional states. *Psychophysiology, 50*, 799–811. doi:10.1111/psyp.12064

LeDoux, J. (1996). *The emotional brain.* New York, NY: Touchstone.

Lee, G. R., Seccombe, K., & Shehan, C. L. (1991). Marital status and personal happiness: An analysis of trend data. *Journal of Marriage and the Family, 53*, 839–844.

Lykken, D., & Tellegen, A. (1996). Happiness is a stochastic phenomenon. *Psychological Science, 7*, 186–189.

Mandler, G. (1975). *Mind and emotion.* New York, NY: Wiley.

Markman, H. J., & Floyd, F. (1980). Possibilities for the prevention of marital discord: A behavioral perspective. *American Journal of Family Therapy, 8*, 29–48.

Matook, S., Cummings, J., & Bala, H. (2015). Are you feeling lonely? The impact of relationship characteristics and online social network features on loneliness. *Journal of Management Information Systems, 31*(4), 278–310. doi:10.1080/07421222.2014.1001282

Moreno, M. A., Jelenchick, L. A., Egan, K. G., Cox, E., Young, H., Gannon, K. E., & Becker, T. (2011). Feeling bad on Facebook: Depression disclosures by college students on a social networking site. *Depression and Anxiety, 28*(6), 447–455. doi:10.1002/da.20805

Nezlek, J. B., & Kuppens, P. (2008). Regulating positive and negative emotions in daily life. *Journal of Personality, 76*, 561–580. doi:10.1111/j.1467-6494.2008.00496.x

Nichols, N. B., Backer-Fulghum, L. M., Boska, C. R., & Sanford, K. (2015). Two types of disengagement during couples' conflicts: Withdrawal and passive immobility. *Psychological Assessment, 27*, 203–214. doi:10.1037/pas0000045

Noller, P. (1984). *Nonverbal communication in marital interaction.* New York, NY: Pergamon.

Peterson, C., Ruch, W., Bermann, U., Park, N., & Seligman, M. E. P. (2007). Strengths of character, orientations to happiness, and life satisfaction. *Journal of Positive Psychology, 2*, 149–156. doi:10.1080/17439760701228938

Piaget, J. (2001). *Studies in reflecting abstraction.* Hove: Psychology Press.

Planalp, S. (1999). Communicating emotion: Not just for interpersonal scholars anymore. *Communication Theory, 9*, 216–228. doi:10.1111/j.1468-2885.1999.tb00358.x

Roseman, I. J., Spindel, M. S., & Jose, P. E. (1990). Appraisals of emotion-eliciting events: Testing a theory of discrete emotions. *Journal of Personality and Social Psychology, 59*, 899–915.

Rotenberg, K. J., Shewchuk, V. A., & Kimberley, T. (2001). Loneliness, sex, romantic jealousy, and powerlessness. *Journal of Social and Personal Relationships, 18*, 56–79. doi:10.1177/0265407501181003

Saffrey, C., Summerville, A., & Roese, N. J. (2008). Praise for regret: People value regret above other negative emotions. *Motivation & Emotion, 32*, 46–54. doi:10.1007/s11031-008-9082-4

Sanford, K., & Grace, A. J. (2011). Emotion and underlying concerns during couples' conflict: An investigation of within-person change. *Personal Relationships, 18*, 96–109. doi:10.1111/j.1475-6811.2010.01317.x

Schacter, S., & Singer, J. (1962). Cognitive, social, and physiological determinants of emotional state. *Psychological Review, 65*, 379–399.

Schwartz, N., & Clore, G. (1988). How do I feel about it? Informative functions of affective states. In K. Fiedler & J. Forgas (Eds.), *Affect, cognition, and social behavior* (pp. 44–62). Toronto, Canada: C. J. Hogrefe.

Shackelford, T. K., Voracek, M., Schmitt, D. P., Buss, D. M., Weekes-Shackelford, V. A., & Michalski, R. L. (2004). Romantic jealousy in early adulthood and in later life. *Human Nature, 15*, 283–300.

Shapiro, A. F., & Gottman, J. M. (2005). Effects on marriage of a psycho-communicative-educational intervention with couples undergoing the transition to parenthood, evaluation at 1-year post intervention. *Journal of Family Communication, 5*, 1–24. doi:10.1207/s15327698jfc0501_1

Sheldon, P. (2013). Voices that cannot be heard: Can shyness explain how we communicate on Facebook versus face-to-face? *Computers in Human Behavior, 29*, 1402–1407. doi:10.1016/j.chb.2013.01.016

Sheldon, P., & Newman, M. (2016). *Instagram and American teens: Understanding motives for its use and relationship to depression and narcissism.* Presented at the National Communication Association annual meeting, Philadelphia, PA.

Shields, S. A. (1987). Women, men, and the dilemma of emotion. In P. Shaver & C. Hendrick (Eds.), *Sex and gender: Review of personality and social psychology* (pp. 229–250). Beverly Hills, CA: Sage.

Simpson, J. A., Collins, W. A., Tran, S., & Haydon, K. C. (2007). Attachment and the experience and expression of emotions in romantic relationships: A developmental perspective. *Journal of Personality and Social Psychology, 92*(2), 355–367. doi:10.1037/0022-3514.92.2.355

Smith, C. W., & Lazarus, R. S. (1990). Emotion and adaptation. In L. Pervin (Ed.), *Handbook of personality* (pp. 609–637). New York, NY: Guilford.

Stets, J. E., & Henderson, D. A. (1991). Contextual factors surrounding conflict resolution while dating: Results from a national study. *Family Relations, 40*, 29–36.

Stets, J. E., & Straus, M. (1990). Gender differences in reporting marital violence and its medical and psychological consequences. In M. A. Straus & R. J. Gelles (Eds.), *Physical violence in American families: Risk factors and adaptations to violence in 18,145 families* (pp. 151–165). New Brunswick, NJ: Transaction Books.

Verduyn, P., Lee, D. S., Park, J., Shablack, H., Orvell, A., Bayer, J., & … Kross, E. (2015). Passive Facebook usage undermines affective well-being: Experimental and longitudinal evidence. *Journal of Experimental Psychology: General, 144*(2), 480–488. doi:10.1037/xge0000057

Volkova, S., & Bachrach, Y. (2015). On predicting sociodemographic traits and emotions from communications in social networks and their implications to online self-disclosure. *Cyberpsychology, Behavior & Social Networking, 18*(12), 726–736. doi:10.1089/cyber.2014.0609

Weiss, R. L. (1984). Cognitive and strategic interventions in behavioral marital therapy. In K. Hahlweg & N. S. Jacobson (Eds.), *Marital interaction: Analysis and modification* (pp. 337–355). New York, NY: Guilford.

Zajonc, R. B., & Markus, H. (1984). Affect and cognition: The hard interface. In C. E. Izard, J. Kagan, & R. B. Zajonc (Eds.), *Emotions, cognition and behavior* (pp. 73–103). London: Cambridge University Press.

CHAPTER THREE

Generating and Maintaining Relationships Through Imagined Interactions

From the book thus far, one might be tempted to conclude that people are somewhat obsessed with thoughts about their past, current, or anticipated romantic relationships. Certainly, private conversations with close associates may support the idea that people spend a great deal of time thinking about the state of their intimate relationships. However, an overlooked fact about relationships is that people imagine conversations with partners in order to feel connected.

Imagined interactions (IIs) refer to a process of social cognition in which individuals imagine and therefore indirectly experience themselves in anticipated and/or past communicative encounters with others (Honeycutt, 2003, 2010, 2015). IIs focus and organize individuals' thoughts on communication. Furthermore, we can plan the relationship: we can think back over encounters and try to work out what went wrong with them or what we can learn from them. This out-of-interaction fantasy or thought work is important in building and destroying relationships.

Creating Relationship Scripts Through Imagined Interactions

Honeycutt (2015) discusses how the term "imagined interaction" is strategically used for "imaginary conversation" or "internal dialogue" because "interaction" is a broader term that takes into account nonverbal and verbal imagery as well as

Internet communication including Facebook. Visual imagery reflects the scene of the interaction (e.g., office, den, and car). Verbal imagery reflects lines of dialogues imagined by self and others (e.g., I recall answering my cell phone when my sister told me that she had just been promoted in the state treasurer's office. I congratulated her with a pun saying, "They invested wisely in you.").

IIs serve as major wellsprings that create expectations for relationship development. In essence, they are internal dialogues with significant others that allow individuals to review relational encounters, and they also serve a rehearsal function for future relational encounters. IIs also create and sustain habitual scripts for various encounters (Honeycutt, 1993). In this regard, imagining what one will say on a first date, when proposing marriage, and when making a disclosure about some personal problem results in expectations regarding anticipated scenes of the interaction and the accompanying scripted lines of dialogue. The process of imagining conversations with relational partners keeps the relationship alive even when the individual is not in the physical presence of the partner; IIs are an integral part of the ongoing ebb and flow of romance.

In this chapter, IIs are discussed as a mechanism for mentally creating relationships, as well as for reliving old memories with ex-partners. The chapter also includes a discussion of the use of imagined dialogue for creating parasocial relationships in times of social isolation, for example, as when viewers fantasize about having a close relationship with a television star. The role of emotions in imagined conversations, in particular how individuals can reexperience prior emotions associated with relational events, is then examined. The chapter concludes with a discussion of gender differences in imaging and offers the results of a study on topics of imagined dialogue in marriage.

Main Features of Imagined Interaction Theory

Deeply ingrained schemas, prototypes, scripts, and personal constructs are reflected in everyday thought processes outside of conscious awareness (Singer, 1985). These may take the form of passing thoughts, fantasies, and daydreams. Daydreaming is one way people sustain interest and arousal while enduring boring situations, such as attending a committee meeting or listening to that well-intentioned professor drone on and on. Indeed, some jobs are particularly conducive to daydreaming (e.g., lifeguards, truck drivers). According to Klinger (1987), daydreaming serves the purposes of planning ahead and reviewing past events as people find relief from the monotony of doing the same thing again and again. Daydreaming appears to be a mechanism by which people often initiate proactive and retroactive IIs in order to rehearse anticipated interactions and relive previous encounters

(Honeycutt, 2014). In addition to rehearsal and reliving of prior conversations, IIs also serve such functions as catharsis, enhancing self-understanding, and keeping relationships alive in people's thoughts.

IIs also have their foundations in cognitive scripts (Honeycutt, 2015). Cognitive researchers argue that much information is stored (sometimes unconsciously) in propositional form; the way in which information is processed is called "computational thinking" (Zagacki, Edwards, & Honeycutt, 1992). Yet propositional information located deep within the human mind may itself be transferred to or represented in phenomenal awareness in a variety of ways. One way is through IIs. Thus, when people experience IIs, they may be experiencing a representation of scripted or partially scripted knowledge, with the information being brought directly into explicit awareness for review. Hence, activating the script through an II may help to reconstitute the existing script. Our memories about relationships form later scripts or expectancies for appropriate behaviors in relationships (Honeycutt, 2003, 2010).

A major function of IIs is compensating for the lack of real communication. From their early development, IIs have been purported to serve in the place of real interaction when it is not possible to actually communicate with a given individual. In their discussion of IIs used for counseling, Rosenblatt and Meyer (1986) indicate that an individual may choose to use IIs in place of actually confronting a loved one in fear that the loved one would be hurt by the message. Furthermore, Honeycutt (1989) found that some elderly residents of a retirement home imagined conversations with friends living in close proximity to their own unit rather than imagining conversations with estranged children who rarely visited. Instead, they created new social families at the retirement home rather than ruminating about the past.

The catharsis function of IIs has to do with their ability to relieve tension and reduce uncertainty about another's actions (Honeycutt, 1989). Rosenblatt and Meyer (1986) proposed IIs as a means of emotional catharsis in counseling sessions having found that IIs served as an outlet for their patients to release unresolved tension. Patients had noted feeling less relational tension after having experienced IIs. Allen and Berkos (2010) describe how individuals use IIs as a means of "getting things off their chest" when they know that certain behaviors or the expression of certain emotions is inappropriate in actual interactions. Van Kelegom and Wright (2013) examined IIs in terms of uncertainty reduction which they examined it as a personality trait as well as their episodic use of IIs in response to an impactful conversation with a romantic partner. Correlations were stronger for imagined interaction functions including catharsis than for attributes, suggesting that the reasons for using episodic IIs are related to one's tendencies while the attributes appear mainly impacted by situational factors. Hence, we may have IIs to manage uncertainty as it helps prepare people for what to say and it can be a way to look back and reexamine a situation. Yet, too much can be dysfunctional and cause too much stress (Honeycutt, 2010).

We often imagine conversations with our friends and may tell them hurtful things. For example, one of our students reported envying a work associate who was recognized for achievement in getting new contracts even though the student had gotten more contracts. The student imagines using an assumed identity and going on Facebook broadcasting how undeserving the award winner was compared to others whose contract publicity was ignored.

McCann and Honeycutt (2006) discussed how individuals may feel "emboldened" in situations where there are sanctions for voicing opinion in a comparison of Americans, Thai, and Japanese. They found that the Japanese used IIs more to suppress communication with and as a means for voicing disagreement because they felt empowered in their imaginary conflicts since there would be no repercussions. McCann and Honeycutt (2006) concluded that IIs might have served as a "safe," punitive-free outlet for self-expression for their Japanese participants because to the Thais and Americans, who perhaps operate under comparatively less rigid norms for individual expression, this "safe" II outlet may not have been as necessary.

IIs have a number of characteristics that are similar to real conversations in that these internal dialogues may be fragmentary, extended, rambling, repetitive, or incoherent. Similarly, everyday discourse often exhibits the same sorts of patterns. And even in relatively formal or structured conversational encounters, interaction may be anything from disjointed to well-orchestrated and is often mirrored in the proactive and retroactive IIs that people initiate in their heads. For example, individuals even have IIs in counseling situations with their therapists (Honeycutt, 1995).

Studies of relational partners indicate that IIs occur in all sorts of contexts, ranging from romantic partners (33%), to friends (16%), to family members (12%), to individuals in authority (9.4%), to work associates (8%), to ex-relational partners (6%), and to prospective partners (4%) (Edwards, Honeycutt, & Zagacki, 1988; Honeycutt, Zagacki, & Edwards, 1989; Zagacki, Edwards, & Honeycutt, 1992). Depending on the differing values people place on their assorted relationships, some people have IIs with many different individuals, whereas others have recurring IIs with only certain individuals about a limited number of topics. Indeed, we know that socioemotional processes which allow us to make sense of other people and predict their behavior in terms of empathy and mental imagery reveal intriguing overlap with the brain regions that are activated when people's minds wander (Poerio & Smallwood, 2016). Whether or not the similarity in brain regions reflects the fact that people engage in socioemotional processing when the mind is not constrained by external demands and/or whether this neural similarity is reflective of more general processes that occur during social cognition and daydreaming (e.g., internally generated cognition) is an open question. Nevertheless, much of our "idle time" is spent generating thoughts about other people, which can impact on socioemotional well-being. People often think about others when the external world permits presumably because of the importance of social relationships (Baumeister & Leary, 1995).

The earlier chapter on physiology is relevant to studies of daydreaming and IIs in terms of fMRI studies. Indeed in the last 20 years advances in cognitive neuroscience have resulted in a transformation toward the systematic study of internally generated unconstrained cognition. This has much to do with the discovery of the Default Mode Network (DMN; Greicius, Krasnow, Reiss, & Menon, 2003), which showed that at "rest" when participants are not performing any external task, the brain remains active consuming between 60–80% of all brain energy (the so-called "brain's dark energy"; Raichle, 2010). The DMN is a large-scale constellation of distributed brain regions which include the medial prefrontal and cingulate cortex, the medial temporal lobe, the lateral parietal cortex, as well as areas of the cerebellum and the striatum (Buckner, Andrews-Hanna, & Schacter, 2008). At rest these regions exhibit a pattern of coherent temporal behavior (Greicius et al., 2003) and are deactivated during cognitively demanding and externally focused tasks (Fox, Spreng, Ellamil, Andrews-Hanna, & Christoff, 2015).

Third-Party IIs

In a dissertation directed by the senior author, Porter (2010) found that third-party IIs (TPIIs) result when an individual observes through mental imagery an interaction between other individuals. The experience is an II if the event includes the self or a TPII if the event does not include the self. A good example is when we wonder what two other people are saying about us behind our back. The data revealed that individuals are more satisfied when they imagine that they are part of the conversation compared to when they are the observers because uncertainty is reduced by having been part of the conversation. Additionally, 55.5% of the participants indicated that they had experienced a TPII the day of the study or the previous day, a figure just under 4% less than those who had experienced IIs. It appears that people engage in both TPIIs and direct IIs on a regular basis. Figure 3.1 demonstrates how IIs influence communication in our interpersonal relationships.

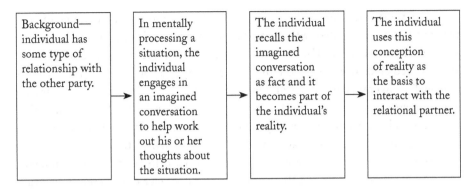

Figure 3.1. Process by which imagined conversations influence future interactions. ("From Third-Party Imagined Interactions," by M. A. Porter, 2009, http://etd.lsu.edu/docs/available/etd-10302009-131200, Copyright 2009 by Marcus A. Porter. Used by permission of the author.)

The finding of higher satisfaction in IIs should be investigated farther. It may be the self is in the II making it more satisfying thus more pleasant, or the self makes it more pleasant thus more satisfying. A third issue may also be that TPII as interactions between others brings out a negative effect that makes them less pleasant. It may be people imagine the worst in the conversation of the TPII more than the II. The third theorem of II conflict-linkage theory suggests people tend to have intruding negative IIs (Honeycutt, 2003). It is possible that individuals believe these negative thoughts will be less constrained in the conversation outside of their presence. This catastrophizing effect (Honeycutt, 2010) would lead to rating TPIIs more negatively.

Relational Maintenance Function of Imagined Interactions

IIs help maintain relationships as people think about their relational partners outside of their physical presence. Research reveals that relational happiness is associated with having pleasant IIs (Honeycutt & Wiemann, 1999). Furthermore, engaged couples who were more likely to live apart used IIs to compensate for the absence of their partner compared to married couples. Research across the lifespan reveals that people of all ages and family backgrounds put a certain level of effort to maintain important relationships in their lives. However, older people are more likely to exert the effort for relational maintenance in long-term friendships even when they do not perceive reciprocity compared to middle-aged adults (Lang, Wagner, Wrzus, & Neyer, 2013).

Honeycutt and Keaton (2013) found that having more specific, frequent, and pleasant IIs was associated with relational quality along with the increased uses of proactive and retroactive IIs. In terms of personality preferences, relational quality was predicted by extraversion and being a judger based on the Myers-Briggs personality inventory in which judging reflects placing a premium on organized environments, competence, performance, and independence. The finding that extraversion has been more typically associated with positive affect and well-being would signify a positive association with relationship satisfaction.

Interestingly, covert narcissism is associated with the relational maintenance function of IIs as well as using them to compensate for lack of real communication (Honeycutt, Pence, & Gearhart, 2013). Covert narcissism reflects a hypersensitivity to criticism and overcompensating with inflated self-exaggeration. These findings may reflect the cultural idiom in which narcissists "want to have their cake and eat it too." The IIs of some narcissists may reflect the desire to control the interaction partner. This interpretation is buttressed by the finding that self-dominance was associated with covert narcissism.

Ruminating about conflict was associated with covert narcissism. Furthermore, as noted by Wallenfelsz and Hample (2010), it may be difficult for a person who has a tendency to take conflict personally to imagine a conflict that is not personal. Serial arguing, or the persistence of conflict within a relationship, would seem to be decidedly antisocial in nature, but that is not always the case. Previous literature on serial conflict within relationships showed that the most important feature of serial arguing is not the number of times a disagreement has occurred, but rather the degree to which partners believe that they are making progress toward resolution (Johnson & Roloff, 2000).

Additional research on the compensation function of IIs in which people compensate for the lack of real communication by imagining conversations with those who are in geographical, close proximity reveals that some long-distance couples idealize their partners. Idealization is the tendency to describe the relationship (and one's partner) in unrealistically positive terms. Idealization may be a reason that research has revealed long-distance relationships to be more stable, committed, and of higher quality than geographically close relationships (Stafford & Merolla, 2007). The data revealed that long-distance couples scored significantly higher than geographically close couples in love, idealistic distortion, and positive reminiscences, perceived agreement, and communication quality even though the actual communication is less in long-distance relationships compared to geographically similar couples. Part of this may be due to avoiding taboo topics such as relational concerns and being positive when actually talking with the absent relational partner. Yet, two-thirds of these long-distance relationships end when the partners are in the same geographical proximity.

Guldner (2003) reports involving interviews with deployed soldiers and the aftermath of their return. While deployed, they found that only 37% of couples reported that the physical separation prompted them to talk about the relationship, while 50% of couples said reunion did. It is possible that people avoid talking about the relationship while they are apart out of fear that this will prompt a breakup. Yet, during reunion, relational talk is unavoidable. Furthermore, research on military separations suggests that many more couples divorce or break up after they reunite than during the actual separations.

Positive emotions may be attributed to the excitement that accompanies relational initiation and growth (Honeycutt et al., 1989). Individuals may imagine pleasant activities with their relational partners, such as engaging in small talk, planning dates, and discussing shared interests. For instance, the journal entry in Box 3.1 was written by a 25-year-old woman who imagines seeing a lover who has been away on a trip. This represents the compensation function in which individuals think about their relational partners outside of their physical presence. It compensates for the lack of text-messaging or face-to-face communication. In addition, the II serves cathartic, rehearsal, and relational maintenance functions within the same coherent episode.

Box 3.1. Imagined Interaction Journal Entry about Seeing a Long-Distance Lover

Andy and I both have had numerous IIs concerning our relationship. An imagined interaction is a process that helps people in the construction of social reality. A person may develop visual or verbal scripts in her head to help them deal with certain situations. IIs serve specific functions: rehearsal for actual upcoming communication situations, evaluation after an important encounter, obtaining a greater sense of our own feelings, and improving our own self-knowledge. Perhaps the best example of IIs being used in Andy's and my relationship occurred during our separation last summer.

It was a very difficult time for both of us because we missed each other so much. The thing that helped each of us deal with the pain was the use of IIs. I was amazed to discover that we both had IIs over the same thing the moment that we would be reunited at the end of the summer. Whenever I was feeling lonely or especially missing Andy, I would think about the moment we would be able to see each other again. I would imagine the inevitable embrace, kiss, and words of love that we would give to each other. I would rehearse over and over again in my head the things that I would tell Andy at that moment. Things like "I love you more than anything else in the world." At the actual moment, we did hug, kiss, and give romantic proclamations of love to one another, but then there was an awkward moment of silence for two reasons.

First, we had each gone over in our head that moment so many times that we neglected to think about what would come next. Second, we were still in shock that we had finally been reunited. Now, we both laugh when we think of that moment because we realize how rehearsed the whole thing was on both of our parts. Nevertheless, imagining conversations with each other and being together again helped us survive the separation. Through the process we learned a lot about how we felt about each other also.

Imagined Interactions with Ex-partners

IIs sometimes feature ex-partners. In fact, this represents the final stage of decaying relationships as individuals think about their former partners. We refer to this as post-termination awareness. This is likely to happen when individuals have been unable to find comparison alternatives or interests; hence they may have retroactive IIs reliving prior conversations. Indeed, in the cases of joint custody of children, it is common for parents to know about the lives of their ex from sharing custody of their children. Hence, the old relationship is redefined in terms of coparenting. For example, a woman in one study (Honeycutt et al., 1989) reported an II with an ex-lover who had terminated the relationship. In the II he apologized for the hurt he had caused her and confessed that he was wrong to let her go. She responded that she hated him and that she was better off with her new boyfriend. This is an example of an II occurring in what might be referred to as the post-termination awareness of an ex-partner. IIs after a romance has soured can create valued psychological contact with the ex-partner. This is a type of reminiscence that often occurs during the process of de-escalating relationships when people remember the good times. It may be that individuals are likely to have these retroactive IIs and be in this post-termination phase until an alternative relationship develops or the individual diverts attention to other endeavors such as hobbies, friends, or work. The journal entry in Box 3.2, written by a 33-year-old man, supports this thesis.

Box 3.2. Imagined Interaction Journal Entry about an Ex-Girlfriend

I had a relationship in high school with a girl that was serious as far as high school relationships go. We dated for almost a year and then broke up. Even though I was the one who terminated the relationship, I was also the one who was the loneliest afterwards. I can remember keeping up with the girl through our mutual friends. I wanted to know who she was dating, what they were doing and whether or not she still liked me. I would have IIs with this girl where I would tell her the things that bothered me about her. She would change the behaviors that I did not like and then we would get back together.

For whatever reasons, I was not able to come straight out and talk to her about the problems I was having with her. Instead I just terminated the relationship. I often still imagined being with these girl years afterwards and would go over in my mind things we had said and what could have been said different. Sort of a cross between fantasizing and imagined interaction. A couple of years after high school and probably four years since we had dated, we met in a college town and had a few dates. Within a very short time, maybe two weeks, our relationship was right back to where it was before I terminated it with her in high school.

Again she showed behavior that was close to that which I had not been able to accept in high school and again I terminated the relationship. This time, however, we both sort of broke contact and did not make an effort to reach one another. Although I still think about this person on occasion, it is only because she was a big part of my past and I tend to reflect on my past experiences and relationships at times.

Comparisons Between Friends and Friends with Benefits

IIs have been examined between friends and friends with benefits (FWBs). Mongeau, Knight, Williams, Eden, and Shaw (2013) found many FWBs represent a desire to transform the relationship from friends to a romantic partnership. Hence, when thinking about a FWB, the IIs may reflect catharsis in an attempt to deal with the anxiety or tension of transforming the relationship. Relatedly, there may be more conflict linkage due to this anxiety as well as relational maintenance to the extent that one becomes obsessed with thinking about the partner outside of his/her absence (Fisher et al., 2002). Self-understanding may be used in an effort to understand the etiology of this type of relationship and the benefits or costs that accrue from it. The data reveal that IIs used for self-understanding with friends were higher than self-understanding IIs used in reference to FWBs. However, there is similarity between friends and FWBs in the use of relational maintenance, catharsis, and conflict linkage.

Self-understanding allows for the individual to evaluate aspects of themselves in order to gain self-clarification (Honeycutt, 2014). However, the reason for FWBs being weaker in self-understanding could be attributed to the lack of self-disclosure and intimacy, but also due to the addition of sexual encounters that meet physical needs rather than social and intimate needs.

Imagined Interactions and Social Isolation: Parasocial Relationships

While IIs may help people to think about their relationships with friends, romantic partners, or family members, they also may be used dysfunctionally to imagine a relationship with someone with whom a person has never communicated in face-to-face interaction. Caughey (1984) discussed cases in which individuals fantasized that they were involved with a celebrity. A well-publicized and unfortunate case of this type of dysfunctional behavior became public in April 1981 when John Hinckley attempted to assassinate President Ronald Reagan. Hinckley had seen the movie *Taxi Driver* and had become infatuated with the actress Jodie Foster, who was one of the film's stars. Hinckley wrote love letters to her and began to imagine that he had a personal relationship with her. He eventually began to believe that he could win her love by killing the president. It is interesting to speculate about the types of IIs Hinckley may have had with Foster in the time leading up to the assassination attempt.

One-sided imagined relationships, such as Hinckley's, reflect extreme cases of parasocial relationships. More common are parasocial relationships in which individuals imagine talking to television characters portrayed by celebrities. However, in some cases, the individuals are infatuated by the celebrity him or herself, rather than the character that he or she plays. Individuals in parasocial relationships are often lonely and isolated from real-life interactions (Caughey, 1984). Edwards et al. (1988) found that loneliness is negatively correlated with having IIs; lonely individuals are less likely to experience such mental conversations. Loneliness is also negatively correlated with how well IIs prepare a person to talk about feelings or problems in later actual conversations ($r = -.40$), and with their being able to make a person feel more confident ($r = -.30$). There is also a weak but positive correlation between loneliness and the discrepancy between IIs and real encounters. Greater loneliness is associated with a greater difference between actual and IIs. Loneliness is also associated with less social support and more anxiety among adolescents, which is even more true for boys who report receiving more cumulative support in which parents offered the most protection compared to other support groups including peers (Cavanaugh & Buehler, 2015).

Lonely individuals experience less satisfaction and more negative emotions in IIs than do nonlonely individuals (Honeycutt, 2014). These results suggest that the tendency to have IIs is affected by various personality characteristics, such as locus of control, sensitivity to conversations, and communication competence (Honeycutt, 2003). One reason that lonely individuals may have fewer IIs is that they have fewer *actual* conversations to review and rehearse. However, one resource available to a lonely individual is to engage in an imagined dialogue with a celebrity, thereby creating a parasocial relationship that is fostered through IIs.

Not all imaginary relationships are associated with loneliness or dysfunctional cognitions. Related to the idea of parasocial relationships are what have been referred to as imaginary playmate (IP) relationships among children. IPs are the partners in imagined relationships in which they talk with a chimerical significant other, such as a make-believe friend, companion, or mentor (Connolly, 1991). There is also research on adults who report about the IPs they had while growing up. For example, Connolly interviewed 69 community college students and discovered that 24 (34%) admitted to having had an IP. Those students who had had IPs had higher grades in school than those who had not had them. Connolly summarized studies that reveal positive profiles for children reporting IPs, suggesting that they are more self-reliant, more socially cooperative, less bored, less impulsive, smile more frequently, watch less TV, and do not have greater or fewer emotional and behavioral problems than children without IPs. In addition, Singer (1979) has found that children as young as 3 and 4 who have IPs are happier, have more advanced linguistic skills, and exhibit more ability to concentrate than children without IPs. Thus, as with most aspects of human cognition, the IIs that accompany IPs should be viewed as processes that are neither good nor bad and whose value can only be seen in the social context that surrounds interpersonal communication.

Affect and Imagined Interactions

IIs can help to maintain relationships by allowing people to think about previous encounters and reexperience the positive emotions associated with them. People become closer to those they care about through mental rehearsal and anticipation. Furthermore, pleasant emotions are associated with having more IIs that are similar to actual encounters rather than being different from actual interactions (Honeycutt, Edwards, & Zagacki, 1989–1990). Data collected using thought-sampling research, in which individuals were given beepers and told to write down in a small diary what they were feeling at the time they were beeped, reveal that subjects' thoughts are concerned with present-life concerns 67% of the time and with the past or future concerns 24% of the time. Thoughts about the past tend to involve reviewing previous events and using critical evaluation (Klinger, 1987). Thoughts about the future tend to be in the form of rehearsals and setting up alternative scenarios for anticipated events.

Support for Klinger's (1987) notion that emotion is concerned with current concerns is provided in the findings of additional research. For example, Zagacki et al. (1992) had subjects evaluate the level of emotional intensity (1 = low intensity, 2 = medium, 3 = strong) in a recently recalled II, the level of emotional feeling associated with the II (1 = positive, 2 = neutral, 3 = mixed feelings, 4 = negative), and the level of communication satisfaction they felt with the II. Analysis indicated that highly intense IIs featured romantic partners and family members, whereas less-intense IIs featured work partners. High intensity was also associated with

II topics that had to do with relational conflict. Medium intensity was associated with topics related to school, work, and small talk. So it seems that the most prominent IIs are associated with intimate relationships, even though they may attend a wider range of potential interaction contexts.

Negative affect in IIs may be linked with Sherman and Corty's (1984) *simulation heuristic*. According to this heuristic, individuals who narrowly fail to achieve certain goals may find it easier to construct counterfactual scenarios that would have led to their success. To the extent that retroactive IIs can simulate earlier unsuccessful experiences, the individual may imagine the same events with more successful outcomes. People often wonder "If only I had said ..." and find that such wishful thinking results in them mentally kicking themselves for not having the foresight of hindsight.

Use of Imagined Interactions in Linking Together Prior Conversations

Linked IIs occur when an individual connects a series of conversations together in the human mind from the past while anticipating the future. When a person has flashbacks, this is a retroactive II which is often seen in television shows. Conversely, when a person is anticipating conversations, before they occur, this is a proactive II. However, they can be linked together when recalling prior conversation while simultaneously envision upcoming interaction. For example, Roxanne recalls arguing with her roommate Chris about his not cleaning the kitchen well. Yet, Roxanne is also waiting for Chris to come home and how she will show him how to clean it better. Hence, the conversations are linked together in Roxanne's mind.

Repetitive, stimulus-relevant cognitions may be related to linked IIs in which multiple functions are served. In the case of long-standing conflict between parents and children or between romantic partners, conflict may be kept alive and maintained in the absence of the other person by having retroactive and proactive IIs. Even though a retroactive II is experienced, it may be immediately linked with a proactive II (e.g., "Last time, I bit my lip. Next time I see him, I am going to say exactly how I feel."). Given that IIs tend to occur with significant others, it may be that many of them are linked and occur between encounters as a means of reviewing and previewing conversations. Box 3.3 contains a sample protocol from a 21-year-old wife in which she described a recent II. She felt positive while imagining it, although the II was a reconstruction of a prior conversation with her husband in which she felt ignored.

Box 3.3. Sample II Protocol Linking a Prior Conversation to an Anticipated One

Gender: Female
Age: 21
Relationship of other participant: Husband
How long ago the II took place: 10 minutes
Scene of II: home
Topic(s) discussed: My expectations and his attitude toward me
Self-reported emotions about the II: Felt better because I had an idea about what I was going to say.
Me: You know, you really hurt my feelings by your comments a few minutes ago.
Husband: Why? That's stupid! They had nothing to do with you. You shouldn't be so sensitive.
Me: They had everything to do with me. When you snap at me like that, when I'm just being concerned, it hurts my feelings. It makes me feel like you have something to hide. I mean, I just asked you a simple question and you get all sarcastic. I don't understand why you have to react that way.

The linking of a series of actual interactions through IIs helps explain why it is often difficult to counsel people in conflict-habituated marriages. Conflict may be kept alive through IIs in such a way that a conflict theme emerges within the relationship. For example, out of the presence of a spouse, one partner may keep conflict alive by reliving the conflict scenes and rehearsing what he or she wants to say at the next encounter. Thus, conflict may pick up where it left off. At the next encounter, couples in such marriages need to be instructed about how to produce more positive images of interactions with their spouse and enact the positive, imagined messages in an actual encounter.

Croghan and Croghan (2010) review research on IIs in organizations and report that experienced managers use a variety of IIs with different subordinates in order to facilitate friendly relations and enhance profit potentials. Furthermore, they report on a study in which experienced managers used IIs to aid in counseling session for both rehearsal and catharsis. Although the managers were more likely to use IIs to rehearse for a counseling situation, they still frequently used IIs to release emotions related to the counseling session.

Acitelli (1993) speculated that married couples in conflict are less likely to remain in conflict if their actual conversations shift from individual blaming to discussion that is more relationally oriented. One way to do this is to welcome positive IIs and to practice talking in the plural using we, for example, and saying

"We've got a problem," instead of "You've got a problem." In doing so, romantic combatants might be better able to focus on the interdependent nature of relational conflict while avoiding the personalization of problems that are typically rooted in the dynamic between the two parties.

Research has revealed that the self talks more during IIs (Honeycutt, 2003). In IIs, people have easier access to their own thoughts and know their own attitudes better. It is easier to think about their own attitudes than to accurately predict another's speech or action. In this regard, there is evidence that married couples often reenvision egocentric attributions as to who is responsible for various behaviors in marriage. For example, individuals tend to assume more responsibility for giving compliments and trying to resolve problems in their relationships compared to how much credit they give their partners.

The domination of the self in IIs is consistent with findings in attribution theory. Attribution theorists (Nisbett & Ross, 1980; Ross, 1977) examined the *fundamental attribution error*, in which there are actor and observer differences in accounting for the cause of behavior. Attributional studies reveal that information about an individual is more available to him or herself than information about others, and that the individual is relatively unable to take the perspective of others. Therefore, individuals process primarily their own roles and thoughts when imagining actions and dialogue with others.

As noted earlier, in addition to psychologically maintaining relationships and linking a series of interactions, IIs serve the functions of catharsis and enhancing self-understanding (Honeycutt, 2008). Catharsis relieves tension and reduces uncertainty about another's actions during the imaging process. Individuals imagine interacting with others in such a way that messages are explored and tested for their effect on others. Individuals may feel better while imagining. The account in Box 3.4 provided by a 22-year-old man who kept a journal on IIs for a 7-day period illustrates this point. The account also reveals the discrepancy between an II and a real interaction.

Box 3.4. Imagined Interaction Journal Account of a Man Encountering a Woman after Long Absence

Last summer I met a girl in Florida and we wrote each other for quite some time. We both kept saying we wanted to see each other, but our plans never materialized. Finally, in September she was going to fly to New Orleans to see me. From the moment she told she was coming to visit, I began imagining what it would be like when we saw each other. I figured we would embrace passionately at the airport and have a million things to say to each other. I figured we would go out Friday night to the French Quarter and go to bars. She had never been to a bar before. At the time the drinking age was 18 in New Orleans and 21 in Alabama (her home state). Saturday I planned for us to go to the Riverwalk all day and then go out again that night. Sunday morning I was supposed to bring her to Biloxi, where she had a ride home to Alabama.

Well, welcome to reality. When she got off the plane, we kind of half-hugged each other and really didn't know what to say to each other. Most of our conversation was small talk. After we got to my house and showered, we went to the French Quarter. We probably didn't stay there any longer than an hour before we decided that we were exhausted and ready to get some sleep. Surprisingly, Saturday was pretty much like I had planned. We spent the whole day at the Riverwalk and really enjoyed ourselves. However, Saturday night was a different story. We began the night as I had planned by going to bars. Then the real excitement began. At about one o'clock in the morning she told me she had to make a phone call. After she got off the phone, I was informed that she had to leave for Biloxi right then. Instead of spending a nice evening out with her, I spent most of the night going to Mississippi. This was definitely a good example of an imagined interaction being quite different than the actual experience.

Fortunately, all of my IIs were not this disappointing. Because my present girl-friend is living in New Orleans this semester, I often have IIs about the two of us. For instance, I often imagine us embracing and kissing when we see each other on Fridays. These IIs are often fulfilled and then some. I also imagine things we are going to say to each other and these dialogues are also fulfilled. We often tell each other how much we thought about each other and how much we missed each other.

Gender Differences in Imagined Interactions and Memory

There are a number of gender differences in the use of IIs (Honeycutt, 2003). Edwards, Honeycutt, and Zagacki (1989) found that women have more frequent and pleasant IIs than do men. Women also talk more in these imagined dialogues than do men. Both genders tend to recall both the lines of dialogue and the visual scenes of IIs, rather than only the imagined dialogue. However, women reported that they were able to see the surroundings in their IIs and recall the scene in which the II took place much more often than men did. Men were twice as likely to have IIs with female partners rather than with other men. Yet, due to the increased frequency of IIs among women, women still were three times more likely than men to have opposite-gender partners in their IIs.

Of course, the vividness and specificity of women's IIs are largely consistent with other studies revealing that women think more often than men do about relationship processes. Women are more aware of problems in a relationship, are less surprised when a relationship is terminated, and have more vivid memories of relational events (Hill, Rubin, & Peplau, 1976; Ross & Holmberg, 1992). Edwards et al. (1989) surmised that women are more socialized to think about the socioemotional aspects of relationships than are men. This is reflected in II topics about dating that are pleasant. Edwards et al. found in their sample that the primary II topic for both genders was dating. They decided that one cause of gender differences in relationship awareness may be that messages for interactions are derived by observing the actual conversations of others, after which the messages are incorporated into IIs. Another possibility is that men and women approach communication about relationships differently and that these different approaches are reflected in thoughts about communication, whether in IIs or in actual encounters. Scott, Fuhrman, and Wyer (1991) speculated that women may be likely to view their conversations as relationship-relevant and to store the conversation as a relationship memory, whereas men see the conversations in terms of the issue discussed. If this is correct, this hypothesis might account for the robustness of women's IIs because, presumably, people have imagined conversations with a *person* in a relationship about an issue rather than with an *issue* itself, and it is those interpersonal dimensions that women tend to focus on.

Acitelli (1992) interviewed married couples about their lives, an analytic device known as collecting an oral history of the marriage (Gottman, 1994). One of the benefits of this kind of interview is that even unhappily married couples often relive pleasant events that occurred in the early stages of their marriage. Couples were asked to tell the story of their relationship from the time they first met to what they thought their future will be like. The spontaneous expression of feelings or needs while telling a story was considered to be an expression of the couples' important concerns. Acitelli coded the partners' responses for relationship talk. Wives' marital and life satisfaction was positively associated with their husbands' relational talk and less with their own relational talk. Wives tended to talk more about their marital relationships than did their husbands. They also reported thinking more about their marriages than did their husbands.

Acitelli (1992) reported that relationship talk in the first year of marriage is related to relationship quality in the third year of marriage. Statements reflecting relationship awareness (e.g., "We were very much in love at that point. We wanted to get along better.") correlated positively with marital stability and happiness in the third year of marriage. In addition, the husband's ease, reflected in lack of tension, resentment, and positive adjustment to marriage, was a mediating factor between the spouses' perspective at the end of the first year together and their opinions of marital quality in their third year. A direct effect between relation-ship talk in the first year of marriage and marital well-being in the third year remained for wives, in addition to the effects the husband's ease variable had for both partners. Hence, Acitelli concluded that relationship awareness influences marital quality only if it leads to the husbands' ease of adjustment. For wives, this relational awareness happens, but need not occur for the relationship perspective to influence her marital quality. Men value relationship talk if it is instrumental in solving a problem, whereas women value relationship talk in pleasant and unpleas-ant situations.

There are also gender differences in using IIs to maintain roommate rela-tionships. Honeycutt and Patterson (1997) surveyed college roommates about how they maintained smooth relations in which they liked their roommates and the role of IIs in maintaining the relations. They found that women liked their roommates more than men did and that liking roommates was associ-ated with having more IIs that were pleasant and specific, as opposed to being filled with abstract images. Women also imagined more positive outcomes in their internal dialogues than did men. Liking one's roommate was associated with including the roommate in social activities and occasionally disclosing personal information about one's feelings, fears, or insecurities. Women who imagined conversations with their roommates tended to report acting in warm, caring, and empathic ways. The finding that women think about conversations with their roommates than do men is consistent with other research that women monitor their personal relationships more compared to men and think about relational events or problems (Harvey, Flannery, & Morgan, 1986; Honeycutt, 1993, 1995).

Imagined Interactions in Marriage

Additional gender differences in IIs and memory in marriage have begun to accu-mulate. Box 3.5 lists the most frequent II topics from the Survey of Relational Issues (Honeycutt, 2001), as well as the number of responses and the rank orders for the topics, which were coded using a list of categories that commonly have been identified in marital research as problematic issues in marriage (Spanier, 1976). The results are based on surveys issued to 136 couples. Interestingly, the topic discussed most often by the wives was how the couple communicated. The topics most discussed by both partners were future plans and goals. The next topic most discussed by husbands and wives was sexual relations, followed by how they communicate.

Box 3.5. Rank Order of Spousal Imagined Interaction Topics

Topics	Combined Rank Order	Male	Female
Future plans and goals	1	1 (12)	2 (7)
Sex life	2*	2 (8)	4 (5)
How we communicate	2*	6 (4)	1 (9)
Financial management	4	3 (6)	4 (5)
Our social life	5*	6 (4)	3 (6)
Our relationship	5*	3 (6)	6 (4)
Children	7*	6 (4)	8 (3)
My job	7*	5 (5)	10 (2)
Feelings and emotions	7*	9 (3)	6 (4)
Fantasies	10	9 (3)	8 (3)

Note: Numbers in parentheses reflect raw frequencies. Asterisk (*) denotes ties.

Imagined Interactions Among Engaged and Married Couples

Honeycutt and Wiemann (1999) conducted a study among engaged and married couples who were distinguished on the basis of Fitzpatrick's (1988) types of marriage. Fitzpatrick (1988) developed a polythetic classification scheme of marriage in which individuals are categorized according to their ideologies about marriage, degree of sharing, and engagement in conflict. There are three marital types: traditionals, independents, and separates. *Traditionals* have conventional beliefs about marriage such as emphasizing stability, sharing a lot of activities, and arguing over serious topics. *Independents* have a moderate amount of sharing, willingly engage in conflict over numerous topics, and endorse more contemporary ideologies about marriage, such as believing that marriage should not hinder an individual's autonomy in any way. *Separates* are ambivalent about family values, share few activities, and tend to avoid conflict. The separates have been described as emotionally divorced due to the lack of sharing.

Honeycutt and Wiemann (1999) also found that traditionals reported that discrepant IIs were used less for rehearsing messages for anticipated encounters than did independents. Because little rehearsing is taking place, there could be more discrepancies in conversational outcomes from what was expected in an II. The research of Sillars, Burggraf, Weisberg, and Wilson (1987) revealed that traditionals have more communal or sharing themes that are reflected in their conversations compared to independents. However, traditionals and independents also differ in intrapersonal communication processes insofar as the characteristics of IIs are concerned. Other research found that individuals who are sensitive to conversations also see themselves as having a great deal of communication competence (Honeycutt, Zagacki, & Edwards, 1992–1993). In turn, communication competence is negatively associated with having a lot of discrepant IIs, whereas conversational sensitivity is associated with a variety of IIs that are specific and occur after real encounters.

Recall that in a discrepant II, a message that is imagined is not communicated during an actual encounter. Traditionals may imagine encounters with their partners to rehearse messages that also inhibit misinterpretation, misunderstanding, or confusion that result in active conflict. Traditionals engage in arguing and conflictual encounters less than independents. Fitzpatrick (1988) reviewed research indicating that traditionals tend to avoid conflict except over serious issues, whereas independents are more likely to disagree about a variety of topics.

Little research has been conducted examining how the functions of talk are associated with characteristics of IIs among engaged and married couples. Many individuals report spending from 85% to 100% of their time thinking about their partner (Fisher, 1994). Intrusive thinking involves IIs with the partner. Given the strategic functions of communication, such as providing information, interpersonal influence, and impression management, IIs may be used to rehearse message strategies or replay prior messages in order to prepare for future encounters.

In terms of the rehearsal function, it has been found that a secure attachment style in which persons are optimistic and confident in forming and sustaining relationships is predicted by rehearsal as compared to other attachment types (Honeycutt, 1999). Perhaps strategic planning for various encounters enhances security in relationships. This use of IIs seems also to be linked to cognitive editing, which allows adjustments to messages after their potential effects on a given relationship have been assessed (Meyer, 1997). The implication here is that individuals rehearse messages, presumably through the use of IIs, and make changes as necessary for achieving desired outcomes.

Honeycutt and Wiemann (1999) found that there was an association between enjoying serious discussion, talking about the events of the day, equality of talk, and having frequent and pleasant IIs that followed expectations with the relational partner. In his marital interaction research program, Gottman (1994) discussed how talking about the events of the day reveals differences between couple types. The discussion of daily events was related to meta-talk or talk about communication and talk about love. Furthermore, the importance of intrapersonal communication is demonstrated through these findings because the functions of talk are linked with specific characteristics of IIs.

Honeycutt and Wiemann (1999) also found that relational satisfaction was associated with being engaged and having pleasant IIs. Thus, internal cognition in which an engaged individual imagines talking with his or her partner predicts happiness in this type of relationship. This finding is important in terms of social cognition because it reveals that a common outcome of close relationships, relationship happiness, is reflected in the minds of individuals internally in the form of intrapersonal communication in which individuals imagine pleasant interactions with relational partners. Hence, communication occurs internally as well as dyadically.

It was found that engaged partners had more IIs, IIs that were pleasant, and IIs that were used to compensate for the lack of real interaction than did marital partners. These findings can be interpreted in terms of the old maxim, "absence makes the heart grow fonder." There may be less rehearsal among the engaged partners due to less conflict in the honeymoon phase of their relational development.

Honeycutt (1995) discussed how one function of IIs is conflict linkage, which explains why conflict is kept alive in the absence of actual interaction. Individuals rehearse for the next episode which may reflect a self-fulfilling prophecy insofar as an episode of conflict is imagined and conflict-escalating statements are uttered, with the outcome being that the conflict picks up where it left off in a prior encounter. The conflict is kept alive outside of real encounters through imagined dialogue.

Honeycutt and Brown (1998) also investigated the use of IIs to rehearse the telling of jokes in marriage. They found that traditionals used IIs to rehearse jokes and that traditionals reported a greater sense of humor compared to independents and separates. Furthermore, traditional wives laughed at their husbands' jokes more than did the other marital types. Perhaps, amateur comedians in marriage may not feel a strong need to rehearse jokes. In this regard, Crawford (1989) showed that wives tend to laugh at their husbands' jokes in order to signal affiliation. Yet in order to allow a joke to realize its full impact, the joke-teller must rehearse the joke. Husbands imagined more joke telling than did their wives. The husbands' jokes are laughed at by their wives, which encourages more jokes. Men use humor more for self-presentation and women use humor to enhance intimacy (Crawford, 1989).

Imagined Interactions in Virtual Relationships

Internet social networking sites have grown exponentially in rapid fashion offering unprecedented opportunities for developing virtual friendships and romantic relationships. This suggests new research protocols for questions concerning thoughts about interacting with individuals one has never actually met. One of the most popular, Facebook, was developed as a social networking site by 22-year-old Mark Zuckerberg. It began exclusively as a site for college students to access information regarding friends with whom they had established relationships, but has expanded to include "friendships" with someone who has been allowed to access one's information on his/her page. To "friend" someone does not imply actual interaction. In fact, in Facebook jargon, the word "friend" has evolved from a noun to a verb. Bruno (2007) suggests, "Facebook might well be changing the nature of relationships, making them both more intrusive and yet somehow less intimate at the same time" (p. 9).

Results of an exploratory study recently have been reported by Bryan (2008) from an online survey of over 300 Facebook users. While discrepancy or the difference between one's II and an actual encounter has been found to be significant in relationships (Edwards, Honeycutt, & Zagacki, 1988), this characteristic appears also to have implications for virtual encounters. People who reported lower discrepancy between their II conversations and face-to-face encounters apparently were engaged in virtual relationships that were more likely to develop into successful actual relationships.

Summary

Imagined interactions (IIs) help create relational expectations and thereby contribute to people's memories about romantic pairings. Expectations regarding relationships can be envisioned as the knowledge or memory structures for relationships. Memory structures for relationships help people make sense of behaviors that they observe in other people and in their own relationships, and they provide a sense of the trajectory relationships are taking. IIs, consequently, provide an important bridge between romantic behavior and the way in which those statements and actions function in the sense-making of the mind.

A romance can be kept alive when the partners are away from each other by their thinking about it. Individuals in long-distance or commuter relationships report that they often think about their partners. Individuals also have IIs concerning romantic partners they see every day. People imagine conversations with relational partners in which they rehearse anticipated encounters, replay prior encounters, and even keep interpersonal conflict alive. IIs can bring up a variety of emotions that depend on the outcome of the imagined conversation. In addition to rehearsing events and keeping conflict or relationships alive, IIs serve a number of other functions including enhancing self-understanding and catharsis, and compensating for a lack in the actual time spent with one's significant other. In some cases, individuals have parasocial relationships in which they imagine talking with a celebrity or fabricated associate. However, most IIs occur with significant others, including relational partners, family members, and friends. Finally, women seem to produce more stalwart IIs than do men, suggesting that their IIs may exert a stronger influence on the type of communication that occurs in romantic relationships.

IIs help engaged couples maintain the relationship in terms of intrusive thinking. Having positive intrapersonal communication in the form of IIs helps couples maintain their marriages, particularly the traditional marital types. Joke telling also is done by traditionals, husbands use IIs to rehearse jokes, whereas their wives laugh at the jokes even if they are not that funny. Humor helps to maintain people's relationships in the face of adversity.

Discussion Questions

3.1. Recall the most recent imagined interaction (II) you have had with an individual who is very important in your life. When was it? What was said? How did you feel about the II? What purpose did it serve (e.g., rehearsal for an ensuing encounter, catharsis, enhancing your own understanding, keeping conflict alive, or keeping the relationship alive in your mind)? If the II was before an anticipated encounter, what happened in the encounter? Was the II different from or similar to the actual encounter?

3.2. Discuss any recurring IIs you have with long-lost loves of the past. How often do these occur? Why do you believe you reminisce about these people?

Applications

3.1. Interview three couples about their IIs with each other. How often do they imagine talking with their partners? Do they enjoy the IIs? What purpose did the IIs serve (e.g., keeping conflict alive, replaying love scenes, or reliving pleasant memories)? Are there differences between partners on the topics of the IIs and the vividness of memory about the IIs? Are the IIs similar to or different from later interaction scenes? If the IIs were used to rehearse for anticipated encounters with partners, how successful were the actual encounters?

3.2. Interview three men and three women about IPs they recall having had as children. Who were these playmates? How old were they when they imagined the playmates? What purposes or functions did the IPs serve (e.g., companionship, rehearse messages for real-life others, or escapism)? How did the relationship end? Did the person stop imagining the playmate at a certain age or time period? Did the IP teach them anything about human relationships?

3.3. Interview a couple in a long-distance relationship. Ask each one separately to explain how they maintain their relationship despite the distance between them. Are their responses the same? Are they familiar with imagined interactions? Write a one-page paper summarizing your data.

References

Acitelli, L. K. (1992). Gender differences in relationship awareness and marital satisfaction among young married couples. *Personality and Social Psychology Bulletin, 18*, 102–110. doi:10.1177/0146167292181015

Acitelli, L. K., Douvan, E., & Veroff, J. (1993). Perceptions of conflict in the first year of marriage: How important are similarity and understanding? *Journal of Social and Personal Relationships, 10*, 5–19. doi:10.1177/0265407593101001

Allen, T. H., & Berkos, K. M. (2010). Imagined interaction conflict-linkage theory: Examining accounts of recurring imagined interactions. In J. M. Honeycutt (Ed.), *Imagine that: Studies in imagined interaction* (pp. 31–41). Cresskill, NJ: Hampton.

Baumeister, R. F., & Leary, M. R. (1995). The need to belong: Desire for interpersonal attachments as a fundamental human motivation. *Psychological Bulletin, 117*(3), 497–529. doi:10.1037/0033-2909.117.3.497

Bruno, D. (2007). A mother and her daughter face up to Facebook. *Christian Science Monitor, 99*(36), 9–9.

Bryan, S. P. (2008, April). *Thinking about virtual relationships*. Paper presented at the 78th Annual Convention Southern States Communication Association, Savannah, GA.

Buckner, R. L., Andrews-Hanna, J. R., & Schacter, D. L. (2008). The brain's default network. *Annals of the New York Academy of Sciences, 1124*, 1–38. doi:10.1196/annals.1440.01

Caughey, J. L. (1984). *Imaginary social worlds*. Lincoln, NE: University of Nebraska Press.

Cavanaugh, A. M., & Buehler, C. (2015). Adolescent loneliness and social anxiety: The role of multiple sources of support. *Journal of Social and Personal Relationships, 33*, 149–170. doi:10.1177/0265407514567837

Connolly, J. F. (1991). Adults who had imaginary playmates as children. In R. G. Kunzendorf (Ed.), *Mental imagery* (pp. 113–120). New York, NY: Plenum.

Crawford, M. (1989). Humor in conversational context: Beyond biases in the study of gender and humor. In R. K. Unger (Ed.), *Representations: Social constructions of gender* (pp. 155–164). New York, NY: Baywood.

Croghan, T. L., & Croghan, J. M. (2010). Visualizing success: Imagined interactions in organization contexts. In J. M. Honeycutt (Ed.), *Imagine that: Studies in imagined interaction* (pp. 99–114). Cresskill, NJ: Hampton.

Edwards, R., Honeycutt, J. M., & Zagacki, K. S. (1988). Imagined interaction as an element of social cognition. *Western Journal of Speech Communication, 52*, 23–45. doi:10.1080/10570318809389623

Edwards, R., Honeycutt, J. M., & Zagacki, K. S. (1989). Sex differences in imagined interactions. *Sex Roles, 21*, 259–268. doi:10.1007/BF00289906

Fisher, H. (1994). *The natural history of monogamy, adultery and divorce.* New York, NY: Fawcett.

Fisher, H., Aron, A., Mashek, D., Li, H., Strong, G., & Brown, L. L. (2002). The neural mechanisms of mate choice: A hypothesis. *Neuro Endocrinology Letters, 23*(Suppl.), 492–97.

Fitzpatrick, M. A. (1988). *Between husbands and wives.* Newbury Park, CA: Sage.

Fox, K. C., Spreng, R. N., Ellamil, M., Andrews-Hanna, J. R., & Christoff, K. (2015). The wandering brain: Meta-analysis of functional neuroimaging studies of mind-wandering and related spontaneous thought processes. *Neuroimage, 111*, 611–621.

Gottman, J. M. (1994). *What predicts divorce?* Hillsdale, NJ: Lawrence Erlbaum.

Greicius, M. D., Krasnow, B., Reiss, A. L., & Menon, V. (2003). Functional connectivity in the resting brain: A network analysis of the default mode hypothesis. *Proceedings of the National Academy of Sciences, 100*(1), 253–258.

Guldner, G. T. (2003). *Long distance relationships.* Los Angeles, CA: JF Milne Publishers.

Harvey, J. H., Flannery, R., & Morgan, M. (1986). Vivid memories of vivid loves gone by. *Journal of Social and Personal Relationships, 3*, 359–373. doi:10.1177/0265407586033007

Hill, C. T., Rubin, Z., & Peplau, L. (1976). Breakups before marriage: The end of 103 affairs. *Journal of Social Issues, 32*, 147–168. doi:10.1111/j.1540-4560.1976.tb02485.x

Honeycutt, J. M. (1989). A functional analysis of imagined interaction activity in everyday life. In J. E. Shorr, P. Robin, J. A. Connelia, & M. Wolpin (Eds.), *Imagery: Current perspectives* (pp. 13–25). New York, NY: Plenum.

Honeycutt, J. M. (1993). Memory structures for the rise and fall of personal relationships. In D. Duck (Ed.), *Individuals in relationships* (pp. 60–86). Newbury Park, CA: Sage.

Honeycutt, J. M. (1995). Predicting beliefs about relational trajectories as a consequence of typicality and necessity ratings of relationship behaviors. *Communication Research Reports, 12*, 3–14. doi:10.1080/08824099509362033

Honeycutt, J. M. (1999). Differences in imagined interactions as a consequence of marital ideology and attachment. *Imagination, Cognition, and Personality, 18*, 269–283. doi:10.2190/DF9M-R77U-EH6P-93KV

Honeycutt, J. M. (2001). Satisfaction with marital issues and topics scale (SMI). In J. Touliatos, B. F. Perlmutter, & M. A. Straus (Eds.), *Handbook of family measurement techniques* (Vol. 1, p. 92). Thousand Oaks, CA: Sage.

Honeycutt, J. M. (2003). *Imagined interaction: Daydreaming about communication.* Cresskill, NJ: Hampton.

Honeycutt, J. M. (2010). Forgive but don't forget: Correlates of rumination about conflict. In J. M. Honeycutt (Ed.), *Imagine that: Studies in imagined interaction* (pp. 17–19). Cresskill, NJ: Hampton.

Honeycutt, J. M. (2014). Imagined interactions. In C. R. Berger & M. E. Roloff (Eds.), *Interpersonal communication* (pp. 249–271). Berlin: Walter de Gruyter.

Honeycutt, J. M. (2015). Imagined interaction theory: Mental representations of interpersonal communication. In D. O. Braithwaite & P. Schrodt (Eds.), *Engaging theories in interpersonal communication* (2nd ed., pp. 75–87). Thousand Oaks, CA: Sage.

Honeycutt, J. M., & Brown, R. (1998). Did you hear the one about? Typological and spousal differences in the planning of jokes and sense of humor in marriage. *Communication Quarterly, 46*, 1–11. doi:10.1080/01463379809370106

Honeycutt, J. M., Edwards, R., & Zagacki, K. S. (1989–1990). Using imagined interaction features to predict measures of self-awareness: Loneliness, locus of control, self-dominance, and emotional intensity. *Imagination, Cognition, and Personality, 9*, 17–31. doi:10.2190/02L8-1GMP-JV5C-JQ7X

Honeycutt, J. M., & Keaton, S. A. (2013). Imagined interactions and personality preferences as predictors of relationship quality. *Imagination, Cognition, and Personality, 32*, 3–21. doi:10.2190/IC.32.1.b

Honeycutt, J. M., & Patterson, J. (1997). Affinity strategies in relationships: The role of gender and imagined interactions in maintaining liking among college roommates. *Personal Relationships, 4*, 35–46. doi:10.1111/j.1475-6811.1997.tb00129.x

Honeycutt, J. M., Pence, M. E., & Gearhart, C. C. (2013). Using imagined interactions to predict covert narcissism. *Communication Reports, 26*, 26–38. doi:10.1080/08934215.2013.773051

Honeycutt, J. M., & Wiemann, J. M. (1999). Analysis of functions of talk and reports of imagined interactions (IIs) during engagement and marriage. *Human Communication Research, 25*, 399–419. doi:10.1111/j.1468-2958.1999.tb00451.x

Honeycutt, J. M., Zagacki, K. S., & Edwards, R. (1989). Intrapersonal communication and imagined interactions. In C. Roberts & K. Watson (Eds.), *Intrapersonal communication processes: Original essays* (pp. 167–184). Scottsdale, AZ: Gorsuch Scarisbrick.

Honeycutt, J. M., Zagacki, K. S., & Edwards, R. (1992–1993). Imagined interaction, conversational sensitivity and communication competence. *Imagination, Cognition, and Personality, 12*, 139–157. doi:10.2190/B9PC-51RJ-1D7N-4M94

Johnson, K. L., & Roloff, M. E. (2000). Correlates of the perceived resolvability and relational consequences of serial arguing in dating relationships: Argumentative features and the use of coping strategies. *Journal of Social and Personal Relationships, 17*, 676–686. doi:10.1177/0265407500174011

Klinger, E. (1987). *What people think about and when they think it*. Paper presented at the annual meeting of the American Psychological Association, New York, NY.

Lang, F. R., Wagner, J., Wrzus, C., & Neyer, F. J. (2013). Personal effort in social relationships across adulthood. *Psychology and Aging, 28*, 529–539. doi:10.1037/a0032221

McCann, R. M., & Honeycutt, J. M. (2006). An intercultural analysis of imagined interaction. *Human Communication Research, 32*, 274–301. doi:10.1111/j.1468-2958.2006.00276.x

Meyer, J. R. (1997). Cognitive influences on the ability to address interaction goals. In J. O. Greene (Ed.), *Message production: Advances in communication theory* (pp. 71–90). Mahwah, NJ: Lawrence Erlbaum.

Mongeau, P. A., Knight, K., Williams, J., Eden, J., & Shaw, C. (2013). Identifying and explicating variation among friends with benefits relationships. *Journal of Sex Research, 50*(1), 37–47. doi:10.1080/00224499.2011.623797

Nisbett, R. E., & Ross, L. (1980). *Human inference: Strategies and shortcoming of human judgement.* Englewood Cliffs, NJ: Prentice-Hall.

Poerio, G. L., & Smallwood, J. *(2016)*. Daydreaming to navigate the social world: What we know, what we don't know, and why it matters. *Social and Personality Psychology Compass, 10*, 605–618. *doi:*10.1111/spc3.12288.

Porter, M. A. (2010). Third-party imagined interactions: Expanding mental imagery to the experience of others' communication. *Imagination, Cognition, and Personality, 30*, 147–169. doi:10.2190/IC.30.2.d

Raichle, M. E. (2010). The brain's dark energy. *Scientific American, 302*(3), 44–49.

Rosenblatt, P. C., & Meyer, C. (1986). Imagined interactions and the family. *Family Relations, 35*, 319–324.

Ross, L. (1977). The intuitive psychologist and his shortcomings: Distortions in the attribution process. In L. Berkowitz (Ed.), *Advances in experimental social psychology* (Vol. 10, pp. 173–220). New York, NY: Academic Press.

Ross, M., & Holmberg, D. (1992). Are wives' memories for events in relationships more vivid than their husbands' memories? *Journal of Social and Personal Relationships, 9*, 585–604. doi:10.1177/0265407592094007

Scott, C. K., Fuhrman, R. W., & Wyer, R. S. (1991). Information processing in close relationships. In G. J. O. Fletcher & F. D. Fincham (Eds.), *Cognition in close relationships* (pp. 37–67). Hillsdale, NJ: Lawrence Erlbaum.

Sherman, S. J., & Corty, E. (1984). Cognitive heuristics. In R. S. Wyer, Jr. & T. K. Srull (Eds.), *Handbook of social cognition* (Vol. 1). Hillsdale, NJ: Lawrence Erlbaum.

Sillars, A. L., Burggraf, C. S., Weisberg, J., & Wilson, E. A. (1987). Content themes in marital conversations. *Human Communication Research, 13*, 495–528. doi:10.1111/j.1468-2958.1987.tb00116.x

Singer, J. L. (1979). *Proceedings, international year of the child.* New Haven, CT: Yale University Press.

Singer, J. L. (1985). Private experience and public action: The study of ongoing thought. Henry Murray Lecture, *Symposium on Personality.* Symposium conducted at Michigan State University, East Lansing.

Spanier, G. B. (1976). Measuring dyadic adjustment: New scales for assessing the quality of marital adjustment. *Journal of Marriage and the Family, 42*, 15–27.

Stafford, L., & Merolla, A. J. (2007). Idealization, reunions, and stability in long-distance dating relationships. *Journal of Social and Personal Relationships, 24*, 37–54. doi:10.1177/0265407507072578

Van Kelegom, M. J., & Wright, C. N. (2013). An investigation of episodic and partner-specific imagined interaction use. *Imagination, Cognition, and Personality, 32*, 319–338. doi:10.2190/IC.32.4.b

Wallenfelsz, K. P., & Hample, D. (2010). The role of taking conflict personally in imagined interactions about conflict. *Southern Communication Journal, 75*, 471–487. doi:10.1080/10417940903006057

Zagacki, K. S., Edwards, R., & Honeycutt, J. M. (1992). The role of mental imagery and emotion in imagined interaction. *Communication Quarterly, 40*, 56–68. doi:10.1080/01463379209369820

Physiology and Relationships

Over the course of history it has been artists, poets, and playwrights who have made the greatest progress in humanity's understanding of love. Romance has seemed as inexplicable as the beauty of a rainbow. But these days scientists are challenging that notion in terms of neurochemicals being conducive to love and understanding conflict. Following is a brief assumption of communibiology and how it explains communication behavior in everyday life followed by reasons for studying physiology in relationships.

Communibiology Assumptions

Communibiology is a paradigm for studying communication by studying the genetic and neurobiological foundation of communication (Heisel, 2014; McCroskey, 2006). Pence, Heisel, Reinhart, Tian, and Beatty (2011) using a technique known as meta-analysis examined a variety of communication behaviors in relation to resting alpha asymmetry in the prefrontal cortex and found evidence for communibiology assumptions for aggressive response to insults, anger, defensiveness, and social competence.

In terms of parental–child relationships, research reveals that when parents are better able to empathize with their children it results in better health outcomes for children including less depression and aggression as well as better psychological profiles and a greater ability to use perspective-taking themselves (Manczak, DeLongis, & Chen, 2016). Furthermore, the psychological conditions of a family environment is associated with aggressiveness in the offspring such that those who grow up in an environment where the parents communicate little warmth as well as engaging in risky parenting practices display more low-grade inflammation of illness including elevations in interleukin 6 and C-reactive protein. The reason for this may be that the availability of support and comfort from parents helps to calibrate children's biological response systems in beneficial ways. Interestingly, parents who were more empathic had greater psychological well-being and higher levels of health inflammatory markers including IL-1ra and IL-6. Giving support to others reduces stressor-evoked SNS activity for systolic blood pressure (Inagaki & Eisenberger, 2016).

Research is also shedding light on some of the more extreme forms of sexual behavior. And, controversially, some utopian fringe groups see such work as the doorway to a future where love is guaranteed because it will be provided chemically, or even genetically engineered from conception (http://www.oxytocin.org/oxytoc/love-science.html).

Imagined Interactions (IIs) Conflict-Linkage Theory

Honeycutt (2003) relates communibiology assumptions in his examination of how ongoing, daily conflict in personal relationships is manifested. Recall from Chapter 3 that *imagined interactions* (IIs) are used to maintain relationships as well as deal with conflict where individuals imagine talking with relational partners over a variety of topics as well as anticipating future encounters or reliving prior conversations. Imagined interaction conflict-linkage theory contains three axioms and nine theorems explaining how interpersonal conflict endures and is managed. This theory explains how individuals manage daily conflict through productive or unproductive means. Ultimately, therapists and counselors might apply the research to relationships for the purpose of educating relational partners as to the roots of their conflicts.

Theorem six of imagined interaction conflict-linkage theory states that recurring conflict is reflected in physiological arousal in which anxiety is triggered and persons "fight" or "take flight" in terms of the sympathetic nervous system (SNS; Honeycutt, 2015). Communication theorists indicate the importance of biological factors in determining communication traits such as communication apprehension and verbal aggression. For example, 50–80% of communication apprehension is explained by genetic factors (Beatty, McCroskey, & Heisel, 1998; Boren & Veksler, 2011). The idea to be drawn from this research is support for the idea that there is a biological link to conflict, particularly verbal aggression (Beatty & McCroskey, 1997). If certain communicative characteristics such as communication apprehension have been linked to biological determinants, then it seems logical that likelihood to engage in conflict could be linked to such factors as well.

Indeed, there is qualified physiological support for argumentative skills deficiency in romantic couples in which couples are discussing an area of conflict in their relationship (Aloia & Solomon, 2015). Communication skills deficiency determines whether people diffuse hostility or increase it. People who lack the ability to engage in rational argumentation get frustrated and use verbal aggression (also see Honeycutt, 2015). People with an inability to diffuse conflict use more criticisms as opposed to focused complaining, use sarcasm, and show increased stress through salivary cortisol. Furthermore, loudness was positively associated with stress increase as revealed through cortisol for females while disagreement and sarcasm were positively associated with cortisol stress for males. Additionally, additional salivary cortisol studies reveal that conflict intensity is associated with the amplitude of stress reactivity in arguments among college-aged dating partners (Aloia & Solomon, 2014). It is interesting how a history of exposure to familial verbal aggression affects stress reactivity such that the magnitude of the positive association between conflict intensity and stress reactivity is reduced when a history of exposure to family aggression is high rather than low.

Beatty, McCroskey, and Pence (2009) discuss how cognition and personality do not exist independently of neurological or physiological properties. Hence, conflict in relationships, particularly verbal aggression, has biological components. Any explanation of a cognitive phenomenon such as that of thinking or dwelling on arguments must acknowledge the impact of neurology and physiology. In our interaction lab, we have seen the rise in heart rate variability as relational partners relive and express ongoing grievances with each other.

A current script for the development of relationships is that love is hard-wired in various areas of the brain and is driven by neurotransmitters in the brain. Relatedly, damage to the amygdala is associated with an impaired ability to recognize emotional faces and a reduction of affect, especially anger, rage, and fear (Adolphs & Tranel, 2003; Morris et al., 1998). Hence, love and the display of emotions are a matter of brain chemistry and chemicals. Yet, the rationale for studying physiology in relationships should first be established. This is briefly discussed next followed by stages of biological love in terms of chemicals.

Why Study Physiology in Relationships?

Physiological data can complement existing methods for interviewing or observing couples. Consider a study of positive and negative affect in discussing issues in intimate relationships such as exclusive daters and engaged and married couples. At the Louisiana State University, we have an interaction lab that is euphemistically referred to as the "Match Box" (see Picture 4.1). The lab resembles a comfortable living room complete with leather couch, wingback chair, paintings, magazines, and games. Relational partners can sit across from each other at right angles or adjacent to each other. However, we are observing them through a concealed video and microphone. We have measured the physiological arousal of couples that were asked to imagine either discussing a topic that they were highly pleased with (e.g., sharing time together) or displeased with (e.g., how they communicate) and then to actually discuss the topics. A typical approach might include surveys (e.g., pre- and postinteraction ratings of affect) and observational data (e.g., behavioral coding of the interaction).

Consider an interaction that is mostly positive except for a brief highly negative exchange in the middle. We often see both positive and negative interaction in our behavioral research lab. One task that we give couples is to complete a list of

Picture 4.1. Mutual gaze and gesturing while speaking with fiancé in Interaction Lab.

topics (Honeycutt, 2001) in which they indicate how satisfied they are with them (e.g., social life, time spent together, how decisions are made, temperament) and they are taped while discussing a pleasing/displeasing topic while being connected to our physiological equipment. While pre and postratings of affect would not capture the variability in this case, continuous physiological data could reveal a spike in arousal during and after the negative exchange. In fact, our physiological monitors allow us to instantly mark any point during a conversation where there is a topic change (e.g., they move on from discussing a positive to a negative topic). We can capture the behavioral variability in this example using observational coding, which also can be informed by physiological data.

Couples may behave atypically in the laboratory (Foster, Caplan, & Howe, 1997), and a calm demeanor may belie significant internal emotion and physiological arousal. This will be discussed further in this chapter when showing the heart rate graphs of a couple discussing a pleasing and displeasing topic. Indeed, a conversation that appears positive on the surface could be the product of two angry people putting on their best performance. Physiological measures offer a window into the alleged internal turmoil that a conversation might create. Most physiological measures are not under conscious control. Hence, physiological measures offer a means of circumventing the self-presentation bias that is endemic to observational studies of communication.

Common Physiological Measures of Arousal

Physiological arousal involves the autonomic nervous system in a state of adrenalin release and includes pulse (heart rate beats per minute), interbeat intervals (IBI), and somatic activity measured in terms of an actigraph that is worn on the wrist. *Somatic activity* tracks wrist and hand movements used while gesturing. It reflects kinetic energy release and tension release through motion. Additional types of somatic activity are the use of nonverbal self and object adapters (Knapp, Hall, & Horgan, 2014). Adaptors are behaviors designed to deal with anxiety, stress, and tension. For example, nervous individuals may play with jewelry, tap a pen, or gesture with a cell phone (object adaptors). Self-adaptors are a type of somatic activity involving touch directed toward one's own body including scratching, preening behavior in the form of playing or stroking the hair, and shaking of the ankles or legs. In this regard, restless leg movement is an extreme form of tension release.

Interbeat intervals is a measure of the time in milliseconds between adjacent heart beats. High IBI rates are related to increased levels of adrenalin, anxiety, and arousal (Porges, 1985a, 1985b). The lower the IBI value, the shorter the cardiac beat, which reflects a faster heart rate. Under normal conditions, the heart's rate is under control of the parasympathetic nervous system (PNS). Generally, resting heart rates for men are 70 and 80 for women according to the American Heart Association. Heart rates above 105 are high and above the effects of exercise (Rowell, 1986). Your resting heart rate typically decreases with age. It is also affected by environmental factors; for example, it increases with extremes in temperature and altitude. We always take a baseline measure of heart rate before engaging in experimental stimuli. We use the baseline measure and age as a covariate in analyzing subsequent mean differences. Research on conflict and storytelling indicates that heart rate is correlated with feeling conflict and stress as opposed to discussing positive stories (Honeycutt, Bannon, & Hatcher, 2014; Revina, 2006). Positive stories provide hope that couples can survive difficult times. Furthermore, a study revealed that optimists live longer while pessimists die earlier (Seligman, Parks, & Steen, 2006).

Additional measures of physiology include respiration, muscle movements, *blood pressure, electrodermal analysis* also referred to as galvanic skin conductance, and electroencephalogram (EEG). Moreover, there are wet measures of physiological activity involving cortisol (saliva) and blood glucose. Skin conductance represents a change in the electrical properties of the skin in response to stress or anxiety; can be measured either by recording the electrical resistance of the skin or by recording weak currents generated by the body. The EEG involves attaching electrodes to the head of a person to measure and record electrical activity in the brain over time. Gottman (1994) reviews studies indicating that under normal conditions, correlations among measures vary. Even though the measures range from none to moderate correlations (.00–.36), there is evidence of patterning. In terms of blood glucose, it has been reported that there is a strong, negative association between the expression of affection and glycohemoglobin, which reflects the average blood glucose level over a three-month period (Floyd, Hesse, & Haynes, 2007).

An intriguing study of blood pressure in married couples reveals that a happy marriage is good for your blood pressure, but a stressed one can be worse than being single. Holt-Lunstad, Birmingham, and Jones (2008) studied 204 married people and 99 single adults. Most were white, and it is not clear whether the same results would apply to other ethnic groups. The participants wore portable devices that recorded their blood pressure at random times over 24 hours. Married participants also filled out questionnaires about their marriage. The analysis found that the more marital satisfaction and adjustment spouses reported, the lower their average systolic blood pressure was over the 24 hours and during the daytime. However, spouses who scored low in marital satisfaction had higher average blood pressure than single people did. During the daytime, their average systolic pressure was about five points higher, entering a range that's considered a warning sign.

An additional measure that we use is *mean arterial pressure*. This measure reflects the weighted average of systolic and diastolic blood pressure (Peckerman et al., 2003).[1] When referring to blood pressure, many people do not consciously think about the differences between the systolic and diastolic numbers and what they mean. Systolic blood pressure essentially reflects pressure *within* a heartbeat. It is the pressure in your aorta, the large artery that received blood coming out of the heart. Diastolic blood pressure is the pressure in the aorta and its main branches *between* beats.

The HeartMath LLC discusses research that reveals how emotions drive activity into coherence or chaos. In response to the perception of threat, the corresponding emotions are fear, worry, anxiety, or anger. A Harvard Medical School Study of 1623 heart attack survivors found that when they got angry during emotional conflicts, their risk of subsequent heart attacks was more than double that of those who remained calm (Anderson & Anderson, 2003).

Oxytocin and the Physiological Development of Love

Oxytocin is a hormone produced naturally in the hypothalamus in the brain. Oxytocin is associated with our ability to mediate emotional experiences in close relationships and maintain healthy psychological boundaries. Conversely, testosterone increases antisocial behavior, dominance, egocentricity, and decreases collaboration (Wright et al., 2012). Being touched anywhere on the body causes a rise in oxytocin levels, initiating a series of events that lead to biological and psychological arousal, including a rush of endorphins (the body's natural pain relievers) as well as a spike in testosterone levels (the hormone that kick-starts sex drive). Oxytocin heightens a warm and fuzzy bonding feeling, increasing sexual receptiveness and intimacy.

Recall from Chapter 2 that sex and physical attraction to a new partner stimulate the release of hormones designed to keep couples together for long enough to reproduce successfully. We are attracted to people who are like us or like our parents in some way (genetics and smell/pheromones both come into play here) and who have characteristics that make us believe they are likely to be a good partner in terms of producing children. Initial desire or lust is brought on by surges of sex hormones including estrogen and testosterone. These produce a relatively indiscriminate desire for physical gratification. When you fall in love, increases in secretion of PEA or b-phenylethylamine, creates natural "high" and helps mask any failings of your potential mate. This can last for the first 2–4 years of the relationship. Gradually over this period, the levels of PEA return to normal.

Similarly, dark chocolate is believed to be good for you. Chocolate carries high levels of chemicals called phenolics. These are antioxidant chemicals that prevent cholesterol from oxidizing and clogging the blood vessels. Indeed, research performed in London suggests that these antioxidants help decrease stress and protect against disease. In addition to its beneficial effect on blood cholesterol levels, recent research has shown that cocoa contains a wealth of phytochemicals and polyphenols, which have significant antioxidant properties and may help to reduce the risk of developing cancer. According to Chocolate.org, chocolate contains small amounts of our love drug, "PEA." *Phenylethylamine*—or "PEA"—is a naturally occurring trace ammine in the brain. PEA is a natural amphetamine that can cause stimulation and contributes to that kick-up-your-heels, on-top-of-the-world feeling that attraction can bring.

The physiological development of love across cultures has been made popular by Dr. Helen Fisher (2004), a cultural anthropologist. She has studied oxytocin. She is the author and presenter of the BBC World Service Love series. Table 4.1 summarizes some of the key findings of Fisher's (2004) research on the physiology of love.

She concludes that romantic love is a universal experience—deeply embedded in the human brain. For example, Fisher believes that people everywhere, from the ancient Sumerians and Chinese to contemporary Tanzanians, Eskimos, and Arabs, express the same mental and physical traits when madly in love. By scanning people's brains, Fisher (2004) suggests that love comes in three stages: lust, romantic love, and long-term attachment. There is overlap, but these are separate phenomena, with their own emotional and motivational systems, and accompanying chemicals. These systems have evolved to enable, respectively, mating, pair-bonding, and parenting.

Lust, of course, involves a craving for sex. The aftermath of lustful sex is similar to the state induced by taking opiates. An interesting mix of chemical changes occurs, including increases in the levels of serotonin, oxytocin, vasopressin, and endogenous opioids (the body's natural equivalent of heroin). These chemicals serve many functions, to relax the body, induce pleasure and fulfillment, and perhaps induce bonding to the very features that one has just experienced all this with. For example, kissing reduces oxytocin levels in men while increasing it in women. Kissing also has a calming effect on both sexes.

Cortisol and Stress in Relationships

The presence of cortisol is associated with stress. Cortisol is present in saliva. During stress, the hypothalamus activates the pituitary gland through the bloodstream by carrying the adrenocorticotropic hormone (ACTH) which stimulates the adrenal cortex to secrete cortisol. Levels are highest in the morning hours and continue to fall throughout the day. Consequently, researchers, interested in studying cortisol and stress, often gather saliva samples in the afternoon. Research among 68 intimate, nonmarital couples who were asked to think about and talk about getting married with their partners found that their cortisol levels increased after finding out they would have the marriage discussion and peaked around the midpoint of the discussion (Loving, Gleason, & Pope, 2009). Other research on the transition of falling in love reveals that there is the release of neurotrophin nerve growth factor, a biological marker linked to social bonding (Emanuele et al., 2005). Research has revealed that kissing provides stress relief by reducing cortisol (Wilson & Hill, 2007). Over the long term, it serves to maintain the bond lovers feel for one another. Forms of it have also been observed in other species including elephants who shove their trunks in each other's mouths. Much information is exchanged when lips meet, with potential "lovers" unconsciously tapping into chemical, tactile, and bodily cues. Regions of the brain are stimulated when you get a good kiss, given that a huge amount of our brain is dedicated to picking up information from our mouths. Kissing has other primal effects on us as well. Visceral marching orders boost pulse and blood pressure. The pupils dilate, breathing deepens, and rational thought retreats, as desire suppresses both prudence and self-consciousness. Hence, Wilson and Hills (2007) confirm the intuitive script that the first kiss can make or break a budding romance for both sexes. Some social scientists argue for a kissing compatibility theory in which we are biologically "programmed" to lock lips better with certain individuals.

Evolutionary psychologists have speculated that the kiss may be one way by which we determine reproduction and whether a would-be lover is genetically compatible. The exchange of saliva during kissing may have biological ramifications, helping to explain why men like to go for the moist kiss. This is even more fascinating when you consider that male saliva contains measurable amounts of testosterone, one of our sex hormones, which can affect libido.

The second stage is attraction, or the state of being in love (what is sometimes known as romantic or obsessive love). This is a refinement of lust that allows people to focus on a particular mate. This state is characterized by feelings of exhilaration, and intrusive, obsessive thoughts about the object of one's affection. Some researchers suggest this mental state might share neurochemical characteristics with the manic phase of manic depression. Fisher's (1994, 2004) work suggests that the actual behavioral patterns of those in love—such as attempting to evoke reciprocal responses in one's loved one—resemble obsessive compulsive disorder (OCD).

Reciprocity raises the question of whether it is possible to "treat" this romantic state clinically, as can be done with OCD. The parents of any infatuated teenager may want to know this. Fisher suggests it might be possible to dampen feelings of romantic love, but only at its early stages. OCD is characterized by low levels of serotonin. Drugs, such as Prozac, work by keeping serotonin hanging around in the brain for longer than normal, so they might fight off romantic feelings. This also means that people taking antidepressants may be interfering with their ability to fall in love. But once romantic love begins in earnest, it is one of the strongest drives on Earth. Fisher (1994) says it seems to be more powerful than hunger. Wonderful though it is, romantic love is unstable—not a good basis for child-rearing.

The third stage is long-term attachment with the desire for parental bonding. This stage allows parents to cooperate in raising children. Attachment theory has been widely discussed in the literature (see Bowlby, 2005) in terms of secure, avoidant, and dismissive types. A secure attachment is characterized by feelings of calm, security, comfort, and emotional union. Fearful avoidant attachments are fearful of long-term relationships and have low self-esteem (Ainsworth, 1989) because of failed relationships in the past and they have formed internal scripts that may act as self-fulfilling prophecies. Hence, lack of commitment may be expected because of the history of short-term relationships. Dismissive attachments have high self-esteem and are self-reliant, believing that they can survive with few, if any, close relationships. They often deny needing close relationships. Some may even view close relationships as relatively unimportant. Not surprisingly, they seek less intimacy with relationship partners, whom they often view less positively than they view themselves.

A final attachment style is anxious-preoccupied. These scripts reflect the idea that other people are better than the self. People with this style of attachment seek high levels of intimacy, approval, and responsiveness from their partners. They sometimes value intimacy to such an extent that they become overly dependent on their partners—a condition colloquially termed *clinginess*. Compared to securely attached people, people who are anxious or preoccupied with attachment tend to have less positive views about themselves. They often doubt their worth as a partner and blame themselves for their partners' lack of responsiveness. They also have less positive views about their partners because they do not trust in people's good intentions. People who are anxious or preoccupied with attachment may experience high levels of emotional expressiveness, worry, and impulsiveness in their relationships.

Because the love stages are independent, they can work simultaneously—with dangerous results. As Fisher (2004) explains, "you can feel deep attachment for a

Table 4.1. The physiology of love (Adapted from http://www.bbc.co.uk/worldservice/specials/1524_love/page3.shtml).

Lust

The craving for sexual gratification—is associated primarily with testosterone in both men and women.

Romantic attraction

The passion, adrenaline, obsessive thinking, focused attention, and yearning of new, fresh love—is associated with elevated brain activities of dopamine and norepinephrine, natural stimulants, and low activity of a related brain chemical, serotonin. Yet, low serotonin levels are related to anxiety, depression, anger, and aggression (see Chapter 13).

Attachment and Oxytocin

The serenity and calm that one often feels with a long-term partner—is associated with oxytocin and vasopressin. Oxytocin in females, as well as the closely related vasopressin in males, is the key to pair bonding. "You first meet someone and they are passable. The second time you go out with the person and they are OK. The third time you go out with him/her, sex is more likely to happen. And from that point on you can't imagine what life would be like without them. Since the release of oxytocin can be classically conditioned, after repeatedly having sex with the same partner, just seeing that partner could release more oxytocin, making you wanting to be with that person all the more, and you bond."

---

long-term spouse, while you feel romantic love for someone else, while you feel the sex drive in situations unrelated to either partner." This independence means it is possible to love more than one person at a time.

Diffuse Physiological Arousal in Couples

Gottman and Levenson (1988) were pioneering social scientists to study marital interaction and physiological arousal systematically as well as longitudinally, sometimes conducting follow-up data analyses on couples over a 14-year period (Gottman & Levenson, 2002). In the past 25 years Gottman and his associates have gathered a wealth of data on the role of physiological arousal in marital dissolution. Physiological arousal is also referred to as physiological linkage because in relationships, emotions are often very correlated (Timmons, Margolin, & Saxbe, 2015). For example, if you are in a relationship with someone and they are feeling anxious, you might start feeling the same way. There is voluminous literature on how people who live together use facial mimicry such that if you live with a person who frowns, you subconsciously mimic facial expressions (Seibt, Mühlberger, Likowski, & Weyers, 2015).

Another leader in this field, Kiecolt-Glaser, Bane, Glaser, and Malarkey (2003) and Kiecolt-Glaser et al. (2005) have accumulated compelling data on the effects of marital conflict on immune and endocrine functioning. Sometimes, their conclusions differ. For example, Gottman claims that physiological arousal is more punishing for men, while Kiecolt-Glaser et al. (2003) argue that it is the women who suffer physiologically from the ill-effects of marital duress (also see Kiecolt-Glaser & Newton, 2001). Therefore, Gottman argues that men are more likely to withdraw from discussing sensitive topics in unhappy marriages because subliminally, they are trying to prevent arousal and the release of adrenalin. Once the man is aroused, it takes longer for his heart rate to return to a basal resting state (Gottman, 1994).

Diffuse physiological arousal (DPA) occurs in terms of adrenalin pumping into the cardiovascular and endocrine systems. It is reflected by elevated heart rate, perspiration, blood pressure, and pulse. DPA can be very high during heated arguments. The research on the stress response and its effect on the human body and performance suggest that as the stress response intensifies, the body may enter into the fight or flight mode with eventual reduction in performance. Gottman's research into DPA with couples in conflict suggests that there are significant changes in the body and brain that inhibited the couples' ability to listen, take in new information and change old thinking, responding, and behaving patterns. Overarousal supports attack, defend, and withdraw reactions when couples hold different positions that lead to conflict. Married couples' blister wounds heal more slowly after a conflictive interaction versus supportive marital interaction (Kiecolt-Glaser et al., 2005). Repeated failure to communicate effectively about important issues in the relationship, coupled with active or passive hostility, leads to disconnection and a negative view of the partner and the relationship. Continual negative feelings and beliefs undermine the health, happiness, and stability of the couple and opens the door to verbal, emotional, and physical abuse. In such an environment, affairs and divorce are likely.

Yet, the ability to calm down when in DPA is absolutely critical for couples. Healthy, happy, and stable relationships are created in a field of positive emotions and interactions. The leading research in marriage and relationship supports this important reality in couple interactions. The Institute of HeartMath's 17 years of thorough research into the power of positive emotions (see www.heartmath. com) supports the research of Gottman (1994), Johnson (2004), and other leading researchers in this field. In fact, the HeartMath Institute offers a biofeedback device in which individuals can immediately trace their heart rate rhythms with a simple ear or finger sensor and use breathing exercises to self-sooth and calm them, thus activating the PNS. A critical role for the PNS is to control arousal and emotional expression. Hence, it is your "chill out" ability in a social context.

Greater heart rate variability leads to the use of adaptive regulation and coping strategies.

The PNS as reflected in heart rhythm facilitates social interaction, which is highly involved in our ability to create relationships. Conversely, reduced heart rate variability has negative outcomes including anxiety, depression, emotional dysregulation, and withdrawal from relationships (O'Connor, Heron, Golding, Beveridge, & Glover, 2002). For example, autistic kinds live in a state of hyperalertness and have lower heart rate variability and a poor PNS. The PNS is associated with recovery and relaxation while the SNS is associated with responding to an external threat such as having an argument, anxiety, arousal, conflict, tension, and adrenalin. Activation of the PNS implies more heart rate variability, which is associated with better overall health. Indeed, the polyvagal theory of Stephen Porges (2001) states how the PNS is associated with relaxation and calmness, while the SNS is associated with tension, anxiety, fear, arousal, and aggression. Gottman and Silver (2015) discuss how marital conflict shows a pattern of *Demand* change and *Withdraw* from the discussion. Furthermore, research by Gottman, Coan, Carrere, and Swanson (1998) reveals that women are more likely to begin with *Harsh Startups* while men are more likely to become *Flooded* and *Stonewalled*, and to rehearse stress-inducing thoughts (see Chapter 3 on IIs). This leads to Gridlock, which may be resolved in one of two ways: Disengagement, which spells a slower divorce that ends at 12+ years, or a high-conflict period marked by the 4 *Horsemen*, which spells a faster divorce in 5–7 years. The 4 horsemen of the apocalypse, as Gottman and Silver (2015) call them, lead to divorce over 94% of the time. They are criticism, contempt, defensiveness, and stonewalling.

- Criticisms—They are global, personal attacks that often include "You always" and "You never" statements. They demean a partner's personality or character (e.g., You're always late. Why can't you be responsible?) Conversely, complaints are good and reflect specific statements about the specific behavior at which a partner failed (e.g., Why were you late arriving at the appointment? Was the traffic bad?)
- Contempt—Sarcasm, insults, name-calling, mockery, and nonverbal behaviors including wrinkling the nose, and raising the upper lip signal contempt. Contempt—"I would never be so low as to do something like that!"
- Defensiveness—Upon receiving criticisms, people are likely to be defensive. They feel that they are being picked on and may even whine. Whining is often heard as a high-pitched, irritating nasal voice tone. Whining is close to crying and related to sadness (Gottman, 1994). Gottman and Silver

(2015) note that criticism, contempt, and defensiveness often function like a relay match handing the baton off to each other, repetitively.

- Stonewalling—Also known as withdrawal, stonewalling reflects avoidance of discussion and lack of responsiveness. The person turns away by being silent or even leaving the room. It reflects shutting down and is associated with high physiological arousal and efforts to self-soothe with thoughts like "I can't believe she's saying this!"

It is possible that gender differences in some relationships make women less powerful, and thus more likely to begin an argument more harshly as a way to communicate "I can't take it any more"; however, such criticisms often ignore why gender differences leave men feeling they have to "Buckle down and take it" when arguments become emotionally overwhelming or even abusive to them. Historical research by Komarovsky (1962) in blue-collar marriages reveals that the wives complained of the husband's withdrawal from serious discussion of grievances, particularly work and money. Similarly, in the middle of the 20th century, Locke (1951) found that divorced men complained of nagging while the wives complained about the husband's emotional withdrawal. These stereotypes still persist today as witnessed in YouTube videos, Internet news reports, and cable TV dramas.

There are consistent individual differences in physiological arousal including marital distress being associated with heart rate variability. To the extent that conflict is characterized by negative behavior, it is physiologically arousing. Unhappy couples typically exhibit greater reactivity in laboratory interactions than happy couples because they engage in more negative and less positive behavior. It should be noted, however, that even happily married newlywed couples exhibit elevated stress hormones after conflict (Kiecolt-Glaser et al., 2003). Robles, Shaffer, Malarkey, and Kiecolt-Glaser (2006) found that high levels of husbands' positive behaviors (e.g., describing problems, compromise, humor, smiling/laughter, agreements, accepting responsibility, assent, positive mind reading) during discussions of relational issues among newlyweds were associated with decreases in two stress hormones, ACTH and cortisol for husbands, while low levels of wives' positive behavior were related to flatter declines in wives' cortisol.

In one study examining attachment styles on abusive tendencies, Diamond, Hicks, and Otter-Henderson (2006) found that avoidant women were more abusive than avoidant men. Avoidance attachment reflects the script that relationships are to be avoided for fear of losing control or self-identity. According to attachment theories, adults raised in a family with poor personal relationships tend to have avoidant or anxious attachment style later in their life. Specifically, *anxiously* attached individuals tend to experience and show more negative emotions, while *avoidantly* attached individuals minimize or suppress negative emotions.

Avoidant women may ruminate about negative emotions longer after an interaction has occurred. Furthermore, Kiecolt-Glaser et al. (1996) argue that women are more vulnerable to negative life events than men. This is the opposite of what Gottman and previous research claimed—that men are more vulnerable to stress. Aside from sample and methodological issues, one explanation may be in the changing roles of women. In the last 25 years women have started to compete with men at the workplace and in the public sphere, so that they are often forced to act "rational," even when they feel "emotional" (also see Tannen, 2005).

In order to be perceived equal to men, many women suppress their emotions, and thus psychologically suffer more than men who are raised, and to some extent born, "rational." Another explanation for avoidant women to react more strongly than men is their role in society. In previous generations, women were taught to be subordinate to men or to take "one down" role (Woods, 2008). Such a position can cause the accumulation of stress in women, especially ones who are thought to desire only equity with men. Diamond and her colleagues (2006) argue that in terms of the relationship between testosterone levels and conflict tactics, women's behavior is more socially moderated than biologically determined (also see Baumeister, 2002).

Both research and clinical practice demonstrate the resiliency of negative emotions on heart rate. For example, Ironson and his associates (1992) showed that cardiovascular disease is associated with remembering anger episodes. Hence, the HeartMath Institute in California promotes training in positive emotions (see Chapter 14) as a tool for health as well as controlling heart rate variability (Childre & McCraty, 2001). In terms of biofeedback, it has been recommended that it is possible to retrain heart rhythms that transform people in relationships and their emotions (MacLean, 2004). A variety of programs are offered including thinking positively through IIs and mental imagery as well as music therapy in which positive music is used (Honeycutt & Eidenmuller, 2001), muscle relaxation, and other types of mediation (Baer, 2003; Moss, 2004).

A Physiological Script for Relational Deterioration

Based on his comprehensive studies of taping and observing couples while they are arguing as well as discussing events of the day and providing an oral history of how they first met, Gottman (1994) has presented a physiological, cascade model of divorce that essentially can be viewed as a script for how many relationships end. Indeed, his physiological, cascade model of divorce can be applied to a variety of long-term, interpersonal relationships.

Physiological responses including elevated heart rate and increases in blood pressure accompany the inability to soothe oneself when a person has elevated adrenalin and is subconsciously trying to avoid escalation of conflict. Physiological arousal leads to flooding and negative attributions. Flooding reflects feeling overwhelmed by criticisms and that you feel helpless. The physiological signs of flooding are increased heart rates above 100. Gottman and Silver (2015) even provide an example of an increased heart rate as high as 165 after controlling for initial, basal resting rates. Blood pressure as well as sweating increases. The ability to process information is reduced and it is harder to pay attention to what your partner is saying. When flooded, there are two basic responses: fight (acting contemptuously or defensive) or flight (withdrawal, silence, and stonewalling). Gottman notes that in 85% of marriages, the stonewaller is male. Evolutionary heritage explains this because of different anthropological development where lives were restricted to rigid sex roles in terms of surviving in harsh climates (e.g., disease, food shortage). Gottman and Silver (2015) provide examples of relaxed nursing mothers lactating more than stressed mothers. Relaxation fuels the release of oxytocin in the brain. Natural evolutionary processes would favor women who could quickly soothe themselves and calm down after distress. Yet, for early hominid males, natural selection favored adrenalin being release quickly in order to hunt and maintain vigilance for survival. Another explanation for male withdrawal is the socialization of males to not communicate a variety of emotions while growing up except for anger. Fearful boys are not reinforced since they may be labeled as "sissy." There are a variety of negative terms for communicating too much emotion.

Current relational happiness reflects how one recalls the past history of events in relationships. The oral history interview asks couples about how they first met, initial impressions, and remembrances about going out (Gottman, 1994; Honeycutt, 1995, 1999). Additional questions ask for recall of fondest and harsh moments, how they deal with ups and downs in the relationship, and a comparison of their relationship with a couple that they know who has a particularly good and bad relationship. How similar or different is their relationship to the comparison couples. They are also asked to compare their relationship to their parents' marriages if they can. Some individuals have single-parent families and cannot respond to this because they never knew one of the parents. Box 4.1 contains a copy of questions from the Oral History Interview.

Box 4.1. Oral History Interviewing Form for Couples

This interview is based on the work of Studs Terkel. Terkel was interested in creating radio programs, so he invented an interviewing style that is very different from a clinical interview. He avoided the usual vocal backchannels ("um hmm," etc.) that clinical interviewers and therapists employ, because these are annoying on a radio show. At the end of the subjects' responses Terkel would gesture and respond with great energy and emotion, and then ask another question and be quiet. He could then splice himself out of the tapes and have a long segment of just the subject talking.

This is a semi-structured interview, which means that you will memorize the questions. However, the subjects may answer Question 10 as they are answering Question 2, and that is OK in a semi-structured interview. The important thing is to get answers to all the questions, but the order is not important. You will go with the natural course of conversation, and try to get the subjects to be expansive and involved as possible.

A bad interviewer, like many people naturally are, merely gets answers to the questions, but a good interviewer makes sure to get into the subjective world of the people being interviewed. For example, suppose that a couple describes a period in their relationship when he went to college but she stayed in high school one more year to finish. She says that she visited him a few times during this year. A good interviewer wonders about the inner experience of this period. Was the situation one in which he was embarrassed by her visits, viewing her as a kid or a yokel, and she felt the rejection? If so, how did they cope with these feelings? Or, was this a situation in which he felt great showing her the world of college and she was proud and excited? We want to know about these inner experiences.

We-ness. You will find some couples who emphasize we-ness in these interviews, while some couples do not. Sometimes one person will be talking about the "we" with the other emphasizing separateness and difference.

Glorifying the struggle. Some couples will express the philosophy that marriage is hard, that it is a struggle, but that it is worth it.

Gender differences. See if you can identify differences between spouses that relate to gender differences in emotional expression, responsiveness, and role.

Conflict-Avoiding versus Conflict-Engaging Couples. Some couples minimize the emotional side of their marital interaction, either positive or negative affect. They tend to avoid disagreements. They tend to speak about the events of the day in terms of errands rather than feelings. Self-disclosure is minimized. Their roles tend to be fairly stereotyped and prescribed by cultural norms.

Part I: History of the Relationship

Question 1. Why don't we start from the very beginning....Tell me how the two of you met and got together?

Do you remember the time you met for the first time? Tell me about it. Was there anything about your partner that made him/her stand out? What were your first impressions of each other?

Question 2. When you think back to the time you started going out, what do you remember? What stands out?

  What were some of the highlights? Some of the tensions? What types of things did you do together?

Question 3. Tell me about how you decided to have an exclusive relationship.

  Of all the people in the world, what led you to decide that this was the person you wanted to be exclusively devoted to? Was it an easy decision? Was it a difficult decision? (Were they ever in love)?

Note: These questions only apply to married couples:

Question 4. Do you remember your wedding? Tell me about your wedding. Did you have a honeymoon? What do you remember about it?

Question 5. When you think back to the first year you were married, what do you remember? Were there any adjustments to being married?

  What about the transition to being parents? Tell me about this period of your marriage. What was it like for the two of you?

Question 6. Looking back over the years, what moments stand out as the really good times in your relationship? What were the really happy times? (What is a good time like for this couple)?

Question 7. Many of the couples we've talked to say that their relationships go through periods of ups and downs. Would you say that this is true of your relationship?

Question 8. Looking back over the years, what moments stand out as the really hard times in your relationship? Why do you think you stayed together? How did you get through these difficult times?

Question 9. How would you say your relationship is different now from when you started seeing each?

Part II: The Philosophy of Relationships

Question 10. We're interested in your ideas about what makes a good relationship work. Why do you think some relationships work while others don't? Think of a couple you know that has a particularly good relationship and one that you know who has a particularly bad one. (Let them decide together which two couples these are.) What is different about these two relationships? How would you compare your own relationship to each of these couples?

Question 11. Tell me about your parents' marriages. (Ask of each partner). What was (is) their marriage like? Would you say it's very similar or different from your current relationship?

Keep notes on a separate sheet for recording answers to each question. Be sure to identify who said what for each question. We need to keep a running count if the male or female's perspective is being stated. In addition, use the following rating scales to evaluate the partner's inner experiences as described at the top of this questionnaire. Note that some of the endpoints for the scales are reversed on some items. This is done in order to enhance careful reading and thought about each individual question.

1a). What amount of "we-ness" in the interview did the male have?
A very small amount __:__:__:__:__:__:__ A very large amount
1b). What amount of "we-ness" in the interview did the female have?
A very small amount __:__:__:__:__:__:__ A very large amount

Common themes of the oral history include admiration for the partner, use of "we-ness" as opposed to "I" or "You" which signifies differentiation from the partner, and glorifying the struggle of the relationship. Other themes reflect volatility in terms of the propensity to argue with intensity. However, other themes reflect the perseverance and satisfaction of overcoming adversity and strife in their relationships. This reflects a "work-it-out" relational script in which relationships are maintained by hard work and commitment (e.g., If people would just put in the effort, most marriages would work). Research reveals that individuals espousing a "soulmate" script in which they believe that attraction is based on passion and chemistry such that there is the belief of a "perfect love match" for them are actually less committed to their relationships because they are more likely to end a relationship when they believe that their partner is not their "soulmate" (Franiuk, Dov, & Pomerantz, 2002).

Flooding results in biased memory of how the couple first met. We conclude this section with a script for marital interaction based on the research of physiological arousal and discussions of pleasing and displeasing topics in relationships. Box 4.2 integrates some of the research on heart rate physiology, communibiology, IIs, and biofeedback during relational discussions. It was written by one of our doctoral students in the form of satirical, research-inspired wedding vows. Essentially, wedding vows reflect a script for marital relationships as the bride and groom espouse their values and views on marriage. While Box 4.2 represents humorous satire, the sentiments are based on social science research.

Box 4.2. Based on Studies of Physiology and Communication

Written by Anne-Liese Juge Fox
Wedding Vows

Groom: I _____ take you _____ to be my wife. I promise to buffer you from environmental stress thus promoting your health. I honor your comunibiology and emotionality, which influence you to escalate conflict and you place a higher value on talking things over. I understand that my diffuse physiological arousal during conflict lowers constructive behavior and leads to behavioral escalations. When my autonomic nervous system is aroused, I will use heart rate variability biofeedback techniques to balance my parasympathetic nervous system and sympathetic nervous system in order to optimize my ability to problem solve and implement higher order planning and counteract my greater excitability to negative affect. When your EEG readings show more activity in the right frontal region of the brain, I will use conciliatory, rational, and withdrawal tactics in order to reduce my risk of cardiovascular disease and premature mortality and protect you from poor health due to distress in marriage. I promise to play a de-escalating role in low conflict discussions and will practice IIs in order to anticipate your issues and find solutions to our conflicts. I will minimize situations where I release catecholamine and cortisol. I understand that your longevity is related to your connections to friends and will support your friendships outside of our marriage. I will avoid attempting to influence you as it negatively impacts my cardiovascular response but rather to disagree with you and will recognize when I perceive your resistance as an attempt to challenge my status, dominance, or control.

BRIDE: I _____ take you _____ to be my husband. I promise to buffer you from environmental stress thus promoting your health. I understand that your longevity is dependent on being married and marital satisfaction and that heightened physical arousal before and during marital conflict contributes to decline in marital satisfaction. I will avoid Gottman's four horsemen of the apocalypse: criticism, defensiveness, withdrawal, and contempt. I will attempt to recognize and reduce my participation in conflict linkage and encourage high levels of positive behaviors for decreases in your adrenocorticotropic hormone and cortisol. I honor that you are not as resilient, tough, or as adaptive as I am to a climate of negative effect. That you have heightened physiological reactivity and are less equipped for recovery from upset than I and that you are less resistant to infectious diseases and environmental stresses than me. In order to avoid marital dissatisfaction and emotional withdrawal on your part, I will do my best to ensure that we spend no more than 16 hours per year in conflict with heated conflicts occurring only 1.3 times per month and lasting no more than .52 hours on each occasion. I promise to play a de-escalating role in high conflict discussions and have constructive IIs in order to prepare for serious discussions so that I can better ensure a high level of marital satisfaction.

Study of the Impact of Imagined Interactions and Arguing Among Couples on Heart Rate

We conducted a study of 123 romantic couples in which the partners had been exclusively seeing each other ranging from 2 months to 52 years with an average duration of 7 years and 5 months. The age of the sample ranged from 19 to 77 with an average age of 32.29 years. The relational demographics of the sample revealed that 31% were nonmarried, yet exclusively involved with each other while 7% were engaged and 58% were married. An additional 4% were living together.

Procedure

Participants were recruited from communication studies courses at the Louisiana State University (LSU) Matchbox Interaction Lab and asked to bring their romantic partner with them in order to complete an interview on couple conflict behaviors. They were offered communication skills training as an incentive. They were separated for the first portion of the experiment. One partner was given a distracter task in order to keep her or his mind off of the coming interaction. The other partner was given various tests to measure state of physiological arousal upon beginning the experience. These measures included blood pressure and heart rate beats per minute. We calculated mean arterial pressure from the systolic and diastolic blood pressure readings.

He or she was then taken through the imagined interaction, using a role play procedure in which the actual interaction was orally reported in front of a video camera in one of our rooms at the LSU Matchbox Lab. The interaction described was a conflict situation on the topic of the participant's choosing. The participant was asked to talk through both sides of the conversation for a five-minute period. Discussion topics were derived from Honeycutt's (2001) list of issues for marital and relational partners (see Box 4.3). The partners are asked to rate how satisfied or dissatisfied they are with issues reflecting a variety of dimensions including communication, social life, chemical dependency, financial management, hobbies, social life, and sexual compatibility. After reporting their scores, they then are asked to choose the most pleasing and displeasing topics.

Individuals in the displeasing condition are instructed to take up to 5 minutes and role-play by talking out loud as they imagine a conversation with their partner about the topic that most displeases you. Speak out loud and have a conversation with your partner. Imagine what he or she would say in terms

Box 4.3. Satisfaction with Relational Issues

In the following items, indicate the degree of satisfaction you feel for each of these aspects of your relationship.

	Extremely dissatisfied		Average				Extremely satisfied
1. Moral and religious beliefs and practices	1	2	3	4	5	6	7
2. Self or partner's job	1	2	3	4	5	6	7
3. How we communicate	1	2	3	4	5	6	7
4. My partner's attitudes about having children	1	2	3	4	5	6	7
5. How the house is kept	1	2	3	4	5	6	7
6. The amount of influence I have over the decisions we make	1	2	3	4	5	6	7
7. Our social life	1	2	3	4	5	6	7
8. How open my partner is in communicating with me	1	2	3	4	5	6	7
9. Amount of money coming in	1	2	3	4	5	6	7
10. How we express affection for each other	1	2	3	4	5	6	7
11. How we raise children	1	2	3	4	5	6	7
12. How we manage our finances	1	2	3	4	5	6	7
13. Our sex life	1	2	3	4	5	6	7
14. How we fight	1	2	3	4	5	6.	7
15. Our shared goals or interests	1	2	3	4	5	6	7
16. Our sexual compatibility	1	2	3	4	5	6	7
17. My partner's faithfulness	1	2	3	4	5	6	7
18. The fun or excitement in our relationship	1	2	3	4	5	6	7
19. How my partner treats drugs or alcohol	1	2	3	4	5	6	7
20. Issues of equality	1	2	3	4	5	6	7
21. How parents or in-laws are treated	1	2	3	4	5	6	7
22. Time spent together	1	2	3	4	5	6	7
23. How often we talk about daily events	1	2	3	4	5	6	7
24. How much we watch TV, videos, or use electronics including I-phones, internet, computers)	1	2	3	4	5	6	7
25. Amount of time my partner listens to me	1	2	3	4	5	6	7
26. State of the family	1	2	3	4	5	6	7
27. Information about people in the news	1	2	3	4	5	6	7

The topic(s) that I most **pleased** with are_____ (Write the item number of the topics).

The topic(s) that I am most concerned about and **displeased** with are _____ (Write the item number of the topics that most concern you in preceding space in the order of the most serious).

of counter-arguments. We have found that this procedure works well for more talkative individuals. We have also used a procedure in which they write down alternating lines of dialogue similar to what is found in a play script in which each speaker is identified in alternating sequences. Both procedures are effective in reflecting the content of imaginary interactions. The role-playing procedure is excellent in that nonverbal elements of dialogue are observed as individuals sometimes change their tone of voice, pitch, articulation, and volume to mimic the responses of their partners.

Afterward, both partners were joined together in another room of the lab. Picture 4.1 reflects a sample couple who is in our lab on a leather couch. Notice, the blur in the picture in which she is gesturing with her left hand. She is wearing a wrist monitor that measures wrist movements. Wrist movements may reflect a type of nonverbal body motion signaling arousal, excitement, anxiety, or release of subliminal tension. This couple was discussing how much they missed each other when she was an exchange student in the Caribbean the previous semester.

Both partners were measured for state of arousal and asked to discuss the displeasing topic chosen by the imagined interaction participant. Afterward, their blood pressure and heart rate was again measured. They were then asked to fill out a series of questionnaires regarding the relationship and the interaction. Table 4.2 presents a hierarchical regression in which heart rate beats per minute is predicted by baseline measures of heart rate and characteristics of IIs. When couples come to our lab, we initially measure their heart rate in order to use this as a control or baseline rate before they are exposed to the experimental conditions (distracter or induced imagined interaction task, actual discussion of a displeasing topic).

Table 4.2. Predicting heart rate and mean arterial pressure as a consequence of imagined interaction variables when discussing displeasing topics.

Dependent Variable	F	Step	r^2	Predictor(s)	Beta	t value*
Conversational	(7, 241) = 46.32	1	.54	Baseline HR	.24	3.30
Heart Rate (HR)		1	.54	Induced HR	.54	7.47
		2	.55	II Discrepancy	.11	2.51
		3	.56	II Rehearsal	−.16	−3.09
		4	.57	II Catharsis	.10	2.08**
Conversational	(7, 241) = 30.61	1	.42	Baseline MAP	.40	5.59
Mean Arterial		1	.42	Induced MAP	.30	4.26
Pressure (MAP)		2	.47	II Conflict-linkage	.19	3.68

Note: All t-values are significant at the .002 alpha level unless otherwise indicated; *p < .01, **p < .039.

The Beta values in Table 4.2 represent standardized regression coefficients ranging from −1 to 1. As expected, heart rate and mean arterial pressure are best predicted by preexisting values (see baseline Betas). Yet, it is intriguing that we found that imagined interaction features do not predict heart rate or mean arterial pressure while having the induced imagined interaction. However, the functions of IIs significantly predict heart rate after the actual conversation involving the conflictual discussion of the displeasing topic. More specifically, the relational partner's heart rate immediately after their actual discussion was predicted by IIs that are discrepant as well as individuals not having rehearsed what they are going to say (see the negative Beta coefficient in Table 4.2). Conversely, anxiety and uncertainty is reduced (catharsis function) which subsequently predicts heart rate. This reflects the old maxim of "Think before You Speak." Hence, it can be recommended that when arguing, it is prudent to plan ahead. Rehearsing messages allows an individual to have lower discrepancy when the actual conversation takes place (Honeycutt, 2010a; Honeycutt et al., 1989–90). Blood pressure as represented in terms of mean arterial pressure is associated with ruminating about past grievances (also see Honeycutt, 2010b).

Case Study of a Couple Discussing Pleasing and Displeasing Topics

We are currently conducting research in the Relation Station Lab in which couples' physiology is measured while discussing both positive and negative topics. Following the procedures discussed above, the couple comes to our lab and there baseline heart rate is gathered. However, one partner is asked to imagine discussing one of the topics that he/she is most satisfied with while the other is asked to imagine discussing one of the topics that he/she is most displeased with. After the induced imagined interaction, they are joined together and asked to discuss the topics.

Agenda Initiation

We have heard the classic statement, "I have good and bad news. Which one do you want to hear first?" The concept of agenda initiation is concerned with setting the agenda for discussion of topics. In this regard, Gottman and his associates (1998) report a tendency for wives to initially bring up sensitive or conflictual topics for discussion while the husband defers. Gottman et al. (1998) hypothesized that the initiation of conflict was a critical issue and that marriages would be more successful if women would soften their start up by not escalating from neutral to negative during the discussion. Denton and Burleson (2007) report a tendency for women to bring up sensitive issues in relational discussions. In addition, Kim, Capaldi, and Crosby (2007) found that men showed higher levels of escalation during the discussion of the issues selected by their partners, and women (but not men) showed significantly higher frequencies of negative start up during the discussion of the issue they selected. However, women showed a higher frequency of de-escalation of partner's high-intensity negative affect during discussion of the issue they selected themselves. Given that one of the partners thought of a pleasing topic and the other ruminated about a displeasing topic, we were interested in which topic would be discussed first.

A case study from our laboratory involves a couple where the husband reported lower marital happiness than the wife (also see Honeycutt, 2010b). She is 24 and he is 27. It should be noted that their level of marital happiness may be considered atypical from a plethora of studies showing a trend for women to report lower levels of relational happiness compared to men (e.g., Burnett, 1990; Duck, 2007; Gottman, 1994). Furthermore, court documents often reveal that more women file for divorce than men in order to obtain custody in western societies such as the United States and Australia (Braver, 1998).

The wife was in the second trimester of her second pregnancy at the time of the oral history interview. When asked what first attracted her to him, she had difficulty responding. However, he responded by saying how her humor, wit, and blue eyes attracted him. Indeed, in our lab, there was a pattern noted by one of our research assistants in which there was a pattern of unilateral eye gaze in which he was more attentive to her in the discussion of events of the day and gazed more at her; while she looked around and did not return gaze very much. Essentially, his patterns of eye gaze were not reciprocated or matched.

Figures 4.1 and 4.2 reflect graphs of wrist movement, heart rate beats per minute, and heart rate variability from the husband and wife, respectively. The most displeasing topic for him was compatibility while her concern was privacy and withholding communication. The most pleasing topic for him was how they were raising their son while she was pleased with the perceived equality in their marriage. The couple has been married for 4 years and 8 months. A measure of relational happiness Norton's (1983) Quality Marital Index based on a 7-point Likert-type scale, revealed that his level of marital happiness was lower ($M = 3.5$, $SD = .55$) compared to hers ($M = 5.33$, $SD = .52$).

The couple came to the Relation Station interaction lab and individually filled out the surveys dealing with pleasing and displeasing aspects of their relationship (see Box 4.3). Both partners are fitted with an elastic chest belt just underneath the chest muscles to measure heart rate beats per minute and IBI. After a baseline time period, we press a marker button on our physiological monitor to start data

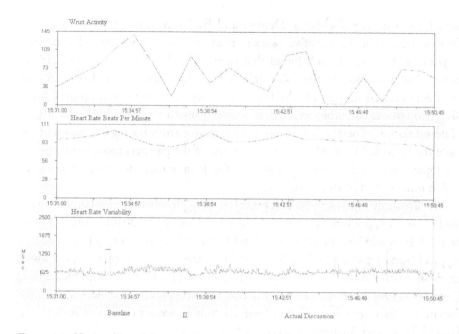

Figure 4.1. Husband imagining and discussing pleasing topic with wife.

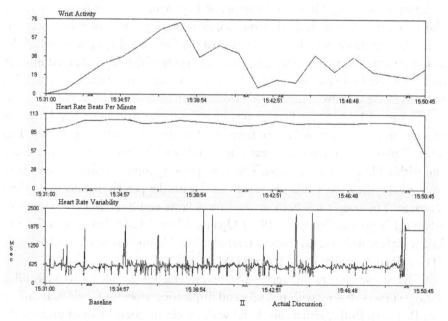

Figure 4.2. Wife imagining and discussing displeasing topic with husband.

collection and to note critical time periods. The first time arrow reflects (Δ) a basal resting period and denotes a time period when the partners were in separate rooms. While separated, she was asked to imagine discussing the most displeasing topic; lack of openness in communication with her partner that she had chosen from the list. Conversely, he was asked to imagine discussing his most pleasing topic: raising their son.

The second time arrow reflects the time period of their having the imagined interaction. Both partners role-played the II using the talk aloud procedure discussed earlier. Then, they were reunited together and instructed to discuss their topics for a few minutes. The third time arrow denotes the beginning of the actual discussion while the fourth arrow ends the exercise.

In terms of *agenda initiation*, we were interested in the contrast between discussing sensitive issues or pleasant topics, first. They were told to decide which topic to discuss first. Following Gottman et al.'s (1998) pattern, the agenda was initiated by the wife when she immediately began by asking him if he wanted to discuss his topic first. However, he deferred and they discussed communication difficulties for 3 minutes, 45 seconds. She did most of the talking while he used many vacuous acknowledgements (e.g., "yes," "um-huh," "right") during this discussion. This discussion was followed by the topic of how they raised their son. This discussion lasted for 2 minutes.

The upper graph of Figure 4.1 shows motor activity in his wrist. Wrist activity means did not differ across the time segments. However, across all time periods, he had substantially more wrist movement (M = 66.14, SD = 37.70) than she did (M = 19.04, SD = 15.86; t (27) = −5.96, p < .001). In a postconversation interview, he indicated that he often gestures to help him relax. Indeed, this proved to be the case as his heart rate was lowered during the discussion. Hence, somatic activity in the form of wrist movements may alleviate cardiac arousal.

The second graph in the figures reflects heart rate. As earlier noted, resting heart rates are about 80 beats per minute for women. Across the time segments, her heart rate was higher (M = 97.69, SD = 9.66) than his (M = 92.58, SD = 7.68; t (25) = 2.37, p < .026). As noted earlier, heart rate beats over 100 are high and reflect arousal (Porges, 1985a). His highest rate is 103 during the induced II while hers is 108. However, as revealed in Figure 4.2, her rate is higher in the induced II (M = 105.50, SD = 3.54) than in actual conversation (M = 100. 40, SD = 2.97). It actually peaks at time period 15.42:51 as portrayed in Figure 4.2. Conversely, his heart rates averaged 86 beats per minute in both the induced II and the actual conversation.[2] He indicated that he is quieter than she is while she complains about this. Indeed, this is a prototypical example of Gottman's (1994) discussion of male withdrawal from marital conflict. Gottman (1994) surmises that relative to arguing over sensitive issues in marriage "males use whatever means possible (which are usually withdrawal, avoidance, and rationality) to manage the levels of negative affect so it does not escalate" (p. 251).

The third graph reflects heart rate IBI in milliseconds. This graph reflects the peaks and valleys of IBI in relation to positive and negative imagination. It is the amplitude of the peaks and valleys that are of interest. Her IBI has more variability particularly during the baseline period and actual conversation (see time arrow 3). In terms of the actual conversation, there were significant differences between their IBIs, $t(288) = 21.88, p < .001$. Her cardiac IBI was shorter ($M = 593.91, SD = 125.27$) than her husbands ($M = 653.90, SD = 72.24$) which reflects a faster heart rate on her part. Hence, she is more aroused discussing the displeasing topic than he is. During a postinterview, he revealed he used wrist movements to relax him.

Summary

The study of physiological variables in interpersonal relationships is important in explaining the daily sources of anxiety and frustration as well as happiness. Indeed, many types love including selfless, agape, and familial love are variations of brain systems intermix in various ways. Furthermore, physiological variables including blood pressure, heart rate variability, and body movements are robust indicators of underlying tension. Hence, a calm demeanor may mask internal emotion and physiological arousal. While verbal statements and socially desirable responses to questionnaire items are easy to fabricate, physiological data are more resilient even with training in biofeedback.

A great body of research has revealed that happy and unhappy couples differ in heart rate variability when discussing events of the day as well as grievances in their relationships. DPA occurs in terms of adrenalin pumping into the cardiovascular and endocrine systems. It can be very high during heated arguments. Research has revealed that heart disease is associated with remembering arguments. A number of studies conducted in our lab have revealed that proactive IIs where a person imagines a conversation beforehand influences heart rate during the actual conversation. For example, the relational partner's heart rate immediately after their actual discussion was predicted by IIs that are discrepant as well as individuals not having rehearsed what they are going to say. This reflects the old maxim of "Think before You Speak."

Case studies in our lab were discussed accompanied by graphs of heart rate variability over the course of the conversations. The physiological data reveal changes in IBI related to the topics and if the topics were pleasing or a source of grievances. In conclusion, the study of physiology in interpersonal relationships is exciting. In order for emotions to be expressed, there has to be physiological arousal. However, if the arousal is moderate, then it may be labeled as positive or pleasing. If the arousal is intense, then negative emotions are more likely such as fear, disgust, or anger.

Discussion Questions

4.1. Think about the cliché of falling in love. Discuss the role of oxytocin when feeling romantic love. Should people eat chocolate to feel love given that it contains the amphetamine, PEA? After all, we are advertised to buy your lover "chocolate" on Valentine's Day? Is this good or bad? Why or why not?

4.2. Discuss the role of biofeedback in controlling heart rate variability through meditation, breathing, or listening to tranquil music. Does nice music have a calming effect on a "romantic evening?"

4.3. Have a retroactive imagined interaction in which you recall an argument over a serious issue with someone derived from Box 4.3. Who was the argument with (e.g., mother, father, sibling, intimate relational partner, best friend)? Are you typically nervous before discussing sensitive issues or does it depend on the nature of your relationship with the aforementioned partners? Did you sweat, feel hot/cold, gesture a lot/little, or notice changes in your breathing? Were you calm?

4.4. Discuss Fisher's distinctions between lust and romantic attraction from Table 4.1 in terms of different chemicals. Do you believe that love is often affected by a "chemical imbalance" that can be stabilized by psychotropic medicine on the basis of psychiatric prescriptions?

Applications

4.1. Video tape a couple discussing events of the day or pleasing/displeasing topics of their choice derived from Box 4.3. Review the tape carefully and identify any of the 4 horsemen of the apocalypse present during their conversation. What does each partner contribute to the relationship? How could each partner improve to make their relationship better?

4.2. From Box 4.1, copy the oral history interview and interview a couple whom you consider has an intimate relationship.

4.3. Observe somatic activity (body, leg, wrist, or arm movements) as well as nonverbal, self, or object adaptors (e.g., scratching, playing with jewelry, moving the legs, gesturing) of individuals who are arguing in a YouTube video or from a film. Do they manifest a lot of somatic behaviors or do they remain relatively motionless, unemotional, or calm? Do the adaptors act as reliable physiological markers of underlying anxiety while arguing?

4.4 Think of anyone you know who has coronary heart disease. Is it genetically inherited? Do they have many social contacts or are they relatively isolated? Do they live by themselves or with someone? Do you believe they are in a happy relationship?

Notes

1. The formula for calculating mean arterial pressure (MAP) at normal resting heart rates is: MAP = [(2 × diastolic) + systolic]/3. Diastole counts twice as much as systole because 2/3 of the cardiac cycle is spent in diastole. At high heat rates, MAP is more closely approximated by the average of systolic and diastolic pressure because arterial pressure pulse becomes narrower.

2. The heart rates are based on an average per minute. Hence, there are not enough time points to statistically test differences on the basis of heart rate and wrist movement because the actual conversation was 5 minutes. Conversely, IBI is measured in milliseconds yielding more time points in which statistical comparisons can be made.

References

Adolphs, R., & Tranel, D. (2003). Amygdala damage impairs emotion recognition from scenes only when they contain facial expressions. *Neuropsychologia, 41*, 1281–1289.

Ainsworth, M. D. S. (1989). Attachments beyond intimacy. *American Psychologist, 44*, 709–716.

Aloia, L. S., & Solomon, D. H. (2014). Conflict intensity, family history, and physiological stress reactions to conflict within romantic relationships. *Human Communication Research, 41*, 367–389. doi:10.1111/hcre.12049

Aloia, L. S., & Solomon, D. H. (2015). The physiology of argumentative skill deficiency: Cognitive ability, emotional competence, communication qualities, and responses to conflict. *Communication Monographs, 82*, 315–338. doi:10.1080/03637751.2014.989868

Anderson, N. B., & Anderson, P. E. (2003). *Emotional longevity: What really determines how long you live.* New York, NY: Viking.

Baer, R. A. (2003). Mindfulness as a clinical intervention: A conceptual and empirical review. *Clinical Psychology: Science and Practice, 10*, 125–143. doi:10.1093/clipsy.bpg015

Baumeister, R. F. (2002). Yielding to temptation: Self-control failure, impulsive purchasing, and consumer behavior. *Journal of Consumer Research, 28*, 670–676. doi:10.1086/338209

Beatty, M. J., & McCroskey, J. C. (1997). It's in our nature: Verbal aggressiveness as temperamental expression. *Communication Quarterly, 45*, 446–460.

Beatty, M. J., McCroskey, J. C., & Heisel, A. D. (1998). Communication apprehension as temperamental expression: A communibiological paradigm. *Communication Monographs, 65*, 197–219. doi:10.1080/03637759809376448

Beatty, M. J., McCroskey, J. C., & Pence, M. E. (2009). Communibiological paradigm. In M. J. Beatty, J. C. McCroskey, & K. Floyd (Eds.), *Biological dimensions of communication: Perspectives, methods, and research* (pp. 3–16). Cresskill, NJ: Hampton Press.

Boren, J. P., & Veksler, A. E. (2011). A decade of research exploring biology and communication: The brain, nervous, endocrine, cardiovascular, and immune systems. *Communication Research Trends, 3*, 1–31.

Bowlby, J. (2005). *The making and breaking of affectional bonds.* New York, NY: Routledge Classics.

Burnett, R. (1990). Reflection in personal relationships. In R. Burnett, P. McGhee, & D. Clarke (Eds.), *Accounting for relationships: Explanation, representation and knowledge* (pp. 73–94). London: Methuen.

Braver, S. (1998). *Divorced dads—Shattering the myths.* New York, NY: Penguin Putman.

Childre, D., & McCraty, R. (2001). Psychophysiological correlates of spiritual experience. *Biofeedback, 29*, 13–17.

Denton, W. H., & Burleson, B. R. (2007). The initiator style questionnaire: A scale to assess initiator tendency in couples. *Personal Relationships, 14*, 245–268. doi:10.1111/j.1475-6811.2007.00153.x

Diamond, L. M., Hicks, A. M., & Otter-Henderson, K. (2006). Physiological evidence for repressive coping among avoidantly attached adults. *Journal of Social & Personal Relationships, 23*, 205–229. doi:10.1177/0265407506062470

Duck, S. (2007). *Human relationships.* Thousand Oaks, CA: Sage.

Emanuele, E., Politi, P., Bianchi, M., Minoretti, P., Bertona, M., & Geroldi, D. (2005). Raised plasma nerve growth factor levels associated with early-stage romantic love. *Psychoneuroendocrinology, 20*, 1–5.

Fisher, H. E. (1994). *Anatomy of love: A natural history of mating, marriage, and why we stray.* New York, NY: Norton.

Fisher, H. E. (2004). *Why we love: The nature and chemistry of love.* New York, NY: Henry Holt.

Floyd, K., Hesse, C., & Haynes, M. T. (2007). Human affection exchange: XV. Metabolic and cardiovascular correlates of trait expressed affection. *Communication Quarterly, 55*, 79–94. doi:10.1080/01463370600998715

Foster, D. A., Caplan, R. D., & Howe, G. W. (1997). Representativeness of observed couple interaction: Couples can tell, and it does make a difference. *Psychological Assessment, 9*, 285–294. doi:10.1037/1040-3590.9.3.285

Franiuk, R., Dov, C., & Pomerantz, E. M. (2002). Implicit theories of relationships: Implications for relationship satisfaction and longevity. *Personal Relationships, 9*, 345–367. doi:10.1111/1475-6811.09401

Gottman, J. M. (1994*). What predicts divorce?* Mahwah, NJ: Lawrence Erlbaum.

Gottman, J. M., Coan, J., Carrere, S., & Swanson, C. (1998). Predicting marital happiness and stability from newlywed interactions. *Journal of Marriage and the Family, 60*, 5–22. doi:10.2307/353438

Gottman, J. M., & Levenson, R. W. (1988). The social psychophysiology of marriage. In P. Noller & M. A. Fitzpatrick (Eds.), *Perspectives on marital interaction* (pp. 182–200). Clevedon, England: Multilingual Matters.

Gottman, J. M., & Levenson, R. W. (2002). A two-factor model for predicting when a couple will divorce: Exploratory analyses using 14-year longitudinal data. *Family Process, 41*, 83–96.

Gottman, J. M., & Silver, N. (2015). *The seven principles for making marriage work.* New York, NY: Harmony.

Heisel, A. D. (2014). Asymmetry in the brain: Communication, personality, and health. In J. M. Honeycutt, C. R. Sawyer, & S. A. Keaton (Eds.), *The influence of communication on physiology and health* (pp. 171–187). New York, NY: Peter Lang.

Holt-Lunstad, J., Birmingham, W., & Jones, B. Q. (2008). Is there something unique about marriage? The relative impact of marital status, relationship quality, and network social support on ambulatory blood pressure and mental health. *Annals of Behavioral Medicine, 10*, 1160–1165. doi:10.1007/s12160-008-9018-y

Honeycutt, J. M. (1995). Imagined interactions, recurrent conflict and thought about personal relationships: A memory structure approach. In J. Aitken & L. J. Shedletsky (Eds.), *Intra personal communication processes* (pp. 138–151). Plymouth, MI: Midnight Oil & Speech Communication Association.

Honeycutt, J. M. (1999). Typological differences in predicting marital happiness from oral history behaviors and imagined interactions. *Communication Monographs, 66*, 276–291. doi:10.1080/03637759909376478

Honeycutt, J. M. (2001). Satisfaction with marital issues and topics scale (SMI). In J. Touliatos, B. F. Perlmutter, & M. A. Straus (Eds.), *Handbook of family measurement techniques* (Vol. 1, p. 92). Thousand Oaks, CA: Sage.

Honeycutt, J. M. (2003). Imagined interaction conflict-linkage theory: Explaining the persistence and resolution of interpersonal conflict in everyday life. *Imagination, Cognition, and Personality, 23*, 3–25. doi:10.2190/240J-1VPK-K86D-1JL8

Honeycutt, J. M. (2010a). Forgive but don't forget: Correlates of rumination about conflict. In J. M. Honeycutt (Ed.), *Imagine that: Studies in imagined interaction* (pp. 17–29). Cresskill, NJ: Hampton.

Honeycutt, J. M. (2010b). Physiology and imagined interactions. In J. M. Honeycutt (Ed.), *Imagine that: Studies in imagined interaction* (pp. 43–64). Cresskill, NJ: Hampton.

Honeycutt, J. M. (2015). Physiological arousal in families. In J. M. Honeycutt (Ed.), *Diversity in family communication* (pp. 141–152). San Diego, CA: Cognella.

Honeycutt, J. M., Bannon, B., & Hatcher, L. C. (2014). Effects of positive family conflict-renewal stories on heart rate. In J. M. Honeycutt, C. R. Sawyer, & S. A. Keaton (Eds.), *The influence of communication on physiology and health* (pp. 11–31). New York, NY: Peter Lang.

Honeycutt, J. M., Edwards, R., & Zagacki, K. S. (1989-1990). Using imagined interaction features to predict measures of self-awareness: Loneliness, locus of control, self-dominance, and emotional intensity. *Imagination, Cognition, and Personality, 9*, 17–31.

Honeycutt, J. M., & Eidenmuller, M. E. (2001). An exploration of the effects of music and mood on intimate couples' verbal and nonverbal conflict-resolution behaviors. In V. Manusov & J. H. Harvey (Eds.), *Attribution, communication behavior, and close relationships* (pp. 37–60). London: Cambridge University Press.

Inagaki, T. K., & Eisenberger, N. I. (2016). Giving support to others reduces sympathetic nervous system-related responses to stress. *Psychophysiology, 53*, 427–435. doi:10.1111/psyp.12578

Ironson, G., Taylor, C. B., Boltwood, M., Bartzokis, T., Dennis, C., Chesney, M., ... Segall, G. M. (1992). Effects of anger on left ventricular ejection fraction in coronary artery disease. *American Journal of Cardiology, 70*, 281–285.

Johnson, S. M. (2004). *The practice of emotionally focused couple therapy: Creating connection.* Levittown, PA: Brunner-Routledge.

Kiecolt-Glaser, J. K., Bane, C., Glaser, R., & Malarkey, W. B. (2003). Love, marriage, and divorce: Newlyweds' stress hormones foreshadow relationship changes. *Journal of Consulting and Clinical Psychology, 71,* 176–188. doi:10.1037/0022-006X.71.1.176

Kiecolt-Glaser, J. K., Loving, T. J., Stowell, J. R., Malarkey, W. B., Lemeshow, S., Dickinson, S. L., & Glaser R. (2005). Hostile marital interactions, proinflammatory cytokine production, and wound healing. *Archives of General Psychiatry, 62,* 1377–1384. doi:10.1001/archpsyc.62.12.1377

Kiecolt-Glaser, J. K., & Newton, T. L. (2001). Marriage and health: His and hers. *Psychological Bulletin, 127,* 472–503. doi:10.1037/0033-2909.127.4.472

Kiecolt-Glaser, J. K., Newton, T., Cacioppo, J. T., MacCallum, R. C., Glaser, R., & Malarkey, W. B. (1996). Marital conflict and endocrine function: Are men really more physiologically affected than women. *Journal of Consulting and Clinical Psychology, 64,* 324–332. doi:10.1037/0022-006X.64.2.324

Kim, H. K., Capaldi, D. M., & Crosby, L. (2007). Generalizability of Gottman and colleagues' affective process models of couples' relationship outcomes. *Journal of Marriage and the Family, 69,* 55–72. doi:10.1111/j.1741-3737.2006.00343.x

Knapp, M. L., Hall, J. A., & Horgan, T. G. (2014). *Nonverbal communication in human interaction* (8th ed.). Belmont, CA: Wadsworth.

Komarovsky, M. (1962). *Blue-collar marriage.* New York, NY: Random House.

Locke, H. J. (1951). *Predicting adjustments in marriage: A comparison of a divorced and a happily married group.* New York, NY: Henry Holt.

Loving, T. J., Gleason, M. E. J., & Pope, M. T. (2009). Transition novely moderates daters' cortisol responses when talking about marriage. *Personal Relationships, 16,* 187–203. doi:10.1111/j.1475-6811.2009.01218.x

MacLean, B. (2004). The heart and breadth of love. *Biofeedback, 32,* 15–18.

Manczak, E. M., DeLongis, A., & Chen, E. (2016). Does empathy have a cost? Diverging psychological and physiological effects within families. *Health Psychology, 35,* 211–218. doi:10.1037/hea0000281

McCroskey, J. C. (2006). The role of culture in a communibiological approach to communication. *Human Communication, 9,* 31–35. doi:10.1080/03634520009379187

Morris, J. S., Friston, K. J., Buchel, C., Frith, C. D., Young, A. W., Calder, A. J., & Dolan, R. J. (1998). A neuromodulatory role for the human amygdala in processing emotional facial expressions. *Brain, 121,* 47–57.

Moss, D. (2004). Heart rate variability (HRV) biofeedback. *Psychophysiology Today, 1,* 4–11.

Norton, R. W. (1983). Measuring marital quality: A critical look at the dependent variable. *Journal of Marriage and the Family, 45,* 141–151.

O'Connor, T. G., Heron, J., Golding, J., Beveridge, M., & Glover, V. (2002). Maternal antenatal anxiety and children's behavioral/emotional problems at 4 years. Report from the Avon Longitudinal Study of Parents and Children. *British Journal of Psychiatry, 180,* 502–508.

Peckerman, A., LaManca, J. J., Qureishi, B., Dahl, K. A., Golfetti, R., Yamamoto, Y., & Natelson, B. H. (2003). Baroreceptor reflex and integrative stress responses in chronic fatigue syndrome. *Psychosomatic Medicine, 65,* 889–895.

Pence, M. E., Heisel, A. D., Reinhart, A., Tian, Y., & Beatty, M. J. (2011). Resting prefrontal asymmetry and communication apprehension, verbal aggression, and other social interaction constructs: A meta-analytic review. *Communication Research Reports, 28,* 287–295. doi:10.1 080/08824096.2011.615959

Porges, S. W. (1985a). Respiratory sinus arrhythmia: An index of vagal tone. In J. F. Orlebeke, G. Mulder, & L. J. P. Van Dornen (Eds.), *Psychophysiology of cardiovascular control: Models, methods, and data* (pp. 437–450). New York, NY: Plenum.

Porges, S. W. (1985b). Spontaneous oscillations in heart rate: Potential index of stress. In P. G. Moberg (Ed.), *Animal stress* (pp. 97–111). Bethesda, MD: The American Physiological Society.

Porges, S. W. (2001). The polyvagal theory: Plyogenic substrates of a social nervous system. *International Journal of Psychophysiology, 42,* 29–52.

Revina, N. E. (2006). Heart rate variability as an autonomic index of conflict-induced behavior of individuals under emotional stress. *Human Physiology, 32,* 182–186. doi:10.1134/ S0362119706020101

Robles, T. F., Shaffer, V. A., Malarkey, W. B., & Kiecolt-Glaser, J. F. (2006). Positive behaviors during marital conflict: Influences on stress hormones. *Journal of Social and Personal Relationships, 23,* 305–325. doi:10.1177/0265407506062482

Rowell, L. B. (1986). *Human circulation-regulation during physical stress.* New York, NY: Oxford University Press.

Seibt, B., Mühlberger, A., Likowski, K. U., & Weyers, P. (2015). Facial mimicry in its social setting. *Frontiers in Psychology, 6,* 1122. doi:10.3389/fpsyg.2015.01122

Seligman, M. E. P., Parks, A. C., & Steen, T. (2006). A balanced psychology and a full life. In F. Huppert, B. Keverne, & N. Baylis (Eds.), *The science of well-being* (pp. 275–283). Oxford: Oxford University Press.

Tannen, D. (2005). *Conversational style: Analyzing talk among friends* (2nd ed.). Oxford, England: Oxford University Press.

Timmons, A. C., Margolin, G., & Saxbe, D. E. (2015, July 6). Physiological linkage in couples and its implications for individual and interpersonal functioning: A literature review. *Journal of Family Psychology, 29,* 720–731. doi:10.1037/fam0000115

Wilson, C., & Hill, W. (2007, November). *Affairs of the lips: Why we kiss.* Paper presented at the annual meeting of the Study for Neuroscience, San Diego, CA.

Woods, J. T. (2008). *Gendered lives* (8th ed.). Stamford, CT: Cengage Learning.

Wright, N. D., Bahrami, B., Johnson, E., Di Malta, G., Rees, G., Frith, C. D., & Dolan, R. J. (2012). Testosterone disrupts human collaboration by increasing egocentric choices. *Proceedings of the Royal Society B Biological Sciences, 279,* 2275–2280. doi:10.1098/ rspb.2011.2523

Bases of Relational Scripts

Chapter 5   Schemata, Scenes, and Scripts for Relationships
Chapter 6   Development of Relationships: Stage Theories and Relational Script Theory

Our early experiences have profound effects on the manner in which we negotiate relationships throughout our lives. How are these mental models formed and stored? What happens to these early models as we continue to interact with others: forming, intensifying, and dissolving relationships? These chapters discuss the foundations of relational scripts, including early experiences with friends and family, memorable messages, the influence of culture, and gender influences. Examples of the manner in which our present experiences are shaped by our past experiences provide an insight into communication behaviors that have unintended consequences, both positive and negative.

Chapter 5   Schemata, Scenes, and Scripts for Relationships
Chapter 6   Development of Relationships: Stages, Theories, and Paradigms

CHAPTER FIVE

Schemata, Scenes, and Scripts for Relationships

One way of exploring the mental creation of relationships is to examine how individuals categorize information about behavior in their relationships. The model of relational expectations, presented at the end of Chapter 1, reflects how such information about relationships is stored in and retrieved from memory. Integral to this process is the way in which people pigeon-hole what they observe in their daily lives. In this chapter, various types of categorization schemes, known to cognitive researchers as schemata, scenes, scripts, and prototypes, are represented.

As noted earlier, Duck (1986) believed that relationships should be regarded not as fixed states of being that are evaluated clinically, but as changing mental and behavioral expectations that involve a good deal of subjectivity. One person, for example, may expect a developing romance to include instances of hugging or holding hands in public, whereas another, based on her or his experience, may not anticipate such public displays of affection. One way to think about the expectations encompassed in developing relationships is to analyze the components of memory and its organization. Memory provides a frame of reference for experiences; it also creates expectations for relationships.

Memory components are called *knowledge structures*, which are defined as coherent and organized clusters of information that are based on experience (Fletcher & Fitness, 1993). Scripts emanate from these knowledge structures that are classified into two types: declarative and procedural knowledge. *Declarative knowledge* is open to conscious inspection, as when an individual chooses his or her words with great care so as not to, say, let a date know that he or she disapproves of a hair style (e.g., "That cut certainly accents your facial features!"). Declarative knowledge is directly expressed and includes any communication act that provides information. It can include verbal communication and nonverbal communication. Baldwin (1992) defined *procedural knowledge* as descriptions about objects or people. Procedural knowledge reflects the routines that people use to pursue personal goals, such as attracting a romantic partner or making sense out of what is being said. Procedural knowledge is contained within the action. This knowledge is automatically activated and operates subconsciously (Simpson, Gangestad, & Lerman, 1990). For example, eyebrow flashes, smiling, body positioning, and canting the head, subconscious behaviors indicating social engagement, are used by individuals to draw attention to themselves and present themselves as stimulating, competent, or socially skilled (Simpson et al., 1990). In fact, Fisher (1994) suggests head canting may be a universal symbol of flirting and notes that even opossum females can't their heads to indicate sexual receptivity to a courting male.

Sex Differences in Interpreting Flirtatious Signs

In terms of flirtatious signaling, there are sex differences in attributing the meaning behind these cues. The sexual schema for males is that they are likely to assign sexual meaning to flirtatious behavior while women may use a friendship schema. Research reveals that men were more accepting of sexual goals during first dates compared to women who were likely to endorse friendship and fun goals when going out on initial date (Mongeau, Serewicz, & Therrien, 2004). Moreover, when women initiate a first date, men are more likely to believe that sex will occur compared to male-initiated dates (Mongeau, Carey, & Williams, 1998). Error-management theory emanates from an evolutionary, psychological perspective and explains why men and women make errors about the intentions behind flirtations. Haselton and Buss (2000) describe how false positives (e.g., perceiving there is sexual intent when there is not) and false negatives occur based on the idea that individuals have committed the error that is least costly. In terms of adapting from evolutionary pressures, it is more beneficial for men to overestimate women's levels of seductiveness and promiscuousness in order to spread their genes. If he commits a false negative error, then he misses a reproductive opportunity resulting in a large evolutionary price. Indeed, it has been found across numerous studies in the social sciences that the data are consistent with error-management theory. Indeed, it appears that men, more than women, perceive both sexes as more flirtatious, seductive, and promiscuous (La France, Henningsen, Oates, & Shaw,

2009). Conversely, women underestimate men's desire for commitment in order to protect themselves from single motherhood.

Memory, stored in knowledge structures, assists in guiding people's beliefs and thoughts about, as well as their behavior in, relationships. Miller and Read (1991) discussed how knowledge structures reflect the ways in which the mind organizes memory as these structures emphasize various qualities of perception, kinds of content, and modes of mental processing. Regardless of kind or quality, knowledge structures categorize the behavior and observations people experience every day. They are influenced by gender, culture, and even chronological age. For example, Barr, Bryan, and Kenrick (2002) suggest that most people believe that women reach their sexual peak later than men, but older women (as compared with younger women) believed the difference in age between men's and women's sexual peak is greater.

Researchers have developed classifications and models of memory, extrapolated from observed behavior, dialogue, and reports that appear to reflect the function and organization of the sense-making process. In their comprehensive review of the research on social cognition and interpersonal relationships, Fletcher and Fitness (1993) pointed to the interface between personal experience and socially shared knowledge structures. Stereotypes, social norms, and rules reflect culturally shared schemata, whereas beliefs about one's own marriage may be private and not shared by others. Furthermore, people's beliefs about themselves activate beliefs about others and relationships. Miller and Read (1991) provided a hypothetical scenario of John and Mary, who meet at a bar and have some drinks. John believes that others are untrustworthy and he has to hurt others before they hurt him while Mary believes the opposite and feels she can depend on others. John has ambivalent feelings about being attached to someone else, whereas Mary finds security in such an attachment. In this scenario, imagine what would happen if Mary discloses something personal to John. John may not affirm her disclosures, assuring the relationship progresses no further.

A Comparison of Memory with the Organization of a Computer

The primary function of a script is to process new experiences and assign them to a particular type of structure or context necessary for understanding them (Schank, 1982). For example, a dating script can include a number of typical dating scenes, such as going to a movie or restaurant. The existing script serves as a reference that enables the individual to judge if a new dating experience is similar to or different from what happens on a typical date. Scripts can be modified by experiences and conversely are used to interpret experiences. They can influence perceptions: Lenton and Bryan (2005) discovered that almost all (98.7%) of the college students who were read a scenario regarding either a casual sexual encounter or committed relationship encounter demonstrated false memories concerning these scenarios when asked to recall details later. That is, once an individual has a script for an encounter, he/she expects certain things to happen and these expectations influence perceptions of an actual encounter. An individual will fill in the blanks when necessary using her own scripts.

Schemata

The term *schemata* is frequently used in a global sense to indicate structures of memory or knowledge. Schemata are categorized according to the function and content of scenes, scripts, and prototypes. Andersen (1993) defined schemata as knowledge structures that stem from prior experience and organize the processing of information. Schemata also guide behavior in the form of expectations.

Schemata represent the mental organization of information: the storage of language and experience in memory. They can be conceptualized as mental file folders which contain information about particular events, ideas, or concepts. Like file folders, the schemata serve both as storage devices in which we store information used to interpret experiences and also they can be modified through those experiences. Each individual schema is a language-based grouping of ideas, such as shopping for groceries, preparing dinner, and cleaning the kitchen, in which the groupings reflect some commonality or similarity in the primary theme within a broader schema, such as "Routine responsibilities in the home."

Cognitive researchers point out that schemata are used to organize the processing of future tasks (Scott, Fuhrman, & Wyer, 1991). Andersen (1993) expands the definition of schemata, indicating that schemata create expectations, anticipatory assumptions, and contingency rules to guide future behavior. In short, *schemata* is a broad term for knowledge structures: organized groupings of information in memory that summarize past experience and guide future behavior.

Relational Schemata

The term *relational schemata* refers to units of organized information stored in memory, which act as repositories for fundamental beliefs and expectations regarding the development of relationships. Relational schemata provide the sources of people's most fundamental beliefs about the characteristics of relationships. As Flannagan, Marsh, and Fuhrman (2005) discovered, these fundamental beliefs derived from relational schemata significantly influence one's interpretation of events and subsequent attributions. The college students who participated in their study made more positive attributions in a given situation when the target was a friend or romantic partner than when the target was unknown. Thus relational schemata bias our perceptions without conscious reflection or forethought. People's beliefs about how relationships develop are derived from direct experience gained by participating in relationships or from indirect experience gained vicariously by watching others or reading about the experiences of other.

Fletcher and Fitness (1993) agreed that memories, beliefs, thoughts, expectations, and attributions reside in knowledge structures and remarked that people typically develop relatively elaborate theories, beliefs, and expectations about relationships. An example of an elaborated schema for marriage is presented in Box 5.1, in which a 27-year-old, engaged female student reports on her expectations for marriage and how these expectations were formed. She indicates that her expectations may be altered during the daily realities of married life. She mentions nine themes as part of her marriage schema. Each of the themes that the student mentions in her schema may be considered a schema sub-file in the broader marriage schema file. For example, part of her religion subschema includes a belief in God and attending church. The young woman indicates that her schema for commitment includes sub-schemata, such as talking about problems and seeking marital counseling, if necessary, before splitting up.

Box 5.1. Sample Marriage Schema of an Engaged Female Student

We as individuals all have some kinds of expectations, whether they are from work, a dating partner, marriage partner, or children. Unfortunately, some of us have expectations that others are incapable of fulfilling. I have expectations of my upcoming marriage and partner, including:

Finances. There will be one checking account and savings account, which will include both of our names. In order to keep the records straight, I will have the only checkbook. I will be responsible for paying bills and for giving Kyle money or checks when needed.

Careers. Kyle will continue to work and be the main provider during the marriage. I will work as a teacher and will be free to have designated weekends, holidays, and summers off. I will also continue to work during pregnancy, but will take off from work the appropriate amount of time allowed. The decision not to work will be mine alone, if financial matters allow it.

Children. We agree to wait for at least two years or until we are mentally and financially ready for a baby. We also agree to have no more than two children. The sex of the children has no bearing, as long as they are healthy. Child rearing and responsibilities will be shared as much as possible.

Recreation. We both agree that recreation is important. Therefore, we will try to set aside as many weekends as possible to devote to each other. We will also remember that we as individuals need time to ourselves. This time can be spent alone or in the company of friends.

Religion. This subject has not yet been decided by either of us. I am Baptist and Kyle is a Catholic. Therefore, we will have to choose the religion in which our belief is the strongest and in which we will raise our children. We both agree that the main point is that a person believes in God and attends a church.

Housekeeping. I will be responsible for the care of the inside of the house, while Kyle is responsible for the outside. Kyle will pick up his personal belongings (clothes, shoes, etc.) and put them in their proper place. I will be responsible for the meals during the week. Kyle likes to cook, so he will have the weekends to do so. The cleanup of the meals and table will be the responsibility of both.

In-Laws. We will not live with either set of parents, unless there is no alternative. They can visit, within reason, anytime. We agree not to let them interfere or control our relationship. It is our marriage during good and bad times. We also agree to spend Thanksgiving and Christmas Day with my mother. We will on occasion go to New Orleans to spend one of these holidays with my father. We will go to Kyle's parents' house that afternoon and/or night during the time of the two holidays.

Commitment/Faithfulness. I promise to be faithful throughout the entire marriage and expect the same from him, because we love and have chosen each as a partner before God. If one partner does break this promise, we will try to find out what the problem is and correct it. After considerable trying, if the problem is not correctable, we will separate and then take legal steps for a divorce. If we have other marital problems and both wish for the marriage to continue, we agree to seek professional counseling.

Communication. A marriage cannot last if partners cannot confide in one another. Therefore, I feel that it is very important to be able to communicate and be open about our feelings with each other. A spouse should be not only a partner, but a best friend as well.

I know that life or marriage can't and doesn't follow a set of rules or guidelines. I know that my expectations will be altered to a certain degree during the "everyday" of life. I can't say that one person or thing has helped me form these expectations. I have seen and learned a lot from my parents, friends, and school. Even though I have come to understand the wrongs and rights through my experiences, that doesn't mean I will have the perfect marriage. Marriage is something I just have to try and then hope for the best.

Scenes

Scenes are scripts often linked with information about a specific physical setting. Scenes can also refer to an entire complex episode: the setting, activities, and people involved. Schank (1982) defined a scene as a general description of a setting and activities in pursuit of a goal relevant to that setting. Scenes also may contain thought patterns of dialogue and action (or scripts) based on experiences that have occurred in that particular environment. They reflect imagery about a specific situation and provide a physical setting that serves as the basis for the reconstruction of memory. If an individual can remember the setting in which an event occurred (the scene), it is then easier to access specific dialogue and actions (the script).

Schank (1982) termed an ordered array of related scenes a *memory organization packet*. Collections of such scripts constitute *metamemory organization packets*. Schank indicated that memory organization packets occur at the physical, societal, and personal levels. Physical scenes represent mental or visual images of particular surroundings at a specific point in time. A societal scene reflects a relationship between individuals who are pursuing a common goal at the same time, with a communication link between them. The actions and the interaction between the participants define the scene (Schank, 1982).

An example of one contemporary societal scene is the increasing use of the Internet to communicate with others having similar interests. For example, there are groups dealing with loneliness, finding a relationship partner, coping with divorce, and gender issues. Such Internet groups allow people to retain their individual identities and conceal their appearance. For those who regularly use this type of web-based venue for relationships, scripts are created that order the various scenes contained therein.

Personal scenes are idiosyncratic and may be thought of in terms of repetitive private goals or strategies. For example, a dating script may reflect an encounter at a specific movie theater (physical scene) or a disclosure in the environment of a restaurant environment (societal scene) that creates greater intimacy in an escalating relationship (personal scene).

Schank's physical scene is similar to the notion of a scene in the theatrical metaphors of Burke (1962). Burke's five-part model of communication (agent, act, scene, agency, and purpose) parallels the five key elements of journalism (who, what, where, when, and how). Schank's (1982) reference to societal scenes is analogous to Burke's notion of the act (what transpired), whereas the personal scene is reflected in the notion of purpose (why something occurred). The physical scene corresponds to Burke's notion of scene (the context in which an action occurs). Boxes 5.2 and 5.3 demonstrate how these elements may be arrayed in terms of the types of questions people could ask themselves, either in general or in reference to an escalating romantic relationship.

Box 5.2. Fundamental Questions That Process Behavior in Scenes

Physical Scene.

> What physically happened?
> Where did it happen?

Societal Scene.

> What societal conventions or norms were used?
> What was said? How was it said?
> What effect did the behaviors have on the individual's social position?

Personal Scene.

> Were the individuals personally affected?
> What goals were achieved by the behaviors?

Box 5.3. Questions That Process Behavior in Developing Relationships

Physical Scene.

> What physically happened the first time my partner said, "I love you?"
> Where were we?

Societal Scene.

> What was said?
> How was "love" communicated nonverbally?

Personal Scene.

> How did I react?
> Did I expect this disclosure from my partner?

Scripts

A *script* comprises a set of sequential step-by-step instructions for accomplishing a specific task (Abelson, 1981; Bower, Black, & Turner, 1979; Schank & Abelson, 1977). Scripts are derived from interactions in one's family and culture and provide instructions for behavior in specific situations (Fiske & Taylor, 1984). Scripts are mindless in that they are well learned and the behavior is somewhat habitual. People have innumerable scripts for relationship interactions, such as what to say when meeting a stranger, introducing a friend, requesting a favor, asking for a date, saying goodbye, making sexual overtures, or offering an apology. Such scripts reflect social behaviors learned through personal experience, observation of family and peers, and accessing information from the Internet and the media, including movies, music, and television shows.

Relational script theory provides a system that peoples can use to evaluate the development of a relationship and to convey fundamental paradigms about communication in relationships. We have scripts for the how relationships should function in terms of their development (e.g., fast versus slow development), online and/or face-to-face communication, maintenance (e.g., do we work it out or redefine the relationship when there are incompatibilities, conflict, or disinterest), and dissolution (e.g., do I tell the person that it's over or say nothing hoping they will figure it out and just leave me alone). Hence, if memory about prior relationships contains more positive scenes, then we are more likely to be optimistic about relationships (Honeycutt, 2010). Stephen (1987) demonstrated that individuals who share similar schemata for the value and conception of different gender roles facilitate the quality of interpersonal relationships. Further, Duck and Miell (1986) point out that people have internalized expectations for relationships that are part of their mental constitution and exist independently of their participation in a specific relationship. These values and expectations can be advantageously explored as part of the therapeutic process.

Unfortunately, there are individual differences in scripts associated with the diversity of relationships based on racial homogamy. Recall from Chapter 1 that the matching hypothesis states that people are attracted to others who are similar in values, attitudes, background, and looks. Yet, there is racial and sexual discrimination in scriptural acceptance concerning attitudes toward interracial relationships by college student. For example, the approval of interracial relationships is lower for those in same-sex relationships compared to cross-sex relationships (Field, Kimuna, & Straus, 2013). The profile of a person whose marriage script does not allow for interracial marriage is someone who is older, less educated, lower income, more conservative, White, and live in areas with smaller black populations (Campbell & Herman, 2015). Younger people approve of more interracial relationships. Yet, the approval of interracial marriage and dating is lower for Black/White unions than for Asian American/White unions. Whites are more disapproving of interracial relationships than Blacks which is qualified by a sex difference. Interestingly, black women are less approving of Black/White unions compared to Black men.

Honeycutt (1996) investigated the popularity of reading various magazines in order to learn about relationships. Respondents were asked to list any magazine they read for information on romantic relationships. Fashion magazines were the most popular (73%), followed at a dramatic distance by health magazines (13%) and news magazines (5%). Some of the magazines were *Voque, Elle, Cosmopolitan, Mademoiselle, Glamour, Brides, Young Miss, and Maxim.* When asked to rank the sources of relational information from an extensive list, respondents listed friends, parents, siblings, magazines, and movies as the top five.

Scripts act as a type of automatic pilot and provide guidelines on how to act when one encounters new situations. To access a script from memory, an individual first thinks of a general category of action (such as overcoming a crisis in a relationship) and then recalls a scene. Once a scene is envisioned, actions, behaviors, or dialogue that occurred within that scene can be recalled. Scenes can thus be considered as entryways to scripts and other memory structures. Recalling a specific scene allows the temporal ordering, or time sequencing, of specific scripted behaviors and actions to occur. Scenes, then, point to ordered and sequential (scripted) activities.

As step-by-step instructions for any given behavior, scripts make it possible to plan and execute everyday activities and aid in the recognition of the familiar activities of others (Bower et al., 1979). For example, scripts provide instructions for greeting grandparents or significant others, or for what to say during a job interview or when arriving at a party. Because scripts are sequential, they frequently reflect a logical order. Scripts are stereotypic representations of behavioral actions and reflect approaches acceptable in a given culture or subculture.

In many ways, ongoing relationships may be thought of as more-or-less scripted routines that follow predictable patterns. Scripts allow us to be mindless. Mindlessness refers to situations in which individuals consider available information rigidly with preconceptions, incompletely, and thoughtlessly.

Mindlessness Versus Mindfulness

Think of inane pick-up lines that men use on women. They use them over and over in the face of rejection and failure. Yet they keep using them because they are so ingrained in their language practices. They use them without thinking. Burgoon and Langer (1995) discussed how routine language encourages mindlessness, and how mindlessness also causes certain kinds of language use. Mindlessness entails limited information processing and the failure to process new information (Langer, 1989). Conversely, when mindful, individuals draw distinctions and create categories because they are sensitive to changes in context. People have expectancies for each of the following roles: a pickup, committed dating partner, fiancé, and spouse. The script that is accessed to process what comes to mind for these roles is affected by a number of factors that precipitate mindlessness.

The first factor is certainty. Research by Langer (1989) shows how certainty results in mindlessness; uncertainty may have the opposite effect. Strong beliefs minimize the need to reflect on new or even contradictory information. Planalp and Honeycutt (1985) described situations in which uncertainty increases in long-term relationships cause concurrent decreases in mindlessness. For example, a change in one's partner's personality, betraying confidences, or leaving with no explanation may increase uncertainty about what motivates the partner. For example, saying "I love you" during the development of romance may show one's partner that one really feels close intimacy, but over time saying this loses its uncertainty-reduction value. Consider the reaction to the following. A major expectation in intimate relationships is fidelity. In fact, the violation of this expectation may lead to the rapid termination of the relationship (Knapp, Vangelisti, & Caughlin, 2014). Suppose a spouse tells his or her partner at the end of the day, "I was faithful to you today." Instead of the statement reducing uncertainty, it momentarily increases uncertainty because the other partner may question what heretofore was taken for granted: fidelity. At this moment, the partner is immediately mindful and desperately wants more information to further reduce uncertainty.

A second cause of mindlessness is dichotomization (Burgoon & Langer, 1995). In order to take action, clear choices are made. The need for action is based on well-defined alternatives that lead people to dichotomize. Antonyms such as attractive/unattractive, caring/uncaring, sensitive/insensitive, secure/insecure, and quiet/loud fail to note the nuances and gradations within these categories, not recognizing that most choices are not either/or, but represent continuums. Underlying ambiguities are conveniently ignored. People are faced with hundreds of choices every day and often must make these choices quickly in order to take action. "Love me or leave me" is a common demand that ignores the variety of factors affecting commitment.

A third cause of mindlessness is habitual responding. Habits are not necessarily all bad. For example, brushing and flossing every night makes one's dentist happy. Relational habits, though, may be destructive. Perhaps Friday nights are pizza nights enjoyed with a significant other. These once a week rituals may become so ingrained in one's behavior they cause a failure to notice subtle cues that perhaps a partner might enjoy some other type of activity. Continuing this behavior that has become a habit may result in negative consequences when this person begins to seek out more adventurous activities, perhaps with someone else! Yet, some ritualism in relationships is important in sustaining and maintaining the relationship despite the mindless repetition. It is ritual to give an anniversary card on the date of one's anniversary. An example of violating a ritual would be for someone to forget to give the card.

A fourth cause of mindlessness is premature cognitive commitment (Chanowitz & Langer, 1981). What this means is that often decisions are made based on initial impressions without waiting for additional information. This is partially a function of living in a society where speed is paramount.

When people are presented with information they have no motivation to question, they cling to their initial impressions. Later, if additional or new information is supplied, people often do not reconsider the initial information in terms of the new information and change their impressions. For example, if people are shown a tape of a couple telling jokes about each other and told that they are happily married, then the jokes are seen as kidding around. Later, the serious moments tend to be ignored. If people are shown the same tape and told that the couple is unhappily married and having some problems in their relationship, then the jokes are seen as teasing, mockery, or put-downs. This recall represents a confirmatory bias that is mindless because of the premature cognitive commitment that the couple is "happy" or "unhappy."

The rigid use of schemata for interpreting new information reflects mindlessness. People do this in the interests of cognitive efficiency because to process all the new information available would be too time consuming and mentally draining. People have language labels to describe others who are mindful, reflecting a range from positive to negative feelings (i.e., creative, imaginative, absorbed, retentive).

According to Langer (1978), mindlessness is more common when situations are familiar and uninvolving, when little effort is required, when behaviors are not interrupted, and when the consequences are similar to previous ones.

The following sections review the research on scripts that are accessed during various phases of a relationship. These scripts include initial interaction scripts, scripts for dating, sexual scripts, interactive scripts, memorable messages, and relational rules.

Initial Interaction Scripts

Although there is considerable research on script generation, there is much less information about the functions of scripts in terms of the conduct of personal relationships. According to Ginsburg (1988), scripts for particular scenes of interaction can be expected to reduce the effort of interaction because they function as a form of mental automatic pilot. Once a behavior is scripted and then called up, the individual proceeds automatically until a barrier to the script is encountered.

Scripts also coordinate action and reduce the necessity of paying attention to the small details that tend to clutter everyday interaction.

Scripts appear to increase people's security in unfamiliar social situations by providing appropriate initial responses available for recall (Stafford & Daly, 1984). And although social situations vary in their degree of unfamiliarity, people encounter communication opportunities every day in which they are thankful that their minds can provide some tacit guidance. In fact, individuals appear to be more satisfied with their relationships when they adhere to their culturally sanctioned scripts (Holmberg & MacKenzie, 2002). It appears that in world filled with uncertainty, individuals appreciate any opportunity for predictability. For example, Kellermann, Broetzmann, Lim, and Kitao (1989) analyzed how the topics people used in initial interactions with strangers are fairly common and accompanied by an appropriate order for discussion. The analysis revealed a progression of topics for initial encounters that is relatively consistent and can be adapted to situational needs. Because scripts appear to be culturally bound, intercultural couples encounter additional difficulties when negotiating their relationships. Cools' (2006) interviews with six couples who represented intercultural pairings revealed communication challenges ranging from having to communicate in one's nonnative tongue to differences in scripts for child-rearing.

One particular relationship script that has been researched involves statements used when meeting someone for the first time. Douglas (1984) examined initial interaction scripts that are reflected in language (greetings), topics (such as current events), and general conversational behavior (such as compliments). Stafford and Daly (1984) found that although participants' reports of specific conversations are sometimes inaccurate, their recall of recurrent conversations is generally on target. For example, a college student whose mother regularly asks her how she is doing in her course work will recall that she consistently responds, "Plugging away," in order to avoid giving a detailed account of her activities. And when interactions are purposeful, Stafford and Daly found that some participants are able to articulate their purpose consciously. For example, a woman interested in the possibility of a particular relationship may say, "I told him about my interest in classical music in order to see if we shared any common interests." However, many if not most simple interactions are found to be relatively automatic and performed without much strategic planning or forethought (Kellermann, 1992). For instance, when someone asks "What's up?" the reply is usually "Oh, not much" or the like, as opposed to "The sky, I suppose" or "Everything that's not down." It is as if people have adopted a series of little rituals that allow them to both process and produce communication without a second thought. And the same may hold true for even more extensive and complex interaction routines.

Scripts for Dating

Scripts for dating appear to be rather routine and mundane. For example, four stud-ies were conducted by Pryor and Merluzzi (1985) to determine male and female scripts for Getting a Date and The First Date. In the first study, 30 male and 21 female undergraduate students were asked to generate a list of 20 actions that typically occur when a man asks a woman for a date and when they go on a first date. The results of the study reveal that the participants agreed on the contents and meaning of the Getting a Date and The First Date scripts. Typical actions reported in the Getting a Date script included the man observing the woman, eye contact and staring between them, smiling, other behaviors signaling interest, and information seeking about one another through friends. Other actions included potential partners manipulating events to create an accidental meeting or being introduced by a friend, the man initiating conversation, the couple exploring inter-ests through conversation to find compatibility, and the man asking the woman for her phone number and then phoning her for a date. Yet the dating behaviors described in the study clearly implied a willingness on the part of the woman to be asked out. Of course, these actions could be perceived as negative if the woman did not desire them, but then how would an initiator know this before the fact? It is important to note that a number of the actions associated with male initiative in asking for a date could be perceived as a Sexual Harassment or Stalking script.

In Pryor and Merluzzi's (1985) study of typical scripts for a first date, the reports of sequences of behavior were consistent, implying cultural consensus on expected, or typical, behaviors. The study attributed the following sequence to the cultural consensus of a typical first date: the man goes to the woman's residence, the woman greets him, the man meets her family or roommates, and they engage in small talk and decide where to go. If they decide, for example, to go to a movie, the typical script includes waiting in line, buying refreshments, and getting some-thing to eat after the movie. The man then takes the woman home and walks her to her door. The couple summarizes the evening at the end of the date. The man may ask to call again; the woman may hope he asks to call again; they kiss, say good night, and thank each other for the evening, and the man departs.

Note that these scripts occur in context and reflect the customs and values of both the society and sub culture in which they occur. There can be significant differences in the scripts for dating and courtship in urban, small-town, and rural cultures. Differences, for example, would be observed between the dating customs in New Orleans and with those of a village in France or in rural Malaysia. Sub-culture and socioeconomic status also influence scripts. There could be variations in the dating scripts for Hispanic, African-American, Asian, Native American, or white couples on a first date, even though they all lived in the same city. Yet most often the same physical, societal, and personal scenes are recalled and envisioned in order to access a variety of scripts.

Sequences of Dating Behavior

The second study by Pryor and Merluzzi (1985) examined the underlying sequence of behaviors in Getting a Date and The First Date scripts. The study participants were distinguished on the basis of their dating expertise. *Dating experts* were defined as those who reported having dated six or more different people in the past year. *Novices* were considered those having dated three or fewer different people in the past year. This criterion identified only a small number of women as experts. Consequently, the sample of participants with dating expertise was restricted to a group of 58 men. The participants were asked to create a sequential order for a stack of shuffled index cards, each card describing a typical example of behavior that occurs when asking for a date or going out on a first date. The behaviors were selected from the lists of the 20 actions that typically occur when a male asks a female for a date and when going on a first date that were generated in Pryor and Merluzzi's first study. The participants were instructed to read through the entire set of cards and arrange them into a logical order of events that might typically occur.

The results demonstrated that men with more dating experience were able to create logical sequences of dating behaviors with the cards more rapidly compared to men who had little dating experience. Apparently, the dating experts used their cognitive representations to create order from a random sequence of events. The cohesion of their scripts allowed them to recognize a sequence of random events rapidly and to categorize them into a socially acceptable logical order.

The third study by Pryor and Merluzzi (1985) was designed to distinguish necessary and typical behaviors that accompany dating scripts. Some behaviors in a script are necessary in order for the script to continue. For example, ordering food is necessary for a restaurant script to be invoked. On the other hand, some behaviors may be quite typical in a script but not necessary. Ordering coffee at the end of a meal is typical, though not necessary for the script to proceed.

Pryor and Merluzzi (1985) surveyed 30 men and 20 women, who were asked to rate how typical a given behavior was from the Getting a Date and The First Date scripts. Most of the script components were considered more typical than necessary. Thus, smiling was mentioned by 20% of participants when they were freely generating lists of behaviors. Yet when a different group of individuals was asked to rate the typicality of smiling, they rated it as just as typical as other behaviors that actually had been mentioned more frequently in the script generation task. Actions considered as necessary in the Getting a Date script included the initial greeting by the woman, the man's initiation of conversation, and man's initiation of requesting a date.

Sequence-Grouping in Dating Behavior

The fourth study by Pryor and Merluzzi (1985) revealed patterns that appear to indicate an underlying grouping of sequences in scripts. Students were asked to read two stories that corresponded to each script; the stories contained sentences that represented each sequence of the reported scripted behaviors. Participants were told that the story could be interpreted as consisting of several natural sections, or themes. They were asked to identify the distinct sections of the story by placing a slash mark, indicating a boundary, wherever they recognized a shift in theme. Boxes 5.4 and 5.5 contain the fictional stories the researchers used as scripts. The frequencies of slash marks or boundary notations identified by the participants are shown in parentheses.

Box 5.4. Sequence-Grouping in the Getting a Date Script: Getting a Date—Greg Meets Susan

Greg was eating at the dining hall when he noticed Sue standing at the salad bar; (2) and Sue also saw Greg. (1) Greg pointed Sue out to a friend. (0) They each caught the other one staring. (13) Then they smiled. (0) They both tried to find out as much as they could about each other from their friends. (11) They also thought of ways in which they could "accidentally" run into each other. (4) Then a mutual friend introduced them to each other at a party. (2) Greg and Sue said hello to one another. (2) Greg began the conversation. (5) They talked of their interests, attempting to find common ones. (0) Then Greg asked Sue if she would be interested in going out. (14) She gave him her phone number. (0) Greg called her later. (10) He began the phone conversation with "small talk." (0) Then he asked her out, and the actual arrangements for the date were made. (16)

Note: Numbers in parentheses indicate the frequency of subjects marking boundaries. Adapted from "The Role of Expertise in Processing Social Interaction Scripts," by J. B. Pryor and T. V. Merluzzi, 1985, *Journal of Experimental Social Psychology, 21*, pp. 362–379. Copyright 1985 by Academic Press, Reprinted with permission.

Box 5.5. Sequence-Grouping in the First Date Script: Dave and Lisa's First Date

Dave arrived at Lisa's dorm room right on time. (0) Lisa greeted him, asking him in. (0) They talked for a little while. (1) Then Lisa introduced him to her roommates, and Dave and Lisa left the dorm. (17) As they were driving to the theater, they talked about the movie they were going to see. (1) They engaged in "small talk," discussing their common interests. (15) Dave and Lisa then watched the movie, and Dave bought refreshments. (10) Afterward, they talked about the movie. (1) They went to a nice restaurant/lounge, where they had something to eat and drink. (1) Meanwhile they continued their conversation. (17) Dave then took Lisa back home. (0) He walked her to her dorm. (2) They exchanged their positive impressions of the evening. (2) Dave asked if he could call her again, and Lisa gladly consented. (4) They kissed. (3) Then they said "goodnight." (2) Lisa thanked Dave, and he thanked her in return. (4) Finally, Dave went back to his dorm. (20)

Note: Numbers in parentheses indicate the frequency of subjects marking boundaries. Adapted from "The Role of Expertise in Processing Social Interaction Scripts," by J. B. Pryor and T. V. Merluzzi, 1985, *Journal of Experimental Social Psychology, 21*, pp. 362–379. Copyright 1985 by Academic Press, Reprinted with permission.

Pryor and Merluzzi indicated that the participants were generally consistent in their agreement on the placement of boundary marks. The typical placement of the boundaries in the text demonstrated that the Getting a Date script yielded four basic sequence groupings, or themes: (a) noticing each other, (b) trying to meet each other, (c) getting to know each other, and (d) making a date. The First Date script yielded five basic sequence groupings or themes: (a) meeting the date, (b) warm-up conversation, (c) main-event activity (such as going to a movie), (d) post main-event activity (such as going to a restaurant), and (e) bringing the date to a close. Notably, each of these sequence groupings contains sub goals that are part of the hierarchical organization of the scripts.

The results of the story-reading procedure revealed that participants frequently agreed in their interpretation of actions. There was also a consensus on the grouping of sequences together according to themes. This agreement reflects culturally influenced schemata, *implying that there are agreed-on scripts within a society.* The influence of culture is apparent when researchers consider what the various schemata would be in such differing societies as Seattle, Bangkok, and Copenhagen. In addition, customs change rapidly in societies linked by media, perhaps as rapidly as every decade.

Sexual Scripts

For some individuals, a part of their dating script may include expectations of sexual contact. Sexual scripts refer to the cultural norms for sexual relations (Gagnon & Simon, 1973) and may include such stereotypes as that men initiate sexual relations, and that these activities should occur in private. As Sprecher and McKinney (1994) indicated, the idea of sexual scripts implies that little sexual involvement is truly spontaneous, even though couples develop their own couple-specific scripts;

however, as Cate (2006) has found, sexual scripts are influenced by context. In an investigation of date rape blame attribution, he discovered that attribution of blame for date rape incidents was associated with whether the victim and/or perpetrator had been using illegal drugs prior to the act. Within the context of a culturally sanctioned partnership such as marriage, rape does not appear to be part of the script (Gelles, 1977).

Traditionally, formal courtship scripts reflected male prerogatives for sexual initiatives. Thus, research by Ard (1977) and Regan and Atkins (2006) revealed that even in marriage husbands reported a significant gap between the amount of sex they wanted and how much they had. The wives' answers indicated that they felt less discrepancy what they wanted and how often they had sex. A cross-cultural review of research on the human sex drive reveals that there is a standard script for sex between first-time partners that depends on the woman signaling sexual interest. Baumeister (2000) discussed how in nearly all known human societies, as well as in nonhuman primate societies, women constitute the restraining force on sex to the extent that they refuse offers or chances for sexual activity. Buss and Schmitt (1993) documented that in heterosexual attraction, men are typically ready for sex long before women are. Men are more willing to have sex with someone they have just met (e.g., Herold & Mewhinney, 1993).

Men also fall in love faster than women and hence are likely to feel loving affection and the accompanying sexual desire at an earlier point in the relationship (e.g., Baumeister, Wotman, & Stillwell, 1993; Huston, Surra, Fitzgerald, & Cate, 1981). Evidence from direct communication was provided by Clark and Hatfield (1989). Men and women were approached by an opposite-gender research confederate who invited the participant to have sex that same evening. All the women refused this invitation, whereas most of the men accepted. By the same token, Mercer and Kohn (1979) found that both men and women rated all the communication strategies of avoiding sex as more typical of women than men, whereas all communication overtures for initiating and obtaining sex were rated as more typical of men than women. Clearly, the participants associated sex with masculinity and refusing sex with femininity. Additionally, it has been found that non acceptance of rape myths (e.g., a woman is enticing a partner if she goes on an expensive date, dresses provocatively, invites her partner into her place) is a strong indicator of rape perceptions such as blaming a perpetrator (Basow & Minieri, 2011).

Because sexual scripts embody socially appointed rituals and rules of social appropriateness, they are tricky to negotiate. Discussing sexual encounters in a relationship is not always easy because of the emotional vulnerability that may occur. Yet, open communication about sexual desires with relational partners is significantly related to sexual satisfaction as well as overall satisfaction with the relationship (Montesi, Fauber, Gordon, & Heimberg, 2011).

Sexual scripts exist in order to establish emotional and sexual rapport and to save face when one is confronted with unreciprocated desires or emotional needs. Unfortunately, a conflict arises when one person's dating script includes an expectation of intercourse and the other's does not. Such a miscommunication can result in the anguish of acquaintance or date rape. Box 5.6 reflects a scenario, in which a student shared her friend's experience where different interpretations of behavioral cues lead to serious consequences.

Box 5.6. How Miscommunication Can Result in Date Rape

Two of my friends went on a date in high school that turned out to be a tragedy as they misinterpreted certain behavioral cues. He had expectations of sexual intercourse in his dating script and she didn't.

Melissa and I grew up together. We became best friends in kindergarten and attended the same schools throughout high school. Toby and I met through our parents, who were good friends. He was the type of guy who would take me out when I needed a date. One night I introduced the two of them, thinking they would be a great match. That night at the party they hit it off. The next day, Melissa called, excited, saying that she had the best time last night talking and hanging out with Toby and that he had asked her out for Friday night. I later talked to Toby, who was also excited yet he tried to be calm and cool about the situation. Toby didn't talk much about their conversation the night before. All he could talk about was her body, how big her breasts were and how long her legs were.

I was actually having fun being the go-between. All week Melissa talked about what she was going to wear and asked nonstop if Toby had mentioned her. Toby on the other hand, wrestled with the question of what to do on the date. By Friday they had worn me out. I could have cared less about the date.

Friday evening Melissa called me again to ask what she should wear, "Should I go sexy or conservative?" she asked. I told her to go a little sexy, something I still regret. Saturday morning Melissa called me very early. I immediately knew something was wrong. My heart pounded as I tried to make sense of what she was saying. Her words were broken up with loud sobs as she told me about their date. She told me they went out to a movie and dinner. Melissa said that they were getting along great and that she felt really comfortable with him. She thought Toby was a complete gentleman, so she didn't worry about getting a little tipsy at dinner. Afterward, Melissa said they parked on the levee and drank a bottle of wine. She said they continued to talk and he kissed her. By this point, Melissa was drunk and when Toby invited her back to his house she thought it was a good idea. Toby's parents were out of town, so they had the house to themselves. Melissa said things were blurry, but that she remembered telling Toby that she wanted to take a little nap. So she lay down on his bed and they made out for a while. She said that things got a little carried away, but that she knew all along that she didn't want to have intercourse. Melissa said she struggled and yelled, "NO!" but that she was too drunk and weak to do anything, so she gave in. By this point I felt guilty

Box 5.1. (*Continued*)

and really angry. When Melissa and I hung up, I called Toby to yell at him. He didn't answer the phone, so I decided to go to his house. When I saw Toby, I yelled at him for five minutes solid and I even threw a shoe at him.

After he calmed me down he told me his side of the story. Toby said that when he picked her up she was practically hanging out of her skirt. He said they had a good time during dinner and a movie afterward. Then he said he kissed her and she didn't seem to mind his fondling her breasts. Toby told me that Melissa continued to ask, "What do you want to do now?" That's when he invited her back to his house. He said that going to his house was never in the plans and the only reason it came up was because Melissa wasn't ready to go home. When they got to his place, he offered her something to eat to sober up, but she declined. Melissa had crawled in bed to take a nap while he ate. Toby went into his room to find Melissa in his bed with only her T-shirt and panties on. He claims they started kissing and one thing led to another. He swears that he never thought that she would have sex on the first date, but that he wasn't about to turn it down. Toby did say that Melissa cried a little and said, "No," but that was after he was already in her. I asked if he felt Melissa struggle and he said that she wasn't struggling, she was just a little rough in bed.

After hearing both sides, I believe that they were both being honest. Toby acted on what he thought Melissa wanted and Melissa did not do a good job of communicating with Toby. Miscommunication and misinterpretation of behavioral cues can lead to horrible results.

Sex with Androids

It is common for crews of astronauts and cosmonauts to be mixed sex. Men and women may spend long time periods on space missions. While the American National Aeronautics Space Administration has not officially conducted studies of sexual relations in space travel, it inevitably has occurred. In fact, futurologists have speculated that the sexual script will be altered to include human beings having sex with robots or androids. Indeed, the idea of romance between humans and artistic or mechanical creations dates back to ancient times with the Greek myth of Pygmalion falling in love with the ivory female statue of Galatea to which the goddess, Venus gave life.

Hooking Up

Traditional dating in college has sometimes been supplanted by "hooking up" which is a casual, sexual encounter between individuals that occurs outside of a romantic relationship but does not necessarily involve penetrative sex (Kuperberg & Padgett, 2015). Students in Greek organizations have higher rates of hookups and dates. Women who attend religious services at least once a month were least likely to have hooked up, but there were no differences in dating or having long-term relationships compared to students who had never attended religious services. Conversely, attending religious services for men resulted in having more hook-ups and dated than non-attenders (Kuperberg & Padgett, 2015). However, other research reveals that religiosity is associated with less casual sex while depression and alcohol use, more loneliness and viewing oneself as less sexually warm and romantic are associated with more hook ups (Manthos, Owen, & Fincham, 2014).

According to Bogle (2008), there are gender differences in terms of the negative effects of hooking up. First, women are far more likely than men to get a bad reputation for how they conduct themselves in the hookup culture. Women can get a bad reputation for many different things, including how often they hook up, who they hook up with, how far they go sexually during a hookup, and how they dress when they go out on a night where hooking up may happen. Men who are very active in the hookup culture may be called a "player"; women, on the other hand, get labeled a "slut" (also see Wood, 2008).

Bogle (2008) also claims that women are not getting what they want from hooking up on the premise that women are more likely seeking relationships and are dissatisfied with how often hooking up does not result in longitudinal, stable relationships. Bogle (2008) also notes that this puts women in a difficult situation. If they do not hook up at all, they are left out of the dominant culture on campus and will likely have difficulty finding opportunities to form sexual and romantic relationships with the opposite sex. Ironically, if they hook up, they have to walk a fine line to make sure they do so in a way that makes them a part of the mainstream on campus without crossing the line and getting negatively labeled.

Various studies cited by Bogle (2008) indicate that traditional dating is surviving alongside of hooking up in the larger culture, but on college campuses hooking up is a substitute for dating as a mechanism to meet and form sexual and romantic relationships. This does not mean that students never go out for dinner and a movie. The "date" still exists among college students, but the term refers to couples who are already in an exclusive relationship. In other words, the trajectory to a boyfriend-girlfriend relationship where a couple might go on a date may begin with hooking up. In the dating era, students would go on a date, which might lead to something sexual happening; in the hookup era, students hook up, which might lead to dating. This is a reversal of scripts that could be considered more traditional.

Another major problem with hooking up is the failure to use a reliable, updated script for dating for post-college relationships. Bogle (2008) interviewed numerous individuals at various universities and colleges who indicated that the transition to the post-college dating scene could be difficult. Many of the men and women were confused over how to act in certain scenarios after college, not knowing if they were on a date or just "hanging out and hooking up." Interestingly, a number of the interviewees had never been on a formal date until after college, so figuring out the rules and script for dating and creating long-term relationships was a big adjustment for them.

Friends with Benefits

Friends with benefits is defined by the urban dictionary as two friends who have casual sex without being emotionally involved. However, it can be a start to an exclusive romantic relationship. FWB relationships share aspects of traditional friendships in terms of shared activities, trust and mutual reliance. Owen and Fincham (2012) found that a quarter of men and 40% of women hoped that a FWB would progress into a more committed relationship. Yet, the social scripts for engaging in FWB relationships are less formal and more ambiguous compared to script for traditional dating relationship and contemporary social norms may promote engaging in FWB relationships. Increased alcohol use and sexually risky behavior (e.g., noncondom use, substance use while having sex, sexually transmitted infections) is also associated with FWBs (Letcher & Carmona, 2015). It is interesting those young adults who started their relationships as FWBs reported lower relationship satisfaction compared to those who started as an exclusive, committed relationship.

Online Relationship Scripts

With the advent of the Internet, social media, and other technologies, relationships and relationship formation have significantly changed. This is especially true in terms of finding romantic partners or "hook up" partners.

Bryant and Sheldon (2017) did a study with 364 college students to examined motives for using online dating websites and mobile dating applications, as well as attitudes toward those platforms. Their survey revealed that the primary reasons for using cyber dating platforms were "Fun," "Relationship," and "Hook Up." There were also differences in the attitudes of those that have experienced cyber dating platforms and those that have not. Nonusers were more likely to hold the "Desperate" attitude. In addition, individuals with high self-esteem were less motivated to use cyber dating to hook up. Older users and women were more likely to use them for relationship reasons, while individuals high in religiosity found them less socially acceptable.

Bryant and Sheldon (2017) argued that people use cyber dating for the "Fun" motive because platforms allow users to scroll through various pictures of people and read different profiles, thus trying new ways to meet people or branching out to meet different types of people. For example, Tinder allows users to go through multiple pictures and "swipe right" if they like someone, and "swipe left" if they do not like someone. In a way, mobile dating apps are like a game.

Additionally, many cyber dating platforms exist to aid people in finding a relationship. Therefore, it makes sense for users to be motivated for relationship reasons. Cyber dating users feel more at ease talking and attempting to form connections with others behind a screen as opposed to face-to-face interactions that feature a plethora of nonverbal cues. When people are denied nonverbal cues, they will express impression and relational messages with cues available through the particular technology-based platform.

Another reason for cyber dating was "Hook Up." Bryant and Sheldon (2017) argued that this cyber dating motive is similar to the seeking sex motive that Couch and Liamputtong (2008) discovered for online dating websites. The "Hook up" motive and "seeking sex" motive insinuate that people use cyber dating platforms primarily for sexual relations without the emotional attachment. Bryant and Sheldon (2017) study also found that due to the more serious nature of online dating websites, people are likely to use them for relationship reasons as opposed to mobile dating applications. Mobile dating apps are also more image-based than online dating websites, and therefore, those motivated by "hook up" reasons are more interested in a platform that provides many pictures of potential "hook ups," as physicality is likely important to them (Bryant & Sheldon, 2017).

Cultural Scripts and Performances for Sex

Both weddings and pornography are cultural performances. Each is filled with scripts that serve to illustrate what society terms legitimate and illegitimate sexual initiatives. Bell (1999) noted how cultural performances of sex, "both weddings and pornography depend on the efficacious enactment of conventions and scripts, performance consciousness of the performers, deliberate manipulation of time and space, and the imposition of frames of belief and play" (p. 175). Both hold consent and sexual intercourse as their *sine qua non*. Because they are mirror doubles, not opposites, they are mutually dependent. Weddings and pornography hold similar constructions of culture, performance, and sex for their existence. If there were no legalized coupling through marriage, there would be no illegitimate coupling through pornography.

Weddings put their participants through ancient rituals to place society's stamp of approval on sex, which occurs out of view but which is often referred to as part of the ritual (e.g., consummating the marriage). In marriage, sex is the physical complement to the communication of action, "I do." Bell (1999) claimed that the centrality of sex to weddings is apparent in its universal acceptance as a cultural practice "until, of course, outsiders question its exclusivity, norms, and privileges" (p. 182). She also argued that sex is considered guilty until proven innocent. Married sex, created through consensual weddings, is the culture's sex "proven innocent" whereas pornography is the culture's "worst possible expression" (p. 180). Pornography carries societal condemnation. Here sex is public in the sense that it is available to be viewed by outsiders, even though the sex may not be real.

Bell (1999) concluded that weddings leave a cultural reminder that the ring must be worn in order to show fidelity, a major part of the marriage script. This reminder is always present when placing a pornographic videotape into a VCR, a reminder that the performance that is about to occur is not approved.

Changes in Interactive Scripts

Scripted routines for interaction include the opportunity for variations on the script, provided the variations are not so great as to destroy the identity of the scripted episode. Such interactive scripts may hinder rather than enhance smooth communication, particularly during episodes of conflict. Each partner's internal scripts are activated during conflict, typically echoing scripts from their families of origin. Thus, in a conflict situation, the tendency to replay old scripts in an automatic manner can be counter-productive. Hearing the internal script, rather than fully hearing the interaction in the moment, prevents partners from responding realistically to the situation at hand.

Butler and Smith (2004) reported that 98% of their respondents reported using a memorable message to assess their behaviors regardless of whether the behavior could be considered positive or negative: for example, providing a ride to someone who was walking (a positive behavior) and leaving a restaurant without paying (a negative behavior). These memorable messages normally provide a means for determining what is appropriate/inappropriate in an interaction, and have even been found to be important in socializing newcomers into organizations (Barge & Schlueter, 2004).

Medved, Brogan, McClanahan, Morris, and Shepherd (2005) discovered that most memorable messages emanated from parents, particularly mothers. They suggest that these messages are part of the socializing process. A list of memorable messages provided by students can be found in Box 5.7.

Box 5.7. Memorable Messages

"Always check out a man's shoes. If he takes good care of his shoes, he's conscientious about taking care of his life." (to female from mother).
"Don't do anything you wouldn't want to read about in the newspaper." (to male from father)
"Notice how a man treats his mother. He will treat his girlfriend the same way." (to female from mother)
"Don't shave your legs on a first date." (to female from friend)
"Never date a woman with teenage children." (to male from friend)
"You will never win an argument with a woman, so don't try." (father to son)
"You will never win an argument with a man, so don't try." (mother to daughter)

Interactive, scripted routines perhaps influenced by memorable messages offer a challenge to both participants. The initiator of the interaction may cue a partner by stating expectations, providing nonverbal signals, or modifying the environment in ways that provide cues. A candlelight dinner at an elegant restaurant, for example, may set the scene and cue the script for romance. Having tacitly agreed that a particular script is in the offing, there can still be violations that will not require a change in the script. For example, there is no violation if a restaurant is too chilly and the man goes to the car to get his date's sweater. Nonetheless, when an individual lacks sufficient information to understand a partner's script, misunderstanding often occurs. An example would be if a man asks a woman to see a movie with him, intending to pick up a video and watch it at her house, and she expects that they will be going to a movie theater; another example is provided in Box 5.8. Of course, either party may adopt other scripts once the misunderstanding is made clear. Sometimes, however, people remain oblivious to the problem because their scripts tell them that they know what is going on. Individuals who expect their partners to read their minds instead of expressing the script they want their partners to follow often find themselves involved in counterproductive interactive scripts. Gottman (1994) discussed how married couples often think they can read the minds of their partners by attributing emotions and feelings (generally without much accuracy) to one another while they are speaking.

Box 5.8. The Effect of Expectations on Interactive Scripts

A woman, stylishly dressed in an outfit specially purchased for the occasion, expects to be taken out for a gourmet dinner. She waits in her living room to be picked up for a first date with a business associate and answers the door with great anticipation. Her date greets her at the door in cutoffs, with a carry-out pizza and a six pack. It is painfully apparent the woman's script has been unexpectedly and negatively violated. In order to determine the script, she could have asked her date how formal the evening was going to be. In order to make his script clearer, her date could have indicated that he planned to order take-out food and have a relaxed evening at home. When expectations are unstated in relational encounters, miscommunication frequently results.

When individuals perform an interactive activity, they often assume unconsciously that their partner in that activity knows what the script is. In reality, one of the tasks in every stage of a relationship is to determine scripts interactively. It is important that individuals communicate their expectations to one another. This interaction entails an enormous amount of negotiation and is often accomplished through trial and error as may be seen in Box 5.9.

Box 5.9. Uncommunicated Interactive Scripts

Woman: "How did your day go?"

Man (sarcastically): "It went fine." His inner script: It was a disaster; I don't really want to talk about it.

Woman: "You don't care about me. We don't communicate. If your day went so badly, why don't you just say it, instead of saying, 'Fine.'"

Her inner script: "Why doesn't he think enough of me to express his true feelings?"

The woman's script represents a desire for open communication. It may also reflect gender bias in that women seem to prefer talking about feelings and emotions more than men do.

Changes in the status of a personal relationship are also likely to be occasioned by changes in the scripts that cue new behavior, as when a couple's relationship shifts from dating to engagement or from engagement to marriage. Ginsburg (1988) noted that alterations in the verbal content of scripts can be expected as a relationship evolves. Changes in a relationship are reflected in changes in the language used to discuss the relationship. When two people begin thinking of themselves as a couple, for example, they may begin using the first person plural pronouns (we, us) rather than the singular pronouns (I, me).

In summary, a significant problem in changing relationships is that individuals act out cognitive scripts and expectations. They may expect their partners to understand their expectations automatically, without even realizing they are doing so. Because these scripts operate below the level of conscious inspection and can be influenced by so many variables, misunderstandings are common. Even one's self-esteem (Koch, 2002) can influence interpretation of events and the scripts that ultimately emanate from these interpretations. Individuals with low self-esteem appear to have scripts for social occasions that automatically include rejection. In order for one's partner to get the script, it is important to communicate as clearly as possible.

Summary

Schemata influence how people perceive events in relationships. For example, going to college football games may mean spending quality time to one person in a relationship, whereas his or her partner may view it as a sacrifice in order to please the other. Expectations about relationship activities and the development of intimacy are based on the recall of scenes and scripts pertaining to particular activities; for instance, expectations for how one breaking bad news may be based on the recall of what was done the last time a similar situation was faced.

The use of schemata reflects mindlessness, in which people habitually do not process new information and use old stereotypes as guides to how to act in situations. People are often mindless when it comes to thinking about communication in their relationships because they do not think of alternative ways of thinking.

People have sexual scripts derived from culture, socialization, and evolution. Cross-culturally, sexual initiatives are associated with masculinity, whereas refusing sex is associated with femininity. Hence, part of the script for courtship involves women changing their desire for sex from no to yes (Baumeister, 2000).

There are cultural scripts for legitimate and illegitimate sex that are seen in examining weddings and pornography. Consummation is legitimized when it is done in private. Pornography is illegitimate because it is viewed publicly by outsiders.

Scripts for initiating interaction, getting a date, what to do on a date, and communication about sexual arousal each contribute to what people typically think goes on in a relationship. Cultural relationship scripts involve jokes about opening lines, asking for a date, common behaviors on dates, proposing marriage, and communicating terms of endearment such as "I love you." Yet scripts may be personal and unique to the extent that people's experiences are not shared by others, and thus researchers always face the challenge of determining how two people view themselves as an independent couple.

Discussion Questions

5.1. Discuss the specificity of the sample marriage schema. What happens if one's expectations for marriage are rigid, versus remaining flexible? What would you advise the woman to do concerning her expectations from her fiancée?

5.2. Discuss how men and women might interpret nonverbal communication cues differently on a first date. For example, how can a woman communicate, "No," to sexual overtures?

5.3. Discuss the differences between the male and female sex drives. What are examples of communication strategies designed to initiate sex? What are examples of strategies designed to refuse sex?

5.4. How will robots change humanity and civilization? Is marriage to robots inevitable or repulsive?

Applications

5.1. Interview four people about the term "dating." What does it mean to them? Is dating now an obsolete term, given the informal sharing of time that many individuals do while studying, doing errands, and helping one another? Or does it involve a greater degree of intimacy and commitment than it did before?

5.2. Interview two men and women about their experiences or opinions on "hooking up." What are different types of hooking up? Are there any positive or negative consequences to this method of attachment?

5.3. In the initial interaction script, what do you believe are appropriate lines of introduction other than "Hi" or "Hello?" Interview four friends and compare their responses.

References

Abelson, R. P. (1981). Psychological status of the script concept. *American Psychologist, 36,* 715–729. doi:10.1037/0003-066X.36.7.715

Andersen, P. A. (1993). Cognitive schemata in personal relationships. In S. Duck (Ed.), *Individuals in relationships* (pp. 1–29). Newbury Park, CA: Sage.

Ard, B. N. (1977). Sex in lasting marriages: A longitudinal study. *Journal of Sex Research, 13,* 274–285.

Baldwin, M. W. (1992). Relational schemas and the processing of social information. *Psychological Bulletin, 112,* 461–484. doi:10.1037/0033-2909.112.3.461

Barge, J. K., & Schlueter, D. W. (2004). Memorable messages and newcomer socialization. *Western Journal of Communication, 68,* 233–256. doi:10.1080/10570310409374800

Barr, A., Bryan, A., & Kenrick, D. T. (2002). Sexual peak: Socially shared cognitions about desire, frequency, and satisfaction in men and women. *Personal Relationships, 9,* 287–299. doi:10.1111/1475-6811.09305

Basow, S., & Minieri, A. (2011). "You owe me": Effects of date cost, who pays, participant gender, and rape myth beliefs on perceptions of rape. *Journal of Interpersonal Violence, 26,* 479–497. doi:10.1177/0886260510363342

Baumeister, R. F. (2000). Gender differences in erotic plasticity: The female sex drive as socially flexible and responsive. *Psychological Bulletin, 126,* 347–374.

Baumeister, R. F., Wotman, S. R., & Stillwell, A. M. (1993). Unrequited love: On heartbreak, anger, guilt, scriptlessness, and humiliation. *Journal of Personality and Social Psychology, 64*, 377–394. doi:10.1037/0022-3514.64.3.377

Bell, E. (1999). Weddings and pornography: The cultural performance of sex. *Text and Performance Quarterly, 19*, 173–195.

Bogle, K. A. (2008). *Hooking up: Sex, dating, and relationships on campus.* New York, NY: New York University Press.

Bower, G. H., Black, J. B., & Turner, T. J. (1979). Scripts in memory for text. *Cognitive Psychology, 11*, 177–200. doi:10.1016/0010-0285(79)90009-4

Bryant, K., & Sheldon, P. (2017, in press). Cyber dating in the age of mobile apps: Understanding motives, attitudes, and personality of users. *American Communication Journal.*

Burgoon, J. K., & Langer, E. J. (1995). Language, fallacies, and mindlessness-mindfulness in social interaction. In M. E. Roloff (Ed.), *Communication yearbook* (Vol. 18, pp. 105–132). Beverly Hills, CA: Sage.

Burke, K. (1962). *A grammar of motives and a rhetoric of motives.* Cleveland, OH: World.

Buss, D. M., & Schmitt, D. P. (1993). Sexual strategies theory: An evolutionary perspective on human mating. *Psychological Review, 100*, 204–232. doi:10.1037/0033-295X.100.2.204

Butler, E. J., & Smith, S. W. (2004). Memorable messages as guides to self-assessment of behavior: A replication and extension diary study. *Communication Monographs, 71*, 97–119. doi:10.1080/03634520410001691456

Campbell, M. E., & Herman, M. R. (2015). Both personal and public: Measuring interethnic marriage attitudes. *Journal of Social Issues, 71*, 712–732. doi:10.1111/josi.12145

Cate, K. L. (2006). The attribution of responsibility in acquaintance rate involving ecstasy. *North American Journal of Psychology, 8*, 411–420.

Chanowitz, B., & Langer, E. (1981). Premature cognitive commitment. *Journal of Personality and Social Psychology, 41*, 1051–1063. doi:10.1037/0022-3514.41.6.1051

Clark, R. D., & Hatfield, E. (1989). Gender differences in receptivity to sexual offers. *Journal of Psychology and Human Sexuality, 2*, 39–55.

Cools, C. A. (2006). Relational communication in intercultural couples. *Language & Intercultural Communication, 6*, 262–274. doi:10.2167/laic253.0

Couch, D., & Liamputtong, P. (2008). Online dating and mating: The use of internet to meet sexual partners. *Qualitative Health Research, 18*, 268–279. doi:10.1177/1049732307312832

Douglas, W. (1984). Initial interaction scripts: When knowing is behaving. *Human Communication Research, 11*, 203–219. doi:10.1111/j.1468-2958.1984.tb00045.x

Duck, S. (1986). *Human relationships: An introduction to social psychology.* London: Sage.

Duck, S., & Miell, D. (1986). Charting the development of personal relationships. In R. Gilmour & S. Duck (Eds.), *The emerging field of personal relationships* (pp. 133–143). Hillsdale, NJ: LEA.

Field, C. J., Kimuna, S. R., & Straus, M. A. (2013). Attitudes toward interracial relationships among college students: Race, class, gender, and perceptions of parental views. *Journal of Black Studies, 44*, 741–776. doi:10.1177/0021934713507580

Fisher, H. (1994). *The natural history of monogamy, adultery and divorce.* New York, NY: Fawcett.

Fiske, S. T., & Taylor, S. E. (1984). *Social cognition.* Reading, MA: Addison-Wesley.

Flannagan, D., Marsh, D., & Fuhrman, R. (2005). Judgments about the hypothetical behaviors of friends and romantic partners. *Journal of Social and Personal Relationships, 22,* 797–815. doi:10.1177/0265407505058681

Fletcher, G. J. O., & Fitness, J. (1993). Knowledge structures and explanations in intimate relationships. In S. Duck (Ed.), *Individuals in relationships* (pp. 121–143). Newbury Park, CA: Sage.

Gagnon, J. H., & Simon, W. (1973). *Sexual conduct: The social sources of human sexuality.* Chicago, IL: Aldine.

Gelles, R. J. (1977). Power, sex, and violence: The case of marital rape. *Family Coordinator, 26,* 339–348.

Ginsburg, G. P. (1988). Rules, scripts and prototypes in personal relationships. In S. W. Duck (Ed.), *Handbook of personal relationships* (pp. 23–39). New York, NY: Wiley.

Gottman, J. M. (1994). *What predicts divorce?* Hillsdale, NJ: Lawrence Erlbaum.

Haselton, M. G., & Buss, D. M. (2000). Error-management theory: A new perspective on biases in cross-sex mind reading. *Journal of Personality and Social Psychology, 78,* 81–91. doi:10.1037/0022-3514.78.1.81

Herold, E. S., & Mewhinney, D. K. (1993). Gender differences in casual sex and AIDS prevention: A survey of dating bars. *Journal of Sex Research, 30,* 36–42. doi:10.1080/00224499309551676

Holmberg, D., & MacKenzie, S. (2002). So far so good: Scripts for romantic relationship development as predictors of relational well-being. *Journal of Social and Personal Relationships, 19,* 777–796. doi:10.1177/0265407502196003

Honeycutt, J. M. (1996). Self-help books and popular literature in personal relationships. *Personal Relationship Issues, 3,* 1–3.

Honeycutt, J. M. (2010). Forgive but don't forget: Correlates of rumination about conflict. In J. M. Honeycutt (Ed.), *Imagine that: Studies in imagined interaction* (pp. 17–29). Cresskill, NJ: Hampton.

Huston, T. L., Surra, C. A., Fitzgerald, N. M., & Cate, R. M. (1981). From courtship to marriage: Mate selection as an interpersonal process. In S. Duck & R. Gilmour (Eds.), *Personal relationships: Developing personal relationships* (Vol. 2, pp. 53–88). New York, NY: Academic Press.

Kellermann, K. (1992). Communication: Inherently strategic and primarily automatic. *Communication Monographs, 59,* 288–300. doi:10.1080/03637759209376270

Kellermann, K., Broetzmann, S., Lim, T. S., & Kitao, K. (1989). The conversation MOP: Scenes in the stream of discourse. *Discourse Processes, 12,* 27–61.

Knapp, M. L., Vangelisti, A. L., & Caughlin, J. P. (2014). *Interpersonal communication and human relationships* (7th ed.). New York, NY: Pearson.

Koch, E. (2002). Relational schemas, self-esteem, and the processing of social stimuli. *Psychology Press, 1,* 271–279. doi:10.1080/152988602760124883

Kuperberg, A., & Padgett, J. E. (2015). The role of culture in explaining college students' selection into hookups, dates, and long-term romantic relationships. *Journal of Social and Personal Relationships, 33,* 1–27. doi:10.1177/0265407515616876

La France, B. H., Henningsen, D. D., Oates, A., & Shaw, C. M. (2009). Social-sexual interactions? Meta-analyses of sex differences in perceptions of flirtatiousness, seductiveness, and promiscuousness. *Communication Monographs, 76*, 263–285. doi:10.1080/03637750903074701

Langer, E. (1978). Rethinking the role of thought in social interaction. In J. Harvey, W. Ickes, & R. Kidd (Eds.), *New directions in attribution research* (pp. 35–58). Hillsdale, NJ: Lawrence Erlbaum.

Langer, E. (1989). *Mindfulness*. Reading, MA: Addison-Wesley.

Lenton, A., & Bryan, A. (2005). An affair to remember: The role of sexual scripts in perceptions of sexual intent. *Personal Relationships, 12*, 483–498. doi:10.1111/j.1475-6811.2005.00127.x

Letcher, A., & Carmona, J. (2015). Friends with benefits: Dating practices of rural high school and college students. *Journal of Community Health, 40*, 522–529. doi:10.1007/s10900-014-9966-z

Manthos, M., Owen, J., & Fincham, F. D. (2014). A new perspective on hooking up among college students. Sexual behavior as a function of distinct groups. *Journal of Social and Personal Relationships, 31*, 815–829. doi:10.1177/0265407513505932

Medved, C. E., Brogan, S., McClanahan, A. M., Morris, J. F., & Shepherd, G. J. (2005). *Reproducing the gendered boundaries between work and family: An analysis and critique of family socialization memorable messages*. Paper presented at the International Communication Association 2005 Annual Meeting, New York.

Mercer, G. W., & Kohn, P. M. (1979). Gender difference in the integration of conservatism, sex urge, and sexual behaviors among college students. *Journal of Sex Research, 15*, 129–142. doi:10.1080/00224497909551031

Miller, L., & Read, S. J. (1991). On the coherence of mental models of persons and relationships: A knowledge structure approach. In G. J. O. Fletcher & F. Fincham (Eds.), *Cognition in close relationships* (pp. 69–99). Hillsdale, NJ: Lawrence Erlbaum.

Mongeau, P. A., Carey, C. M., & Williams, M. L. M. (1998). First date initiation and enactment: An expectancy violation approach. In D. J. Canary & K. Dindia (Eds.), *Sex differences and similarities in communication: Critical essays and empirical investigations of sex and gender in interaction* (pp. 413–426). Mahwah, NJ: Lawrence Erlbaum.

Mongeau, P. A., Serewicz, M. C. M., & Therrien, L. F. (2004). Goals for cross-sex first dates: Identification, measurements, and the influence of contextual factors. *Communication Monographs, 71*, 121–147. doi:10.1080/0363775042331302514

Montesi, J. L., Fauber, R. L., Gordon, E. A., & Heimberg, R. G. (2011). The specific importance of communicating about sex to couples' sexual and overall relationship satisfaction. *Journal of Social and Personal Relationships, 28*, 591–609. doi:10.1177/0265407510386833

Owen, J., & Fincham, F. D. (2012). Friends with benefits relationships as a start to exclusive romantic relationships. *Journal of Social and Personal Relationships. 29*, 982–996. doi:10.1177/0265407512448275

Planalp, S., & Honeycutt, J. M. (1985). Events that increase uncertainty in personal relationships. *Human Communication Research, 11*, 593–604. doi:10.1111/j.1468-2958.1985.tb00062.x

Pryor, J. B., & Merluzzi, T. V. (1985). The role of expertise in processing social interaction scripts. *Journal of Experimental Social Psychology, 21*, 362–379. doi:10.1016/0022-1031(85)90036-8

Regan, P. C., & Atkins, L. (2006). Sex differences and similarities in frequency and intensity of sexual desire. *Social Behavior and Personality, 34*, 95–102.

Schank, R. C. (1982). *Dynamic memory*. New York, NY: Cambridge University Press.

Schank, R. C., & Abelson, R. P. (1977). *Scripts, plans, goals, and understanding*. Hillsdale, NJ: Lawrence Erlbaum.

Scott, C. K., Fuhrman, R. W., & Wyer, R. S. (1991). Information processing in close relationships. In G. J. O. Fletcher & F. D. Fincham (Eds.), *Cognition in close relationships* (pp. 37–67). Hillsdale, NJ: Lawrence Erlbaum.

Simpson, J. A., Gangestad, S. W., & Lerman, M. (1990). Perception of physical attractiveness: Mechanisms involved in the maintenance of romantic relationships. *Journal of Personality and Social Psychology, 59*, 1192–1201. doi:10.1037/0022-3514.59.6.1192

Sprecher, S., & McKinney, K. (1994). Sexuality in close relationships. In A. L. Weber & J. H. Harvey (Eds.), *Perspectives on close relationships* (pp. 193–216). Boston, MA: Allyn & Bacon.

Stafford, L., & Daly, J. A. (1984). The effects of recall mode and memory expectancies on remembrances of natural conversation. *Human Communication Research, 10*, 379–402. doi:10.1111/j.1468-2958.1987.tb00127.x

Stephen, T. (1987). Taking communication seriously: A reply to Murstein. *Journal of Marriage and the Family, 49*, 937–938.

Wood, J. T. (2008). *Gendered lives* (8th ed.). Stamford, CT: Cengage Learning.

CHAPTER SIX

Development of Relationships

Stage Theories and Relational Script Theory

Scholars studying personal relationships have maintained that relationships develop through a series of phases or stages that reflect an individual's different levels of intimacy with another, ranging from impersonal interactions to intimate relations. Stage models have withstood the test of time and existed for nearly half a century (e.g., Murstein, 1970). Kelley et al. (1983) indicated that "when a relationship changes markedly in a property, it is reasonable to say that it has moved to a new stage or level" (p. 38). The stages reflect different expectations for behavior in a period in a relationship. For example, an initiation stage occurs at an initial meeting and the discovery of shared interests. The individuals may see one another again and become acquaintances, develop friendship, or become romantically involved.

A common element of these models involves an assumption that there is systematic movement through stages of interaction, even though there is difficulty in accounting for alternating periods of growth and decline over the life history of relationships (Surra, 1990). Movement may occur forward, backward, and laterally. This assumption has been ignored by critics of stage models who claim that the models posit linear movement in which individuals proceed from one phase to another in a regular sequence. However, stage models allow individuals to enhance intimacy and decrease intimacy at various times and in a variety of contexts. For example, opposing dialectic needs can be used to calibrate the intimacy that is seen as comfortable in a relationship at any time. If one person feels another is coming on too strong or being impulsive, the person may distant him or herself, hoping to set the intimacy at a lower level. *Filters* and *phases* are terms in the literature that are synonymous with developmental stages.

This chapter reviews a number of stage models of relationship development, discussing their contributions and limitations, and how the models have been revised. The chapter concludes with a brief discussion of the role of cognition in reflecting stages in the minds of individuals, followed by sample male and female expectations about intimate relationships.

Developmental Models of Relationships

Many of the labels that people use to describe relationships (e.g., strangers, acquaintances, friends, best friends, lovers, fighting couple, separated couple, and ex-partners) reflect stages of intimacy. In an examination of 166 cultures, Jankowiak (1995) found evidence of romantic love in 88% of them. Moreover, there are also systematic stages of romance in these cultures. Following are two developmental models based on physiology and communication behavior, respectively.

Chapter 1 mentioned the classic biochemical work of Fisher (1994), in which she argued that brain physiology drives romantic stages. In this regard, she discussed three stages of romantic love that occur cross-culturally and that are based on brain physiology associated with infatuation, attachment, and detachment that has evolved as part of a primordial mating system. The first stage, infatuation, begins the moment another individual takes on special meaning. This person may be an old friend viewed in a new light or a stranger. The characteristics of this stage include intrusive thinking in which many individuals report spending from 85% to 100% of their time thinking about their partners. Negative traits of the beloved are overlooked, whereas positive traits are aggrandized. Many emotions are felt at this stage, including elation, hope, apprehension, uncertainty, shyness, fear of rejection, helplessness, irrationality, uncontrollability, and longing for reciprocity.

Tennov (1980) measured the distance from the moment that infatuation started to the moment of feeling of neutrality. She found that this stage typically lasts from 18 months to 3 years. The end of infatuation may be linked to brain physiology because the nerve endings in the brain become habituated to the natural stimulants or the levels of these amphetamine-like substances begin to drop (also see Chapter 4 on physiology). Studies in brain imaging use fMRI technology have confirmed this in which people look at pictures of others with whom they have close relationships with compared to strangers (Honeycutt, Sawyer, &

Keaton, 2014). Moreover, viewing pictures of a romantic partner has been shown to reduce experimental thermal pain because it is associated with neural activations in reward-processing centers in the brain (Younger, Aron, Parke, Chatterjee, & Mackey, 2010).

As infatuation declines, the second stage of romantic love, attachment, begins. The end of infatuation may be linked to changes in brain physiology because the nerve endings become habituated to the level of neurotransmitters in the brain. Fisher (1994) cited researchers who hypothesized that endorphins give partners feelings of safety, peace, and stability. Contentment characterizes this stage. The duration of attachment is not known.

Detachment is the third stage of romance. The physiology that accompanies detachment has not been analyzed. However, Fisher (1994) suggested that the brain's receptor sites for the endorphins or other neurochemicals become further desensitized or overloaded after the decline of attachment. This decline sets up the mind for separation from the partner. As noted in Chapter 1, Fisher (1994) proposed that there is a tendency for men and women to pair and remain together for about 4 years, which reflects an ancestral reproductive strategy to cooperatively raise a single helpless infant.

Fisher noted that in many cultures, divorce occurs regularly during and around the 4th year of marriage. Men and women tend to divorce in their 20s, the height of their reproductive years. Men and women are more likely to abandon relationships that have produced no children or one dependent child. In addition, many divorced individuals of reproductive age remarry. According to Fisher (1994), the longer a marriage lasts, the older spouses get, and the more children they have, the more likely they are to remain together. Although, there are obvious exceptions, these characteristics persist across cultures regardless of the standard of living.

The brain physiology for stages of romance may have evolved to fuel the human primordial mating system. Fisher (1994) discussed the emergence of serial monogamy more than 4 million years ago, when male hominids were unable to obtain enough food to sustain a harem, but could provide food and protection for a single female hominid. The pair-bonding during the infancy of a child was critical for human women and practical for men, and monogamy evolved.

Fisher (1994) posited that as a couple aged, as the length of their pair-bond increased, or as a couple bore successive young, the flexible neural circuits in the brain helped to sustain the pair-bond. With the expansion of the human cerebral cortex over 1 million years ago, humans began to build on the core of primal cyclic emotions by adding other feelings, cultural rituals, and beliefs about attraction, attachment, and detachment.

Fisher (1994) also discussed how culture plays an important role in infatuation. By the teenage years, people carry with them an unconscious mental template or love map that consists of physical, psychological, and behavioral traits that an individual finds attractive in a mate. Mental templates for relationships are discussed in detail in this chapter in terms of relationship schemata.

Other models of relational development concentrate on the communication behaviors of the individuals. In this regard, Knapp, Vangelisti, and Caughlin (2013) defined relationship stages in terms of the amount of repetitive communicative behaviors over time. For example, physical affection, self-disclosure, and dating occurring within a time period reflect the intensification of a relationship. Their model contains five stages of communication growth:

1. Initiating—Two individuals meet and communication is stylized to allow the individuals to talk with little knowledge of one another.
2. Experimenting—There is the use of small talk and interaction rituals in order to discover similarities with one another. Norms of politeness characterize these interactions and individuals present a desired image of themselves.
3. Intensifying—A close friendship develops, intimate disclosure increases, and private symbols are used to identify the couple as a unique dyad.
4. Integrating—Personalities fuse, social networks merge, and the couple is seen as a couple by outsiders. A jointly constructed view of the world emerges and plans are made with one another in mind.
5. Bonding—There is a serious discussion about commitment. There are public rituals that announce that the commitments are formally contracted, such as exclusively seeing one another, becoming engaged, or getting married.

Knapp and his colleagues also discussed five stages of decay in which communication progressively becomes restricted and eventually, ceases to exist. We added an additional stage that takes into account long-term memory and intermittent awareness:

1. Differentiating—Partners begin to remind one another of how different they are. There may be a repetitive cycle of breaking up and making up, as partners move from bonding to differentiating, back to integrating, and so on.
2. Circumscribing—There is less communication, both in the number of interactions and the depth of the topics discussed. Familiar phrases are "Let's not talk about this anymore." "I have nothing to say."

3. Stagnating—Communication is at a standstill. As a result, there may be imagined interactions about topics because they feel they know how the encounters will go. It is useless to communicate because the encounters are perceived to be unproductive. Knapp and his associates (2013) indicated that communication becomes more stylized, difficult, rigid, hesitant, awkward, and narrow.
4. Avoiding—There is a physical separation of the partners. The other person is seen less and reasons may be given about why one individual cannot see his or her partner.
5. Termination—Relationships can terminate immediately, after a greeting, or over many years. There may be a summary statement reviewing the relationship's history and providing the reasons for the ending of the relationship.

An additional stage of decay could be called *post-termination awareness* of the ex-partner. This stage happens when the individual thinks about the ex-partner or the relationship and recalls events in the relationship. Individuals are likely to be in this stage to the extent they have not found alternative interests or partners that allow them to focus externally on other stimuli. Even remarried individuals with children from a prior marriage are aware of their ex-partner through visitation encounters and reports from their children about the ex-partner.

Additionally, it has been found that couples in de-escalation stages report less idioms, and use idioms with less frequency, than couples in the escalation stages (Dunleavy & Booth-Butterfield, 2009). The use of positive idioms is associated with relational satisfaction while couples in de-escalating stages use confrontation, nickname, and teasing insult idioms with more negative effects than escalating couples.

Movement is basically sequential in the stage models, as individuals tend to progress through adjacent stages rather than skipping stages. Knapp and his associates (2013) indicated that each stage contains important conditions for ensuing stages such that sequencing makes forecasting adjacent stages easier while skipping stages is a risk on the uncertainties presented by the lack of information that could have been learned in the skipped stage. Additionally, some social norms do not condone skipping stages. For example, even though sexual intercourse may occur as an isolated event for individuals getting to know each other as discussed earlier in terms of hookups or Friends with Benefits, it is often associated with couples in an intensifying stage, due to its repetition.

Although movement tends to be orderly, it may occur at various speeds in various directions with a variety of results. In addition, there are many paths on the road of relational escalation and de-escalation that may lead to the continual recalibration of the relationship or to its ending. Consider couples who argue a great deal compared to couples who argue only intermittently. Repetitive arguing reflects the differentiating stage, in which the relational partners are distancing themselves and stressing individual needs (Knapp et al., 2013). Intermittent arguing could be subsumed under another stage label, depending on what preeminent behaviors characterize the communication of the relational partners.

The developmental models represent a relational life cycle symbolizing the evolution of different kinds of relationships, from initial meeting to final encounter in some cases. Developmental models have helped researcher to understand relationship dynamics by describing the role of communication (e.g., self-disclosure, reading one's partner's nonverbal cues, sending clear nonverbal cues, resolving conflict in constructive manners) in defining the current state or stage of a relationship (Knapp et al., 2013). The amount of self-disclosure in a relationship reflects the importance and intimacy of the relationship as well as reducing the uncertainty about attitudes and roles (Baxter & Wilmot, 1984; Berger & Bradac, 1982).

The developmental models have great appeal because they help people to reduce uncertainty about the type of personal relationships people may find themselves in. Yet the models have been criticized for emphasizing thinking about relationships and observing oneself and one's partner's actions or reactions. On the other hand, college students exposed to these models often report that they are able to recognize behaviors and make sense of what is happening in their current relationships or to attribute meaning to behaviors in their previous relationships. The recognition of behaviors involves memory recall of events in relationships. Relational schemata are activated in order to make sense of the progression of events, behaviors, or activities in personal relationships, and one way this is done is by conceptualizing relational development in terms of stages.

The identification of recurring behaviors and the categorization of these behaviors into categories reflecting developmental stages provide individuals with a vocabulary to assist in their understanding the movement and dynamics of relational development. For example, increased dating may be categorized as reflecting the intensification of a relationship if one wonders about reciprocal intimate feelings from one's partner. Relationships may also intensify after partners overcome some type of relationship crisis, such as feeling insecure or jealous about one another's activities (Planalp & Honeycutt, 1985). Hence, developmental models serve a critical function in symbolizing motion in relationships. Movement is based on need, exchange of rewards, social background, and shared relational scripts based on similar experiences.

Duck (1990) discussed how motion is the fundamental property of relationships rather than a steady state. However, couples often present an image to others of orderly, routine, or predictable patterns of communication in order to stabilize that perpetual motion. In addition, individuals often tell stories about relationship events to provide order for time-ordered events (Askham, 1982). The provision of order reflects a desire for structure and predictability.

People's memories of relational events often reflect stage-like qualities because individuals tell stories about meeting for the first time, developing intimacy, getting married, dealing with conflicts in the relationship, and ending prior relationships. Yet if someone is asked to tell the story about his or her marriage, the person will look bewildered and may reply, "Well, what do you want to know about my marriage; the story of how we met, the wedding, the time we went to Cancun, or the time we were both in the hospital?" Stories about events bring order to the passage of time and punctuate the relationship into a series of identifiable events that often can be viewed as reflecting stages of intimacy. In essence, the developmental models have advanced people's understanding of the temporal organization of relationships.

Criticisms of Developmental Models

Critics of stage models have argued that the stages are hard to identify, may be skipped, are arbitrarily defined, and simply represent the passage of time in relationships. It is argued the stages do not really exist because movement through them is capricious and depends on the individual relationship. Despite the problems of precisely identifying stages, as well as the direction and rate of movement through the stages, a variety of models have been proposed. In fact, a saturation point seems to have been reached with the diversity of models (e.g., Altman & Taylor, 1973; Baxter, 1985; Duck, 1982; Knapp et al., 2013; Lee, 1984; Levinger, 1974; Murstein, 1974).

Early models of relational development were simple. Levinger (1974) proposed a three-stage awareness model. In unilateral awareness, the individuals are not aware of each other in a reciprocal fashion; a man may be aware of a woman but the woman is unaware of the man. Bilateral awareness involves small talk; relationships between acquaintances represent this type of awareness. Mutual awareness is more intimate and involves a shared dependency between the people. Additional three-stage models have been proposed. For example, Duck (1986) described a physical appearance stage followed by an assessment of the other person's attitudes and compatibility with the other person's personality.

Levinger (1980, 1983) revised the three-stage awareness model and proposed a five-stage model that includes: (a) initiation and awareness of the other person, (b) building the relationship, (c) continued interaction that may lead to marriage, (d) deterioration or decline of the bond, (e) and ending of the relationship through death or some type of separation. These five stages correspond to three states of growth, maintenance, and termination.

A three-stage model that has received a great deal of attention and criticism over the years is the stimulus-value-role (SVR) model. The assumptions of this model were debated in research journals (e.g., Leigh, Holman, & Burr, 1984; Murstein, 1974, 1986, 1987; Rubin & Levinger, 1974; Stephen, 1987). Murstein (1987) proposed that individuals who initially encounter another are in the stimulus (S) stage in which an individual evaluates an encountered person in terms of physical qualities and nonverbal inferences based on voice or clothing. The second stage, value (V), is presumed to exist when the individuals share basic attitudes regarding a variety of opinions or beliefs on issues such as religious beliefs, politics, abortion, euthanasia, and so on. The final stage is the role compatibility (R) stage in which the partners evaluate the functions of roles that have evolved in relation to each other. For example, individuals may perceive themselves as co-equal decision makers, supporters, lovers, guardians, and so on relative to one another.

SVR theory has received continued attention even though the basic premises of the theory have been questioned. Individuals may require information about stimulus, values, and roles continuously. It appears that the rate of acceleration in which information is acquired defines each stage. Stephen (1987) argued that a model that proposes that values and attitudes are created through communication is a problem for stage theorists because communication theories assume individuals can value different kinds of information unequally. Some individuals value stimulus information above all else (physical appearance), whereas others may examine role information first.

The SVR sequence is not the same from individual to individual. Further, what happens if two individuals who meet have different sequences? Does that relationship end, do the individuals negotiate sequences, or does one person follow the sequence preferences the other? Individuals are likely to be more compatible when they have similar expectations about relationship development.

Another problem with the SVR model is role classification. What roles are partners assigned to, friend, lover, best friend, and so on? Leigh et al. (1984) had difficulty classifying individuals in the value and role stages using Murstein's (1986) model. The recognition of this difficulty in classification has resulted in an attempt to set more precise standards for categorization.

The problems associated with the SVR model apply to other developmental models. Lewis (1973) posited a stage sequence in which individuals initially |notice similarities to one another, develop rapport and begin to self-disclose, and cast themselves into roles vis-a-vis one another. Finally, the bond between the partners is crystallized or cemented. Yet the movement may not be sequential because individuals can develop rapport and then notice dissimilarities from one another.

In addition to the problems associated with the SVR model, the developmental models present a view of relationships as being relatively predictable, orderly, and rational to the extent that individuals progress through stages. This view of relationships has been referred to as the *linear assumption* of the development of relationships. The linear assumption has been criticized by a number of researchers on the basis that individuals seemingly skip some stages, do not progress through all the stages or have different rates of movement through the stages.

The linear assumption has been tested using an additive scale in which the endorsement of certain items is necessary before other items can be endorsed. King and Christensen (1983) modeled relationships using an additive scale. Their scale presumes that an individual will endorse the item "We have spent a whole day with just each other" and "I like you" before reporting "I love you."

Their scale has six stages of relational growth: (a) expression of mutual attraction in terms of the amount and variety of interaction increasing, (b) identification by the social network of the individuals as a couple, (c) increase of emotional investment as the participants identify their feelings as love and avoid rival romantic involvements, (d) projection of the relationship into the future while considering commitment and maximum levels of interdependence, (e) coordination of time, money, and activities for the benefit of joint interests, and (f) commitment to the permanence and exclusiveness of the relationship through engagement, living together, or marriage. Some of these stages are similar to the social-penetration escalating stages model discussed by Altman and Taylor (1973) and Knapp and his associates (2013).

There are a number of examples in the literature of nonsequential movement through the stage of decaying relationships, the stages of breaking up or relational disillusionment. Lee (1984) proposed a five-stage dissolution model; (a) discovery of dissatisfaction in which a problem, conflict, or dissatisfaction threatens the continuance of the relationship, (b) exposure in which dissatisfaction is discussed with friends or the partner, (c) negotiation which begins when serious discussion occurs concerning issues of dissatisfaction, (d) resolution which takes place when one or both partners reach a decision about the relationship and any action to be taken, and (e) final transformation in which a change actually takes place.

Other researchers have found support for the omission of stages calling the linear assumption into question. For example, Lee (1984) analyzed subjects' memories about 112 relational breakups and found that only 17% of disengaging relationships went through all of the stages. Complex scenarios or mixed formats involving stage recycling included 31% of the cases. Other scenarios involved omission of the discussion of dissatisfaction (26.8% of cases). Lee concluded that although the ending of relationships may be messy or uncontrolled, the individuals' retrospective memory recall suggested that the dissolution process occurs in regularities. These regularities include a high association between the dimensions of termination (length of the ending and the conclusiveness or finality of the ending) and the lack of intimacy in the couple.

Termination characteristics were also associated with negative affect during a breakup such as confusion and fear, as well as in post-breakup behaviors when encountering the ex-partner. Lee (1984) also found that individuals reporting little or no communication about issues of dissatisfaction had shorter, less intense relationships that also had less commitment and were more superficial. Little or no communication during a breakup represents the omission of the exposure and negotiation stages in his model of disengaging relationships. The omission of stages highlights the difficulty in identifying transitions between adjacent stages.

The boundary points between stages have been called into question. Duck (1988) indicated that although some sequencing of stages has been demonstrated in a number of models, "no precision or specificity as to their exact operation has been advanced" (p. 73). He viewed process as the essential state of all relationships and apparent stability as only a temporary equalization of opposing forces.

Conville (1991) argued that developmental models have not provided an adequate view of relationship transitions because they fail to give priority to relational partners' personal narratives. On the other hand, Conville believed that the models seem to grant priority to relationship dissolution when relationships are placed in the arenas of intrapersonal, interpersonal, and social interaction. Further, there is no precision or specificity as to the exact operation of the transition between the stages.

The lack of precision about stage transitions is revealed in a study by Hays (1984) in which he examined the development of friendship over a 3-month period among male and female college students. Students were given a series of self-report behavior checklists asking their ratings of individuals whom they believed might become good friends. Dyads that developed into close relationships showed more intimacy of disclosure and more talking about a variety of topics. In the successfully progressing friendships, the number of superficial and casual behaviors engaged in slightly increased from time 1 to time 2 and then decreased until the time 4 was assessed. The number of affection behaviors as revealed in the expression of positive or negative sentiment toward the partner, remained relatively stable as the months passed. However, there was a gender difference: women engaged in more affection and casual communication behaviors with their friends than did men. Finally, behaviors such as providing goods, services, or support were the best predictors of the intensity of the friendship at the end of the 3-month period.

Hays (1984) concluded that some of his findings supported the social penetration model of relational development. The initial interaction of friends was found to correspond to an additive scale that progressed from superficial talk to increasingly intimate levels of behavior. Yet the emergence of intimate behaviors was not gradual. After only 6 weeks, the dyads reached their peak in the reported number of intimate behaviors performed, a pattern no different from that of their nonintimate exchange of behaviors. It was interesting that after 3 weeks of acquaintance, the activity of doing things together was more related to friendship ratings than assessments of how intimate the communication was in the dyad. However, as time passed, the intimacy levels of the dyads' interactions emerged as equally and, in some cases, more associated with ratings of friendship compared to the variety of topics that were discussed. These findings suggest that as friendships develop, and individual expectations about and standards for evaluating friendship may change.

Relational Dialectic Models

The criticisms about linearity and stage definition have resulted in contemporary developmental theorists revising the models (e.g., Baxter, 2011; Baxter & Norwood, 2015). Their goal was to reflect the dialectic view that relationships never really achieve a particular stage or a steady state because there is continual negotiation and recalibration. Altman, Vinsel, and Brown (1981) argued for a dialectic model in which the formation of relationships is characterized by cyclicity in that relationships have elements of stability and change that are cyclical. Thus, sequential movement is insufficient to explain the development or decline of relationships (Altman et al., 1981; Baxter, 1985; Taylor & Altman, 1987). Relationships are filled with inherent contradictions such as one partner wanting to feel close or connected while the other desires autonomy. Other common dialectical needs are novelty-predictability and openness-closeness. The two poles of dialectic are in constant motion with each other. A classic song by the Beatles, "Hello-Goodbye" reflects the autonomy-connection.

There is continual recalibration of relationship roles. Relationship recalibration may be passive or active. For example, two spouses who achieve a certain level of intimacy may give little thought to intensifying the relationship except after arguments or squabbles. On the other hand, a person who wishes to maintain a dating relationship at an existing stage of intimacy, although his or her partner wants to intensify the intimacy, may withdraw from relationship activities, and inform his or her partner of the person's hesitancy in escalating the intimacy in the relationship.

VanLear (1987) found support for dialectic behaviors in the development of college friendships. He audiotaped 15 dyads that initially had no history of interaction. The dyads met once a week for 30 minutes over a 6-week period. They were given no instructions on what to talk about in order to create an environment for naturally occurring conversation. Over time, VanLear found that private or personal disclosures tended to increase, whereas public (small talk and demographics) and semiprivate disclosures (attitudes and opinions) revealed no systematic trend, reflecting an increase or decrease in these disclosure areas. Reciprocity of disclosure at the same level of intimacy was the rule rather than the exception from period to period. Reciprocity of semiprivate disclosure was more frequent and stronger than reciprocity of public or private disclosure. Self-disclosure occurred in concurrent cycles of reciprocal small talk and semiprivate disclosures. Thus, relational development was not a strict linear process regarding the amount and type of disclosures.

Research has revealed that dialectic behaviors (e.g., one partner discloses but the other withdraws from the interaction) often reveal systematic patterns of interaction. This was referred to as the *punctuation problem* in communicative encounters by Watzlawick, Beavin, and Jackson (1967). Current behaviors (e.g., He's withdrawing) are the result of preceding behaviors by a relational partner (e.g., She's nagging because he did not want to discuss problems in the relationship). The cause of a given response is the effect of a preceding message. Hence, messages are linked, and cause and effect are arbitrary labels applied at particular times. In terms of relational dialectics, John may be trying to escalate intimacy in a relationship because he believes that Mary is withdrawing. On the other hand, Mary is withdrawing because she sees John as moving too fast. At one level, these behaviors may seem to be uncoordinated actions and random movement in different stages of a relationship with one person escalating and the other de-escalating. Yet the dialectics are inherent in relationships because individual needs may be contrasted with relational obligations or desires.

Dialectic behaviors in relationships reflect changing interpersonal needs. Indeed, Schutz's (1958) classical interpersonal needs theory stressed that individuals have needs for inclusion, control, and affection in a variety of circumstances. Given individual needs at specific times, movement may occur within stages, such as an individual increasing physical affection but the partner reduces the level of affection in order to stabilize the relationship at a particular level of intimacy. Although movement seems to be random, there is the assumption of movement generally occurring through adjacent stages.

It is impossible to go back to earlier stages of intimacy after reaching a more intimate stage because memory of prior intimate scenes affects how new information is processed. Conville (1991) argued that because of memories the same event cannot occur. Human experience is presented as a spiral. Due to memory, whenever one repeats an experience and recognizes that one has returned to the experience, the fact of recognition proves that one has not returned to the same experience. In essence, memory is the element that individuals bring back to the same place that acknowledge that it is not the same place. Repeated events are not the same event; rather, repeated events are events of the same type (Conville, 1991).

Although acknowledging that movement may be dialectic and nonsequential, some theorists argued that the decline of relationships often follows a reversal of stages that the partners progressed through while developing the intimate bond (Knapp et al., 2013). Yet there is compelling evidence against this reversal hypothesis for declining relationships (Baxter, 1985; Duck & Lea, 1983). On the one hand, Baxter and Montgomery (1996) review research that found support for declining disclosure for individuals reporting on the disengagement of a recent relationship. However, there is not support for the reversal hypothesis on communication characteristics regarding social knowledge of one's partner.

Other research revealed that the diversity of strategies for relationship growth is greater than the number of disengaging strategies (Baxter & Montgomery, 1996). The beginning of a relationship requires the agreement of both partners in order to succeed, whereas disengagement may be accomplished by one party. Baxter (1985) argued that the reversal hypothesis is less useful as one shifts away from emotion-based features of communication to more cognition-based features. Stages of disengagement such as discovery of dissatisfaction, seeing one another less often, and spending less time together (e.g., Knapp et al., 2013; Lee, 1984) do not mirror stages of relational growth. Instead, love and distance are continually being negotiated in relationships. Individuals need varying amounts of love or independence, depending on needs, and circumstances.

Communication provides a mechanism for labeling feelings of love and detachment. Yet, the early stage models have been criticized not only for ignoring dialectic needs but for following what Stephen (1987) referred to as a lock-and-key view of development that ignores communication as an ongoing, dynamic process in which roles emerge through interaction and negotiation. Researchers have typically chosen to treat matching characteristics among individuals as traits rather than as being relationally defined through social interaction.

Criticisms of Relational Dialectic Models

Criticisms of dialectic models have also surfaced. First, they have been criticized for overstating the sequential argument at the expense of ignoring an assumption of developmental models that allows for nonsequential movement. Second, the models have been criticized for misrepresenting the social construction of reality by assuming that this only occurs through the negotiation of meanings at a dyadic level and not within the individual.

Berger (1993) disagreed with dialectical theorists who argue that developmental models do not adequately represent process and change and that dialectical approaches are better able to explain nonsequential movement in relationships as contrasted with smooth trajectories of growth and decay. Berger also criticized the belief of dialectic theorists that developmental models focus on the individual and thus are not capable of explaining relationship-level phenomena as the negotiation of meaning and mutual understanding.

From a dialectic view the negotiation of mutual understanding is a dyadic and not an individual phenomenon. Individuals negotiate meanings to determine their appropriate roles in their relationships and the level of affect that is preferred. Recall from Chapter 1 that Stephen's (1994) discussed happy couples sharing a relationship worldview; he was not clear if this sharing is incidental or negotiated. He indicated that people's conceptions of relationships are transformed by what is brought into the relationship and exposure to one another's constructions of reality. In contrast, Berger (1993) argued that what people commonly call mutual understanding may arise from the joining of individual systems of knowledge. Hence, there is no negotiation, but instead a meeting point or juncture of experiences.

This argument applies to happy couples sharing expectations for the development and maintenance of their relationships, which is an assumption of the relational cognitive approach discussed in the next section. Berger (1993) claimed that "what appear to be 'negotiated meanings' for relationships may in fact simply be the result of overlap of knowledge representation systems that persons bring with them to relationships" (p. 54).

These systems of knowledge include memories about relationships and corresponding expectations for how relationships develop, can be maintained, or die and they vary in complexity depending on one's experiences or exposure to informational sources. Recall from Chapter 1 that much of this knowledge is knowledge of failed relationships, for example, soap opera viewers may expect romance to be whimsical with infidelity a rule, not an exception. As noted in Chapter 2, it is important to examine people's expectations about the rise and demise of romance as part of how they interpret events and communication in close relationships.

Social Cognition: The Script Approach

Relationships are states of mind derived from prior experience, which organizes the processing of information. Andersen (1993) wrote, "We collaboratively can think relationships into and out of existence. Because these relational cognitions exist for both partners and rarely match exactly, relationships are tricky, dynamic, and sometimes frustrating" (p. 29).

Duck (1986) argued that relationships should be regarded as changing mental and behavioral creations of participants, which play a crucial role in creating and sustaining relationships. Similarly, Berger and Roloff (1982) discussed that the development of relationships can best be understood in terms of individuals' existing or emergent scripts that enable the anticipation of what is likely to happen in a relationship. For example, one may have a script for opening lines to introduce oneself to the opposite gender (Kellermann, Broetzmann, Lim, & Kitao, 1989). Expectations for romantic relationships could include behaviors such as walking in a park, periods of touching, intimate communication, and an endless array of actions.

The concept of stage has utility from a cognitive perspective. People have scripts that consist of prototypical behaviors that they expect to occur in escalating and de-escalating relationships (Honeycutt, 1993). The order of the behaviors reflect stages for relationships; thus, the concept of stage may be useful for examining individuals' perceptions or beliefs about what should occur during the course of relationships.

Marriage therapists often contend that a major factor in the decay of marriages is the erroneous expectations that never-married people bring to their marriages. High expectations before marriage may result in unsatisfactory outcomes (Sabatelli, 1988). For example, never-married individuals tend to expect higher levels of sexual activity, interest in sex, discussion of sexual issues, companionship, and affection from their partners. There are similar expectations when comparing married and never-married individuals about dealing with conflict over daily decisions, recreation, friends, arguing over petty issues, agreement on lifestyle, the freedom to pursue friendships, jealousy expressed by partner, and the degree of privacy. Sabatelli (1988) suggested that a reevaluation of expectations should take place after marriage if couples are to continue to be satisfied with their relationships.

The script approach places importance on the mental creations of relationships based on memory, talk, and expectations that sustain individuals in everyday living. In addition, current relational experiences affect the reconstruction of prior events in relationships. Current feelings affect how events are recalled in a relationship. A person who is currently angry is unlikely to recall many positive events from his or her relationship.

The developmental models serve as a heuristic anchor for processing relationship behaviors (Honeycutt, 1993). They help people interpret prior events in relationships and prescribe subsequent events. Other research also revealed that prior expectations may influence how people view current behaviors (Nisbett & Ross, 1980). For example, if an older couple is observed eating lunch, holding hands, and kissing in a park, they may be initially seen as married by a stranger. Yet the couple may be having an affair! The observed behaviors may be associated more with a quality marriage than with having an affair because the behaviors of demonstrating physical affection are part of the observer's script for marriage. Once individuals have developed a script for their own romantic relationship, they appear to be better at discerning whether others are involved in a loving liaison (Aloni & Bernieri, 2004).

Gender Differences in Intimate-Relationship Scripts

There are numerous gender differences in intimate relationship scripts. Historically men have been viewed as success objects reflecting task attraction while women are viewed as sex objects reflecting physical attraction. For example, Davis (1990) found in a study of 328 personal advertisements sampled from a major daily Canadian newspaper that gender differences for desired companion attributes were consistent with traditional sex role stereotypes. Relative to the opposite sex, women emphasized employment, financial, and intellectual status, as well as commitment, while men emphasized physical characteristics. Physical characteristics were the most desired, regardless of sex. Secondary findings were that, for this sample, considerably more men than women placed ads, and that the mean age for both sexes was relatively high. The main findings were similar to those from earlier studies.

Other noteworthy studies reveal that during initial encounters, men are operating with simplistic scripts for what constitutes true, sincere female attraction toward them while the female scripts are considerably more complex. More often than not, guys interpret even friendly cues, such as a subtle smile from a gal, as a sexual come-on and find it difficult to tell the difference between women who are being friendly and women who are interested in something more. Farris, Treat, Viken, and McFall (2008) report that 70% of college women reporting an experience in which a guy mistook her friendliness for a sexual come-on.

Farris and her colleagues examined nonverbal communication in a group of 280 undergraduates, both men and women with an average age of 20 years. The students viewed images of women on a computer screen and had to categorize each as friendly, sexually interested, sad, or rejecting. Each student reported on 280 photographs, which had been sorted previously into one of the categories based on surveys completed by different groups of students. Women categorized more images correctly than men did. When it came to friendly gestures, men were more likely than women to interpret these to mean sexual interest. More surprising, the guys were also confused by sexual cues. When images of women meant to show allure flashed onto the screen, male students mistook the allure as amicable signals. So it appears that women trying to brush off a guy at work or the gym may need to be more direct. Men in the study also had more trouble than women distinguishing between sadness and rejection.

A common explanation for reports of men taking a friendly gesture as "she wants me," is based on men's inherent interest in sex, which is thought to result from their biology as well as their upbringing (Buss, 2003). Additionally, women are viewed as more communicative in personal relationships while men are stereotypically less concerned with communication and view activities and events as key ingredients in their relationships (Wood, 2008). Hence, men in general may be less sensitive to subtle nonverbal behavior than women.

There are additional gender differences in the complexity of relationship scripts. Consider the excerpts in Box 6.1. The first is provided by a 24-year-old woman who indicated her expectations for an intimate relationship in a journal entry; the second is a journal account from a 28-year-old married man. These two students were enrolled in an interpersonal communication course and kept communication journals for a 2-month period. These excerpts were in response to a question concerning personal expectations for intimate relationships. The students were not exposed to the idea of schemata or scripts at the time of their journal keeping, and the excerpts represent the students' thoughts before being exposed to any theory of relational development. Their expectations reflect reconstructions of memory about previous relationships. For example, the woman writes about how her expectation about a partner's honesty has been changed by memories about relationship activities from a prior relationship.

Box 6.1. Sample Male and Female Expectations for Intimacy and Relationships

Female's Expectations:
I have many expectations for intimacy. These expectations have been developed throughout my lifetime and have been derived from my own relationships, the influence of other's relationships, and my basic morals and beliefs. Basically, an intimate relationship should establish a *commitment* from two people to continue to develop a deep, emotional tie which will stimulate and bring happiness to the couple. Another expectation of intimacy I have is the *willingness to try, or give and take*. I learned this the hard way. My boyfriend would always say, "You're only happy when things go your way." I was willing to try, but only enough to satisfy my own needs. Two people are not going to agree on every issue. Therefore, sometimes one person must accept what he doesn't agree with and go on with matters. Disagreements shouldn't always be a battle with one opponent emerging as the winner and the other as the loser.

Another expectation which ties into the idea of trying is *mutual respect*. If there is mutual respect in a relationship, each person can understand the other's beliefs and ideas without necessarily agreeing with them.

The following expectation I hold, may have been influenced by the fact that I live in a small town where this is often seen. The old-fashioned stereotypical roles of the man as the "leader" and the woman as "passive" is an idea which I totally disagree with. I believe in *roles being equal*. The following is an example of this notion. One day a married friend and I went shopping. She repeatedly said she had to be home at a certain time to fix her husband's supper. This is only one example of people still conforming to stereotypical roles. I also feel that my friend probably would think she was not being a "good wife" if she did not conform to these behaviors. My belief on housekeeping is that all duties should be divided equally if both partners are employed.

I would be willing to invest whatever it took (time, patience, emotional support, etc.) to make a relationship work, to the extent that my own identity was not lost in the process. Also, my efforts would be greatly affected by the honesty and sincerity of the other person. Including this idea as well as others I hold have been changed by various memories about relationship activities while being involved in a six-year relationship. Although I may not know exactly what to expect of a relationship such as marriage, I do have a more firm grip on what not to expect.

Male's Expectations:
I have a number of expectations for relationships. With the divorce rate so high, it is evident that very severe problems exist between men and women and society today. Those engaged couples are constantly being reminded of the divorce rate as they prepare to embark on a life-long encounter of their own. At this phase in my life, I thought, "We're different. We're older and more mature than most couples. *We share a lot of common interests* and we really love each other." My wife and I have been married for 2 years and we have experienced few arguments in that time. Most people would say that constitutes a good marriage. I feel like my wife and I have a good marriage;

however, I think that many relationships exist where there are conflicts and there is still happiness because *they can communicate with each other without being defensive.*

Attitudes are important in determining the quality of a relationship. You must learn to recognize strengths and weaknesses in yourself and your partner. The most important point for any two people to realize is that *conflict is inevitable.* No matter how well you think you know a person, you will always be surprised by something that is said or by some behavior that they engage in from time to time. Two people are going to have opposing ideas on certain issues. I think the key to success is to know your partner and be *sympathetic* to their needs. I look at relationships optimistically. My parents have a good marriage and this is probably the reason I feel the way I do about the institution. My views on life in general today are very similar to those of my parents. I can also see resemblances between my wife's behavior and the behavior of her parents. Nevertheless, I think that *understanding* is the key to a successful marriage and this can only be achieved through *effective communication.*

The italicized words in the journal extracts in Box 6.1 represent keywords that reveal a portion of the woman's and man's scripts or expectations for an intimate relationship. Her expectations include commitment, willingness to invest in the relationship, mutual respect, and equal division of labor. These appear to be key ingredients of a satisfying marital relationship for this woman. The man's expectations include sharing common interests, communicating effectively, expecting conflict, being sympathetic, and believing that one understands his or her partner.

The woman's expectations seem to be more detailed than the man's expectations. This is consistent with research indicating that women monitor their personal relationships more closely than do men and are more aware of events during the life cycle of relationships (Rubin, Peplau, & Hill, 1981). The woman mentions learning about relationships from a wide variety of sources, whereas the man mentions only his parents. This is consistent with previously reported gender differences in reported sources of information about relationships. Although both genders report learning about relationships from parents as a major source, women have reported learning more about relationships from siblings than do men (Honeycutt, Cantrill, & Greene, 1989). This has resulted in some social-learning theorists arguing that modeling same-gender behavior is easier for women than for men due to the lesser availability of fathers (Arliss, 1991; Lynn, 1969). Other theorists have speculated that men may use their mothers as counter-role models once they realize their mothers belong to the opposite gender between 24 and 36 months after birth.

The themes in the journal entries in Box 6.1 reflect the components of the various developmental theories discussed in this chapter. The woman in the journal entry is in a premarital-engaged stage, whereas the man is in a stage of the family life cycle referred to as young, childless, married couples (Olson et al., 1983). Social-exchange profits and resources are reflected in the woman's journal entry. The woman refers to her boyfriend believing that she was only happy when her needs were satisfied. In addition, the woman refers to equal division of housekeeping duties, as well as making references to investing time and emotional support in the relationship. The woman refers to the satisfaction of her own needs. This statement reflects interpersonal needs theory in which there is an emphasis on the satisfaction of interpersonal needs, which may include desires for affection, control, and being recognized as a unique individual with self-worth (Schutz, 1958).

The journal entries are compatible with existing research on gender differences in recall about relational events. Women have more vivid memories of relationships events than do men (Harvey, Flannery, & Morgan, 1986). Women are socialized to be more concerned with relationships and to be more aware of the feelings of others than are men (Deaux, 1976), which suggests that they think about relationships differently or have different expectations about them.

Traditionally, the two genders have been socialized differently in terms of gender-role orientation in ways that affect perceptions of relationships. For example, women have been socialized to be cooperative, nurturing, and supportive, and to seek self-identity in terms of their relationships with others, whereas men have been socialized to be competitive, independent, aggressive, and less expressive of emotions (Pearson, Turner, & Todd-Manchillas, 1991). Memories and expectations about relationships as a function of gender are likely to reflect differences in gender-role socialization by parents, peers, and the media.

Summary

There is a long legacy of research in developmental communication based on the idea of relationships developing through a series of stages. Developmental models have been criticized for problems in stage identification; specifying the direction, speed, and rate of movement; and using a researcher's imposed view of what the stages are. As a result of these criticisms, developmental models were modified and expanded.

A cognitive approach addresses some of these problems by looking at the role of expectations for the development of romance. Relationships are initially created in people's minds even though it is communication and observable behavior that constitute the relationship (Duck, 1993). There is evidence of gender differences in relational expectations. Women have a greater recall of relational events and more detailed expectations for relational development than do men.

Despite their limitations, developmental models have extended researchers' understanding of communication across the lifespan of romantic relationships. Communication varies over the course of relationships and serves different functions, such as bonding, increasing intimacy, decreasing intimacy, and reinforcing the relationship. Individuals often ask themselves, "Where is this relationship headed?" The models have provided a reference in which to understand where relationships may be headed in terms of a trajectory.

Discussion Questions

6.1. Discuss your expectations about the following relationships: dating, same-gender best friend, friends with benefits, mentor, parent-child, and same-sex marriage. How complex are these expectations? Have your relationship expectations changed or been relatively stable over the years?

6.2. How is motion the fundamental property of relationships? Why can't couples just walk off into the sunset and live happily ever after as they sometimes do in fairy tales?

6.3. How can high levels of expectations for close personal relationships affect satisfaction with the relationship? Would you counsel individuals to have high or low levels of relational expectations, or no expectations at all, when entering into new relationships?

Applications

6.1. Interview two men and three women. Ask them about their expectations for a relationship based on diverse relationships (e.g., income differences between the partners, partners from different cultures, LGBTQ). Compare the men's responses with the women's responses. Does one group have more or less articulated expectations?

6.2. Ask a mixed-gender group what they think about the idea of love being hardwired in the brain's neurotransmitters. Discuss Fisher's (1994) physiological love stages of infatuation, attachment, and detachment.

References

Aloni, M., & Bernieri, F. J. (2004). Is love blind? The effects of experience and infatuation on the perception of love. *Journal of Nonverbal Behavior, 28*, 287–295. doi:10.1007/s10919-004-4160-0

Altman, I., & Taylor, D. A. (1973). *Social penetration*. New York, NY: Holt, Rinehart & Winston.

Altman, I., Vinsel, A., & Brown, B. (1981). Dialectic conceptions in social psychology: An application to social penetration and privacy regulation. In L. Berkowitz (Ed.), *Advances in experimental social psychology: Vol. 14* (pp. 76–100). New York, NY: Academic Press.

Andersen, P. A. (1993). Cognitive schemata in personal relationships. In S. Duck (Ed.), *Individuals in relationships* (pp. 1–29). Newbury Park, CA: Sage.

Arliss, L. P. (1991). *Gender communication*. Englewood Cliffs, NJ: Prentice-Hall.

Askham, J. (1982). Telling stories. *Sociological Review, 30*, 555–573. doi:10.1111/j.1467-954X.1982.tb00668.x

Baxter, L. A. (1985). Accomplishing relationship disengagement. In S. Duck & D. Perlman (Eds.), *Understanding personal relationship: An interdisciplinary approach* (pp. 243–265). Beverly Hills, CA: Sage.

Baxter, L. A. (2011). *Voicing relationships*. Los Angeles, CA: Sage.

Baxter, L. A., & Montgomery, B. M. (1996). *Relating: Dialogues and dialectics*. New York, NY: Guilford.

Baxter, L. A., & Norwood, K. M. (2015). Relational dialectics theory. In D. O. Braithwaite & P. Schrodt (Eds.), *Engaging theories in interpersonal communication* (2nd ed., pp. 279–291). Los Angeles, CA: Sage.

Baxter, L. A., & Wilmot, W. (1984). 'Secret tests': Strategies for acquiring information about the state of the relationship. *Human Communication Research, 11*, 171–201. doi:10.1111/j.1468-2958.1984.tb00044.x

Berger, C. R. (1993). Goals, plans, and mutual understanding in relationships. In S. Duck (Ed.), *Individuals in relationships* (pp. 30–59). Newbury Park, CA: Sage.

Berger, C. R., & Bradac, J. J. (1982). *Language and social knowledge: Uncertainty in interpersonal relations*. London: Edward Arnold.

Berger, C. R., & Roloff, M. E. (1982). Thinking about friends and lovers: Social cognition and relational trajectories. In M. E. Roloff & C. R. Berger (Eds.), *Social cognition and communication* (pp. 151–192). Beverly Hills, CA: Sage.

Buss, D. M. (2003). *The evolution of desire: Strategies of human mating*. New York, NY: Basic Books.

Conville, R. L. (1991). *Relational transitions: The evolution of personal relationships*. New York, NY: Praeger.

Davis, S. (1990). Men as success objects and women as sex objects: A study of personal advertisements. *Sex Roles, 23*, 43–50. doi:10.1007/BF00289878

Deaux, K. (1976). *The behavior of women and men*. Monterey, CA: Brooks/Cole.

Duck, S. (1982). A topography of relationship disengagement and dissolution. In S. Duck (Ed.), *Personal relationships: Dissolving personal relationships* (Vol. 4, pp. 1–30). London: Academic Press.

Duck, S. (1986). *Human relationships: An introduction to social psychology*. London: Sage.

Duck, S. (1988). *Handbook of personal relationships: Theory, research, and interventions*. John Wiley & Sons.

Duck, S. (1990). Relationships as unfinished business: Out of the frying pan and into the 1990s. *Journal of Social and Personal Relationships, 7*, 5–28. doi:10.1177/0265407590071001

Duck, S. (1993). *Individuals in relationships.* Newbury Park, Calif: Sage Publications.

Duck, S., & Lea, M. (1983). Breakdown of relationships as a threat to personal identity. In G. Breakwell (Ed.), *Threatened identities.* London: Wiley.

Dunleavy, K. N., & Booth-Butterfield, M. (2009). Idiomatic communication in the stages of coming together and falling apart. *Communication Quarterly, 57*, 426–432. doi:10.1080/01463370903320906

Farris, C., Treat, T. A., Viken, R. J., & McFall, R. M. (2008). Sexual coercion and the misperception of sexual intent. *Clinical Psychology Review, 28*, 48–66. doi:10.1016/j.cpr.2007.03.002

Fisher, H. (1994). *The natural history of monogamy, adultery and divorce.* New York, NY: Fawcett.

Harvey, J. H., Flannery, R., & Morgan, M. (1986). Vivid memories of vivid loves gone by. *Journal of Social and Personal Relationships, 3*, 359–373. doi:10.1177/0265407586033007

Hays, R. B. (1984). The development and maintenance of friendship. *Journal of Social and Personal Relationships, 1*, 75–98. doi:10.1177/0265407584011005

Honeycutt, J. M. (1993). Memory structures for the rise and fall of personal relationships. In D. Duck (Ed.), *Individuals in relationships* (pp. 60–86). Newbury Park, CA: Sage.

Honeycutt, J. M., Cantrill, J. G., & Greene, R. W. (1989). Memory structures for relational escalation: A cognitive test of the sequencing of relational actions and stages. *Human Communication Research, 16*, 62–90. doi:10.1111/j.1468-2958.1989.tb00205.x

Honeycutt, J. M., Sawyer, C. R., & Keaton, S. A. (2014). Introduction. In J. M. Honeycutt, C. R. Sawyer, & S. A. Keaton (Eds.), *The influence of communication on physiology and health* (pp. 1–10). New York, NY: Peter Lang.

Jankowiak, W. (1995). Introduction. In W. Jankowisak (Ed.), *Romantic passion: A universal experience?* New York, NY: Columbia University Press.

Kellermann, K., Broetzmann, S., Lim, T. S., & Kitao, K. (1989). The conversation MOP: Scenes in the stream of discourse. *Discourse Processes, 12*, 27–61. doi:10.1080/01638538909544718

Kelley, H. H., Berscheid, E., Christensen, A., Harvey, J. H., Huston, T. L., Levinger, G., ... Peterson, D. R. (1983). Analyzing close relationships. In H. H. Kelley, E. Berscheid, A. Christensen, J. H. Harvey, T. L. Huston, G. Levinger, E. McClintock, L. A. Peplau, & D. R. Peterson (Eds.), *Close relationships* (pp. 20–67). New York, NY: Freeman.

King, C. E., & Christensen, A. (1983). The relationship events scale: A Guttman scaling of progress in courtship. *Journal of Marriage and the Family, 45*, 671–678. doi:10.2307/351672

Knapp, M. L., Vangelisti, A. L., & Caughlin, J. P. (2013). *Interpersonal communication and human relationships* (7th ed.). New York, NY: Pearson.

Lee, L. (1984). Sequences in separation: A framework for investigating endings of the personal (romantic) relationship. *Journal of Social and Personal Relationships, 1*, 49–73. doi:10.1177/0265407584011004

Leigh, G. K., Holman, T. B., & Burr, W. R. (1984). An empirical test of sequence in S. V. R. Murstein's theory of mate selection. *Family Relations, 33*, 225–231. doi:10.2307/583787

Levinger, G. (1974). A three-level approach to attraction: Toward an understanding of pair relatedness. In T. L. Huston (Ed.), *Foundations of interpersonal attraction* (pp. 100–120). New York, NY: Academic Press.

Levinger, G. (1980). Toward the analysis of close relationships. *Journal of Experimental Social Psychology, 16*, 510–544. doi:10.1016/0022-1031(80)90056-6

Levinger, G. (1983). Development and change. In H. H. Kelley, E. Berscheid, A. Christensen, J. H. Harvey, T. L. Huston, G. Levinger, E. McClintock, L. A. Peplau, & D. R. Peterson (Eds.), *Close relationships* (pp. 315–359). New York, NY: Freeman.

Lewis, R. A. (1973). A longitudinal test of a developmental framework for premarital dyadic formation. *Journal of Marriage and the Family, 35*, 16–25. doi:10.2307/351092

Lynn, D. B. (1969). *Parental and sex role identification: A theoretical formulation.* Berkeley, CA: McCitchan.

Murstein, B. I. (1970). Stimulus-value-role: A theory of marital choice. *Journal of Marriage and the Family, 32*, 465–481. doi:10.2307/350113

Murstein, B. I. (1974). Clarification of obfuscation on conjugation: A reply to a criticism of the SVR theory of marital choice. *Journal of Marriage and the Family, 36*, 231–234. doi:10.2307/351148

Murstein, B. I. (1986). *Paths to marriage.* Beverly Hills, CA: Sage.

Murstein, B. I. (1987). A clarification and extension of the SVR theory of dyadic pairing. *Journal of Marriage and the Family, 49*, 929–933. doi:10.2307/351985

Nisbett, R. E., & Ross, L. (1980). *Human inference: Strategies and shortcoming of human judgment.* Englewood Cliffs, NJ: Prentice-Hall.

Olson, D. H., McCubbin, H. I., Barnes, H. L., Larsen, A. S., Muxen, M. J., & Wilson, M. A. (1983). *Families: What makes them work.* Beverly Hills, CA: Sage.

Pearson, J. C., Turner, L. H., & Todd-Manchillas, W. (1991). *Gender and communication* (2nd ed.). New York, NY: Wadsworth.

Planalp, S., & Honeycutt, J. M. (1985). Events that increase uncertainty in personal relationships. *Human Communication Research, 11*, 593–604. doi:10.1111/j.1468-2958.1985.tb00062.x

Rubin, Z., & Levinger, G. (1974). Theory and data badly mated: A critique of Murstein's SVR and Lewis's PDF models of mate selection. *Journal of Marriage and the Family, 36*, 226–231. doi:10.2307/351147

Rubin, Z., Peplau, L. A., & Hill, C. T. (1981). Loving and leaving: Sex differences in romantic attachments. *Sex Roles, 7*, 821–835. doi:10.1007/BF00287767

Sabatelli, R. M. (1988). Exploring relationship satisfaction: A social exchange perspective on the interdependence between theory, research, and practice. *Family Relations, 37*, 217–222. doi:10.2307/584323

Schutz, W. C. (1958). *FIRO: A three-dimension theory of interpersonal behavior.* New York, NY: Holt, Rinehart & Winston.

Stephen, T. (1987). Taking communication seriously: A reply to Murstein. *Journal of Marriage and the Family, 49*, 937–938.

Stephen, T. (1994). Communication in the shifting context of intimacy: Marriage, meaning, and modernity. *Communication Theory, 4*, 191–218. doi:10.1111/j.1468-2885.1994.tb00090.x

Surra, C. A. (1990). Research and theory on mate selection and premarital relationships in the 1980's. *Journal of Marriage and the Family, 52*, 844–865. doi:10.2307/353306

Taylor, D. A., & Altman, I. (1987). Communication in interpersonal relationships: Social penetration processes. In M. E. Roloff & G. R. Miller (Eds.), *Interpersonal processes: New directions in communication research* (pp. 257–277). Newbury Park, CA: Sage.

Tennov, D. (1980). *Love and limerence.* New York, NY: Stein and Day.

VanLear, C. A. (1987). The formation of social relationships: A longitudinal study of social penetration. *Human Communication Research, 13*, 299–322. doi:10.1111/j.1468-2958.1987.tb00107.x

Watzlawick, P., Beavin, J., & Jackson, D. D. (1967). *Pragmatics of human communication: A study of interactional patterns, pathologies and paradoxes.* New York, NY: Norton.

Wood, J. T. (2008). *Gendered lives* (8th ed.). Stamford, CT: Cengage Learning.

Younger, J., Aron, A., Parke, S., Chatterjee, N., & Mackey, S. (2010). Viewing pictures of a romantic partner reduces experimental pain: Involvement of neural reward systems. *PLoS ONE 5*(10), e13309. doi:10.1371/journal.pone.0013309

PART THREE

Relational Escalation and Deescalation

Chapter 7   Scripts for Romantic Development and Decline
Chapter 8   Semantics of Break-ups

What happens when individuals become attached? Are there actually "soul mates"? Why do we attract particular people and not others? Is there one special person for everyone? What is the trajectory of relationship development? These questions are answered in Chapter 6. We believe each of our relationships is unique; however, research has suggested otherwise.

Which communication behaviors are essential for a relationship to develop and decline? Which are typical but not necessary? Chapter 8 presents semantic codes designed to give accounts to other's relationship problems.

CHAPTER SEVEN

Scripts for Romantic Development and Decline

Studies of scripts for romances have unearthed an interesting array of behaviors that characterize their development. This chapter reports on the results of a series of studies that reveal the variety in the amount of repetitiveness found in generating lists of expectations for relational escalation and decline. Redundancy may be associated with having simple expectations for evolving relationships. Individuals cite recurring behavior such as sharing time together and arguing while ignoring other behaviors that may happen infrequently or only once, such as meeting parents for the first time.

Secondly, the results of a study concerning the content of escalating and deescalating scripts as a function of the number of personal relationships an individual reports having had and his or her general beliefs that relationships follow a set pattern are reported. Following this discussion, there is an examination of differences in the typicality and necessity of expected behaviors. Some behaviors may be more or less typical and necessary in order for a relationship to develop. For example, engaging in sexual intercourse before marriage may be typical but not necessary for intimacy to develop. Typicality and necessity ratings of relational behaviors are also examined for their ability to predict individual beliefs that relationships follow a set pattern.

Redundancy and the Complexity of Romantic Scripts

Early studies of script generation made the assumption, in terms of information theory, that the stating of actions is relevant and nonredundant. For example, participants were told to write a list of expected actions for a given situation with each line representing one action. There were individual differences in the number of generated actions, with some subjects writing more actions. The differences were interpreted as the degree of experience in the contextual area. However, counting the number of action lines may not be a good representation of the complexity of the memory-structure actions. Individuals may repeat actions in a number of lines and this repetition of action may reflect the recycling of actions throughout a relationship and the enduring pervasiveness of the actions. For example, arguing may occur throughout the history of a relationship. Yet subsequent arguments will be influenced by the memory of previous arguments; therefore, the same exact event does not occur because of this memory.

Because of memory, whenever individuals go around in a circle of events (e.g., recurrent conversations about the same topic) and seem to wind up where they started, the fact they recognize that they have returned indicates that they have not really returned to the same place. This type of recollection is reflected in statements like, "We've discussed this many times before."

People are not very mindful or bright about what is going on in their relationships because they often do not pause to reflect on their relationships (Honeycutt, 2010). Burnett (1990) asked subjects to think about relationships they recently had thought a lot about. Negative life events such as illness and periods of transition were events that stimulated relational thought. The accounts revealed that personal relationships are thought about frequently but superficially; they were in the form of summary statements and lacked detail. Burnett even wondered about the extent to which participants were biased by the study to the extent they felt they had to come up with something for the experimenter. Additional data revealed that subjects reported on the difficulty of thinking of a reply to a question about writing to a friend about "what your relationship with X is like"? Thus, recycling may reveal the inability to cite a variety of distinct actions and inattention to relational events.

Box 7.1 contains sample male and female scripts that highlight differences in redundancy. Note that these scripts are different in terms of their structure and content from the sample marriage schema in Chapter 5. Relational schemata do not reflect behaviors in a time-ordered sequence, as does the memory structure. At first glance, the man appears to mention 20 actions, whereas the woman refers to 14 actions. Research reveals that women mention more unique actions than do men in terms of their expectations for developing relationships (Honeycutt, Cantrill, & Greene, 1989). However, in the sample male memory structure, note that some of his actions are redundant, such as calling (action lines 3, 10, and 11). Action lines 4, 5, and 7 concern going out. There is a difference in specificity; simply going out (line 4) is more vague than going to a bar (line 5). The woman's memory structure reveals less redundancy (action lines 4 and 5).

Box 7.1. Sample Escalating Memory Structures Illustrating Redundant Actions

Man's Expectations
Participant: Escalating Expectations
18-year-old man, been in 3–5 relationships, talked about relationships with friends and parents

1. Party—meet at friends
2. Get their phone number
3. Call the next day C
4. Go out that night G
5. Go to a bar G
6. Don't talk about anything important.
7. Go to a park, etc. G
8. Mess around (a little)
9. Go home
10. Call the next day C
11. This goes on for a while C
12. Until one day, they find they're committed
13. Forget about their friends
14. See each other every day
15. Break-up and make-up patterns
16. Argue greatly but always seem to go back to each other
17. By now they have gotten into heavier things
18. Parents are annoyed
19. Want to finally break them up
20. Eventually they do and it is over

Woman's Expectations
Participant: 18-year-old woman, been in 1–2 relationships, talked about relationships with friends

1. Meet each other—at a party, in class, or some sort of social gathering
2. Become infatuated or fascinated with each other
3. Begin to talk regularly/semi-regularly
4. Go to a party or social event together G

5. Go out in one on one situations G
6. Start to become emotionally involved with other's feelings and thoughts
7. Some form of intimate contact
8. Decide to have a relationship
9. Relationship intensifies/enjoy each other's company
10. Reach a plateau—sort of a boring time in relationship
11. Stumble on a problem in relationship/occasionally breakup but not permanently
12. Back on track
13. Know each other very well
14. Eventually breakup or marriage depending *on which way the* relationship goes

Note: Redundant actions are indicated by the underlined abbreviations: C, calling, G, going out.

The man's expectations in Box 7.1 refer to cyclical patterns of arguing and getting back together. On the other hand, both memory structures refer to initial meeting, sharing time together, the exclusivity of the developing relationship, overcoming crisis (e.g., arguments, parental interference, and breaking up), and ending the relationship or getting married. These actions reflect common events that a number of individuals mention in their memory structures. These samples highlight the dialectics of escalation in terms of conflict about relational problems. Although there is a progression toward intimacy, there is also the dialectic of the relationship possibly ending (see action lines 20 and 14 in the two memory structures). Further, although arguing is a commonly mentioned behavior for de-escalating memory structures, it is part of relational development.

The script generation instructions assume Grice's (1975) classic maxims of relevance and non-redundancy, in which individuals write or speak in order to be informative without being too redundant. One problem with these assumptions discussed by Rosch, Mervis, Gray, Johnson, and Graem (1976) is that individuals use action-summary terms (e.g., "He kissed her"—to indicate physical affection) rather than discrete, microscopic terms that segment actions (e.g., "He approached her with his eyes fixated on her lips. He touched his lips to her lips. He opened his mouth and extended his tongue to her tongue. The interface between lips and tongue continued for a few seconds."). The action-summary terms are more likely to be redundant, whereas discrete terms are more specific and less likely to repeat. As noted previously, this is apparent in actions 4 and 5 of the man's expectations in Box 7.1 in which action 4, going out is more abstract than action 5, going to a bar.

The memory-structure generation procedure also assumes that Grice's (1975) maxim of non-redundancy leads individuals to describe activities at approximately the same level and that the nature of the generating task motivates them to revealing "normally boring details within a script" (Bower, Black, & Turner, 1979, p. 183). The calculation of a redundancy coefficient reveals that this assumption is not totally supported (Honeycutt et al., 1989). The coefficient is calculated in such a way that higher values reflect less redundancy. It is the ratio of the number of unique actions divided by the total number of action lines a person records in the generation task. The mean redundancy for escalating scripts is .70, which indicates a slight degree of repetitiveness (Honeycutt et al., 1989). The correlation coefficient may range from −1 to 1 and represents the degree of association between two variables; in this case redundancy and the number of total actions. A score of 1.0 would be perfect nonredundancy, in which the number of nonrepeated actions equals the total number of listed actions. As the number of action lines increases, so does the probability of redundancy. The correlation (r) or association between the length of an escalating memory structure and redundancy is significant ($r = -.54, p < .001$; Honeycutt et al., 1989).

A problem with the redundancy measure is that number of actions that a person lists is not revealed in the ratio. For example, a person listing only one statement would have no redundancy (1.00), whereas a person listing four unique and five total statements would have more redundancy (4/5 = .80). People mention an average of 11.53 actions (range: 3–20 actions, standard deviation = 3.93). The measure is valid because a person mentioning one action is not redundant, but is simplistic. Redundancy is not meant to reflect the length of a person's script. However, a person listing more actions with low redundancy has a more complex set of expectations than listing one action. Following are the results of a content analysis of escalating and deescalating romantic scripts.

Content of Romantic Scripts

A classic study on script development involves having people generate a list of up to 20 actions that were typical in developing an intimate relationship and put them in the order in which they occur (Honeycutt et al., 1989). We have used this procedure to measure scripts for Friends with Benefits (FWBs) and casual friendships (Honeycutt, Shimek, & White, 2015). Previous studies used a form with 20 blank lines in order not to make the task cumbersome (Bower et al., 1979; Pryor & Merluzzi, 1985). In addition, in which no limit was specified revealed that no individuals generated more than 20 actions. The average number of listed actions was 12 and the range was from 3 to 20 actions. However, only five individuals used all 20 lines.

Box 7.2 presents the list of actions and underlying phases that characterize a developing romance while Box 7.3 presents relational decline actions. The students were asked to begin the list with two individuals meeting for the first time and end the list with the individuals expressing a long-term, serious commitment to each other. They were instructed to report behaviors (e.g., saying hello) and avoid inferences (e.g., reporting feelings or emotions). The reason for distinguishing between behavioral activities and inferences is that inferences often are an outcome of a series of underlying behaviors. For example, a person listing as an action "Feeling inseparable, more intimate or boredom" is reporting on feelings that may be associated with several underlying behaviors such as self-disclosure, displays of physical affection, and sharing activities together.

Box 7.2. Behavioral Expectations for Escalating Scripts

	Behavioral Expectancy	Subjects Mentioning	Action Stage
1.	Meet for the first time (party, class)*	97%	
2.	Ask for other's phone number and call later*	57%	
3.	*Small talk (discuss weather, school, events)**	*69%*	*Initiating*
4.	Formal Date (dinner, movie, concert, etc.)*	92%	
5.	Show physical affection (kiss, touch, hug, etc.)*	43%	
6.	*Engage in joint activities*	*64%*	*Experimenting*
7.	*Self-disclosure of intimate information*	*52%*	*Intensifying*
8.	Sexual intercourse*	26%	
9.	Meet parents or in-laws*	26%	
10.	Bonding ritual (give flowers, gifts, mementos)*	30%	
11.	Other-oriented statements (communicate interest in each other's orientations, goals)*		
12.	Verbal commitment (both talk about a long-term relationship)	49%	
13.	*Marriage**	*28%*	*Bonding*
14.	Cohabitation	7%	
15.	Overcome crisis (jealousy, uncertainty, arguing)	13%	
16.	Talk about future plans	16%	
17.	Verbal expression of love	18%	
18.	Miscellaneous behaviors	21%	

Note: Asterisk (*) indicates a prototypical memory-structure actions in which 25% or more of participants mentioned the expectation.

Box 7.3. De-escalating Script Expectations

Behavioral Expectation	Percentage of Subjects Mentioning Action
Decreasing Intimacy	
1. Stop expressing intimate feelings* (statements of love, concern, care)	26%
2. Decrease physical intimacy and withhold affection (such as kisses, hugs, touches, petting, etc.)	14%
Aversive Communication	
3. Argue about little things, pet peeves, recurring irritants*	32%
4. Disagree about attitudes, opinions, values, roles, things to do*	20%
5. Verbal fighting and antagonizing the other (e.g., shouting, yelling, profanity, whining)	36%
6. Criticize partner through noting shortcomings in partner, personal attacks	17%
7. Make sarcastic/contemptuous remarks to partner	13%
Decreasing Contact	
8. Call or phone less	12%
9. Spend less time together; see each other less often*	39%
10. Avoid and ignore other in public settings*	40%
11. Give other excuses for not being able to go out or date	11%
Reevaluating Relationship	
12. Trial rejuvenation; Try to smooth things over through discussion; a period of time for readjustment*	32%
13. Talk about etiology and why disagreements occur; discuss source of problems/conflicts	15%
14. Talk about breaking up with partner*	20%
15. Talk with others or friends about relational problems, issues, or conflicts	10%
Comparing Alternatives	
16. Assess and compare alternatives; think of costs and benefits of other arrangements; become interested in others*	23%
17. Spend more time with same-gender friends	13%

Behavioral Expectation	Percentage of Subjects Mentioning Action
18. Start seeing others of the opposite-gender*	23%
19. Develop more outside interests, hobbies, activities unrelated to relationship	13%
Terminating Relationship	
20. Final breakup and termination of the relationship*	58%
21. Miscellaneous behaviors	31%

Note: An asterisk (*) indicates prototypical script actions in which 20% or more of subjects mentioned the behavior.

As revealed in Box 7.2, the most frequently listed escalating activities were meeting, calling (texting), small talk, showing physical affection, dating, engaging in informal activities, self-disclosure, meeting parents, giving gifts (bonding ritual), making a commitment, sexual intercourse, making other-oriented statements, and getting married. Each of these actions was mentioned by 25% or more of the participants.

Box 7.2 also reveals actions mentioned less often. Overcoming a relational crisis including feelings of jealousy, uncertainty, or arguing was listed by 13% of the sample. Talking about the future in terms of a couple or "we" orientation was mentioned by 16% of the participants. In this regard, Knapp, Vangelisti, and Caughlin (2014) discussed that individuals use the plural pronoun "we" in referring to future activities. The verbal expression of love was mentioned by 18% of the sample, whereas 7% reported living together (cohabitation) as an expectancy for relational development.

Bower et al. (1979) used a decision rule of 25% of subjects mentioning an action for its inclusion into a prototypical script. This rule was based on examining the distribution of the frequency of responses and determining where a distinct gap existed. Using the 25% decision rule, a distinct gap was evident in this study between two behaviors mentioned by 26% of the subjects and the next most frequently mentioned behavior at 18%. On this basis, 13 actions constitute the prototypical memory structure.

Some of the escalating memory-structure actions have been reported as turning points in developing romantic relationships. Baxter and Bullis (1986) define a *turning point* in a relationship as any event that is associated with change in the relationship. They surveyed romantic college couples and asked them to identify all of the turning points in their relationships since their first meeting.

Fourteen turning points were identified, several of which appear in the study presented in Box 7.2. "Getting to know the other" occurs in many of the memory-structure activities, such as initial meeting, small talk, dating, sharing time together, self-disclosure, and overcoming crisis. "Quality time," which included meeting the family and special occasions is another of the memory-structure actions. "Passion," which referred to events involving physical or emotional affection between the partners, and intercourse, kissing, and saying "I love you" reflect the memory-structure actions of physical affection and verbal expression of love. "Exclusivity," which consisted of a joint decision to be romantically involved with only one another as well as breaking any romantic liaisons with others except one's partner is reflected in the "verbal commitment" memory-structure expectancy. "Serious commitment," which reflected living together or getting engaged, appears as cohabitation, another of the escalating memory-structure actions. "Sacrifice," which involved offering assistance to one's partner when he or she is experiencing personal problems as well as giving gifts or favors mirrors the bonding-ritual expectation in which relational partners exchange mementos and gifts.

It is interesting that direct talk about the relationship was involved in the turning points of exclusivity, passion, and serious commitment. Thus, disclosure about the status of the relationship was important in the turning points. This is reflected in the escalating memory-structure expectations in the separate actions of self-disclosure and verbal commitment. A number of the other memory-structure actions also reflect direct talk about relationship status, such as the use of partner-oriented statements reflecting interest in the other person's goals and talking about future plans as a couple. Obviously, the statement "I love you" reflects the memory structure expectation of verbal expressions of love.

Deescalating Script

Some of the de-escalating actions in Box 7.3 are similar to classic strategies discussed by Baxter (1985) for ending a relationship. Baxter distinguished between direct and indirect strategies. Direct strategies include fait accompli-actions indicating that the relationship is over with no opportunity for discussion. Action 14 in Box 7.3 is most similar to this strategy. Baxter discussed a state-of-the-relationship talk strategy in which there is an explicit statement of dissatisfaction and a desire to exit the relationship. Action 13 in Box 7.3 is close to this strategy; partners talk about why disagreements occur between them as well as the sources of relational conflict. Another strategy discussed by Baxter is attributional conflict. This strategy is characterized by anger, yelling, or screaming while attributing blame. This strategy appears in the aversive communication cluster and in particular, action 5 where there is shouting, yelling, and whining. Another direct strategy is what Baxter referred to as negotiated farewell, in which there is explicit, non-hostile communication that formally ends the relationship. This appears in action 20, the final breakup and ending of the relationship.

Indirect strategies may be used with the intent of accomplishing the dissolution without an explicit statement of the end of the relationship (Baxter, 1985). Withdrawal is an indirect strategy that is characterized by a reduction of intimacy and contact. Actions 1 and 2 of the decrease intimacy cluster represent this strategy. Another indirect strategy is what Baxter referred to as pseudo de-escalation, in which there is a false declaration to the partner that one desires a transformed relationship of reduced closeness. The de-escalating script most similar to this strategy is action 12, involving a period of attempted rejuvenation to discuss a transformed relationship. Cost escalation is another indirect strategy, which involves behavior toward the partner that increases relational costs. Action 7 is most similar to this strategy, in which the individual expects sarcastic language to accompany or even accelerate the decline of relationships. Gottman and Silver (2015) also gave examples of unhappily married couples using deliberate sarcasm in order to make their partners feel uncomfortable.

The content of the de-escalating script contains actions that are found in the exit-voice-loyalty-neglect model of relational dissatisfaction. Rusbult (1987) discussed four responses to dissatisfaction in relationships: exit (ending or threatening to end the relationship; actions 14 and 20), voice (actively and constructively expressing one's dissatisfaction with the intent of improving conditions; actions 3, 4, 12, and 13), loyalty (passively but optimistically waiting for conditions to improve), and neglect (passively allowing one's relationship to decay; 1, 2, and 8-11).

These categories overlap. Most relational problems extend over time rather than being isolated events and may be associated with several reactions. Rusbult (1987) claimed that exit and neglect are destructive behaviors, whereas voice and loyalty are constructive. Exit and voice are active responses, whereas neglect and loyalty are passive reactions. Rusbult indicated that exit and neglect are destructive of the current relationship, whereas voice and loyalty are constructive to its continuance or reconstitution. On the other hand, Goodwin (1991) found that the responses are not easily classified as active or passive and that the loyalty response contains positive and negative elements. Also, the de-escalating script in Box 7.3 reveals no evidence for loyalty; there were no expectations reflecting this type of response. The closest action to this was trial rejuvenation, but this expectation involved an active attempt to work things out in the relationship.

An example of negative loyalty is topic avoidance where individuals decide not to share information about specific topics (Afifi & Guerrero, 2000). Gottman (1994) discusses this in terms of withdrawing from conflictual discussions in order to control physiological arousal. Moreover, topic avoidance is associated with relational dissatisfaction (Caughlin & Vangelisti, 2006) and even irritable bowel syndrome. Bevan (2009) found that topic avoidance was associated with abdominal difficulty and number of doctor visits in the last month. Similarly, it has been found that when husbands and wives withdraw from conflictual discussions, there is less satisfaction with the marriage (Segrin, Hanzal, & Domschke, 2009). Moreover, if one partner perceives himself/herself as a conflict engager and is likely to argue or being a problem solver, he/she has an attributional bias in which he/she views his/her partner similarly. Self-esteem needs motivate people to make biased perceptions of themselves that enhance their relationships (Gagne' & Lydon, 2004). Segrin et al. (2009) concluded that the more positively people viewed a spouses' conflict styles (e.g., "he rarely explodes and gets out of control," "she rarely shuts down and refuses to talk,") the happier they were with the marriage (p. 223).

Inferences Associated with Relationship Decay

One of the interesting observations about deescalating scripts is that some people intersperse emotional inferences with deescalating actions in their cognitive scripts despite being told not to (Honeycutt, Cantrill, & Allen, 1992). Box 7.4 contains the inferences that were mentioned by at least 11% of the sample. There was little agreement on the inferences, with the exception of feeling bored with the relationship and feeling an increase in uncertainty. After these inferences, the next most-frequently mentioned inference, anger, only had a frequency of 17%. The finding that boredom was frequently mentioned was also observed in other research to be the most-identified contributing factor to the ending of relationships (e.g., Hill, Rubin, & Peplau, 1976). Uncertainty appears to be highly associated with relationship decay. Bachman and Guerrero (2006) surveyed unmarried individuals who had experienced a hurtful event precipitated by a romantic partner and found perceptions of the partner prior to the event had significant implications as to whether the couple remained together or parted ways. Couples who remained together after the hurtful event tended to view their partners as more rewarding than did individuals who broke up because of the hurtful event.

Box 7.4. Inferences Interspersed within the De-escalating Script Actions

Inference	Percentage of Subjects Mentioning Inference
1. Feel angry	17%
2. Feel annoyed, distressed	11%
3. Bitter	11%
4. Feel bored, inattentive, listless, restless	30%
5. Jealous	11%
6. Moody	12%
7. Feel hurt	10%
8. Feel insecure and loss of confidence	22%
9. Miscellaneous	15%

One speculation about the mentioning of inferences is that the subjects may be unable to articulate the source or cause of the emotional inference. The inference probably represents an outcome of an underlying action. It was found that individuals are more redundant in generating emotional inferences than actions (Honeycutt et al., 1992). In order to explain this phenomenon, consider Carlston's (1980) dual-memory model of impression formation, which assumes that individuals select distinctive behaviors for analysis as well as drawing on previously stored inferences. Inferences and interpretations may be made about the behaviors; however, there may be an inability to articulate some actions. Baxter (1986) provided an example of a man who cannot find words to express the absence of romance.

Typicality Versus Necessity in Predicting Beliefs About Relational Development

Prior research has examined the scripted behaviors in which other people rated how typical and necessary each behavior was in order for a relationship to grow and decline. For example, texting may be typical but not necessary when self-disclosing.

Gender and the typicality and necessity activity ratings can be used as predictors of relational development in regression analyses that correlate subjects' beliefs that relationships follow a set pattern, that there are expectations about what should occur in the development of an intimate relationship and that relationships can be thought as developing through a series of stages. In addition, data were gathered on the number of intimate relationships that individuals reported having had.

A sample of individuals was asked to report the exact number of close personal relationships the individuals had ever been involved in. Most individuals reported having been in two relationships. The number of relationships ranged from zero to nine, although few individuals reported having been in more than three relationships (Honeycutt, 1995).

Gender was initially entered in the regression models as a control variable to see whether men and women differed in mentioning any of the escalating activities that, in turn, might be associated with the number of reported relationships. There were no gender differences in predicting developmental beliefs. However, there were significant typicality and necessity predictors, as revealed in the following.

The numbers in parentheses are standardized beta coefficients ranging from −1 to 1. Scores close to 0 show no association, whereas scores around 1 show perfect predictability. Scores around −1 show a perfect negative correspondence between the action and the predicted belief. Hence, these coefficients reflect the magnitude of association among each of the escalating relationship activities and beliefs about relationships. The positive or negative sign preceding each activity reveals if the predicted relationship between the behavior and belief is positive or negative.

Typicality Ratings

- Relationships tend to follow a set pattern = Show physical affection (+.22) minus Self-disclosure (−.19)
- I have a lot of expectations of what should occur in the development of an intimate relationship = Other-oriented statements (+.27) + Show physical affection (+.19)
- I believe that relationships can be thought of as developing through a series of stages = Overcome crisis (+.26) + Dating (+.21)
- Number of relationships = Showing physical affection (+.22) − Getting married (−.18)

Necessity Ratings

- Relationships tend to follow a set pattern = No predictors
- I have a lot of expectations of what should occur in the development of an intimate relationship = Other-oriented statements (+.25)

- I believe that relationships can be thought of as developing through a series of stages = Other-oriented statements (.+27)
- Number of relationships = Talk about future plans as a couple (−.26) minus Meeting parents (−.25) + Self-disclosing intimate and personal information (+.19)

It is interesting that self-disclosure was negatively related to the belief that relationships follow a set pattern, while it was positively related to the number of relationships an individual reported being in. This is consistent with the earlier finding that self-disclosure is viewed as more necessary, yet less typical, in a developing relationships and that it emerges as a separate phase in the development of relationships (Honeycutt et al., 1989).

Other-oriented statements emerged as a predictor in three of the equations. Becoming relationally oriented and communicating this to one's partner is associated with having a lot of expectations about relational development. The emergence of a joint identity as a couple can be enhanced by communicating interest in one's partner's interests, opinions, activities, and goals. Further, other research on variables that predict marital happiness revealed that actively signaling attentiveness to what one's marriage partner is saying is related to effective communication, which in turn, is related to one's spouse's belief that one understands him or her (Honeycutt & Godwin, 1986). Consequently, communication effectiveness and perceived partner understanding predict the level of marital happiness.

It is interesting that the typicality of overcoming a relational crisis was related to the belief that relationships follow through a series of stages. From a dialectic perspective, overcoming a crisis in a relationship could reflect the disengaging of the relationship that has been redefined and the acquisition of memory structures and associated scenes and scripts for relational de-escalation. Support for this interpretation is found in a study by Planalp, Rutherford, and Honeycutt (1987), who reported that some relationships became closer after a period of time when uncertainty was temporarily increased by some behavior or event, ranging from negative events such as discovering one's partner's infidelity to positive events such as discovering that a friend believed the relationship was closer than one originally believed and the feeling was reciprocated. It is interesting that infidelity estimates are very low among dating and married couples.

Research in the expectancy violation tradition reveals that those who have script expectations those reflect an understanding of the risk of infidelity will be more prepared to handle the fallout it brings such that they are less surprised, dismayed, and upset with its occurrence (Watkins & Boon, 2016). A consequence of high expectations for infidelity is less commitment to the relationship. Research involving dating couples in which partners were asked about if their partners had or would cheat on them using an estimated percentage from 0 to 100% revealed that the vast majority of the sample (70%) estimated that their partner had been or ever would be unfaithful was 5% or less.

Predicting Beliefs About Relational Decay

Regression models were also tested for the impact of typicality and necessity ratings as predictors of relationship decay in terms of a belief that relationships follow a set pattern, having expectations of what should occur in the deterioration of an intimate relationship, and predicting the number of intimate relationships a person reported having had. Again, gender was entered in the regression models as a control variable.

Typicality Ratings

- Relationships tend to follow a set pattern = Sarcasm (0.28) + Arguing (0.27)
- I have a lot of expectations of what should occur in the deterioration of an intimate relationship = Arguing (0.23)
- Number of relationships = Discuss breaking up (minus 0.28) + Develop outside interests (0.24)

Necessity Ratings

- Relationships tend to follow a set pattern = Develop more outside interests (0.31)
- I have a lot of expectations of what should occur in the deterioration of an intimate relationship = Call less often (0.29) minus Attempt to rejuvenate relationship (0.25)
- Number of relationships = Develop outside interests (0.25)

The beta coefficients in the equations reveal beliefs that sarcasm and arguing over little things are relatively typical in the deterioration of a relationship and predict the belief that relationships following a set pattern. The typicality of arguing also was associated with having expectations about the deterioration of intimate relationships. Arguing about small things over a period of time has cumulative effects, in terms of creating a lot of expectations for the decline of relationships. Yet these expectations do not necessarily reflect a linear progression of stages. Recall from Chapter 6, the discussion of relational dialectics, that there may be rapidly alternating periods of autonomy versus bonding, disclosiveness versus privateness, and predictability versus spontaneity. In addition, the manner in which the conflict is important. There is an assumption in communication studies that men use more withdrawal in conflict with intimate partners while women use more demanding strategies including nagging (Denton & Burleson, 2007; Gayle, Preiss, & Allen, 2002).

Demand/withdraw patterns in serial arguing can negatively impact resolvability. Characteristics of demanding are nagging, criticisms, or complaints in an argument as outlined by Gottman and Silver (2015). There is a cyclical pattern of demanding resulting in a partner's withdrawal which causes the initiator to continue more nagging and complaining which can actually be used a poor strategy for compliance-gaining (Malis & Roloff, 2006). Interestingly, chronic stress from serial arguing is associated with reduced immune system functioning (Honeycutt, Keaton, Hatcher, & Hample, 2014).

The typicality findings are interesting because they are compatible with findings by Gottman and Silver (2015) that arguing in and of itself does not predict marital quality over time. Rather, the exchange of anger has only temporary effects and may not be harmful in the long run. Johnson and Roloff (2000) discovered if partners engage in confirming behaviors during their arguments and remain optimistic about the relationship there is a higher likelihood that the argument will be resolved and the disagreement is less likely to result in harm to the relationship. Thus, it is the style of arguing that is important, in terms of whether the arguing has negative affect. In terms of sarcasm, Gottman and Silver (2015) also reported that this may be associated with contempt for one's partner and associated with the long-term dissatisfaction, decline, and termination of marital relationships. Marital conflict is associated with depression in spouses and more heart-rate variability (Choi & Marks, 2008; Honeycutt, 2010).

The number of intimate relationships an individual reported being in was predicted by typically not discussing or talking about breaking up, as revealed in the negative beta coefficient. On the other hand, developing outside interests predicted the number of relationships in both typicality and necessity beliefs. This is consistent with social-exchange theory in which individuals may evaluate comparison alternatives with a current relationship and decide if the perceived outcomes from other relationships or activities are more than the outcomes that are currently received (Stafford, 2015). Developing outside interests is a way to do activities exclusive of the relationship that may be a desirable comparison alternative.

Underlying Dimensions of Relational Development and Decline

The scripted behaviors can be used to identify underlying clusters of actions. According to systems theory, no behavior occurs in a vacuum independent of other behaviors. Behaviors may occur simultaneously or in quick succession. Consequently, some actions are interchanged easier than others. For example, the display of physically affectionate behaviors is more related to consummation than is meeting one another's. The underlying dimensions represent conceptual clusters of co-occurring behaviors.

The idea that some actions are more easily exchanged than others is a foundation of Foa and Foa's (2012) interpersonal resource theory, in which actions such as showing love are more easily exchanged and sanctioned than the exchange of disparate actions such as exchanging love for money. They argue that the exchange of particularistic resources (e.g., resources that can only be obtained from particular individuals such as love, services, and status) and the exchange of universalistic resources for another (e.g., resources that can be obtained from a variety of sources such as money, information, and goods) are more likely than exchange of particularistic and universalistic resources. For example, information is universalistic because it is available from a number of sources and tends to be exchanged for other information. Information exchanged for money is called tuition. More intimate relationships involve exchanges of love, status, information, and services rather than goods and money (Foa & Foa, 2012). It is harder to exchange particularistic resources for universalistic resources unless there is a rule or contract for this exchange between individuals (e.g., intercourse for money is prostitution).

One of the outcomes associated with having cognitive scripts for a romance is the ability to recognize the actions and arrange them in a sequential order. The sequential ordering of expected actions may reflect stages from a number of developmental models discussed in Chapter 5. Although individuals can generate memory structures for romance, the memory-generation procedure is limited in telling researchers if individuals agree on the order or sequencing of the activities. For example, some individuals may expect meeting with the other person's parents to occur before a long-term commitment has been made, whereas others may expect a commitment to occur before meeting the other person's parents. Some individuals may believe that self-disclosure comes early, whereas others believe it comes later in the development of a relationship.

Card-Sorting Experiment for Escalating and Deescalating Actions

Two studies were conducted for escalating and deescalating actions, respectively. Participants were given a deck of index cards in which each of the prototypical actions in Boxes 7.2 and 7.3 were listed on a separate card. The participants were given the following instructions in the study for escalation:

> We may have expectations for how a romantic relationship should develop. For example, you may believe that there is a typical sequence of behaviors that reflects an escalating relationship. Enclosed in your envelope is a set of 13 index cards that list various relational behaviors. The cards are in a random order. We want you to sort the cards in what you believe is a logical order and then to record how long it took you to sort the deck. (Honeycutt et al., 1989, p. 75)

For de-escalation, the word "decline" was substituted for "develop" and "de-escalating" for "escalating."

Study 1 was the sorting of escalating actions that involved a sample of 71 men and 78 women students in basic communication courses at Louisiana State University They ranged in age from 17 to 32 with an average age of 20.42. The students were given response sheets on which to record the rank ordering of the 13 prototypical behaviors. They were instructed to open the envelopes at a specified time, sort the cards, record how long it took to complete the task (in seconds), and write their orderings on the response sheet. On the response sheet, subjects indicated how many intimate relationships they had been involved in.

The time it takes to sort the escalating actions is a measure of a person's ability to access a relational memory structure and use it to recognize actions. Sorting time is correlated with previous relationship history, such that those who had been in more relationships seemed to take less time sorting the cards. Thus, they could more easily relate to the prototypical actions they see on the cards and arrange them in an intuitive order.

The following numbers are standard deviations that reveal the extent of disagreement or dispersion on the placement of a given action. They are critical in beginning to demonstrate the existence of underlying stages for developing relationships that exist in the minds of individuals. The higher the standard deviation, the more individuals disagree on the order for a given action. The prototypical ordering of the 13 actions is: meeting (.54), small talk (.52), calling/texting (1.47), dating (1.75), showing physical affection (2.00), sharing time together (2.04), self-disclosure (2.18), sexual intercourse (2.17), meeting parents (2.32), sharing gifts or bonding ritual (1.96), making other-oriented statements (1.88), stating a commitment (2.40), and marriage (2.44).

Students agreed least on the ordering of verbal commitment and marriage, whereas there was wide agreement on the initial ordering of meeting, small talk, and calling the other person on the telephone. The standard deviations also reflect the degree of interchange among actions. For example, the orders of such actions as small talk and making a verbal commitment are less easily interchanged, shown by their lower standard deviations compared to sharing time together, disclosure, intercourse, and meeting parents, which have higher standard deviations.

Cutoff points between clusters of actions were determined by computing adjacent mean difference scores and noting instances of higher differences between adjacent actions. Activities considered to constitute a cluster have lower within mean difference scores compared to the differences between adjacent actions located at the endpoints of respective clusters (Honeycutt et al., 1989). An example is the rank difference (d) between showing physical affection and calling ((d) = 1.82). This difference is higher than the difference between small talk and calling (d = 1.03).

This analysis reveals five underlying phases. Phase one consists of meeting, calling, and small talk. The activities are grouped more closely together and form a cluster that reflects initiation or coming together (Honeycutt et al., 1989). Small talk is characteristic of what Knapp and his associates (2014) called the experimentation stage. During this stage, potential relational partners experiment using different topics in order to determine if more intimate conversation can develop in particular topical areas. The second phase consists of dating, showing physical affection, and sharing time together. These behaviors reflect intensifying the relationship. The third phase consists of disclosure. Disclosure also emerges as a separate stage in the story-reading procedure for identifying stages discussed later (Honeycutt et al., 1989). The fourth phase consists of intercourse, meeting parents or in-laws, and exchanging gifts or mementos. The fifth phase consists of other-oriented statements, verbal commitment, and getting married. These phases are similar to Knapp et al. (2014) social-penetration growth stages of initiation (meeting), experimentation (dating, showing affection), intensifying (disclosure), integrating (meeting in-laws), and bonding (marriage).

Deescalating Clusters

The actions in Box 7.3 that were mentioned by at least 20% of the subjects in the schema-generation study were used as the prototypical behaviors. A sample of 48 men and 54 women were tested, recruited from introductory speech communication classes. The students ranged in age from 18 to 41, an average age of 20.45.

The data revealed a slight positive correlation between processing time and the number of relationships previously redefined or ended by the subject, while also taking into account the number of previous relationships ended by both partners or the other partner ($r = 0.16$, $p < .042$). Even though the magnitude of the correlation is small, this finding is interesting in that an individual who has a number of previous relationships to reflect on may be slowed in processing the actions because each relationship may have gone through the de-escalation process differently (Honeycutt et al., 1992). An anecdotal example of this is from a woman who sorted the de-escalating script expectations in 30 seconds. After the experiment, she told the research assistant that the timing of the experiment was ironic because that afternoon she had ended her relationship with a boyfriend after a long struggle.

When reflecting on previous endings of relationships, the individual may be delayed in sorting the actions as he or she considers the alternative de-escalating paths. Consider an individual who has the following thoughts about two relationships, referred to as Y and Z (the other capital letters refer to various behavior): "In relationship Y, I or my partner used behaviors A, B, C, and so on; but in relationship Z, I or my partner used behaviors J, K, L; and so on. Therefore, I have to be careful to sort the typical sequence." To the extent that the de-escalating script generation task revealed a positive association between relational experience and the absolute number of distinct actions and inferences subjects listed, the relative complexity of an individual's experience-based thought (as opposed to that drawn from movies or novels) may have had a debilitating effect on processing time. Indeed, no significant associations were found between processing time and number of previous relationships ended by the other partner or both partners.

Following the procedures of Honeycutt et al. (1989), four clusters were identified the prototypical de-escalating script. The clusters were identified by computing adjacent mean differences, such that behaviors considered to signify a cluster had lower within-mean differences than the behaviors located at the endpoints of tentatively identified clusters.

The prototypical de-escalating order of events (standard deviations are parentheses) includes stopping the expression of intimate feelings (2.38); disagreeing about attitudes, opinions, or values (1.90); and arguing about little things (2.26). These actions constitute the first cluster of interchangeable actions. Verbal fighting (2.32) and spending less time together (2.45) make up the second cluster of behaviors. The third cluster consists of avoiding each other (2.48), attempts to rejuvenate the relationship (2.13), and talk about breaking the relationship off (2.99). The fourth cluster is distinguished by the partners' actively comparing alternatives to the current relationship. This cluster contains becoming interested in others (2.32), actually seeing others (2.33), and the final breakup (2.21).

An intriguing observation is that compared to the prototypical escalating script actions, there is more agreement on the ordering of escalating actions. In contrast, there is a constant level of dispersion in ordering the de-escalating activities so that the standard deviations are relatively homogenous for the de-escalating actions. "Once a certain action level is reached, there is a spreading activation in which behaviors may co-occur" (Honeycutt et al., 1989, p. 77).

Story-Segmentation Analysis

Further evidence of underlying stages existing in people's relational cognitions was revealed using a story-reading procedure (Honeycutt et al., 1989). Scripts should contain general lines of action that reflect abstract stages of a relationship. Here, the superordinate action represents a breakpoint in an escalating romance. The typical ways to measure this is to have individuals read a story containing actions and segment the story into naturally occurring scenes (e.g., Bower et al., 1979; Pryor & Merluzzi, 1985).

Two stories were written containing 13 sentences each, with each sentence representing a prototypical memory-structure action (Honeycutt et al., 1989). These actions were the actions in Box 8.2 that were mentioned by at least 25% of the subjects. Two stories were used to examine generalizability of results from story to story. A sample of 89 women and 88 men students at Louisiana State University were surveyed. The ages ranged between 18 and 30, an average age of 20.18. Eighty-five students read one romantic story and 92 read a second story. The ratio of women and men readers was balanced for both stories. Readers were given the following instructions:

> Below is a brief story about John (or Linda) and Veronica (or Tom) who are involved in a developing and escalating romance that ends in marriage. Some people feel that romantic stories like these may be divided into several natural parts or stages. We would like you to carefully read the story and decide whether this story may be divided into different parts. If you think that these natural stages exist please identify them by placing a slash mark (/) at the end of each sentence that you think ends a part. These slashes are to indicate the boundaries between parts. (Honeycutt et al., 1989, p. 84)

Box 7.5 reveals the percentage of subjects marking a boundary after each action in the two stories for the escalating script, while Box 7.6 reveals the deescalating stages that are discussed further below. A statistical analysis of the distribution of the slash-mark locations in each story revealed that there were significant boundary points and therefore relationship stages could be identified. Boundary marks were exchanged between sentences two and three in the two stories. More individuals indicated a boundary after the sentence about discussing a biology course (small talk) in the story about Linda and Tom, whereas readers of the John and Veronica story placed a boundary after the sentence about calling for a date. In addition, more readers of the Linda and Tom story indicated a boundary after the sentence about continual dating.

Box 7.5. Phases within the Prototypical Escalating Scripts

John and Veronica:

John and Veronica met for the first time at a party. (8.2%) They engaged in small talk such as commenting on how nice the party was, who they knew at the party as well as learning a little about where each one was from. (24.7%) John asked Veronica for her phone number and if he could call her later to see about going on a date. (81.2%) The first date went well and so they continued dating. (20%) They held hands, kissed, and hugged each other. (20%) They also did informal activities together such as watching television, studying together, playing tennis, and going to lunch. (69.4%) John and Veronica self-disclosed to each other and revealed personal information such as likes and dislikes, successes and failures, values, and the like. (58.8%) They had sexual intercourse. (64.7%) Veronica took John on a weekend trip to her hometown to meet her parents. (28.2%) They gave each other candy, "love cards," and jewelry. (28.2%) They became more interested in each other's goals and lives since they felt like they needed each other and had an exclusive relationship. (49.4%) They made a verbal commitment so they could make the relationship long-term and stable. (57.6%) They got married. (100%)

Linda and Tom:

Linda and Tom met in a biology lab during the fall semester. (19.6%) They talked about the course, their majors and what they wanted to do after graduation. (66.3%) Tom asked Linda if he could call her and see about going on a date to one of the home football games. (38.0%) They enjoyed the game and continued going to games as well as having other dates. (43.5%) They held hands and kissed each other. (21.7%) They did informal activities together such as studying, biking, and jogging. (51.1%) They disclosed personal information about such things as family history, failures, and fantasies. (69.6%) They slept together. (47.8%) Tom invited Linda to visit his hometown and meet his parents. (27.2%) They exchanged little gifts and favors such as jewelry and candy. (20.7%) They talked about the other's needs and how to help each other whenever they could. (48.9%) They told each other they were exclusively committed to each other. (63.0%) They got married. (100%)

Source: Honeycutt et al. (1989).
Note: Numbers in parentheses indicate the percentage of subjects marking boundaries.

Box 7.6. Scenes within the Prototypical De-escalating Scripts

John and Veronica

John and Veronica stopped telling each other intimate feelings and thoughts. (41.7%) They disagreed about the other's attitudes and opinions as well as things to do together. (38.3%) Veronica and John argued about little things. (11.6%) They fought and antagonized each other through shouting, yelling, and whining. (68.3%) They spent less time together. (20.0%) They avoided and ignored each other when encountering the other on the university campus or in public settings. (91.7%) John and Veronica tried to rejuvenate the relationship by talking and attempting to smooth things over. (28.3%) They talked about breaking up or ending the relationship. (68.3%) They became interested in other opposite-gender individuals. (20.0%) Veronica and John started going out with other individuals. (41.6%) They ended their relationship. (100%)

Linda and Tom

Linda and Tom stopped telling each other their private feelings and thoughts. (52.9%) They disagreed over opinions and what to do together. (8.8%) They argued over small things. (17.6%) They shouted, yelled, and whined as well as antagonized each other. (70.5%) Tom and Linda saw each other less. (18.1%) They ignored each other when coming across one another in public. (91.1%) Linda and Tom attempted to work things out through rejuvenating the relationship. (58.8%) They talked about ending their relationship. (47.0%) They became interested in other potential, relational partners. (27.9%) They started seeing others. (51.4%) They ended their relationship. (100%)

Note: Numbers in parentheses indicate the percentage of subjects marking boundaries.

The first stage in both stories of Box 7.5 consists of meeting and small talk. The second phase reflects dating, the display of physical affection, and doing informal activities together. The third phase reflects self-disclosure. The next action, sexual intercourse, was viewed as a separate unit by a sizable percentage of the readers of the John and Veronica story compared to the Linda and Tom story. The fifth phase consists of meeting parents, exchanging mementos, other-oriented statements, and stating a commitment to the relationship. The final phase is marriage.

The difference in the percentages demarcating intercourse as a separate phase may be due to language use and the social desirability of the expression, "sleeping together." Although, this expression is a euphemism for the act of intercourse, "sexual intercourse" sounds more biological or clinical and may not signal passionate emotion, whereas "sleeping together" has a more intimate connotation. Because of this connotation, sleeping together slides into the relationship phase reflecting the intensification or integration of the relationship, as opposed to being a separate phase in itself.

The boundary percentages reinforce the phases identified using the card-sorting procedure. The first phase reflects the social-penetration stages of initiation and experimentation. The second phase resembles the penetration stage of intensifying. The third phase, self-disclosure, was discussed as part of the intensifying stage (Knapp et al., 2014). Sexual intercourse is a separate phase in the stories, whereas the fifth phase appears to represent a combination of intensifying and integrating. The final phase, marriage, simply reflects a legal-bonding stage that in which wedding vows are exchanged.

For the escalating actions about John and Veronica and Linda and Tom, they had gotten married. The story continues so we could determine how individuals segment de-escalating actions into underlying scenes and phases.

Each continuing contained 11 sentences, one sentence for each prototypical de-escalating script expectation. A sample of 60 men and 63 women were surveyed. They ranged in age from 17 to 34 years, with an average age of 21. 25. The subjects were divided into two groups with each group reading one story of a romantic relationship that had started to go sour. Two stories were used in order to generalize beyond the particular characters of one de-escalating story.

The subjects were given one of the stories in Box 7.6 and told that the stories could be divided into underlying parts, as in the instructions in Chapter 8 for the escalating stories. The sentences in the stories were derived from the prototypical actions based on the 20% decision rule discussed earlier for the de-escalating schema-generation study. If subjects thought that the story could be subdivided into natural parts, they were asked to place a slash mark at the end of each sentence that they believed ended a part. If they did not think there were parts to the story, then they were asked to put one mark at the end of the story.

A comparison of slash-mark locations between the stories revealed two significant differences between the stories. Readers of the John and Veronica story were more likely to place slash marks after the second sentence about "disagreeing about the other's attitudes" than were the readers of the Linda and Tom story. Apparently, the word "attitudes" in the first story may have more connotative meaning than the word, "opinions" in the second story. In addition, readers of the Linda and Tom story were more likely to indicate a boundary after the sentence about rejuvenating the relationship than were the readers of the John and Veronica story.

It is interesting that attempting "to work things out through rejuvenating the relationship" elicited more segments (58.8%) than did trying "to rejuvenate the relationship by talking and attempting to smooth things over" (28.3%). Rejuvenation may not have that much psychological meaning for the readers (Honeycutt et al., 1992).

It is also interesting that readers tended to immediately place boundaries after the first scene, unlike readers in Honeycutt et al.'s (1989) escalating-relationship study. Therefore, the first de-escalating action may be a critical segmentation point that starts the process. The first scene consists of stopping self-disclosures and seems to be similar to the circumscribing stage described by Knapp et al. (2014). The second scene involves disagreeing about the one's partner's opinions, arguing over small things, and using aversive statements. The third scene represents the decreasing contact cluster (avoiding the other and seeing less of the other) identified in the de-escalating script generation study. This scene is similar to Cody's (1982) behavioral de-escalation strategy, as well as the avoidance stage of the social-penetration model (Knapp et al., 2014). The fourth scene represents reevaluating the relationship. The fifth scene seems to represent the breaking-up dimensions identified in the factor analyses of the typicality and necessity ratings of the de-escalating actions. In this scene the relationship is ending and interest in others increases. The final scene marks the dissolution of the relationships and is similar to Knapp's termination stage, in which the relationship is redefined or ended.

However, we add an additional stage, "post-termination" awareness as noted in Chapter 6 in which partners have redefined the relationship and are aware of the other's activities. Indeed, this is quite common because some people continue to have imagined interactions with the ex that is facilitated through social network monitoring, reports from third parties, co-custodial arrangements involving children, or a lack of comparison alternatives to keep the mind focused on other activities. Also, 61% of people who ended a relationship reported they remained friends with the former partner. Indeed, the relational investment model reveals that people with greater relational satisfaction, lower alternatives, and more investment in their relationships report more commitment (Tan, Agnew, VanderDrift, & Harvey, 2015).

In order to identify central or critical script actions that are robust in the decline of a relationship, Honeycutt et al. (1992) used five criteria: (a) an action mentioned by at least 20% of the participants in the script-generation task, (b) positive loadings on typicality, (c) positive loadings on necessity, (d) signifying the end of a stage in the card-sorting task, and (e) placement of slash marks in the de-escalating-relationship stories. They concluded: The most important actions seem to be talk about breaking up and final break-up which met all of the criteria. Other robust actions based on meeting four of five criteria were stopping the expression of intimate feelings, arguing about little things, verbal fighting, avoiding the other, and start seeing others of the opposite sex. To use a metaphor, these actions may be like signposts directing an individual of warnings, hazards, and exit points on the highway of decline. Yet, some relationship drivers may be more attuned to the relationship road signs such as those initiating the break-up. On the other hand, persons also tend to believe they began the de-escalating process (Honeycutt et al., 1992, p. 557).

The script model emphasizes the importance of the role of thought and cognition in establishing beliefs about appropriate behavior in personal relationships. It is the structure of cognition that resembles phases rather than the nature of the phase concept itself. Studies revealed that internal cognitions resemble thoughts about the rise and demise of relationships found in researcher-imposed stages. Indeed, the expectations represent intrapersonal guides for behavior that help individuals identify behaviors and label their experiences (Honeycutt, 1993). Thus, developmental models of communication serve a heuristic function in conceptualizing interaction phases.

Gender Differences in Generating and Processing Scripts

There are significant differences between men and women in generating and processing escalating scripts. These differences concern the initiation and termination of relationships. Rubin, Peplau, and Hill (1981) found that men tend to initiate relationships, whereas women end them. This still appears to be true in contemporary society according to studies cited in Fletcher, Simpson, Campbell, and Overall (2013). Additionally, women see a breakup coming sooner than do men. Men are more romantic in their beliefs about relationships because they are more emotionally dependent on relationships (Frazier & Esterly, 1990). Traditionally, men have placed more emphasis on sex, game-playing love, and *agape* love (all-giving, selfless, altruistic love) because they have been more economically independent, while being emotionally dependent on the relationship. Coleman and Ganong (1992) found that women expected prospective husbands to make more money; have higher educational achievements; be more intelligent, successful, and better able to handle things than the women themselves. In contrast, men expected their prospective wives to be relatively similar to the men themselves.

Burnett (1990) found that men reported thinking less about relationships, as well as being less involved in communication about relationships. This is reinforced by a review by Fletcher and his associates (2013) in which were women talk openly about their intimate relationships, more accurately at mind reading, and produce complex explanations for relational decline while men are more likely to adopt a proprietorial attitude toward female sexuality and coitus rather than the inverse, become jealous and are more likely to injure their partners through the enactment of violence.

Women's distinctions between liking and love are also supported by data reported in a study of characteristics of same-gender friendships. On the one hand, Duck and Wright (1993) found that both genders meet with same-gender friends most often just to talk for talk's sake, followed by working on some task, and, least often, to discuss relational issues. An example of men doing this is at a bar (see Picture 7.1). On the other hand, although both men and women were concerned with caring, supportiveness, and encouragement, women were more likely than men to communicate these concerns directly (see Picture 7.2). Duck and Wright (1993) found that women reported voluntary interdependence, supporting one another's ego, affirming a friend's self-concept, security, expressing emotions, and permanence of the relationship as characterizing friendships more often than did men. In addition, they found that women reported same-gender friendships as more important relationships than did men.

Picture 7.1. Men disclose indirectly through humor and liquor.

Picture 7.2. Women directly disclose their concerns.

The lack of discriminating criteria for men has been suggested by Burnett (1990) to be due to a pattern of socialization of men to not demonstrate emotion for fear of revealing vulnerability. Burnett's statement was supported by data from Rubin et al. (1981). They found that women reported being less romantic than men and more cautious about entering into romance. Women were more pragmatic and sensitive about the development of relationships.

Women reported having more general expectations of what should happen in the development of an escalating romance (Honeycutt et al., 1989). Furthermore, women reported being more aware of their reasons for using verbal strategies to escalate intimacy at various stages of relational development (Honeycutt, Cantrill, Kelly, & Lambkin, 1998). In addition, women have more developed scripts for escalating relationships. Women generated an average of 12.11 actions for their escalating scripts, whereas men generated an average of 10.10, without being redundant (Honeycutt et al., 1989). Gender stereotypes lead one to believe that women self-disclose more. Indeed, females rate self-disclosure as more necessary than typical in a growing romance than do men (Honeycutt et al., 1989). Yet Dindia and Allen (1992), reviewing over 200 studies of gender differences in self-disclosure, found that although women tend to disclose more than men, the difference is small. For example, women disclose more than men in same-gender conversations, but there is no difference between the amount that women and men disclose in opposite-gender conversations.

For example, Honeycutt et al. (1989) found that women rate engaging in joint activities, overcoming a crisis, meeting parents, talking about future plans, verbal expression of love, stating a commitment, and making other-oriented statements as more typical than did men. Women rated meeting one another's parents and talking about future plans as more necessary than did men. The only action mentioned by men as being more necessary in an order for intimacy to develop in a relationship compared to women was sexual intercourse. These self-reports are consistent with traditional gender-role stereotypes of women as being more likely to use relational maintenance than men, even though behavioral studies revealed that both genders use strategies of positivity, disclosure, and giving assurances to one another (Stafford & Canary, 1991).

Women monitor their relationships and have more vivid memories of specific events occurring in the relationships (Ross & Holmberg, 1992). Similar to the results of Burnett (1990), Ross and Holmberg also found that wives attributed greater personal importance to the events, reported reminiscing about them more often, and expressed more emotions in describing the events than did their husbands.

Husbands turn to their wives for help in recalling events of the relationship. When recalling events together, husbands were more likely to report memory failures, whereas husbands' and wives' reports of forgetting did not differ when they recalled relational episodes alone (Ross & Holmberg, 1992). The increase in husbands' forgetting in the dyadic situation and attempts to gain information from their spouses is known as transactive retrieval (Wegner, 1987).

Ross and Holmberg (1992) noted that the gender effect in the ratings of vividness disappears when the outcome of a recalled argument is considered. Additional analyses of the argument transcripts distinguished between who initiated and who won the argument. Men and women who lost the dispute reported higher vividness ratings than did the winning spouses. Husbands who lost the dispute tended to have the most vivid recall of all. Wives reported more vivid memories because they were more likely to lose the dispute.

Honeycutt et al. (1989) studies of relational memory-structure processing reveal that individuals who have been in relationships sort randomized actions more efficiently than do individuals who have been in zero relationships. This finding should not be interpreted as implying that individuals in multiple relationships are experts at sustaining relationships. In fact, the very opposite can be surmised, due to the frequent endings of their relationships. In addition, it is possible that the losers in the Ross and Holmberg (1992) study may have analyzed a history of failed strategies. Berger and Kellermann (1986) noted that individuals may use habitual behavioral strategies when trying to gain compliance, even when they are faced with barriers and failure. They speculated that these individuals use a maxim which can be stated as: "Keep doing what usually works even if it isn't and try something new and hope that it will work better" (p. 24).

In general, wives may be more likely than their husbands to evaluate current relational experiences in view of their memories of previous encounters. Ross and Holmberg (1992) provided an example in which a wife exhibits an extreme reaction to an oversight by her husband. He does not understand this. The wife may associate the current disagreement with a previous sequence of actions, whereas the husband may regard her disagreement as an unreasonable response to a single incident.

As revealed in Figure 9.1, men have not been socialized into communicating their vulnerabilities and isolation and often withdraw.

Scripts for Friendships Compared with FWBs

Although there are many recent studies on FWBs, the evaluation of cognitive scripts involved in FWBs has yet to be established. One study (Karlsen & Træen, 2013) investigated sexual scripts in FWBs, their definition of sexual scripts differs from the memory structure approach. Even though there is a clear difference in the conceptualization of scripts, the researchers still state that scripts are needed in FWBs or else individuals would not know how to interact while in them. Thus, the investigation of the scripts operating throughout the course of FWBs is of great importance and concern.

Honeycutt and his colleagues (2015) had college students generate their scripts for friendships and FWBs in order to compare it with the romantic script described earlier. The first research question inquired about the similarities and differences present in cognitive scripts in the development of friendships and FWBs. In order to analyze the cognitive scripts, researchers used the established escalating and deescalating behaviors to code the respondents' scripts as previously detailed above. The deescalating behaviors are described in more detail later.

Friendships and FWBS are both initiated with a meeting, followed by small talk, and proceed to shared time together. The primary difference seems to lie in the development of these relationships past the shared time together behavior. Friendships tend to include self-disclosure, other-oriented statements, and even verbal commitment, whereas FWBs begin to incorporate sexual intercourse and halting the expression of intimate feelings.

Summary

The content of relational memory structures for developing romances reveals gender differences in the complexity of the structure. Women report more expectations about the development of romance than do men. Men may be rather simplistic in their expectations for romance because in action-generation studies they restate actions and mention few unique activities.

Research has revealed that the number of relationships a person reports having been in can be predicted from what they mention as being characteristic of a developing relationship. In addition, most actions that characterize romance are seen as typical; less are seen as necessary. Individuals often label actions as being characteristic of romance, even though they are unable to generate a list of actions on their own. In other words, once the action is presented, it is recognized. The only action rated as more necessary than typical was a desire for self-disclosure.

Men and women can readily identify underlying stages of escalating relationships. A prototypical sequence was derived that resembled some of the social-penetration stages in the staircase model of Knapp and his associates (2014). There is more agreement on the ordering of early actions, such as dating, than on later-occurring actions, such as making a commitment.

In terms of anticipating the ending of a relationship, the data revealed that individuals reported they had initiated more breakups than their partners. This bias reflects a self-serving accounting and does not allow for a joint desire to end the relationship.

Gender differences were evident in the de-escalating studies in which women reported more de-escalating actions and inferences than did men. Furthermore, women processed the prototypical de-escalating actions faster than did men. Women rated talking with friends and verbal fighting higher in typicality than did men. While gender may have a direct effect in how individuals perceive de-escalating relationships, it may also have an interactive effect in combination with personality. For example, women high in extroversion reported their extroverted partners to be condescending, and males reported their extroverted wives as abusive. Personality characteristics of male partners were among the strongest predictors of couple's perceptions regarding conflict communication patters and those men high in Neuroticism were reported to be judging, abusive, unfaithful, moody, and inconsiderate.

Discussion Questions

7.1. Why do women list more expectations for the escalation of romance than men? Are men cognitively simplistic or ignorant about the behaviors that characterize the escalation of romance?

7.2. Look at the list of actions that characterize the escalation and de-escalation of romance. Discuss which of these actions are more easily interchanged or switched in the prototypical sequence. For example, meeting tends to precede marriage, unless the cultural mores establish contractually arranged marriages such as in Egypt or India while arguing tends to proceed leaving.

7.3. Does the presence of social media affect rate of movement through the actions? Why or why not?

7.4. Discuss what may happen if two individuals meet and one has a diversified set of non-redundant expectations for the development and deterioration of romance, whereas the other has a simple set that is not complex.

7.5. Some research indicates that both genders tend to take responsibility for initiating the breakup of a relationship. Relate these findings to your own experiences and discuss the nature of this attributional bias.

7.6. Have you ever tried to rejuvenate a relationship? What type of relationship was it? Discuss what you did and the outcome of the attempted rejuvenation.

7.7. Is it really possible for two individuals who have achieved a certain level or type of intimacy in a relationship to go back and just be friends? Is "being a friend" a euphemism for saying the current state of the relationship is over.

Applications

7.1. Conduct a mini-experiment by asking three male and three female friends to generate a list of behaviors that characterize a close relationship. Compute the redundancy of the listed actions by counting the number of repeated or similar statements made by an individual. Did the men and women have similar levels of redundancy? When you take redundancy into account, did the men and women generate the same number of unique actions? Can you make any conclusions about differences in the complexity of the expectations for a close relationship?

7.2. Conduct a mini-experiment by writing down the descriptions of the behavioral expectations in Box 8.2, each on a separate index card. Shuffle the cards so the expectations are in a random order. Give the deck to three male and three female friends and instruct them to sort the cards in an intuitive logical order. Time them and compare their orders with those in Box 7.2. Was it difficult for them to sort the expectations? Were there any reactions to the experiment? Discuss any gender differences in the sorting times and rank orders of the behavioral expectations.

References

Afifi, W. A., & Guerrero, L. K. (2000). Motivations underlying topic avoidance in close relationships. In S. Petronio (Ed.), *Balancing the secrets of private disclosures* (pp. 165–180). Mahwah, NJ: Lawrence Erlbaum.

Bachman, G., & Guerrero, L. (2006). Relational quality and communicative responses following hurtful events in dating relationships: An expectancy violations analysis. *Journal of Social and Personal Relationships, 23,* 943–963. doi:10.1177/0265407506070476

Baxter, L. A. (1985). Accomplishing relationship disengagement. In S. Duck & D. Perlman (Eds.), *Understanding personal relationship: An interdisciplinary approach* (pp. 243–265). Beverly Hills, CA: Sage.

Baxter, L. A. (1986). Gender differences in the heterosexual relationship rules embedded in break-up accounts. *Journal of Social and Personal Relationships, 3,* 289–306. doi:10.1177/0265407586033003

Baxter, L. A., & Bullis, C. (1986). Turning points in developing romantic relationships. *Human Communication Research, 12,* 469–494. doi:10.1111/j.1468-2958.1986.tb00088.x

Berger, C. R., & Kellermann, K. (1986, May). *Goal incompatibility and social action: The best laid plans of mice and men often go astray.* Paper presented at the annual meeting of the International Communication Association, Chicago, IL.

Bevan, J. L. (2009). Interpersonal communication apprehension, topic avoidance, and the experience of irritable bowel syndrome. *Personal Relationships, 16,* 147–165. doi:10.1111/j.1475-6811.2009.01216.x

Bower, G. H., Black, J. B., & Turner, T. J. (1979). Scripts in memory for text. *Cognitive Psychology, 11,* 177–200. doi:10.1016/0010-0285(79)90009-4

Burnett, R. (1990). Reflection in personal relationships. In R. Burnett, P. McGhee, & D. Clarke (Eds.), *Accounting for relationships: Explanation, representation and knowledge* (pp. 73–94). London: Methuen.

Carlston, D. E. (1980). Events, inferences and impression formation. In R. Hastie, T. M. Ostrom, E. B. Ebbesen, R. S. Wyer, Jr., D. L. Hamilton, & D. E. Carlston (Eds.), *Person memory: The cognitive bias of social perception* (pp. 84–119). Hillsdale, NJ: Lawrence Erlbaum.

Caughlin, J. P., & Vangelisti, A. L. (2006). Conflict in dating and marital relationships. In J. G. Oetzel & S. Ting-Toomey (Eds.), *Sage handbook of conflict communication: Integrating theory, research, and practice* (pp. 129–157). Thousand Oaks, CA: Sage.

Choi, H., & Marks, N. F. (2008). Marital conflict, depressive symptoms, and functional impairment. *Journal of Marriage and the Family, 70,* 377–390. doi:10.1111/j.1741-3737.2008.00488.x

Cody, M. (1982). A typology of disengagement strategies and an examination of the role intimacy reactions to inequity, and behavioral problems play in strategy selection. *Communication Monographs, 49*, 148–170. doi:10.1080/03637758209376079

Coleman, M., & Ganong, L. (1992). Gender differences in expectations of self and future partner. *Journal of Family Issues, 33*, 55–61. doi:10.1177/019251392013001004

Denton, W. H., & Burleson, B. R. (2007). The initiator style questionnaire: A scale to assess initiator tendency in couples. *Personal Relationships, 14*, 245–268. doi:10.1111/j.1475-6811.2007.00153.x

Dindia, K., & Allen, M. (1992). Sex differences in self-disclosure: A meta-analysis. *Psychological Bulletin, 112*, 106–124.

Duck, S., & Wright, P. H. (1993). Reexamining gender differences in same-gender friendships: A close look at two kinds of data. *Sex Roles, 28*, 709–727. doi:10.1007/BF00289989

Fletcher, G., Simpson, J. A., Campbell, L., & Overall, N. C. (2013). *The science of intimate relationships*. Malden, MA: John Wiley & Sons, Ltd.

Foa, E. B., & Foa, U. G. (2012). Resource theory of social exchange. In K. Tornblom & A. Kazemi (Eds.), *Handbook of social resource theory: Theoretical extensions, empirical insights, and social applications* (pp. 15–132). New York, NY: Springer.

Frazier, P. A., & Esterly, E. (1990). Correlates of relationship beliefs: Gender, relationship experience and relationship satisfaction. *Journal of Social and Personal Relationships, 7*, 331–352. doi:10.1177/0265407590073003

Gagne', F. M., & Lydon, J. E. (2004). Bias and accuracy in close relationships: An integrative review. *Personality and Social Psychology Review, 8*, 322–338. doi:10.1207/s15327957pspr0804_1

Gayle, B. M., Preiss, R. W., & Allen, M. (2002). A meta-analytic interpretation of intimate and nonintimate interpersonal conflict. In M. Allen, R. W. Preiss, B. M. Gayle, & N. A. Burrell (Eds.), *Interpersonal communication research: Advances through meta-analysis* (pp. 345–368). Mahwah, NJ: Lawrence Erlbaum.

Goodwin, R. (1991). A re-examination of Rusbult's responses to satisfaction typology. *Journal of Social and Personal Relationships, 4*, 569–574. doi:10.1177/026540759184007

Gottman, J. M. (1994). *What predicts divorce?* Hillsdale, NJ: Lawrence Erlbaum.

Gottman, J. M., & Silver, N. (2015). *The seven principles for making marriage work*. New York, NY: Harmony.

Grice, H. P. (1975). Logic and conversation. In P. Cole & J. L. Morgan (Eds.), *Syntax and semantics: Speech acts* (Vol. 3, pp. 41–58). New York, NY: Seminar Press.

Hill, C. T., Rubin, Z., & Peplau, L. (1976). Breakups before marriage: The end of 103 affairs. *Journal of Social Issues, 32*, 147–168. doi:10.1111/j.1540-4560.1976.tb02485.x

Honeycutt, J. M. (1993). Memory structures for the rise and fall of personal relationships. In D. Duck (Ed.), *Individuals in relationships* (pp. 60–86). Newbury Park, CA: Sage.

Honeycutt, J. M. (1995). Predicting beliefs about relational trajectories as a consequence of typicality and necessity ratings of relationship behaviors. *Communication Research Reports, 12*, 3–14. doi:10.1080/08824099509362033

Honeycutt, J. M. (2010). Forgive but don't forget: Correlates of rumination about conflict. In J. M. Honeycutt (Ed.), *Imagine that: Studies in imagined interaction* (pp. 17–29). Cresskill, NJ: Hampton.

Honeycutt, J. M., Cantrill, J. G., & Allen, T. (1992). Memory structures for relational decay: A cognitive test of sequencing of deescalating actions and stages. *Human Communication Research, 18*, 528–562. doi:10.1111/j.1468-2958.1992.tb00571.x

Honeycutt, J. M., Cantrill, J. G., & Greene, R. W. (1989). Memory structures for relational escalation: A cognitive test of the sequencing of relational actions and stages. *Human Communication Research, 16*, 62–90. doi:10.1111/j.1468-2958.1989.tb00205.x

Honeycutt, J. M., Cantrill, J. G., Kelly, P., & Lambkin, D. (1998). How do I love thee? Let me consider my options: Cognition, verbal strategies, and the escalation of intimacy. *Human Communication Research, 25*, 39–63. doi:10.1111/j.1468-2958.1998.tb00436.x

Honeycutt, J. M., & Godwin, D. D. (1986). A model of marital functioning based on an attraction paradigm and social-penetration dimensions. *Journal of Marriage and the Family, 48*, 651–667. doi:10.2307/352051

Honeycutt, J. M., Keaton, S. A., Hatcher, L. C., & Hample, D. (2014). Effects of rumination and observing marital conflict on observers' heart rates as they advise and predict the use of conflict tactics. In J. M. Honeycutt, C. R. Sawyer, & S. A. Keaton (Eds.), *The influence of communication on physiology and health* (pp. 73–92). New York, NY: Peter Lang.

Honeycutt, J. M., Shimek, C., & White, R. C. (2015, May). *Cognitive, attraction, attachment, and love type differences among friends with benefits.* Paper presented at the annual International Communication Association Conference, San Juan, Puerto Rico.

Johnson, K. L., & Roloff, M. E. (2000). Correlates of the perceived resolvability and relational consequences of serial dating relationships: Argumentative features and the use of coping strategies. *Journal of Social and Personal Relationships, 17*, 676–686. doi:10.1177/0265407500174011

Karlsen, M., & Træen, B. (2013). Identifying 'friends with benefits' scripts among young adults in the Norwegian cultural context. *Sexuality & Culture, 17*, 83–99. doi:10.1007/s12119-012-9140-7

Knapp, M. L., Vangelisti, A. L., & Caughlin, J. P. (2014). *Interpersonal communication and human relationships* (7th ed.). New York, NY: Pearson.

Malis, R. S., & Roloff, M. E. (2006). Demand/withdraw patterns in serial arguments: Implications for well-being. *Human Communication Research, 32*, 198–216. doi:10.1111/j.1468-2958.2006.00009.x

Planalp, S., Rutherford, D. K., & Honeycutt, J. M. (1987). Events that increase uncertainty in personal relationships II. Replication and extension. *Human Communication Research, 14*, 516–547. doi:10.1111/j.1468-2958.1988.tb00166.x

Pryor, J. B., & Merluzzi, T. V. (1985). The role of expertise in processing social interaction scripts. *Journal of Experimental Social Psychology, 21*, 362–379. doi:10.1016/0022-1031(85)90036-8

Rosch, E. R., Mervis, C. B., Gray, W. D., Johnson, D. M., & Graem, P. (1976). Basic objects in natural categories. *Cognitive Psychology, 8*, 382–439. doi:10.1016/0010-0285(76)90013-X

Ross, M., & Holmberg, D. (1992). Are wives' memories for events in relationships more vivid than their husbands' memories? *Journal of Social and Personal Relationships, 9*, 585–604. doi:10.1177/0265407592094007

Rubin, Z., Peplau, L. A., & Hill, C. T. (1981). Loving and leaving: Sex differences in romantic attachments. *Sex Roles, 7*, 821–835. doi:10.1007/BF00287767

Rusbult, C. E. (1987). Responses to dissatisfaction in close relationships: The exit-voice-loyalty-neglect model. In S. Duck & D. Perlman (Eds.), *Intimate relationships: Development, dynamics, and deterioration* (pp. 209–237). Newbury Park, CA: Sage.

Segrin, C., Hanzal, A., & Domschke, T. J. (2009). Accuracy and bias in newlywed couples' perceptions of conflict styles and the association with marital satisfaction. *Communication Monographs, 76*, 207–233. doi:10.1080/03637750902828404

Stafford, L. (2015). Social exchange theories: Calculating the rewards and costs of personal relationships. In D. O. Braithwaite & P. Schrodt (Eds.), *Engaging theories in interpersonal communication* (2nd ed., pp. 403–415). Los Angeles, CA: Sage.

Stafford, L., & Canary, D. J. (1991). Maintenance strategies and romantic relationship type, gender, and relational characteristics. *Journal of Social and Personal Relationships, 8*, 217–242. doi:10.1177/0265407591082004

Tan, K., Agnew, C. R., VanderDrift, L. E., & Harvey, S. M. (2015). Committed to us: Predicting relationships closeness following nonmarital relationship breakup. *Journal of Social and Personal Relationships, 32*, 456–471. doi:10.1177/0265407514536293

Watkins, S. J., & Boon, S. D. (2016). Expectations regarding partner fidelity in dating relationships. *Journal of Social and Personal Relationships, 33*, 237–256. doi:10.1177/0265407515574463

Wegner, D. M. (1987). Transactive memory. In B. Mullen & G. R. Goethals (Eds.), *Theories of group behavior* (pp. 185–208). New York, NY: Springer-Verlag.

CHAPTER EIGHT

Semantics of Break-ups

When an individual ends an intimate relationship, he or she must provide an account of the breakup to members of his or her social network, including work associates, family, and friends. As indicated in Chapter 7, research revealed that these accounts tend to place the onus of responsibility on one's partner for the breakdown of the relationship (Cody, 1982; Harvey, Weber, Galvin, Huszti, & Garnick, 1986). People tend to attribute blame to others, absolving themselves of responsibility. For example, when talking with family members about serious romantic problems, persons tend to give accounts that absolve themselves of blame (McBride & Braithwaite, 2008). Their motivations for doing this are: (a) family members would judge them, (b) the problem in their relationship would reflect negatively on them, and (c) embarrassment.

This system of allocating blame buttresses self-esteem, helps to save face, and presents a positive image to eligible future partners (Harvey et al., 1986). Individuals also develop such accounts to maintain a sense of control over their environment, to aid in emotional purging, and as a reaction to unfinished business (Harvey, Orbuch, & Weber, 1992).

The de-escalating script actions discussed in Chapter 7 reveal an additional intriguing phenomenon in terms of linguistic codes. Some of the actions represent what can be referred to as omissions and commissions. This finding was incidental, but significant. Why do people access one language code for a particular action instead of another? Three explanations will be discussed in this chapter in reference to this type of semantic code referencing: attributional, implicit benefit-of-the-doubt, and rules-based. Results of a study revealing gender differences in accessing the codes will also be discussed.

Linguistic Codes of Omissions and Commissions

Gergen and Gergen (1992) emphasized the importance of the social construction of relationships based on the language used to describe their events. They stated that relationship events exist in the eye of beholder in such a way that "there are an unlimited number of ways of characterizing the same state of affairs, and no single language can justifiably claim transcendence or status as the one true description" (p. 275). Omissions and commissions illustrate that different linguistic codes can be used to describe the same state of affairs.

The 21 actions in the de-escalating metascript presented in Chapter 7 were recoded to reflect either omissions or commissions. For example, one person might write that a typical action indicative of a decaying relationship is that "Individuals do not spend enough time together," whereas another person may write, "Individuals spend too much time on their jobs." The former is an omission, whereas the latter is a commission. Logically, if a person is not spending time with his or her partner, he or she is presumably committing time to something else. But as the example illustrates, some individuals see apples, and others see oranges.

Honeycutt, Cantrill, and Allen (1992) found that one third of the de-escalating actions could be classified as omissions. Words such as "not," "less," "avoid," "decrease," "withholding," and "withdrawal" signal the omission of a behavior. The decrease intimacy (e.g., stop expressing intimate feelings, decrease physical intimacy) and decreasing contact (e.g., call less, avoid other, give other excuses for not being able to go out) clusters discussed in Chapter 7 are omissions. The remaining clusters represented claims of commission to the extent that the language used to refer to active behaviors, such as aversive communication, re-evaluating the relationship, assessing comparison alternatives, ending the relationship.

Semantic Codes of Action

An Attributional Explanation

Attributional biases were discussed in Chapter 7 in terms of attributing the source of one's relational problems to one's partner in unhappy relationships. Honeycutt et al. (1992) used attribution theory to posit a research question on the existence of omissions (Honeycutt et al., 1992). They cited Ross (1977) for his discussion of the fundamental attribution error in which individuals attribute the cause of others' behaviors to dispositional, internal factors and their own behaviors to situational features (e.g., "My boyfriend is late because he is irresponsible." According to the boyfriend, he is late because of bad traffic.). Ross (1977) described a fictional, potentially developing relationship between Jack and Jill in which Jack believes Jill does not like him. He is unable to understand why he feels this way because he can not recall specific actions by Jill that reveal her dislike. But Jack could be focusing on what Jill does not do, such as providing positive feedback and being involved in their interactions. In this fashion, Ross described the informational bias of occurrences versus nonoccurrences.

Individuals tend to notice actions in forming their impressions while neglecting to consider information conveyed when particular actions do not occur. Ross speculated that nonoccurrences may be more noted when an individual has access to active category labels that can be applied to nonoccurring actions, as is true of the behaviors associated with intimate relationships. Following this reasoning,

> In the breaking up of a relationship, there may be "sins" of commission and omission that reflect attributional conflicts due to actor observer differences. The person is both an actor by being in the relationship as well as an observer by noticing the other's actions. In the former case, there is attribution to what the person is doing (e.g., seeing others). In the latter case, a behavior is omitted because it is *not* occurring (e.g., not seeing me). The difference between these may be a matter of semantics. (Honeycutt et al., 1992, p. 535)

> A number of strategies that are used to de-escalate a relationship represent nonoccurrences or omissions. Honeycutt et al. (1992) noted that Cody's (1982) behavioral de-escalation strategy included some null events: "I *never* brought up the topic," and "I *never* verbally said anything to the partner." On the other hand, two samples of this strategy reflect positive labels for null actions: "I avoided contact," and "I avoided scheduling future meetings with him/her." (p. 163)

Baxter (1984) discussed withdrawal as a unilateral, indirect strategy to end a relationship. The withdrawer reduces contact and intimacy with his or her partner. Some of Baxter's sample accounts involve nonevents. For example, "I *never* answered the notes" (p. 36). Baxter also generated a typology of reasons that individuals gave for their relationships ending. A number of Baxter's categories reflect "omissions." For example, the most frequent reasons for a breakup reported by Baxter include lack of similar attitudes or values, lack of supportiveness, lack of openness, lack of fidelity, and lack of romance. Only the desire for autonomy and physical separation were frequent reasons that reflect an affirmative or proactive wording.

An Implicit Benefit-of-the-Doubt Explanation

Another explanation for the choice of language to characterize relational failure is of the flexibility of null language codes; they allow one to consider other explanations in the hope that omission will end. When a person says, "My partner did not spend enough time with me," it may in the hope that his or her partner will start spending more time with him or her. The null event reflects more tentativeness and is a less definitive statement. For example, someone who says, "My partner was not spending enough time with me" implies that his or her partner could spend more time with that person. In contrast, the commission formulation, "My partner was spending too much time doing his hobbies," is more definitive.

Harvey et al. (1992) indicated that one motivation for accounts is to "stimulate an enlightened feeling and greater hope and will for the future" (p. 6). Perhaps, the null event reflects an implicit desire that there could be change, whereas the commission implies that change is not considered. In order to test this idea, it would be necessary to track individuals over time as they go through the process of a relationship breakdown. If this speculation has some foundation, then individuals earlier in the phases of relational decay ought to be more willing to hope for behavioral change than they would be later. Hence, there would be more omissions in early phases of breakdown than in later phases. A Relational Expectancies Survey Test returned by a man (age 28) provides some confirmation that in the early stages of relationship breakdown, when there is still hope for positive changes, omissions predominate over commissions. Under marital status, this respondent checked "married," but placed an arrow directionally toward "separated" with the words "maybe soon" handwritten over the category and "or" with another arrow pointing toward the "divorced" category. Thus he was indicating that at that point he was in a relationship that was beginning to breakdown. His specific responses to a query asking him to list behaviors that are typical of a relationship that has gone sour are found in Box 8.1. Note that of 20 total responses, omissions account for 14 and commissions account for only six. Perhaps this demonstrates "Hope springs eternal," at least in the heart of this husband.

Box 8.1. Responses of 28-Year-Old-Married, "Maybe Soon Separated" Man

1. Not talking*
2. Not making love*
3. Not being considerate of each other*
4. Not supporting each other's decisions*
5. Avoiding spending time with each other*

6. Not planning surprises*
7. Not helping with household chores*
8. Not kissing goodbye*
9. Not kissing hello*
10. Not checking where you are*
11. Not caring if you return*
12. Spending a lot of time with other people*
13. Finding a new partner (male or female)
14. Not ever sending flowers*
15. Not remembering important events*
16. Sleeping separate
17. Rooming separate
18. Living in separate homes
19. Not seeing each other*
20. Divorce or separation

Note: An asterisk (*) indicates an omission.

Gottman (1994) conducted a number of longitudinal investigations of the communication behaviors that characterize happily married and unhappily married couples. He posited a cascade model of corrosive communication behaviors that lead to divorce. These behaviors include complaining and criticizing, which in turn leads to contempt. Contempt leads to defensiveness, which results in stonewalling and relational termination. He was able to predict with considerable accuracy which couples would divorce 3 years later.

Gottman (1994) provided examples of these behaviors, and it should be noted that a number of the examples reflect omissions. Defensiveness involves an attempt to protect one's self from perceived attack. Often, defensiveness is reflected through negative mind reading in which there are attributions of motives, feelings, or behaviors to the partner. Gottman (1994) provided examples such as: "You don't care about how we live," "You never clean up," "You always embarrass me at parties," and "You get tense in situations like that one" (p. 25). In addition, Gottman indicated that mind-reading statements are accompanied by "You always" or "You never" phrases. These types of referents clearly reflect commissions and omissions, respectively.

Gottman discussed whining as a type of defensiveness that reflects dissatisfaction in a childish way. There are several types of whining that he discussed, one contains verbal statements containing omissions. Gottman (1994) provided this omission as an example of the complaint type of whining, "You never take me anywhere" (p. 27).

Individuals may implicitly or subliminally realize that further into the relationship-decay process, their partners are not going to start doing proactive behaviors. In this regard, Gottman (1994) reviewed studies indicating that unhappy couples show greater negativity during discussions of issues in the marriage and also display less humor, less reciprocated laughter, fewer agreements, more criticism, and more putdowns compared to happy couples. This list of differences contains omissions in terms of not showing humor, not laughing together, and disagreeing. Commissions are reflected in the active wording of criticism and the use of putdowns.

It is possible that sins of commission, in proactive wording say, reflect the reduction of uncertainty. Consider the following omission and commission: "Before, my partner was not spending enough time with me. Over time, I realized that the other preferred to spend the time doing God knows what." The omission is ambiguous because the individual does not know what his or her partner is doing; hence, a null event may symbolize a higher level of uncertainty and ambiguity. The wording of commission seems to indicate that a judgment of definitive action has been made and there is less uncertainty.

A Rules-Based Explanation

The third possibility explanation is based on the premise that omissions reflect the violation of a rule. The rules-based approach explains language codes for null events in terms of violations of expectations (Grandin & Barron, 2005). Hence, a rule violation is noted (e.g., "He or she was not showing me affection."). The actual rule is that an intimate should demonstrate affection to his or her partner. As noted in Chapter 5, rules for the rise and demise of relationships may take the form of script expectations. Null behaviors reflect violations of expectations and rules for interaction in personal relationships.

Symbolic interactionists believe that people negotiate rules for appropriate behavior in a variety of relationships based on numerous dimensions including individualism and collectivism, uncertainty avoidance, and power difference (e.g., parent-child, sibling, teacher-student, political adversaries) (Hofstede, Hofstede, & Minkov, 2010). While honestly is universally understood as "telling the truth;" two partners may have different standards and apply it differently depending on the situation, especially when pragmatic concerns make it difficult to be totally honest (e.g., Yes, you look great out in that new outfit even though you are having an imagined interaction with your partner in which you are laughing about how bad you think they look it in). Yet, it has been found that 82% of intimate couples agree on rules for disclosure; yet only 25% discuss these rules (Roggensack &

Sillars, 2014). Furthermore, people assume that their relational partners would agree with them on the value of following obligatory rules such as honesty. Understanding was measured by comparing differences between partners, self-ratings of how much they agreed with the rule. While perceived agreement was a measure of what they believed their partner would answer. Perceived agreement exceeded actual agreement. Hence, it can be argued that rules are an abstraction for observed norms while others argue that rules are only partly conscious because they do not they have followed a rule until it is violated (e.g., You are not aware of the speed limit until you are ticketed.).

Argyle and Henderson (1985) created a list of rules that pertain to a variety of relationships (e.g., teacher-student, intimates, acquaintances, best friends). A number of their rules are prescriptive (e.g., Be polite) in that they often prescribe what should be done in the given relationship. Other rules are restrictive, that is, they indicate what is not permissible. Research (Jones & Gallois, 1989) revealed that recognizing rule violations may be easier than freely generating rules for relationships.

Examples of Argyle and Henderson's (1985) prescriptive rules are respecting the other's privacy, repaying debts, being polite, and speaking in turn. Restrictive rules include not discussing with others what is said in confidence, not criticizing the other person publicly, not embarrassing the other person, and not lecturing or patronizing the other person. Argyle and Henderson presented a list of the nine most important rules; thus breaking these rules contribute to the collapse of friendships. These rules have been broken when one's friend is jealous of one's other relationships, does not keep confidences, is not being tolerant of one's friends, criticizes one in public, does not confide in one, does not volunteer help in time of need, does not show a positive regard for one, does not stand up for one in one's absence, and does not give one emotional support. It is interesting that, seven of the nine are worded to reflect a null event.

Additional research revealed null accounts of why marital and dating relationships ended. Cupach and Metts (1986) conducted a study on the accounts that respondents gave for problems that contributed to the breakups of their relationships. Six underlying dimensions were discovered: the individual's psychological state contributing to relational strain, the enactment of relational roles, relational cohesion, and the regulation of interaction, third-party affairs, and external forces beyond the couple's direct control. Each of these dimensions reflects rules for marriage and dating relationships that partners expect to be followed. The breaking of the rules results in relational strain or the ending of the relationship. Note that rule violation is often stated in terms of null events or what is not happening.

In these problems areas, Cupach and Metts (1986) provided numerous instances of omissions stated in the respondents' own words. Box 8.2 contains examples of the underlying problems in relationships. The dimensions are listed, followed by sample omission statements.

Box 8.2. Reasons for Relationships Breaking Reflecting Omissions

1. References to individual attitudes in the relationship. Former spouse decided he was *un*happy. I *never* intended to have a serious relationship. We made plans to go out that night but she *didn't* show up at the place or time. I became *no* fun.
2. Enactment of relational roles. I was *not* growing as a person. He found *no* joy in being a father. *No* sexual relations. He was *not* for me an adequate dating partner. He said he *wasn't* ready to become a father. We were *not* ready for the responsibility of marriage.
3. Relational cohesion. We *no* longer wanted the same things out of life. Our personalities *didn't* mix. We did *nothing* together as a couple. The feelings of love just *weren't* there.
4. Regulation of interaction. He *wouldn't* listen. I learned about a time she was *not* honest with me.

*Note: Italicized words reflect the null portion in each response, according to Cupach and Metts (1986, pp. 320–321).

In a factor analysis of rules for conflict resolution in Australian married couples, Jones and Gallois (1989) reported five factors, two of which were restrictive rules. These restrictive rules appear to be very similar to Cupach and Mett's (1986) dimension of regulation of interaction among divorcees and former partners. The restrictive rules included a dimension reflecting being considerate of one's partner (e.g., Don't interrupt, Don't humiliate the other person, Don't dismiss the other person's issue as unimportant, Don't talk down to the other person, Don't blame the other person unfairly, Don't push one's own point of view as the sole view, Don't be sarcastic or mimic the other person, Don't hurt the other person, Don't make the other person feel guilty, and Don't talk too much or dominate the conversation). The second restrictive dimension, rationality, included rules about keeping conflict rational (e.g., Don't get angry, Don't raise your voice, Don't be aggressive or lose your temper, Don't get upset and keep calm, Don't argue, and Don't bring up issues that tend to lead to arguments). The remaining three dimensions were prescriptive: self-expression (e.g., Get to the point quickly, and Be consistent), conflict resolution (e.g., Explore alternatives, Make joint decisions), and positivity (e.g., Try to relieve tension in arguments, and Look at each other).

Jones and Gallois (1989), while commenting on rule violation, noted that the married couples in their study "seemed to find it easier to identify rules that they were breaking than to identify the rules they were following" (p. 960). In a study done designed to examine whether Jones and Gallois's rule dimensions extended to an American sample, Honeycutt, Woods, and Fontenot (1993) replicated the restrictive rule-dimensions (rationality and consideration) in samples of engaged and married couples. However, they were not able to replicate the prescriptive rules as clearly as the restrictive rules. Positive understanding and concision emerged as rule dimensions.

Although expectations regarding the rise and demise of relationships can be viewed using a rules-based approach, it is important to note that this approach does not provide the mechanism by which the specific language code is accessed. For example, is it easier to recall restrictive rules? If so, why? Are there individual differences in stating restrictive rules?

Gender Differences in Omissions and Commissions

A re-analysis of the data presented in the de-escalating metascript generation study of Honeycutt et al. (1992) revealed some interesting results regarding the association of commissions and omissions with gender and other variables associated with relational breakdown. The sample consisted of 197 respondents enrolled in introductory communication courses at a large university. The sample was of 44% men and 56% women.

Two frequently mentioned omissions were avoiding the other in public settings and spending less time together. The most-mentioned commission was ending of the relationship followed by verbal fighting and antagonizing. Additional analyses controlling for the degree of redundancy in generating behaviors and inferences, revealed that women came up with a significantly greater variety of commissions (M = 5.13) than did men (M = 4.29) when generating expectations for relational breakdown. There were no significant effects for gender regarding omissions.

Partial correlations that take into account the amount of redundancy in the generated de-escalating script actions reveal a significant association between the total number of unique behaviors and inferences with commissions (Partial correlation = 0.63, p < .001).[1] The partial correlation allows one to describe the association between them, and at the same time to rule out other variables, in this case, the tendency to restate de-escalating behaviors or inferences. The number of omissions was also correlated with the number of unique behaviors and inferences (Partial correlation = 0.42, p < .001). The statistical procedure, the

Z test of correlation differences, was used to determine if the different values of these correlations were statistically significant. Values of Z scores equal to or above 1.96 are statistically significant. This analysis revealed that commissions were more common in the generated de-escalating behaviors and inferences than were omissions. The correlation of 0.63 is significantly higher than the correlation of 0.42 (z = 2.90, p < .004). Yet, the .42 correlation still reflects the subtle incidence of mentioning what is not happening as relationships sour.

Summary

The claims of omission and commission are an intriguing semantic phenomenon. Yet the basic question remains: Why do individuals sometimes reference null events as opposed to active events? More research is needed on the conditions that result in conceptualizing in one code instead of another. We believe that the code accessing occurs subliminally. Rarely does a person say, "I am blaming my partner for what he or she was not doing right, even though I could just as easily have said what they were doing wrong." In this regard, a few theoretical explanations have been offered.

Regarding gender differences, do women notice more null events as relationships are dissolving? This question cannot be answered with these data. However, recall that other research with couples on factors leading to the recent breakup of romances indicated that the ending of these relationships is more of a surprise for the men than for the women (Hill, Rubin, & Peplau, 1976). Because women think more about relational problems and the conditions affecting the relationship, they may notice earlier than men what is not happening (e.g., "He has been avoiding me. He has not been spending as much time with me as he did a few weeks ago."). If this is the case, then they use more omissions because they are simply thinking about the relationship. Recall from Chapter 3 Burnett's (1990) research on the gender differences in thinking about relationships and how this was more difficult for men than women. Men don't know what is going on in terms of noticing and monitoring potential relationship problems.

Discussion Questions

8.1. How often have you noticed claims of omission and commission when things were going badly" in one of your relationships? Was it difficult for you to notice what was not happening? What was the type and nature of this relationship?

8.2. Discuss each of the three explanations for using claims of omission: attributional explanation, implicit benefit-of-doubt and rules-based perspective. Can you think of examples supporting each of these explanations in a relationship that has some problems? What is the nature of these problems? Can these problems be rectified with good communication?

Applications

8.1. Ask three men and three women to generate a list of rules for a happy relationship. Code and compare the number of omissions and commissions between the genders.

8.2. Survey three men and women about how often they notice what a relational partner is not doing when there are tensions or anxieties in the relationship. For example, have they ever thought about or noticed when their partners have quit doing something that they used to do regularly (e.g., kissing goodbye, asking about events in the day, or doing surprise favors).

8.3. Interview a friend about the breakup of a recent relationship. Ask your friend to make a list of the reasons for the breakup. Code the listed reasons as omissions and commissions. Can you make any conclusions about human cognition in terms of noticing behaviors while a relationship is souring? For example, based on your friend's experience, is it more important what one and one's relational partner are not doing or what both are doing in the course of a relationship?

Note

1. Readers with a background in correlation analyses might be interested in knowing that this partial correlation is also an example of an item-total correlation, which results in inflated correlations because the component of one of the variables (total unique behaviors and inferences) is not independent of the number of commissions or omissions generated by a person. Hence, the number of commissions added to the number of omissions is equal to the total number of behaviors and inferences. The higher item-total correlation for commissions is another indication that more commissions were generated than omissions.

References

Argyle, M., & Henderson, M. (1985). The rules of relationships. In S. Duck & D. Perlman (Eds.), *Understanding personal relationships: An interdisciplinary approach* (pp. 63–84). Beverly Hills, CA: Sage.

Baxter, L. A. (1984). Trajectories of relationship disengagement. *Journal of Social and Personal Relationships, 1*, 29–48. doi:10.1177/0265407584011003

Burnett, R. (1990). Reflection in personal relationships. In R. Burnett, P. McGhee, & D. Clarke (Eds.), *Accounting for relationships: Explanation, representation and knowledge* (pp. 73–94). London: Methuen.

Cody, M. (1982). A typology of disengagement strategies and an examination of the role intimacy reactions to inequity, and behavioral problems play in strategy selection. *Communication Monographs, 49*, 148–170. doi:10.1080/03637758209376079

Cupach, C. R., & Metts, S. (1986). Accounts of relational dissolution: A comparison of marital and non-marital relationships. *Communication Monographs, 53*, 311–354. doi:10.1080/03637758609376146

Gergen, M. M., & Gergen, K. J. (1992). Attributions, accounts and close relationships: Close calls and relational resolutions. In J. H. Harvey, T. L. Orbuch, & A. L. Weber (Eds.), *Attributions, accounts, and close relationships* (pp. 269–279). New York, NY: Springer-Verlag.

Gottman, J. M. (1994). *What predicts divorce?* Hillsdale, NJ: Lawrence Erlbaum.

Grandin, T., & Barron, S. (2005). *Unwritten rules of social relationships: Decoding social mysteries through the unique perspectives of Autism.* Arlington, TX: Future Horizons.

Harvey, J. H., Orbuch, T. L., & Weber, A. L. (1992). Introduction: Convergence of the attribution and accounts concepts in the study of close relationships (pp. 1–18). New York, NY: Springer-Verlag.

Harvey, J. H., Weber, A. L., Galvin, K. S., Huszti, H. C., & Garnick, N. N. (1986). Attribution in the termination of close relationships: A special focus on the account. In R. Gilmour & S. Duck (Eds.), *Personal relationships: Vol. 4. Dissolving personal relationships* (pp. 107–126). London: Academic Press.

Hill, C. T., Rubin, Z., & Peplau, L. (1976). Breakups before marriage: The end of 103 affairs. *Journal of Social Issues, 32*, 147–168. doi:10.1111/j.1540-4560.1976.tb02485.x

Hofstede, G., Hofstede, G. J., & Minkov, M. (2010). *Cultures and organizations* (3rd ed). New York, NY: McGraw-Hill.

Honeycutt, J. M., Cantrill, J. G., & Allen, T. (1992). Memory structures for relational decay: A cognitive test of sequencing of deescalating actions and stages. *Human Communication Research, 18*, 528–562. doi:10.1111/j.1468-2958.1992.tb00571.x

Honeycutt, J. M., Woods, B., & Fontenot, K. (1993). The endorsement of communication conflict rules as a function of engagement, marriage, and marital ideology. *Journal of Social and Personal Relationships, 10*, 285–304. doi:10.1177/026540759301000208

Jones, E., & Gallois, C. (1989). Spouses' impressions of rules for communication in public and private marital conflicts. *Journal of Marriage and the Family, 51*, 957–967. doi:10.2307/353208

McBride, M., & Braithwaite, D. O. (2008). *Doing facework while managing private information: Talking with family members about romantic relationship problems.* Paper presented at the annual meeting of the International Communication Association, Montreal, Canada.

Roggensack, K. E., & Sillars, A. (2014). Agreement and understanding about honesty and deception rules in romantic relationships. *Journal of Social and Personal Relationships, 31*, 178–199. doi:10.1177/0265407513489914

Ross, L. (1977). The intuitive psychologist and his shortcomings. In L. Berkowitz (Ed.), *Advances in experimental social psychology* (pp. 173–220). New York, NY: Academic Press.

PART FOUR

Relationship Scripts in Context

Chapter 9   Online Communication and Relational Scripts

Chapter 10   Scripts for Office Romance: Approved or Forbidden?

These chapters reveal how relationships are influenced by context and explore the nuances which evolve from the conditions in which a relationship is negotiated. Almost everyone can relate anecdotes concerning online relationship experiences, but what does the research reveal? How are relationships mediated by technology constituted between partners? Chapter 9 answers these questions, delving deeply into how virtual partners negotiate their relationships. Chapter 10 offers an overview of relationships at work in discussions of voluntary relationships such as those between a mentor and protégé and involuntary liaisons that may result in sexual harassment claims.

CHAPTER NINE

Online Communication and Relational Scripts

In the information technology age, people developed scripts for meeting people online. In fact, computer-mediated communication (CMC) is so ubiquitous that it is another channel for relational development. This chapter reviews the research on online communication.

Cues-Filtered Out Theories and Computer-Mediated Communication

CMC is a format of communication facilitated by computer technologies and is defined as "synchronous or asynchronous electronic mail and computer conferencing, by which senders encode in text messages that are relayed from senders' computers to receivers" (Walther, 1992, p. 52). Traditionally, it includes the computer-mediated forms such as e-mail, chat rooms, and social networking services, but also other text-based interactions such as text-messaging. Social scientists often take a socio-psychological view when studying CMC, focusing on how humans use computers to interact with each other, form impressions, maintain relationships, as well as how CMC impacts their daily lives.

Early research studies emphasized differences between computer-mediated and face-to-face communication (e.g., Culnan & Markus, 1985; Kiesler, Siegel,

& McGuire, 1984; Siegel, Dubrovsky, Kiesler, & McGuire, 1986), suggesting that people using CMC were prevented from gaining impressions due to the lack of nonverbal cues in the medium. This difference has led some to conclude that relationship development is thwarted in CMC (Kiesler et al., 1984). This group of theories is known as cues-filtered out theories. One of the cues-filtered out theories is media richness. According to media richness theory (Daft & Lengel, 1986), face-to-face is the richest medium, richer than online communication. Rich media are those that can support a) multiple-cue systems (nonverbal and verbal), b) simultaneous sender-and-receiver exchanges, c) natural language, and d) message personalization. For example, a Facebook message cannot reproduce visual social cues such as gesture or Skype.

Due to increased use of the Internet for social purposes in the last two decades, other perspectives have emerged suggesting that people can have intimate relationships in the computer-mediated environment as users rely on alternative mechanisms to accomplish these functions (Walther, 1996). The best examples are social network sites (e.g., Facebook, Twitter, Instagram), online dating websites, and mobile dating apps (e.g., Tinder). Walther (1992) proposed social information processing theory, arguing that the need for social bonding is the same in CMC as it is in FTF communication. People can compensate for loss of nonverbal in CMC. As Tidwell and Walther (2002) explained, individuals adapt their communicative behavior in limited-cue environments, using different content and linguistic strategies (e.g., checking another person's profile page on Facebook or Tinder). Over the last decade, emoticons have been used as a nonverbal representation of emotions (Walther, 2006; Walther & D'Addario, 2001; Walther & Tidwell, 1995). In a study of the effects of emoticons on people's responses to negative feedback delivered through CMC, Wang, Zhao, Qiu, and Zhu (2014) found that "liking" emoticons significantly influence feedback acceptance when the feedback is specific.

Due to limited nonverbal and contextual cues, researchers (Sheldon & Honeycutt, 2010; Walther, 1992, 1996) have argued that self-disclosure is important for the formation of online relationships in a computer-mediated environment.

Online Relationships Development

A study by Sheldon and Honeycutt (2010) conducted to examine similarities and differences in relationship development through social network sites versus face-to-face, showed that the process of relationship development was similar in both Facebook and face-to-face relationships (Figure 9.1.)

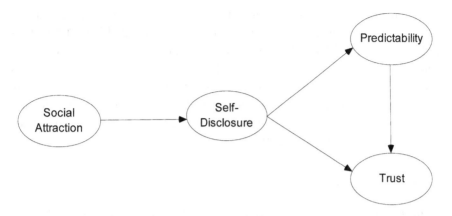

Figure 9.1. Relationship between attraction, predictability and trust in online relationships.

Self-disclosure has been viewed as central to the development and mainte-nance of close relationships. We communicate personal information only to those people whom we trust and whose behavior we can predict. Individual trust is the most influential in predicting self-disclosure, both offline and online (Sheldon & Honeycutt, 2010; Sheldon & Pecchioni, 2014). Sheldon and Pecchioni (2014) applied interpersonal communication theories to understand how people develop relationships through social media.

Uncertainty Reduction Theory

According to uncertainty reduction theory (URT, Berger & Calabrese, 1975), individuals self-disclose to those whose behavior they can predict. Although online communication can lack face-to-face characteristics, such as physical prox-imity, frequent interaction, and physical appearance, people in an online setting can still decrease their uncertainty about one another. For example, we can observe each other's behavior by looking at each other's Facebook or Instagram profiles and photos (Walther, Van Der Heide, Kim, Westerman, & Tong, 2008). This is an example of passive uncertainty strategy. We can also employ active strategy, by asking a third person about the user that they have just added as a Facebook or Instagram "friend" (Sheldon, 2015).

Antheunis, Valkenburg, and Peter (2010) examined which uncertainty reduc-tion strategies (passive, active, interactive) the social network sites users employed to gain information about persons whom they had recently met. They discovered that the passive uncertainty reduction strategy was most commonly used among the users of Hyves, a Dutch site similar to Facebook; however, the interactive strategy (in the form of self-disclosure) was the only strategy that effectively reduced the level of uncertainty. Other researchers (Parks & Floyd, 1996; Tidwell & Walther, 2002) have also argued that in dyadic CMC, participants mostly employed interactive strategies. Several studies have found that unlike other forms of CMC, social network sites encourage users to disclose a great deal of information about themselves (Antheunis et al., 2010), including private information such as hobbies, tastes in music, books, movies, relationship statuses, and sexual preferences (Gross & Acquisti, 2005).

Social Penetration Theory

Altman and Taylor (1973) conceptualized *social penetration theory* to illustrate the process of relationship bonding that moves a relationship from superficial to more intimate. Most relationships follow some particular trajectory to closeness. According to the theory, relationship development is a gradual process, while self-disclosure is at its core. Although some studies have suggested that people disclose significantly more in their Internet relationships than face to face (Parks & Floyd, 1996), recent research (e.g., Tang & Wang, 2012; Sheldon & Pecchioni, 2014) have challenged those ideas. Tang and Wang (2012) surveyed Taiwanese bloggers, exploring the topics that the bloggers disclosed on their blogs, as well as the depth and breadth of their disclosures to three target audiences (online audience, best friend, and parents). They discovered that bloggers made the deepest and widest disclosures of their thoughts, feelings, and experiences to their best friends in the real world—rather than to their parents or online audiences. Sheldon and Pecchioni (2014) also found that college students self-disclose less to their Facebook friends than to their face-to-face friends. This supports cues-filtered out theories.

Consistent with social penetration theory, progress to more and more intimate levels of disclosure is accompanied by increased attraction. Pellegrini, Hicks, and Meyers-Winton (1978) argued that the increased depth of self-disclosure is associated with the motivation to win reciprocal approval or liking. While studying users of social network sites, Antheunis et al. (2010) found that social attraction results from perceived "rewards" that can be obtained through direct interaction and self-disclosure, or from passive observations of the target person. Other researchers (e.g., Collins & Miller, 1994) have suggested that those who disclose intimate secrets tend to be more liked than those who do not. However, it is not just that we disclose to those whom we like; we tend to like them more because we have self-disclosed to them. This finding was true in both exclusive face-to-face and exclusive Facebook relationships in a study conducted by Sheldon and

Pecchioni (2014). They argued that disclosures may not have much to do with the other person, but more about the feelings that friends experience after disclosures (as humans like to talk about themselves). Talking produces a catharsis, a good feeling. People enjoy self-disclosing if they know other people are listening (Sheldon, 2015).

Furthermore, Greitemeyer and Kunz (2013) examined whether Facebook users are more likely to accept friendship requests from other Facebook users with positive (relative to negative) names and who are considered physically attractive (relative to being moderately attractive). Their results revealed that both name-valence and physical attractiveness affected friendship acceptance. People judge and behave more positively toward individuals with positive names and individuals who are physically attractive.

Hyperpersonal Perspective

Walther (1992, 1993) suggested that online relationships are just as real as other relationships, but the relational development occurs over a longer period than in FTF interactions. People are adaptable and can compensate for the decreased social context and nonverbal cues in online settings. According to Walther's hyperpersonal communication theory, CMC allows people to overcome certain limitations of FTF interactions by providing an environment where they can interact with relative anonymity and develop intimate relationships very quickly (Walther, 1996). Research has found that CMC triggers more self-disclosures than FTF communication (Jiang, Bazarova, & Hancock, 2013). Hyperpersonal perspective also suggests that individuals try to adapt to the lack of nonverbal expressive behavior by disclosing more online than they would FTF (Tidwell & Walther, 2002). In addition, CMC users have the ability to edit, delete, and rewrite messages to make themselves more desirable (Walther, 2011). The more desirable the partner is, the more editing occurs (Walther, 2007). Walther (2011) suggests that when receiving messages from others in CMC, an individual tends to exaggerate perceptions of the message sender. Therefore, in the absence of the physical and other cues that FTF interactions provide, receivers fill in the blanks with regard to missing information. This can take the form of idealization and heightened attraction and lead to behavioral confirmation (Snyder, Tanke, & Berscheid, 1977). Behavioral confirmation is a form of self-fulfilling prophecy. When individuals (as perceivers) hold expectations about other people (as targets), they can elicit from these targets behaviors that confirm their expectations, even if these expectations are not target's real characteristics. Tong and Walther (2015) found that behavioral confirmation occurs in CMC when perceivers believed that their partners had a pleasant personality and were in a good mood.

Considering that CMC allow selective self-presentation and editing under asynchronous communication conditions (Toma, Hancock, & Ellison, 2008), hyperpersonal perspective has been applied to understanding online dating. For example, studies have shown that most online daters misrepresent their age, weight, or height online (Hall, Park, Song, & Cody, 2010; Toma et al., 2008). This is now even more possible considering that Instagram and other mobile apps (e.g., BeautyCam, FaceTune) offer a number of filters that can enhance one's physical appearance.

Changing Nature of Friendships

Research from various social science disciplines provides different definitions of friendship. Hartup (1975) defined friends as those "who spontaneously seek the company of another" (p. 11). According to Wright (1984), friendship is a relationship that includes voluntary interaction.

Newer communication technologies have changed the nature of friendships, and social networking individuals have too. Not only are online social networks larger than regular social networks, but they are structurally different as they are not highly influenced by demographic factors, such as income and attractiveness (Acar, 2008). For example, an average Facebook user has several times more friends on Facebook than in real life. It is easier and less risky to accept new members online, but there is also a social desirability factor (positive feeling of online popularity) (Acar, 2008). Furthermore, social network sites scholars suggest that technological tools may assist us in maintaining friendship relationships with more individuals, especially with those whom we consider weak ties, such as colleagues or friendly acquaintances (Ellison, Steinfeld, & Lampe, 2007). Although in "real" life individuals differentiate between close friends, true friends, best friends, good friends, casual friends, work friends, social friends, and friendly acquaintances (Westmyer & Myers, 1996), on social network sites this differentiation is lost. Bryant and Marmo (2009) also reported confusion in the definition of "friend." Some people consider their casual relationships to be friendships, whereas others reserve the term friend for close relationships. Therefore, Bryant and Marmo explored which relational maintenance behaviors are performed on Facebook, and which relationship types comprise college students' Facebook "friend" lists. Their analysis revealed that Facebook "friend" lists are comprised of five distinct types of relationships: close friends, casual friends, acquaintances, romantic partners, and outsiders. Participants in their study explained that most of their offline close friends are also their Facebook friends; however, that category accounted for only a small portion of their Facebook friends. Nearly all of their participants agreed that Facebook is a useful tool to maintain long-distance close friendships. They even referred to such casual friendships as obligations. Participants also reported being friends with people on a non-voluntary basis—such as parents, uncles, grandparents, and bosses on their lists of Facebook friends. However, most participants agreed that most of their Facebook friends are neither close nor casual friends, but simple acquaintances with whom they rarely or never interact with on Facebook. Overall, Bryant and Marmo (2009) concluded that the basic close versus casual friend dichotomy does not adequately describe the diverse number of relationships represented on a person's list of Facebook friends.

Some studies on online personal relationships showed that online friendships are actually deeper and are of better quality than real-life friendships (Bruckman, 1992). In some cases, online relationships have blossomed into romance and marriage. Physical proximity is also not an issue in online relationships, as it is not possible. Rather, the frequency of contact is what is important in the formulation of online relationships (Levine, 2000). Often people feel more comfortable disclosing personal information online than face-to-face (Cooper & Sportolari, 1997). Self-disclosing through social media can have a positive impact. Olson (2012) conducted a study using both a survey and a focus group that asked participants how good they feel when they disclose on Facebook. Most participants (81%) agreed that they feel good when they self-disclose on Facebook. In addition, they said that self-disclosing on Facebook had a positive effect on one's self-esteem.

Niland, Lyons, Goodwin, and Hutton (2015) investigated how young adults in New Zealand make sense of Facebook friendships. They conducted focus groups with 26 women and 25 men aged 18–25 years. Their results showed that all participants used Facebook routinely every day to interact with their face-to-face friends—which contests the notion of friendships on SNSs as "not real." Facebook was used to enjoy friendships and to have "fun times" together. Friendships were reinforced through activities such as posting funny comments, "likes," and tags.

Long before social networking sites existed, Reisman (1981) identified three types of friendships, including the friendships of reciprocity, receptivity, and association. The friendship of reciprocity is the ideal one, characterized by loyalty, self-sacrifice, mutual affection, and generosity. It is based on equality. In the friendship of receptivity, there is an imbalance in giving and receiving. At the lowest level, the friendship of association is often described as a friendly relationship rather than a true friendship. In the majority of cases, Facebook or Instagram friendships are friendships of association. However, they are still important as they help young adults to develop a better sense of self (Bagwell, Schmidt, Newcomb, & Bukowski, 2001).

Romantic Relationships Online

With the advent of the Internet, social media, and other technologies, relationships and relationship formation have significantly changed. This is especially true in terms of finding romantic partners or "hook up" partners. In addition to traditional dating, cyber dating platforms have become common ways to meet people. Cyber dating consists of online dating websites and mobile dating applications. Online dating websites are characterized by detailed profiles and can be difficult to use due to the multitude of features and time spent creating profiles and sending e-mails (Stewart, 2015). Unlike online dating sites, mobile dating apps are accessed from mobile devices such as phones or tablets. A condensed profile is required, or there may be no profile requirement at all (Bryant & Sheldon, 2017).

Cyber dating platforms exist to aid people in finding a relationship (e.g., Bryant & Sheldon, 2017; Couch & Liamputtong, 2008; Lawson & Leck, 2006; Wang & Chang, 2010). Cyber dating users may feel more at ease talking and attempting to form connections with others behind a screen. According to social information processing theory of CMC interaction (Walther, 1992), people want to form impressions, reduce uncertainty, and develop affinity in online settings just as much as they do in offline settings. When people are denied nonverbal cues, they will communicate through private messaging, and perhaps disclose more information than they would in face-to-face interactions (Bryant & Sheldon, 2017). In addition, other reasons for using cyber dating platforms include sexual relations ("hooking up") without the emotional attachment (Bryant & Sheldon, 2017; Couch & Liamputtong, 2008). Cyber dating platforms may allow one to be more forthright about wanting to "hook up" than he or she might be in person. The shallow quality of communication that takes place on cyber dating may be appealing to those who are motivated to "hook up," because they are not interested in an emotional or personal connection. In addition, cyber dating platforms typically allow people a greater chance of finding a person to "hook up" with than they might find in their immediate environment. Bryant and Sheldon (2017) found that the users of mobile apps were more interested in hooking up than the users of online dating websites. The users of dating websites, however, were more interested in creating long-term relationships than the users of mobile apps.

Dating sites typically involve thorough profiles in which people reveal personal information about themselves (Stewart, 2015). Revealing such information gives users a basis for conversation and may aid their ability to form deep connections with others. Reading through cyber dating profiles is an example of a passive uncertainty reduction strategy, meaning that users obtain information about others in an indirect, unobtrusive manner. In addition to profiles, many online dating websites also allow users to search for specific criteria of potential partners. This option eliminates the action of scrolling through various profiles of people in whom users have no interest. Those that are serious about relationships are likely to use these features as they are looking for certain characteristics in a long-term partner (Bryant & Sheldon, 2017).

Since 2010, niche dating sites have become popular in the online dating industry. Those include sites for vegetarians (veggiedate.org), redheads (e.g., DateGinger.com), gay men (e.g., Grindr), seniors (e.g., SeniorPeopleMeet.com, SilverSingles.com, OurTime.com), military (MilitaryCoupid.com). Even mainstream dating services offer specialized sections for various subgroups of users, in order to attract advertising dollars.

Tinder

In September 2012, Sean Rad and Justin Mateen created a mobile matchmaking app at the University of Southern California. Tinder is a location-based dating, social discovery app (using Facebook) that facilitates communication between mutually interested people, allowing matched users to chat. By using Facebook, Tinder is able to build profiles with previously uploaded pictures on the users' Facebook pages. Basic information is gathered from the profiles and the users' social graph is analyzed. Users are most likely to be matched based on geographical location, mutual friends, and common interests. Based on the results, users are able to anonymously like one another by swiping right or pass by swiping left. If two users like each other, it becomes a "match" and then they are able to communicate within the messaging system in the app. In 2014, Tinder reported having upwards of fifty million users where on average, people log into the application eleven times a day. Women spend as much as 8.5 minutes swiping left and right during a single session; men spend 7.2 minutes. All of this can add up to ninety minutes each day (Bilton, 2014). Since the launch of the app back in 2012, Tinder has become one of the most popular mobile dating apps, particularly among adults ages 18–24 years old (Escobar, 2014). In fact, this age group makes up roughly 51% of the people who use Tinder. With location-based technology, it has become easier than ever to connect with people within the user's area.

Who Forms Online Relationships?

Parks and Floyd (1996) also asked about who forms online relationships. They compared people who did and did not have an online personal relationship in terms of their demographic characteristics and patterns of Internet involvement. They found that women were significantly more likely than men to have formed a personal relationship online. Age and marital status were not related to the likelihood of developing a personal relationship online.

Recently, efforts were made to study how teens use social network sites, such as Instagram. Sheldon and Newman (2016) found that excessive reassurance-seeking can explain why teens use Instagram to become popular, to escape from reality, and for creative purposes. Individuals who suffer from excessive reassurance-seeking are insecure and needy and are overly dependent on others (Joiner, 1999). Because they are insecure, they might use Instagram to get positive feedback—"likes"—to validate their sense of self. Reassurance-seeking is a form of depression-related social behavior (Joiner & Metalsky, 2001). In addition, Barker (2009) and Bonetti, Campbell, and Gilmore (2010) found that social network sites may be utilized as a form of social compensation for those youth who are feeling disconnected from their peer group. Teens with excessive reassurance-seeking may thus use Instagram to cope with those shortcomings. Blomfield Neira and Barber (2014) also discovered that youth with lower self-esteem and a greater depressed mood are more invested in their social network sites than their peers. Therefore, social network sites may be providing them with more opportunities to practice social skills.

Interpersonal rejection is another indicator of depression among teens. Sheldon and Newman (2016) found that it was positively related to the escapism motive for Instagram use, explaining 23% of variance. Teens who perceive that nobody loves them and that they cannot be as good as other kids use Instagram for one purpose: to escape from reality and to avoid loneliness. While social compensation or the "poor-gets-richer" hypothesis did not receive much support among social media scholars, Sheldon (2008) found that those individuals who fear anxiety in face-to-face communication use Facebook more to pass time and to avoid feelings of loneliness than other respondents who feel less anxious in face-to-face interactions.

Ward and Tracey (2004) examined the relations between shyness and online and face-to-face relational involvement. One of the possibilities, they said, is that people who get involved in online relationships are those with difficulties in face-to-face communication. Online, they can communicate with others anonymously, at their own pace. Online relationships provide minimized social risk, as one does not have to meet other participants face-to-face (Curtis, 1997). McKenna (1998) found that socially anxious individuals were more likely to form relationships online. Similarly, Ma and Leung (2005) concluded that people who are less willing to communicate in real life also tend to be less open online. Looking at whether anxiety or loneliness are indicators of who is more likely to form an online relationship, Bonebrake (2002) found that the level of loneliness was not a predictor of forming online relationships. Rather, the time was crucial. The more time people spend online communicating with one person, the more new relationships they are likely to form (Bonebrake, 2002). Therefore, she concludes that differences do not exist between Internet users who do and do not form new relationships online.

Ward and Tracey (2004) also found that individuals involved in online relationships score higher on shyness than those not involved in these relationships. However, they discovered that personality variables were less influential in online relationships than the amount of time spent online in general. Their results were consistent with Parks and Floyd (1996) who suggested that the more time people spent online, the more involved they become in online relationships. Sheldon (2013) found that shy individuals disclose more to their face-to-face friends (and more often) than to their Facebook friends. When compared to individuals who are less shy, they disclose less than them to both their face-to-face and Facebook friends. One of the possible reasons why shy individuals do not use Facebook to compensate for the lack of face-to-face interactions might be because there is opportunity to remain anonymous in a social network environment. Ryan and Xenos (2011) also suggested that people with smaller social networks are less motivated to use a website like Facebook.

Generally, two opposing hypotheses have been proposed to explain the relationship between loneliness and Internet use: excessive Internet use causes loneliness vs. lonely individuals who are more likely to use the Internet excessively. Morahan-Martin and Schumacher (2003) concluded that neither of the hypotheses about the direction of a relationship between loneliness and Internet use is sufficient. Instead, the relationship may be bi-directional (p. 669). The first hypothesis suggests that excessive use of the Internet isolates individuals from the real world and deprives them of the sense of belonging and connection with the real world (p. 660). Those individuals often invest in online relationships at the expense of real life relationships. HomeNet study by Kraut et al. (1998) documented increases in loneliness resulting from Internet use.

The second hypothesis claims that lonely people were drawn to the Internet more than non-lonely people. "Loneliness occurs when a person's network of social relationships is smaller or less satisfying than the person desired" (Peplau, Russell, & Heim, 1979, p. 55). Lonely people have poor social skills (Vitkus & Horowitz, 1987), have difficulty making friends, initiating social activity, and participating in groups (Horowitz & de Sales French, 1979), are less likely to be intimate and self-disclose (Berg & Peplau, 1982), and have low self-esteem (Burger, 1997). The Internet provides an ideal social environment for lonely people. They can choose with whom and when to communicate and have time to compose messages (Morahan-Martin & Schumacher, 2003, p. 662). As Joinson (1998) claims, online anonymity and the lack of face-to-face contact promote disinhibition, "an apparent reduction in concerns for self-presentation and the judgment of others" (p. 44). This can lead lonely individuals to self-present more idealized versions of self online.

Peter, Valkenburg, and Schouten (2005) studied how introversion/extraversion, online self-disclosure, the motive for social compensation, and the frequency of online communication influence the formation of adolescent friendships. Introversion is a person's tendency to prefer his or her own company to large social events. Extroversion is a person's inclination to seek company and social interaction (Hamburger & Ben-Artzi, 2000).

Scholars came up with two different hypotheses. The rich-get-richer hypothesis states that the Internet primarily benefits extraverted individuals (Kraut et al., 2002). The social compensation hypothesis, by contrast, proposes that the Internet benefits introverts more (McKenna & Bargh, 2000). The Kraut et al. (2002) findings supported the rich-get-richer hypothesis, while Gross, Juvonen, and Gable (2002) and McKenna et al. (2002) supported the social compensation hypothesis. Studies showed that the Internet's anonymity and reduced cues might stimulate online self-disclosure, because there is no fear of being ridiculed or rejected (Derlega, Metts, Petronio, & Margulis, 1993). This may be particularly appealing to introverts when trying to open up. McKenna et al. (2002) found that introverts were more likely to present their true selves online than extraverts. Lonely people perceived the anonymity of the Internet as liberating (Morahan-Martin & Schumacher, 2003). On the other hand, Peter et al. (2005) found that introversion resulted in less rather than more frequent online communication. In contrast to what both the rich-get-richer and social compensation hypotheses propose, adolescents' degree of introversion (or extroversion) did not directly influence whether they formed online friendships. Rather, introversion (or extroversion) affected online self-disclosure, the frequency of online communication, and the social compensation motive.

Extraverted adolescents self-disclosed and communicated online more often. The Peter et al. (2005) model showed that the possibility to self-disclose in a more anonymous setting did not automatically lead to increased online self-disclosure among introverted adolescents. Introversion had a negative effect on both online self-disclosure and the frequency of online communication. Bryant and Sheldon (2017) found that those with high self-esteem are less motivated to use cyber dating for "hook up" reasons. This idea is plausible as those with a high self-esteem might view themselves too highly to engage in a "one-night stand" or the occasional "hook up." Another study (Paul, McManus, & Hayes, 2000) found that individuals that "hook up" generally have lower self-esteem than those who do not. In relation to age and potential cyber dating motives, older cyber dating users are more likely to use these platforms for relationship reasons and less likely to use them for fun (Bryant & Sheldon, 2017). Single people in their 30s concentrate more on marriage, finding "The One," and starting a family (Taylor, 2015). Conversely, singles in their 20s are less concerned with long-term commitments, and are more interested in finding someone fun (Taylor, 2015). Men are also more motivated to use cyber dating to "hook up," whereas women are more influenced by relationship aspects. These findings match traditional expectations for what men and women desire in terms of romantic relationships and sex (Bryant & Sheldon, 2017).

Attitudes Toward Online Relationships

Literature provides various study results on attitudes toward online relationships. Smith and Duggan (2013) studied cyber dating and found that attitudes toward online dating have changed in the last decade. Results that the authors reported from a survey on Americans' use of the Internet indicate that 59% of Internet users agree that "online dating is a good way to meet people," as opposed to only 44% in 2005 (Smith & Duggan, 2013, p. 3). Other findings show that 53% of people who use the Internet agree that "online dating allows people to find a better match for themselves," compared to 47% in 2005. Other research also showed that there is a positive relationship between those with an affinity for the Internet and the perception of online romantic relationships (Anderson, 2005). Thus, those who enjoy using the Internet are more open to the idea that interpersonal relationships can be formed through online means. However, those with more conventional romantic beliefs are less in favor of online relationships (Anderson, 2005).

Bryant and Sheldon (2017) also found that the most prevalent attitude about cyber dating platforms was the "socially acceptable" attitude. It suggests that most people view cyber dating as something that is permissible. This is likely due to the familiarity with technology that most people have today. For those with cyber dating experience, a socially acceptable attitude is plausible as they are surrounded by other cyber daters on the platforms that they use (Bryant & Sheldon, 2017).

Sheldon (2016) conducted a study with students and faculty from across the United States to investigate factors that influence professors' and students' intentions to add each other as friends on Facebook. The results of the study indicated a change in attitude toward adding students as Facebook friends, as almost 50% of surveyed faculty members said that they are currently a Facebook friend with one or more students. This number was much higher than the number reported in a 2010 study of faculty members' friendships with students at Ohio colleges of pharmacy (Metzger, Finley, Ulbrich, & McAuley, 2010). In addition, most faculty said that they add students because they feel an obligation to do so or because they want to track alumni. Among students, however, the reasons to add professors as Facebook friends were more personal. Most students said that they wanted to get to know the teacher better. DiVerniero and Hosek (2011) also found that having access to instructors' online profiles allows students to see them as "human beings" and "friends."

Summary

Online relationships have similarities and differences with face-to-face relationships. The motivations for forming online relationships mirror the human need for inclusion, companionship, and affection. More women have online friends than men. Also, it appears that extraverts have more friends in real life and online even though introverts spend more time online. In recent CMC scholarship, this blurring and traversing of boundaries has been debated and misunderstood as a negative phenomenon, concentrating on what CMC does not offer, rather than what it does—and rather than looking at the positive possibilities and outcomes. In addition, the definition of Internet usage is too broad, and research should distinguish Internet applications (e.g., e-mail vs. online chat), functions, or settings.

Morahan-Martin and Schumacher (2003) and Sheldon (2013) suggested investigating what the long-term effect of Internet use is for those who are lonely. In addition, the question of cause and effect in terms of loneliness and Internet use remain unresolved. Researchers have suggested conducting longitudinal studies. Furthermore, research that looks at the nature and quality of online relationships—and that compares online relationships with face-to-face relationships among youth—is greatly needed.

Discussion Questions

9.1. What are the advantages and disadvantages of online, virtual relationships compared to face-to-face relationships?

9.2. Some research has suggested that extraverted individuals have more Facebook friends than introverted individuals even though the introverts spend more time using the internet. Do you think this is true?

9.3. Do you know someone who has social media addiction? How is this person's life affected?

9.4. Should parents' control the accessibility of internet websites for children under the age of 12? Why or why not?

9.5. Have you ever used a "fake" or deceptive identity or internet site? How prevalent is deception on the internet based on your experiences?

Application

9.1. Interview 6 people on their views of Face-to-Face communication versus CMC. Which method of communication do they prefer, and why?

References

Acar, A. (2008). Antecedents and consequences of online social networking behavior: The case of Facebook. *Journal of Website Promotion, 3*, 62–83. doi:10.1080/15533610802052654

Altman, I., & Taylor, D. (1973). *Social penetration: The development of interpersonal relationships.* New York, NY: Holt, Rinehart, Winston.

Anderson, T. L. (2005). Relationships among internet attitudes, internet use, romantic beliefs, and perceptions of online romantic relationships. *CyberPsychology & Behavior, 8*, 521–531. doi:10.1089/cpb.2005.8.521

Antheunis, M. L., Valkenburg, P. M., & Peter, J. (2010). Getting acquainted through social network sites: Testing a model of online uncertainty reduction and social attraction. *Computers in Human Behavior, 26*, 100–109. doi:10.1016/j.chb.2009.07.005

Bagwell, C. L., Schmidt, M. E., Newcomb, A. F., & Bukowski, W. M. (2001). Friendship and peer rejection as predictors of adult adjustment. *New Directions for Child and Adolescent Development, 91*, 25–49. doi:10.1002/cd.4

Barker, V. (2009). Older adolescents' motivations for social network site use: The influence of gender, group identity, and collective self-esteem. *Cyberpsychology & Behavior, 12*, 209–213. doi:10.1089/cpb.2008.0228.

Berg, J., & Peplau, L. (1982). Loneliness: The relationship of self-disclosure and androgyny. *Personality and Social Psychology Bulletin, 8*, 624–630. doi:10.1177/0146167282084004

Berger, C. R., & Calabrese, R. J. (1975). Some explorations in initial interaction and beyond: Toward a developmental theory of interpersonal communication. *Human Communication Research, 1*, 99–112. doi:10.1111/j.1468-2958.1975.tb00258.x

Bilton, N. (2014). *Tinder, the fast-growing dating app, taps an age-Old Truth*. Retrieved 2016, February 12, from http://www.nytimes.com/2014/10/30/fashion/tinder-the-fast-growing-dating-app-taps-an-age-old-truth.html?_r=0

Blomfield Neira, C. J., & Barber, B. L. (2014). Social networking site use: Linked to adolescents' social self-concept, self-esteem, and depressed mood. *Australian Journal of Psychology, 66*(1), 56–64. doi:10.1111/ajpy.12034

Bonebrake, K. (2002). College students' Internet use, relationship formation, and personality correlates. *CyberPsychology & Behavior, 5*(6), 551–557. doi:10.1089/109493102321018196

Bonetti, L., Campbell, M. A., & Gilmore, L. (2010). The relationship of loneliness and social anxiety with children's and adolescents' online communication. *Cyberpsychology, Behavior, and Social Networking, 13,* 279–285. doi:10.1089/cyber.2009.0215.

Bruckman, A. (1992). *Identity workshop: Emergent social and psychological phenomena in text-based virtual reality.* Unpublished manuscript, M.I.T. Media Laboratory, Cambridge, MA. Available via anonymous ftp from media.mit.edu in pub/MediaMOO/Papers/identity-workshop

Bryant, E. M., & Marmo, J. (2009). *Relational maintenance strategies on Facebook.* Paper presented at the annual meeting of the National Communication Association conference in Chicago, IL.

Bryant, K., & Sheldon, P. (2017, in press). Cyber dating in the age of mobile apps: Understanding motives, attitudes, and personality of users. *American Communication Journal.*

Burger, J. (1997). *Personality* (4th ed.). Pacific Grove, CA: Brooks/Cole.

Collins, N. L., & Miller, L. C. (1994). Self-disclosure and liking: A meta-analytic review. *Psychological Bulletin, 116,* 457–475. doi:10.1037/0033-2909.116.3.457

Cooper, A., & Sportolari, L. (1997). Romance in cyberspace: Understanding online attraction. *Journal of Sex Education and Therapy, 22,* 7–14.

Couch, D., & Liamputtong, P. (2008). Online dating and mating: The use of internet to meet sexual partners. *Qualitative Health Research, 18,* 268–279. doi:10.1177/1049732307312832

Culnan, M. J., & Markus, M. L. (1985). Information technologies. In: F. Jablin, L. L. Putnam, K. Roberts, & L. Porter (Eds.), *Handbook of organizational communication* (pp. 420–443). Newbury Park, CA: Sage.

Curtis, P. (1997). Mudding: Social phenomena in text-based virtual realities. In S. Kiesler (Ed.), *Culture of the Internet* (pp. 121–142). Mahwah, NJ: Erlbaum.

Daft, R. L., & Lengel, R. H. (1986). Organizational information requirements, media richness and structural design. *Management Science, 32*(5), 554–571.

Derlega, V. L., Metts, S., Petronio, S., & Margulis, S. T. (1993). *Self disclosure.* London: Sage.

DiVerniero, R. A., & Hosek, A. M. (2011). Students' perceptions and communicative management of instructors' online self-disclosure. *Communication Quarterly, 59,* 428–449. doi:10.1080/01463373.2011.597275

Ellison, N. B., Steinfield, C., & Lampe, C. (2007). The benefits of Facebook "friends:" Social capital and college students' use of online social network sites. *Journal of Computer-Mediated Communication, 12,* 1143–1168. doi:10.1111/j.1083-6101.2007.00367.x

Escobar, S. (2014, April 21). *Swipe left: This age group is taking over Tinder*. Retrieved from http://www.yourtango.com/2014213884/sex-dating-age-group-using-hookup-tinder-app

Greitemeyer, T., & Kunz, I. (2013). Name-valence and physical attractiveness in Facebook: Their compensatory effects on friendship acceptance. *Journal of Social Psychology, 153*, 257–260. doi:10.1080/00224545.2012.741629

Gross, E. F., Juvonen, J., & Gable, S. L. (2002). Internet use and well-being in adolescence. *Journal of Social Issues, 58*, 75–90. doi:10.1111/1540-4560.00249

Gross, R., & Acquisti, A. (2005). Information revelation and privacy in online social networks (The Facebook case). *ACM workshop on privacy in the electronic society* (pp. 71–80). Alexandria, VA. doi:10.1145/1102199.1102214

Hall, J. A., Park, N., Song, H., & Cody, M. J. (2010). Strategic misrepresentation in online dating: The effects of gender, self-monitoring, and personality traits. *Journal of Social and Personal Relationships, 27*, 117–135. doi:10.1177/0265407509349633

Hamburger, Y. A., & Ben-Artzi, E. (2000). The relationship between extraversion and neuroticism and the different uses of the Internet. *Computers in Human Behavior, 16*, 441–449. doi:10.1016/S0747-5632(00)00017-0

Hartup, W. W. (1975). The origins of friendship. In M. Lewis & L. A. Rosenblum (Eds.), *Friendship and peer relations* (pp. 11–26). New York, NY: Wiley.

Horowitz, L., & de Sales French, R. (1979). Interpersonal problems of people who describe themselves as lonely. *Journal of Consulting and Clinical Psychology, 47*, 762–764. doi:10.1037/0022-006X.47.4.762

Jiang, L. C., Bazarova, N. N., & Hancock, J. T. (2013). From perception to behavior: Disclosure reciprocity and the intensification of intimacy in computer-mediated communication. *Communication Research, 40*, 125–143. doi:10.1177/0093650211405313

Joiner, T. E., Jr. (1999). A test of the interpersonal theory of depression in youth psychiatric inpatients. *Journal of Abnormal Child Psychology, 27*, 77–85. doi:10.1023/A:1022666424731

Joiner, T. E., Jr., & Metalsky, G. I. (2001). Excessive reassurance seeking: Delineating a risk factor involved in the development of depressive symptoms. *Psychological Science, 5*, 371–378. doi: 10.1111/1467-9280.00369

Joinson, A. (1998). Causes and implications of disinhibited behavior on the Internet. In J. Gackenbach (Ed.), *Psychology and the Internet* (pp. 43–60). San Diego, CA: Academic Press.

Kiesler, S., Siegel, J., & McGuire, T. W. (1984). Social psychological aspects of computer-mediated communication. *American Psychologist, 39*, 1123–1134. doi:10.1037/0003-066X.39.10.1123

Kraut, R., Kiesler, S., Boneva, B., Cummings, J., Helgeson, V., Crawford, A. (2002). Internet paradox revisited. *Journal of Social Issues, 58*, 49–74. doi:10.1111/1540-4560.00248

Kraut, R., Patterson, M., Lundmark, V., Kiesler, S., Mukopadhyay, T., & Scherlis, W. (1998). Internet paradox: A social technology that reduces social involvement and psychological well-being? *American Psychologist, 53*, 1017–1031. doi:10.1037/0003-066X.53.9.1017

Lawson, H., & Leck, K. (2006). Dynamics of internet dating. *Social Science Computer Review, 24*, 189–208. doi:10.1177/0894439305283402

Levine, D. (2000). Virtual attraction: What rocks your boat. *CyberPsychology & Behavior, 3*, 565–573. doi:10.1089/109493100420179

Ma, M., & Leung, L. (2005). Unwillingness-to-communicate, perceptions of the Internet and self-disclosure in ICQ. *Telematics and Informatics, 23*, 22–37. doi:10.1016/j.tele.2005.01.001

McKenna, K. (1998). *The computers that bind: Relationship formation on the Internet.* Unpublished doctoral dissertation, Ohio University, Athens, OH.

McKenna, K., & Bargh, J. (2000). Plan 9 from cyberspace: The implications of the Internet for personality and social psychology. *Personality and Social Psychology Review, 4,* 57–75. doi:10.1207/S15327957PSPR0401_6

McKenna, K. Y. A, Green, A. S., & Gleason, M. E. J. (2002). Relationship formation on the Internet: What's the big attraction? *Journal of Social Issues,* 58, 9–31. doi:10.1111/1540-4560.00246

Metzger, A. H., Finley, K. N., Ulbrich, T. R., & McAuley, J. W. (2010). Pharmacy faculty members' perspectives on the student/faculty relationship in online social networks. *American Journal of Pharmaceutical Education, 74*(10), 188.

Morahan-Martin, J., & Schumacher, P. (2003). Loneliness and social uses of the Internet. *Computers in Human Behavior, 19,* 659–671. doi: 10.1016/S0747-5632(03)00040-2

Niland, P., Lyons, A. C., Goodwin, I., & Hutton, F. (2015). Friendship work on Facebook: Young adults' understandings and practices of friendship. *Journal of Community & Applied Social Psychology, 25,* 123–137. doi:10.1002/casp.2201

Olson, A. M. (2012). *Facebook and social penetration theory.* Master's thesis, Gonzaga University, Spokane, WA.

Parks, M. R., & Floyd, K. (1996). Making friends in cyberspace. *Journal of Communication, 46,* 1–17. doi:10.1111/j.1083-6101.1996.tb00176.x

Paul, E. L., McManus, B., & Hayes, A. (2000). "Hookups": Characteristics and correlates of college students' spontaneous and anonymous sexual experiences. *Journal of Sex Research, 37,* 76–88. doi:10.1080/00224490009552023

Pellegrini, R. J., Hicks, R. A., & Meyers-Winton, S. (1978). Effects of simulated approval-seeking and avoiding on self-disclosure, self-presentation, and interpersonal attraction. *Journal of Psychology, 98,* 231–241. doi:10.1080/00223980.1978.9915966

Peplau, L. A., Russell, D., & Heim, M. (1979). The experience of loneliness. In I. Frieze, D. Bar-Tel, & J. Carroll (Eds.), *New approaches to social problems* (pp. 53–78). San Francisco, CA: Jossey-Bass.

Peter, J., Valkenburg, P. M., & Schouten, A. P. (2005). Developing a model of adolescent friendship formation on the Internet. *CyberPsychology & Behavior, 8,* 423–430. doi:10.1089/cpb.2005.8.423

Reisman, J. M. (1981). Adult friendship. In S. Duck & R. Gilmour (Eds.), *Personal relationships. 2: Developing personal relationships* (pp. 205–230). New York, NY: Academic Press.

Ryan, T., & Xenos, S. (2011). Who uses Facebook? An investigation into the relationship between the Big Five, shyness, loneliness, and Facebook usage. *Computers in Human Behavior, 27,* 1658–1664. doi:10.1016/j.chb.2011.02.004

Sheldon, P. (2008). The relationship between unwillingness to communicate and students' Facebook use. *Journal of Media Psychology: Theories, Methods, and Applications, 20,* 67–75. doi:10.1027/1864-1105.20.2.6

Sheldon, P. (2013). Voices that cannot be heard: Can shyness explain how we communicate on Facebook versus face-to-face? *Computers in Human Behavior, 29*, 1402–1407. doi:10.1016/j.chb.2013.01.016

Sheldon, P. (2015). *Social media: Principles and applications.* Lanham, MD: Lexington Books.

Sheldon, P. (2016). Facebook friend request: Applying the theory of reasoned action to student-teacher relationships on Facebook. *Journal of Broadcasting and Electronic Media, 60,* 269–285. doi:10.1080/08838151.2016.1164167

Sheldon, P., & Honeycutt, J. (2010, November). *Self-disclosure between Facebook friends and face-to-face friends: Similarities and differences.* Paper presented at the annual meeting of the National Communication Association, San Francisco, CA.

Sheldon, P., & Newman, M. (2016). *Instagram and American teens: Understanding motives for its use and relationship to depression and narcissism.* Presented at the National Communication Association conference in Philadelphia, PA.

Sheldon, P., & Pecchioni, L. (2014). Comparing relationships between self-disclosure, liking and trust in exclusive Facebook and exclusive face-to-face relationships. *American Communication Journal, 16*(2). Retrieved from https://www.dropbox.com/s/xnqyywo3z1zbxzm/ACJ%20 2014-025_Pavica.pdf?dl=0

Siegel, J., Dubrovsky, V., Kiesler, S., & McGuire, T. W. (1986). Group processes in computer-mediated communication. *Organizational Behavior and Human Decision Processes, 37,* 157–187. doi:10.1016/0749-5978(86)90050-6

Smith, A., & Duggan, M. (2013, October 21). Online dating & relationships. *Pew Research Center.* Retrieved from http://www.pewinternet.org/files/old-media//Files/Reports/2013/PIP_Online%20Dating%202013.pdf

Snyder, M., Tanke, E. D., & Berscheid, E. (1977). Social perception and interpersonal behavior: On the self-fulfilling nature of social stereotypes. *Journal of Personality and Social Psychology, 35,* 656–666. doi:10.1037/0022-3514.35.9.656

Stewart, G. (2015). Dating apps vs dating sites: 10 questions to ask yourself. *DatingAdvice.com.* Retrieved from http://www.datingadvice.com/online-dating/dating-apps-vs-dating-sites

Tang, J., & Wang, C. (2012). Self-disclosure among bloggers: Re-examination of social penetration theory. *Cyberpsychology, Behavior, and Social Networking, 15,* 245–250. doi:10.1089/cyber.2011.0403

Taylor, J. (2015). Find love at any age. *match.com.* Retrieved from http://www.match.com/magazine/article/5425/Dating-At-20-30-40-50-And-60/

Tidwell, L. C., & Walther, J. B. (2002). Computer-mediated effects on disclosure, impressions, and interpersonal evaluations: Getting to know one another a bit at a time. *Human Communication Research, 28,* 317–348. doi:10.1111/j.1468-2958.2002.tb00811.x

Toma, C. L., Hancock, J. T., & Ellison, N. B. (2008). Separating fact from fiction: An examination of deceptive self-presentation in online dating profiles. *Personality and Social Psychology Bulletin, 34,* 1023–1036. doi:10.1177/0146167208318067

Tong, S. T., & Walther, J. B. (2015). The confirmation and disconfirmation of expectancies in computer-mediated communication. *Communication Research, 42,* 186–212. doi:10.1177/0093650212466257

Vitkus, J., & Horowitz, L. (1987). Poor social performance of lonely people: Lacking a skill or adopting a role? *Journal of Personality and Social Psychology, 52,* 1266–1273.

Walther, J. B. (1992). Interpersonal effects in computer-mediated interaction: A relational perspective. *Communication Research, 19,* 52–90. doi:10.1177/009365092019001003

Walther, J. B. (1993). Impression development in computer-mediated interaction. *Western Journal of Communication, 57,* 381–398. doi:10.1080/10570319309374463

Walther, J. B. (1996). Computer-mediated communication: Impersonal, interpersonal, and hyperpersonal interaction. *Communication Research, 23,* 3–43. doi:10.1177/009365096023001001

Walther, J. B. (2006). Nonverbal dynamics in computer-mediated communication, or :(and the net :('s with you, :) and you :) alone. In V. Manusov & M. L. Patterson (Eds.), *The Sage handbook of nonverbal communication* (pp. 461–479). Thousand Oaks, CA: Sage Publications, Inc.

Walther, J. B. (2007). Selective self-presentation in computer-mediated communication: Hyperpersonal dimensions of technology, language, and cognition. *Computers in Human Behavior, 23,* 2538–2557. doi:10.1016/j.chb.2006.05.002

Walther, J. B. (2011). Theories of computer-mediated communication and interpersonal relations. In M. L. Knapp & J. A. Daly (Eds.), *The Sage handbook of interpersonal communication* (4th ed., pp. 443–479). Thousand Oaks, CA: Sage.

Walther, J. B., & D'Addario, K. P. (2001). The impacts of emoticons on message interpretation in computer–mediated communication. *Social Science Computer Review, 19,* 324–348. doi: 10.1177/089443930101900307

Walther, J. B., & Tidwell, L. C. (1995). Nonverbal cues in computer-mediated communication, and the effect of chronemics on relational communication. *Journal of Organizational Computing, 5,* 355–378. doi:10.1080/10919399509540258

Walther, J., Van Der Heide, B., Kim, S., Westerman, D., & Tong, S. T. (2008). The role of friends' appearance and behavior on evaluations of individuals on Facebook: Are we known by the company we keep? *Human Communication Research, 34,* 28–49. doi:10.1111/j.1468-2958.2007.00312.x

Wang, C., & Chang, Y. (2010). Cyber relationship motives: Scale development and validation. *Social Behavior & Personality: An International Journal, 38,* 289–300. doi:10.2224/sbp.2010.38.3.289

Wang, W., Zhao, Y., Qiu, L., & Zhu, Y. (2014). Effects of emoticons on the acceptance of negative feedback in computer-mediated communication. *Journal of the Association for Information Systems, 15,* 454–483.

Ward, C. C., & Tracey, T. J. G. (2004). Relation of shyness with aspects of online relationship involvement. *Journal of Social and Personal Relationships, 21*(5), 611–623. doi:10.1177/0265407504045890

Westmyer, S. A., & Myers, K. A. (1996). Communication skills and social support messages across friendship levels. *Communication Research Reports, 13,* 191–197. doi:10.1080/08824099609362086

Wright, P. H. (1984). Self-referent motivation and the intrinsic quality of friendship. *Journal of Social and Personal Relationships, 1,* 115–130. doi:10.1177/0265407584011007

Scripts for Office Romance

Approved or Forbidden?

Consider the following story:

> A long workday was ending for two women who crossed paths in the restroom. They both stopped at the basin to wash their hands when the dialogue began. The administrative assistant gave the other woman an accusing look in the mirror, "Everyone in the company knows what you have been doing!" She began angrily. Her puzzled conversational partner replied, "Knows what?"
>
> The conversation initiator continued, "Everyone knows about you and your supervising partner, Chris!" "Everyone knows about Chris and me concerning what?"
>
> "Everyone knows that Chris and you are having an affair. Everyone at work is really angry with you, especially *your* administrative assistant, because Chris' home partner is expecting a baby from in vitro fertilization! How could you do this! Everyone knows you've slept your way to the top!"
>
> The puzzled recipient of these remarks reflected a moment and replied, "Well, I'm not having an affair with Chris and I wouldn't ever sleep my way to the top, but if ever I were to do so it would have to be for a better job than this one!"

This encounter is true; although the names have been changed. The office administrator was the recipient of the totally unwarranted gossip in the early stages of her professional career, accusations that while untrue, contributed to mistrust and ultimately diminished the quality and quantity of work within the division of this organization. This brief encounter demonstrates the pitfalls inherent in workplace relationships, real or imagined. This chapter will examine the scripts elicited in workplace relationships that transcend hierarchy and status.

Workplace romantic relationships appear to be ubiquitous and on the increase.

A study from CareerBuilder revealed that 37% of employees have dated a colleague at one point or another in their career and while most of those relationships eventually come to an end, some result in a sustained long-term relationship such that 33% ended in marriage (retrieved from http://www.businessnewsdaily.com/7764-co-workers-dating.html). Conversely, 5% of workers who have been romantically involved with a coworker ended up not only with a broken heart, but also a new job, because they left their employer after the relationship went south. Rabin-Margalioth (2006) writes, "As many Americans are getting married at an older age and are working longer hours in less sex-segregated work environments, it is inevitable that some workplace interaction will go beyond the purely professional" (p. 237).

Mainiero (1986) defines organizational romances as relationships where two individuals employed by an organization manifest a physical attraction and desire which finds expression in intimacy and/or sexual contact. In addition, she suggests that the awareness of a third party is important, a view shared by Quinn (1977), a pioneer in the field of romantic relationships in organizations, who identified perceptions by coworkers as important to the manner in which the workplace relationship is constituted: "A relationship between two members of the same organization 'perceived by a third party' as characterized by sexual attraction" (p. 30). These definitions suggest three script components inherent in workplace relationships: (1) initial attraction (2) action(s) based on the attraction (3) the action(s) are perceived by another (others). While the overwhelming majority of research focuses on ongoing relationships, some of these encounters between office workers may simply be categorized as "friends with benefits" (Eisenberg, Ackard, Resnick, & Neumark-Sztainer, 2009).

While a relationship might exist without being perceived by others, this is rare in office romances. The third component to this definition becomes the most problematic aspect of romantic relationships at work as discussed by Gomes, Owens, and Morgan (2006) who emphasizes that when third parties become aware of romantic relationships in organizations, these relationships inherently become riskier. While individuals who enter into romantic liaisons attempt to keep their relationship from the notice of coworkers, they are not successful (Anderson & Hunsaker, 1985; Quinn, 1977). It appears coworkers are attuned to violations of workplace norms that signal to them the possibility of a budding romantic relationship (Mainiero, 1986). Even if the partners achieve success in their quest to maintain secrecy, they may experience negative physical and psychological outcomes including diminished self-esteem and increased health problems (Lehmiller, 2009).

In some cases, one of the partners in this relationship may provide hints to coworkers. Quinn (1977) references an occasion where a married male coworker involved in a romantic liaison "who was described as being proud of several earlier conquests" (p. 38) asked a female member of his work group for assistance in selecting woman's apparel. The coworker to whom the request was directed readily agreed, under the impression it was for the man's wife. She was quite surprised to note the dress she had selected being worn by another coworker later that week!

Based on a number of interviews and narratives, Quinn (1977) developed typologies of office romances over 30 years ago that continue to have explanatory powers concerning workplace liaisons. This typology includes factors relating to the initial formation of the relationship, including proximity, work requirements, and contact; motivation for engaging in the relationship including job advancement, sexual excitement, and love; categories of relationships which include "fling, sincere love, and utilitarian relationship" (p. 35); and the characteristics of the work group including how closely the couple is supervised, the organizational norms, and the importance of the work itself. Possible ramifications of a workplace romance include involved individuals becoming less effective at work, losing the respect of others, being tardy or leaving early, reducing attendance at meetings, and making mistakes (Quinn & Lees, 1984). Expanding the work of Quinn and Lees (1984), Tourigny and Dougan (2004) have identified the intrapersonal dilemmas engendered through an office romance for the individuals involved in the liaison that result in inner conflict and subsequent actions that are not congruent with the organizational context. They describe this as a "dialectic between emotions and rationality" (p. 7).

This complex communication-based phenomena, although pervasive, was not studied extensively, until Roy (1974) identified workplace romantic relationships as important but "often overlooked" (p. 44); Riach and Wilson (2007) discovered how both managers and workers viewed romance at work as common behavior in organizations. Anderson and Hunsaker (1985) have compared the workplace to a dating service since it provides many of the antecedent conditions such as proximity and mutual interests important to the development of romantic relationships. It is interesting that a study reported by Campbell (2008) found that 40% of those who were polled acknowledged that they have had an office romance at some point in their work career. The astounding part of this survey was that 66% felt there was no need to hide the relationship.

The workplace may be a rather dysfunctional dating service. Wilson, Filosa, and Fennel (2003) reference a 1998 study by the Society for Human Resource

Management that suggested over 50% of romantic work relationships would conclude in marriage, but over a quarter would precipitate complaints from coworkers and almost a quarter may result in sexual harassment claims and decreased productivity. Thus it appears that workplace relationships, while common, appear to encompass difficulties inherent in both romantic relationships and workplace relationships in a multiplicative rather than additive effect because of unique challenges specific to the context: in only 10% of the cases studied by Quinn (1977) were there positive consequences associated with workplace romances.

Proximity Theory and the Formation of Relationships

As Monge and Contractor (2001) have noted, "proximity facilitates the likelihood of communication by increasing the probability that individuals will meet and interact" (p. 497). Proximity appears to be an underlying factor important to the creation of networks and ties within organizational contexts. Zahn (1991) found that as physical distance between offices increased, the probability of communication decreased.

This appears to be especially likely in the context of a romantic relationship. Physical proximity appears to be an important component of adult romantic attachments (Gur, 2007). Indeed, Overall and Sibley's (2008) examination of diary entries revealed the propensity of some individuals to develop romantic attachments to those in close proximity even while involved in another romantic relationship. In a review of research addressing the development of romantic relationships in the workplace, Mainiero (1986) discovered that being colocated facilitates the development of romantic relationships in the workplace; however, as Pierce, Byrne, and Aguinis (1996) note there is a difference between physical proximity or the colocation of workers and functional proximity which references the ease with which an interaction can occur. Both are important antecedents for the development of romantic relationships. Powell and Foley (1998) have discovered that physical and functional proximity lead to attractions between coworkers.

Quinn (1977) reported that in 63% of the office romances, employees work stations were located near each other. Dillard and Witteman (1985) found that those workers who are similarly located on the organizational hierarchy tended to be colocated and that smaller organizations were less likely to have romantic liaisons (company size less than 20). They discovered organizations containing 21–50 members had the most romantic relationships. The fewest romances were in organizations that had over 500 employees. So perhaps moderately-sized organizations provide colocations and enough possibilities to encourage romantic attachments where larger organizations may be perceived as impersonal and small organizations do not provide sufficient alternatives.

However, while proximity affords individuals opportunities to develop relationships, it is not sufficient in itself for a romantic attachment to occur. This is noted by Hoffman, Clinebell, and Kilpatrick (1997) who write "The increased interaction, proximity, and dependency on each other to meet deadlines have resulted in an increase of an old phenomenon—office dating" (p. 263). For example, propinquity allows individuals to observe the behavior of coworkers in which they may be interested in variety of settings. Hoffman et al. (1997) suggest that the nature of the work itself may reveal whether someone has the potential to be a partner worth pursuing. Often the work requires an individual display a variety of behaviors such as initiative, understanding, maturity, etc. Whether an individual responds to the challenges of his/her workplace with adaptive behaviors can provide important clues to a potential partner as to whether the relationship should be pursued.

Losee and Olen (2007) who married two coworkers wrote a handbook for finding and managing romance on the job. They argue that the workplace is the new intimacy village and therefore, an ideal place to find love. They espouse the belief that there is a growing acceptance of office dating (not to be confused with a hookup) is something of a backlash against dating Web sites. They argue that people need to be physically near each other to feel happier and better in everyday life. Rhetorically, they pose the following question and answer: "Where do we still have that physical proximity of neighborhoodliness?" "It's at the office."

In their model of workplace romance Pierce et al. (1996) founds support for colocation as an important but insufficient antecedent of workplace romance. Other contributing factors which led to the development of romantic relationships included repeated exposure to particular individuals and arousal from factors at work. Additional antecedents included sharing work tasks, involvement in shared activities outside of work, and the perception of similarity. Although nearness may facilitate the development of a relationship, there are many other factors that are inherent in relationship development as discussed in other chapters of this book.

When Mentoring Scripts Include Romance

Although the research on sexual attraction and mentoring relationships is sparse, Morgan and Davidson (2008) note that the closeness of a mentor and protégé could certainly be a catalyst for the development of a romantic attachment.

Kalbfleisch (2002) references the personal nature of a mentoring relationship and suggests that it is "the human connection of two people" (p. 64) delineating both the professional and personal aspects of the relationship. Kalbfleisch (2002) compares a mentoring relationship to a romantic relationship in that they both indicate to the individuals involved that there is a movement toward more commitment. Kram (1985) also notes both the professional and social support endemic to these relationships. The expectations of the protégé and mentor are that both will exhibit specific aspects of their behavior that are viewed favorably in the workplace. McManus (2008) found that clearly defined prototypes regarding both roles exist: The protégé is expected to have a great deal of potential while the mentor is expected to be powerful organizationally and demonstrate strong interpersonal skills; however, as Bozeman and Feeney (2008) have discovered, the perceived social capital generated for the protégé by the relationship with the mentor can be exceptional significant. These are characteristics that can be quite appealing. Udeh and Omar's (2009) focus on the outcome phase of the mentoring relationship reveals the cautions to which both mentor and protégée must adhere when entering into this type of relationship.

Kram (1985) in investigating narratives of mentoring relationships identified four phases: Initiation, or the beginning of the relationship where the mentor and protégé must learn about each other including such things as work styles and preferences; Cultivation, where the mentoring activity becomes central and the majority of learning on both the part of the mentor and protégé take place; Separation, the phase at which the mentor and protégé must part ways, often due to a relocation; and finally, Redefinition, when the mentor and protégé must determine how to negotiate their relationship in a different fashion due to the ending of the mentoring phase.

Certainly, romantic attachments could occur at any of these four phases, but from the preliminary research conducted by Morgan and Davidson (2008), it appears that the Cultivation phase provides the best opportunity for the relationship to develop into a romantic attachment. In an analysis of over 50 interviews with men and women who have been protégés to a mentor "a common finding has been for participants to openly acknowledge that they used flirting with a powerful senior to gain advice, promotions, and sponsorship" (p. S124). A narrative from one young heterosexual woman revealed self-reported flirtatious behavior with her male mentor that continued until she was promoted. Indeed, many of the relationships appear to progress beyond flirting. Collins (1983) discovered that a quarter of the protégés in her study had had sexual relationships with their mentors. None of these women reported that these intimate relationships had been helpful to them either professionally or personally and most expressed regret concerning the relationship.

Morgan and Davidson (2008) conclude that while mentoring relationships can reap benefits for both the protégé and the mentor, there are many aspects that have been underrepresented in research, most likely to the detriment of both parties. They note that these relationships can vary widely in the manner in which they are constituted and there are many times when little direction is provided to either member of this relationship. If the relationship becomes sexual in nature, this tends to be problematic for all those involved and may be detrimental to the organization. Conversely, if the relationship remains distant, the protégé may feel unworthy of the mentor's time and attention. The relationship is therefore fragile and must be constituted carefully. Well-developed interpersonal communication skills are necessitated to negotiate the proper roles and establish boundaries for this relationship.

Gender Scripts in Office Romances

Although almost 57% of women aged 16 years and older are engaged in the work force (United States Department of Labor), it appears there remain differences in the relationship scripts for men and women regarding romantic relationships at work. The differences in the manner in which participants in office relationships are perceived and discussed appear to be constituted at least in part by gender.

Anderson and Fisher's (1991) survey of recent business school graduates revealed significant differences in attributed motivations for office romances between men and women. Almost 80% of participants indicated they were personally aware of at least one work-based romantic relationship, while over 30% indicated personal involvement in such a liaison. Both male and female participants suggested significantly different attributions for office romances based on the gender of the partner. Females who entered into romantic relationships at work were perceived to do so in order to advance their careers or for romantic involvement where the motivations of males included the satisfaction of their egos and for the sexual excitement and experiences.

These attitudes do not appear to have changed significantly with the passage of time. Riach and Wilson (2007) used a narrative technique to discern possible gendered practices regarding heterosexual relationships in organizations. They discovered that recent hires appear to be the most likely "targets" for romance and even when infidelity was a contributing factor to the dissolution of a relationship, each participant in the relationship was expected to behave in a resilient manner. Yet this did not mean that coworkers perceived the losses of the partners as equal. Both inherently and explicitly, women were consistently relegated to the position of "losing" when participating in non-platonic relationships, regardless of their positions. It appears that females tend to be the "losers" in real terms as well. Quinn (1977) reported that women in romantic liaisons lost their jobs through termination as a rate twice that of men.

Many decisions about the legitimacy of a relationship were judged through the forecasting of future consequences (Riach & Wilson, 2007). In such instances, participants relied on traditional discussions of sexual behavior where the women's behavior is classified as either virtuous or sinful: the woman is either unable to control her emotions or is literally embodying her power through manipulative and sexual predatory behavior. Interestingly, when scenarios are presented that cast the female participant in heterosexual romantic relationships as higher in the organization's hierarchy, attributions as to her behavior are more likely to include love (Jones, 1999).

Gay relationships appear to be constituted to significant others in a different manner, with few attributions. Extensive in-depth interviews with employees of pubs in the U.K. conducted by Riach and Wilson (2007) revealed that while romantic relationships at work were viewed as a natural outcome of individuals working together, gay relationships were considered not natural. Gay employees were cautioned to keep their relationships private, "a girlfriend of hers was banned from coming into the pub as she 'looked like a lesbian' and 'was the wrong kind of clientele'" (p. 86).

Hierarchy Differences

Dillard and Miller (1988) suggest that work relationships between individuals at different hierarchical levels are more pervasive than those between peers, but unfortunately these are viewed less favorably than peer romances by third parties (Anderson & Hunsaker, 1985). Riach and Wilson (2007) also note that romantic liaisons between peers are viewed by coworkers as acceptable behavior unless it interferes with the work itself. Non-peer romantic relationships can create an additional set of issues in which the dynamics of power and dependency are evoked (Mainiero, 1986). Indeed, Powell and Foley (1998) suggest "hierarchical and utilitarian romances present the greatest threat" (p. 445). Perhaps this is because as Mainiero (2003) suggests a romance that involves individuals at different levels in an organization offers an opportunity for an unscrupulous employee to advance his/her career through the relationship.

Mainiero's (1986) review of literature reveals a social exchange perspective in situations where romantic partners represent different levels of the organizational hierarchy. She suggests that an individual at the higher level has more resources at his/her disposal to exchange. This higher level individual is consequently less dependent upon the relationship because of receiving fewer benefits. She suggests dependencies manifest themselves in a number of ways within the complex organizational context. The first exchange she identifies involves task dependency, that of needing others in the organization to complete a job. Exchanges are also made in career dependency, where an individual is dependent upon a manager for feedback that will assist career advancement. For example, an employee may exchange task work for career advancement.

When a couple enters into a romantic liaison, a third type of dependency is added to the dynamics of the workplace, that of a personal/sexual dependency. This includes all the aspects of romantic relationships, closeness, affection, companionship, etc. which are associated with close interpersonal ties. This addition of the personal/sexual dependency creates an imbalance in the dynamics of the workplace suggests Mainiero (1986). That is, coworkers become concerned that additional exchanges will take place in the personal/sexual areas (for example, sexual favors exchanged for a job promotion) to which they are not privy. A disruption in the workplace occurs because the employee involved in the liaison with a manager is able to negotiate exchanges not available to anyone else. In addition, workplace romances are markedly different from other types of workplace relationships in that they are not officially sanctioned in the manner of workgroup relationships (Powell & Foley, 1998).

An analysis of cases of romantic liaisons reported by participants (Quinn, 1977) lends support to Mainiero's contentions. He suggests that in most cases a workplace romantic relationship is more exchange-oriented in nature. When hierarchical disparities exist, the individual who is lower in the hierarchy (usually the female) is able to influence workplace transitions to which under normal circumstances this individual would not be privy. "Because she provides ego rewards to the male in exchange for organizational rewards, she is able to influence the contracts and transactional positions that other have established in such potent areas as organizational identity, communication, and power" (p. 44).

Powell (2001) notes that the situation is exacerbated when one or both partners in the office romance are married to someone else: The senior-level executive in a hierarchical WR is likely to be older than the lower-level employee because of the considerable work experience required to attain a senior level in most organizations. As a result, the senior-level executive is more likely to be married than the lower-level employee. Coworkers may perceive a hierarchical extramarital affair as a more serious and disruptive issue than a hierarchical WR between two single people (p. 1521).

Powell (2001) found support for this contention in a study involving 275 participants enrolled in graduate business courses. Eighty-nine percent of these individuals were employed full-time, thus having expectations framed by experience.

The participants were provided different scenarios of workplace romances where the gender and hierarchical levels were manipulated. Analysis revealed that there were no negative responses to romantic liaisons in the work place in general; however, when the attachment disrupted the work itself, the relationship was valanced negatively. In the scenarios where there were negative consequences to the workplace tasks, participants tended to assess the situation more negatively than when there were no adverse task consequences association with the relationship. The most negative responses to the relationship were associated with a situation involving a female participant who was at a lower level than the male participant. Male participants were more likely than female participants to indicate that they would take some action personally, although belief in the seriousness of the situation did not differ significantly between the genders. Very few participants indicated they would report the situation to the management of the organization. Indeed, reporting the relationship may not be a fruitful endeavor. As Quinn (1977) notes many managers are reluctant to interfere in this area of an employee's life without substantial proof that the relationships exists and this often is lacking; however, Foley and Powell (1999) suggest that coworkers are interested in management intervening in situations where a romantic liaison has resulted in unfair practices.

However, the issue of workplace policies regarding romantic relationships and consequent responses to these may be more complex than suggested by either Quinn (1977) or Foley and Powell (1999): Karl and Sutton (2000) found that measured responses to workplace romances based on a number of contextual factors were considered the most fair responses by coworkers. They found support for disciplinary action when work performance was affected or when the romance was obvious; however, respondents did not believe that simply angering coworkers was a sufficient cause to warrant punishment, but instead recommended counseling as the preferred organizational response. Respondents indicated that peer relationships of individuals from different divisions of the company rarely required managerial intervention but did support the policy that clearly elucidated expectations concerning workplace romantic relationships.

Sexual Harassment Scripts

Unfortunately, workplace sexual harassment is quite common. It even occurs among female doctors as 30% report facing it on the job while only 4% of male doctors reported it (Jagsi et al., 2016). Some organizations require yearly online videos and to take a course in sexual harassment signs and rules which is an attempt to create an organizational, harassment script. You then receive a certificate. The definitions of workplace romantic relationships appear to encompass only those relationships willingly entered into, precluding harassing or stalking types of relationships that may evolve within the workplace context. Recall that sexual harassment is distinguished from liaisons willingly entered into by mutual consent as it includes unwelcome sexual advances, requests for sexual favors, and other physical or verbal conduct of a sexual nature that is unwanted. In addition, the behaviors must interfere with the accuser's work or create a work environment that is hostile or intimidating. The law includes any behaviors or items that make the work environment offensive. These behaviors have been considered violations of Title VII of the Civil Rights Act of 1964 (US EEOC, 1990) since this argument was accepted by the Supreme Court in 1986 (Clarke, 2006). Two types of sexual harassment have been identified by the courts: (1) the first, "quid pro quo" harassment, is that which occurs when an employee is expected to submit to the sexual advances of a coworker or supervisor in order to maintain the job or be eligible for promotion; (2) the second, a "hostile work environment," is created by pervasive instances of intimidation or insult (Browne, 2006). Solomon (2006) writes that the over 15,000 charges of sexual harassment filed every year do not begin to reflect all of the instances; many are unreported.

Chamberlain, Crowley, Tope, and Hodson (2005) note that sexual harassment can comprise a number of different behaviors, all of which are based in communication. These include verbal behaviors such as overt remarks that are either sexual in nature or sexist and nonverbal aspects of communication that include environments containing sexually oriented objects. Homophobic slurs and remarks about men who were perceived to be gay were a common type of verbal harassment against males (McDonald & Charlesworth, 2015).

More extreme examples include overt solicitation of sex, inappropriate contact, and even forced sexual acts. In spite of the courts repeated attempts to specify exact behaviors that constitute sexual harassment, there appear to be no conceptualizations that are consistently accepted (Chamberlain et al., 2005). The results of sexual harassment can be quite detrimental to the victim and include negative psychological, physiological, and employment outcomes (Vijayasiri, 2008).

The evolutionary underpinnings of sexual harassment are identified by Browne (2006) who suggests that since females bear reproductive responsibility for allowing sexual access, they are necessarily more selective. Regarding the contention that harassment concerns power relationships, he writes, "rather than men using sex to obtain power, it is much more accurate to say that they use power to obtain sex…[the result being] a substantial sexual asymmetry in investment… leading to a significant disparity in the potential consequences of a particular act of intercourse" (p. 145). As a consequence, this creates an overwhelming likelihood for misunderstandings where a female's friendly interest is misinterpreted by a male as a sexual come-on. For example, significantly more women than men report that their causal comments inadvertently have been perceived by male colleagues as being sexual in nature (Browne, 2006).

Harassment complaints can involve individuals who had no previous romantic attachment or conversely, can involve individuals who were involved in a sexual liaison. Although many harassment complaints arise from individuals who have no previous attachments, Clarke (2006) echoing many feminist scholars, questions since women often are in positions subordinate to men in the workplace whether a romantic liaison can ever be consensual. She notes that regardless, the potential for harassment to occur is certainly greater when the individuals involved are at different levels within the organizational hierarchy.

Pierce and Aguinis (2001) suggest that harassment may occur as a result of the dissolution of consensual romantic workplace liaisons, particularly those of a hierarchical nature leading to more negative perceptions of these relationships. They suggest three scenarios that represent possibilities for dissolved hierarchal relationships to evolve into sexual harassment complaints. The first, if the relationship is terminated by the individual at a higher level, the direct report may lodge a complaint of sexual harassment as a retaliatory effort, especially if the direct report had employment related concerns for entering the relationship; the second, the lower-level individual initiates the break-up and the manager aggressively attempts to rekindle the romance; the third, the higher-up tries to manage the break-up by relocating or firing the subordinate regardless of who initiated the dissolution.

Pierce and Aguinis (2001) have developed a framework for increasing understanding and predicting the likelihood of sexual harassment claims emanating from the termination of this type of relationship. Their model suggests there are a number of factors that contribute to whether there is a greater or lesser likelihood of the ending of a relationship resulting in a sexual harassment claim. The first is the type of workplace romance: whether the motives for entering the relationship were similar or dissimilar and what was represented by the motives. They suggest five types of motives: (1) companionate love (where both parties are motivated by love); (2) passionate love (where both parties are motivated by both love and ego); (3) fling (both parties motivated by ego); (4) mutual user (both parties motivated by their jobs); and (5) utilitarian (where one party is motivated by ego and the other is motivated by the job).

These types of romances are influenced by whether the organization's tolerance for sexual harassment is low or high; whether the partner's social power is personal or positional; whether the relationship was dissolved by one or both parties;

whether the male partner has a likelihood to engage in sexual harassing behaviors; and whether the partners' affect subsequent to the dissolution of the relationship is positive or negative. They suggest that all these factors work together to determine whether sexual harassment will occur and whether it will constitute a hostile environment or the more egregious quid pro quo complaint. For example, they posit that dissolutions of utilitarian and mutual user relationships are more likely to result in quid pro quo behaviors while relationships that had been based on companionate and passionate motivations might result in hostile environment claims. According to this model, the ending of liaisons where both parties are motivated by ego (flings) is the least likely to elicit any type of sexually harassing behavior (Pierce & Aguinis, 2001).

Pierce, Aguinis, and Adams (2000) tested portions of this model in a study involving 226 employees of a sheriff's department who were presented with different harassment scenarios and asked to make judgments concerning responsibility and subsequent disciplinary action. They found little difference between male and female perceptions of harassment complaints made subsequent to the dissolution of a romantic relationship. This may have been due to the fact that their sample of participants had received extensive training concerning issues of sexual harassment; however, participants' perceptions concerning the romance motives of the couple significantly influenced subsequent judgments about the nature of a complaint. When the accused individual had an ego motive and the accuser had a love motive, the accused was judged very severely by the participants; however, when the accused had a love motive and the complainant had a job-related motive, the accused was judged as least responsible for the harassment. In addition, participants believed that disciplinary action was most appropriate for cases in which the parties had been involved in a hierarchical romance as opposed to a relationship comprised of peers.

Harassment claims can emanate from individuals who have never considered a romantic relationship with the harasser to those who have shared a personal relationship. There are instances of harassment encompassed under the concept of hostile work environment. For example, sexual favoritism, where a worker is granted organizational benefits because of participation in a romance with the manager can be the impetus for a suit alleging a hostile work environment. A decision made by California Supreme Court in 2005, *Miller v. Department of Corrections*, has indicated that favoritism in an organization may be considered sexual harassment of employees who are not favored. The Court has indicated that the instances of favoritism must be both pervasive and severe to warrant the claim.

Sexual harassment is not only a function of perception and communication regarding the individuals involved in the complaint, it is a function of juries' perceptions, especially regarding socially desirable attributes (Wuensch & Moore, 2004). Unattractive defendants were two and a half times more likely to be found guilty by individual mock jurors than were attractive defendants. The jury was more sympathetic to claims of attractive plaintiffs, charging the defendant with guilt almost three times more frequently than when the plaintiff is unattractive. In addition, the mock jurors considered sexual harassment more likely when the defendant is unattractive and/or the plaintiff is attractive. If a male plaintiff is attractive jurors are twice as like to find in his favor and are more certain of the guilt of the female defendant. Female jurors favored the physically attractive male plaintiff only when the female defendant was unattractive; male jurors favored the attractive male plaintiff only when the female defendant was physically attractive. There was little difference between female jurors and male jurors when the litigants were similarly attractive. This has significant implications for jury trials and is information that must be transmitted to jurors to ameliorate the possible biasing effect that appearance may have on perceptions of guilt or innocence.

As noted by theorists who study sexual harassment in the workplace (Browne, 2006; Pierce et al., 1996; Solomon, 2006) organizational culture may play an important role regarding the constitution of such relationships and serve in an inhibitory fashion or a facilitating fashion, regardless of actual intent. Schaefer and Tudor (2001) suggest that workplaces that ensure humane and equitable treatment of all employees and provide equal advancement opportunities are less likely to experience occasions of sexual harassment.

So far, this discussion has presumed that sexual harassment occurs among opposite-sex workers. Yet, a brief discussion on same-sex harassment is warranted due to its legal recognition and increase in the reporting of it.

Same-Sex Sexual Harassment

Harassment is conduct; the gender of the parties involved is irrelevant. Most workplace harassment is male to female. According to EEOC statistics, in 1992, males filed 9.1% of the sexual harassment charges that were filed with the EEOC and state and local Fair Employment Practices agencies around the country. This figure has increased slightly every year. In 2001 the percentage of charges filed by men was 13.7%. The percentage reflects both societal norms (men usually are expected to be the aggressor in intimate relations) and workplace norms (men usually have more organizational power than women). As these norms change, the way sexual harassment is played out at work probably will also change.

Harassment also occurs from females to males, males to males, and females to females. All these forms of harassment are prohibited and the same standards are applied to allegations of same-sex sexual harassment as to harassment between a male and a female. Same-sex harassment does not depend on the sexual orientation of any party. For example, a heterosexual male could be harassed by another heterosexual male and it could still constitute sexual harassment.

In *Oncale-v-Sundowner Offshore Servs., Inc.*, the Supreme Court determined that same-sex sexual harassment violates antidiscrimination laws when it is motivated by the individual's gender. It is difficult to predict when same-sex sexual harassment will be considered based on gender as opposed to some other reason. Therefore, the investigator should not be concerned with what a court of law will do but rather should focus on whether the behavior violates work rules prohibiting harassment. Also, remember that while most sexual harassment is male to female, a female can harass a male.

This becomes more complex with the myriad of state case decisions involving a variety of same-sex harassment claims. According to Robinson, Epermanis, and Frink (2005–2006) the courts continue to struggle with same sex sexual harassment claims primarily concerning the legal interpretation of "sex" which references a physiological/biological manifestation rather than an orientation. The law precludes an individual receiving disparate treatment because of his/her biological sex; all employees should be treated the same regardless of biological sex. As a consequence to be a violation of Title VII, a victim must prove that the unwanted behavior was based on his/her sex. They reference a recent case *Holman v. Indiana* where Steven and Karen Holman, a married couple, complained that they had both individually been harassed by a bi-sexual supervisor. The court found that this was not a violation of Title VII since neither victim was treated differently because of biological sex. "Since different treatment was ruled out, the Seventh Circuit concluded that there could be no violation of Title VII" (p. 87).

The issue of sexual harassment has been and continues to be a workplace issue based in the communication or more likely miscommunication of individuals who share a common work environment. It appears to be dependent upon a number of factors including gender and is especially difficult to discern during allegations of hostile work environments since the term is subject to a variety of interpretations.

Intercultural Differences

The interpretation of romantic relationships at work and the communication that ensues appears to be significantly influenced by the culture of the organization which in turn is influenced by larger cultural manifestations. Emanating from the early work of Hofstede (1984) concerning the variations of power distance among countries, it becomes apparent that the influence of culture on interpretations of romantic relationships at work is pervasive.

Mano and Yiannis (2006) suggest organizational culture embedded in a larger cultural context may impact the manner in which relationships are constituted through narratives that represent these relationships. These researchers collected narratives of workplace romances from participants representing two organizations located in different countries. They suggested that organizational climate, a component of organizational culture, can influence the manner in which romantic relationships are constituted through dialogues: cold climates dissuade romantic relationships and if these do occur they do not appear to be readily discussed; in comparison, hot climates view romantic relationships as extensions of the sexualization that occurs in the organization itself. A third type of organizational climate, termed "temperate" neither facilitates nor impedes the development of romantic relationships in the work place.

The authors investigated organizations in both Taiwan and Israel and found that country of origin was a predictor of the narratives that were recounted concerning workplace relationships. Israel narratives were more explicit where the Taiwanese participants appeared more reticent to share information, perhaps due to cultural norms. Israel participants related narratives in which individuals appeared responsible for their behaviors while narratives from Chinese counterparts attributed the formation of romantic relationships to fate, suggesting that the organization should not become involved in the relationship. The researchers also discovered that the "hotter" organizational cultures lent themselves to more explicit narratives that romanticized these relationships.

Summary

Workplace romantic attachments occur with great frequency, but tend to be problematic for a number of reasons. They appear to violate the organizational norms concerning roles within the organization, in that the role of romantic partner is not one that is officially sanctioned in the workplace. In addition, they add a third element to workplace dynamics involving exchanges between two individuals, denying other coworkers access to these exchanges. As Mainiero (2003) has succinctly written, "The problem is that sex is a commodity that can be traded for power" (p. 151).

Discussion Questions

10.1. Have you been involved in an office romance? Did you attempt to keep it hidden from your coworkers? What was the result?

10.2. Do you think the attitudes of individuals entering the workforce such as yourselves are different from older workers concerning work place romantic relationships? In what ways do you think the attitudes may differ? To what do you attribute these differences?

10.3. What factors in a mentoring relationship could facilitate development into a romantic relationship? What would be the cautions? Can you identify any benefits?

10.4. Discuss the issue of romantic relationships at work with your friends. If you were the manager of a work group, how would you address this issue? Would you forbid dating, set rules, or ignore the relationship?

10.5. Do you believe most relationships that begin at work represent committed partners or are the simply "friends with benefits"?

10.6. Sexual harassment is a critical issue in organizations. Liability to an organization can be extensive if the organization is shown to have neglected training or did not respond promptly to an accusation. (For example, in a historic case in 1999, Robert Lockley was awarded $3.75 million in damages because the New Jersey correctional facility where he worked had failed to respond to his complaints about being sexually harassed by a fellow guard). Have you been a victim of sexual harassment? Was it a result of the dissolution of a consensual relationship or not? How did you respond? How did your organizational respond? Was the response effective?

Application

10.1. David who is unmarried is a new employee in a unit that processes components for notebooks. His supervisor, Margaret, is married with children. Margaret has approached David on two separate occasions noting his excellent physical attributes, suggesting that they, "take the time to get to know each other better." David is gay and uninterested in a relationship with a married woman, but uncertain as to whether Margaret's behaviors constitute sexual harassment since he has not told her these advances are unwelcomed. He approaches you, his supervisor, to discuss the situation. What would you say to David? What actions, if any, would you take?

References

Anderson, C. I., & Hunsaker, P. L. (1985). Why there's romancing at the office and why it's everybody's problem. *Personnel, 62*, 57–63.

Anderson, C. J., & Fisher, C. (1991). Male-female relationships in the workplace: Perceived motivations in office romance. *Sex Roles, 25*, 163–180. doi:10.1007/BF00289852

Bozeman, B., & Feeney, M. (2008). Public management mentoring: What affects outcomes? *Journal of Public Administration Research & Theory, 19*, 427–452. doi:10.1093/jopart/mun007

Browne, K. R. (2006). Sex, power, and dominance: The evolutionary psychology of sexual harassment. *Managerial and Decision Economics, 27*, 145–158. doi:10.1002/mde.1289

Campbell, D. (2008). *Marital infidelity: Office romance takes flight*. Retrieved 2008, June 16 from http://www.buzzle.com/articles/marital-infidelity-office-romance-takes-flight.html

Chamberlain, L. J., Crowley, M., Tope, D., & Hodson, R. (2005). *Sexual harassment in context: Organizational and occupational foundations of abuse*. Paper presented at the annual meeting of the American Sociological Association, Philadelphia, PA.

Clarke, L. (2006). Sexual relationships and sexual conduct in the workplace. *Legal Studies, 26*, 347–368. doi:10.1111/j.1748-121X.2006.00020.x

Collins, N. W. (1983). *Professional women and their mentors: A practical guide to mentoring for the woman who wants to get ahead*. Englewood Cliffs, NJ: Prentice-Hall.

Dillard, J. P., & Miller, K. I. (1988). Intimate relationships in task environments. In S. W. Duck (Ed.), *Handbook of personal relationships* (pp. 449–65). New York, NY: Wiley.

Dillard, J. P., & Witteman, H. (1985). Romantic relationships at work: Organizational and personal influence. *Human Communication Research, 12*, 99–116. doi:10.1111/j.1468-2958.1985.tb00068.x

Eisenberg, M. E., Ackard, D. M., Resnick, M. D., & Neumark-Sztainer, D. (2009). Casual sex and psychological health among young adults: Is having "Friends with Benefits" emotionally damaging? *Perspectives on Sexual & Reproductive Health, 41*, 231–237. doi:10.1363/4123109.

Foley, S., & Powell, G. (1999). Not all is fair in love and work: Coworkers' preferences for and responses to managerial interventions regarding workplace romances. *Journal of Organizational Behavior, 20*, 1043–1057. doi:10.1002/(SICI)1099-1379(199912)20:7<1043::AID-JOB1>3.0.CO;2-A

Gomes, G. M., Owens, J. M., & Morgan, J. F. (2006). The paramour's advantage: Sexual favoritism and permissibly unfair discrimination. *Employee Rights Journal, 18*, 73–88. doi:10.1007/s10672-006-9006-y

Hoffman, L., Clinebell, S., & Kilpatrick, J. (1997). Office romances: The new battleground over employees' rights to privacy and the employers' right to intervene. *Employee Responsibilities and Rights Journal, 10*, 261–275. doi:10.1023/A:1025607232517

Hofstede, G. (1984). *Culture's consequences: International differences in work-related values*. Beverly Hills, CA: Sage.

Jagsi, R., Griffith, K. A., Jones, R., Perumalswami, C. R., Ubel, P., & Stewart, A. (2016). Sexual harassment and discrimination experiences of academic medical faculty. *Journal of the American Medical Association, 315*, 2120–2121. doi:10.1001/jama.2016.2188.

Jones, G. (1999). Hierarchical workplace romance: An experimental examination of team members' perceptions. *Journal of Organizational Behavior, 20*, 1057–1073. doi:10.1002/(SICI)1099-1379(199912)20:7<1057::AID-JOB956>3.0.CO;2-O

Kalbfleisch, P. (2002). Communicating in mentoring relationships: A theory for enactment. *Communication Theory, 12*, 63–69. doi:10.1111/j.1468-2885.2002.tb00259.x

Karl, A. A., & Sutton, C. L. (2000). An examination of the perceived fairness of workplace romance policies. *Journal of Business and Psychology, 14*, 429–442. doi:10.1023/A:1022928216431

Kram, K. E. (1985). *Mentoring at work.* Boston, MA: Scott, Foresman, and Company.

Lehmiller, J. L. (2009). Secret romantic relationships: Consequences for personal and relational well-being. *Personality and Social Psychology Bulletin, 35*, 1452–1466. doi:10.1177/0146167209342594

Losee, S., & Olen, H. (2007). *Office mate: Your employee handbook for finding—and managing—romance on the job.* Adams Media. Retrieved 2008, June 16 from http://www1.pressdemocrat.com/article/20071030/NEWS/710300308

Mainiero, L. A. (1986). A review and analysis of power dynamics in organizational dynamics. *Academy of Management Review, 11*, 750–762. doi:10.5465/AMR.1986.4283926

Mainiero, L. A. (2003). On the ethics of office romance: Developing a moral compass for the workplace. In R. J. Burke & M. C. Mathis (Eds.), *Supporting women's career advancement.* Cheltenham: Edward Elgar.

Mano, R., & Yiannis, G. (2006). Workplace romances in cold and hot organizational climates: The experience of Israel and Taiwan. *Journal of Human Resources, 59*, 7–35.

McDonald, P., & Charlesworth, S. (2015). Workplace sexual harassment at the margins. *Work, Employment & Society, 30*, 118–134. doi:10.1177/0950017014564615

McManus, S. (2008). Cognitive prototypes of the mentor and protégé roles. *Dissertation Abstracts International: Section B: The Sciences and Engineering, 68*, 7011.

Monge, P. R., & Contractor, N. S. (2001). Emergence of communication networks. In F. M. Jablin & L. L. Putnam (Eds.), *The new handbook of organizational communication: Advances in theory, research, and methods* (pp. 440–502). Thousand Oaks, CA: Sage.

Morgan, L. M., & Davidson, M. J. (2008). Sexual dynamics in mentoring relationships: A critical review. *British Journal of Management, 19*, 120–129. doi:10.1111/j.1467-8551.2008.00577.x

Gur, N. (2007). A cognitive priming approach to the study of adult attachment. *Dissertation Abstracts International: Section B: The Sciences and Engineering.* Cornell University.

Overall, N., & Sibley, C. (2008). Attachment and attraction toward romantic partners versus relevant alternatives within daily interactions. *Personality & Individual Differences, 44*, 1126–1137. doi:10.1016/j.paid.2007.11.006

Pierce, C. A., & Aguinis, H. (2001). A framework for investigating the link between workplace romance and sexual harassment. *Group and Organization Management, 26*, 206–229. doi:10.1177/1059601101262005

Pierce, C. A., Aguinis, H., & Adams, S. K. R. (2000). Effects of a dissolved workplace romance and rater characteristics on responses to a sexual harassment accusation. *Academy of Management Journal, 43*, 869–880. doi:10.2307/1556415

Pierce, C. A., Byrne, D., & Aguinis, H. (1996). Attraction in organizations: A model of workplace romance. *Journal of Organizational Behavior, 17*, 5–32. doi:10.1002/(SICI)1099-1379(199601)17:1<5::AID-JOB734>3.0.CO;2-E

Powell, G. N. (2001). Workplace romances between senior-level executives and lower-level employees: An issue of work disruption and gender. *Human Relations, 54*, 1519–1544. doi:10.1177/00187267015411005

Powell, G. N., & Foley, S. (1998). Something to talk about: Romantic relationships in organizational settings. *Journal of Management, 24*, 421–448. doi:10.1177/014920639802400306

Quinn, R. E. (1977). Coping with cupid: The formation, impact, and management of romantic relationships in organizations. *Administrative Science Quarterly, 22*, 30–45. doi:10.1177/105960117700200311

Quinn, R. E., & Lees, P. L. (1984). Attraction and harassment: Dynamics of sexual politics in the workplace. *Organizational Dynamics, 13*, 35–46. doi:10.1016/0090-2616(84)90017-2

Rabin-Margalioth, S. (2006). Love at work. *Duke Journal of Gender Law & Policy, 13*, 237–254.

Riach, K., & Wilson, F. (2007). Don't screw the crew: Exploring the rules of engagement in organizational romance. *British Journal of Management, 18*, 79–92. doi:10.1111/j.1467-8551.2006.00503.x

Robinson, R. K., Epermanis, K., & Frink, D. D. (2005–2006). Narrowing the legal definition of "homosexual": Establishing sexual desire as a motive for same-sex sexual harassment, *Journal of Individual Employment Rights, 12*, 83–95.

Roy, D. (1974). Sex in the factory: Informal heterosexual relations between supervisors and work groups: In C. Bryant (Ed.), *Deviant behavior: Occupational and organizational bases* (pp. 44–66). Chicago, IL: Rand McNally.

Schaefer, C. M., & Tudor, T. R. (2001). Managing workplace romances. *S.A.M. Advanced Management Journal, 66*, 4–10.

Solomon, D. H. (2006). A relational framing perspective on perceptions of social-sexual communication at work. In B. A. LePoire & R. M. Dailey (Eds.), *Applied interpersonal communication matter: Family, health and community relations* (pp. 271–298). New York, NY: Peter Lang.

Tourigny, L., & Dougan, W. I. (2004). *More than love and work: A critique of existing treatments of organizational romance.* Paper presented at the 2004 Annual Conference of the Midwest Academy of Management, Minneapolis, MN.

Udeh, I., & Omar, A. (2009). Strategic versus gratuitous mentoring: A preliminary investigation. *Allied Academies International Conference: Proceedings of the Academy of Strategic Management, 8*, 44–47.

United States Department of Labor (2006). *Employment status of the civilian noninstitutional population by age and sex, 2006.* Retrieved 2008, June 8, from http://www.bls.gov/cps/wlf-table1-2007.pdf

United States Equal Employment Opportunity Commission. (1990). *Policy guidance on current issues of sexual harassment*. Retrieved 2008, June 9, from http://www.eeoc.gov/policy/docs/curentissues.html

Vijayasiri, G. (2008). Reporting sexual harassment: The importance of organizational culture and trust. *Gender Issues, 25*, 43–61. doi:10.1007/s12147-008-9049-5

Wilson, R. J., Filosa, C., & Fennel, A. (2003). Romantic relationships at work: Does privacy trump the dating police? *Defense Counsel Journal, 70*, 78–89.

Wuensch, K. L., & Moore, C. H. (2004). Effects of physical attractiveness on evaluations of a male employee's allegation of sexual harassment by his female employer. *Journal of Social Psychology, 144*, 207–217. doi:10.3200/SOCP.144.2.207-217

Zahn, G. L. (1991). Face-to-face communication in an office setting: The effects of position, proximity, and exposure. *Communication Research, 18*, 737–754. doi:10.1177/009365091018006002

Cautions and Recommendations

Chapter 11   Dysfunctional Scripts for Abusive Relationships

Chapter 12   The Dark Side of Social Media Communication

Chapter 13   Scripts for Constructive Communication

Chapter 11 provides an overview of dysfunctional scripts that may result in abuse. The communication manifestations of abuse are acknowledged in the differences between argumentation and verbal aggression focusing on the interrelationship between verbal aggression, arguing, and physical coercion. The role of mental imagery, imagined interactions, in abuse is explained through the research of the lead author of this text. Chapter 12 discusses the dark side of social media, including online harassment, social media addiction, narcissism, and the declining quality of interpersonal relationships.

After this discussion of the cautions in relationships, the final chapter provides guidelines for the development of healthy relationships. While not discounting effects due to hardwired genetically based behaviors, the authors suggest many ways to improve relationships based on developing your verbal and nonverbal communication competence.

CHAPTER ELEVEN

Dysfunctional Scripts for Abusive Relationships

The scripts for abuse are pervasive and may blame the victim. Indeed, a stereotypical script described by students in focus-groups contains the following: Abuser blame partners for problems. He/she stews or simmers. The abuser strikes after the partner makes an egregious mistake. Later, the partner may feel some remorse and promises not to do it again. The cycle repeats.

Intimate partner abuse is a pervasive problem depending on the area. The World Health Organization estimates that is estimated that 35% of women worldwide have experienced either physical or sexual violence by a non-partner at some point in their lives. However, some national studies show that up to 70% of women have experienced physical and/or sexual violence from an intimate partner in their lifetime (Violence Against Women, 2015).

Table 11.1 presents various statistics about relational violence. Additionally, according to, intercultural data presented by Straus (2001) across 23 nations and various states, Louisiana had the most cases of physical assault in dating relationships (44.7% total assault rate) while Utah had the lowest (17.7%). The percentages have not changed much in the past 15 years when you examine various sites. Estimates of its occurrence range from 960,000 incidents of violence against a current or former spouse, boyfriend, or girlfriend per year to three million women who are abused physically by their husband or boyfriend per year (http://www.endabuse.org/resources/facts/). It is interesting that 82% of parents feel confident

Table 11.1. Selected statistics about relational violence.

General Statistics and Facts

- About 25% of women will experience an abusive relationship.
- Women ages 18 to 34 are at greatest risk of becoming victims of domestic violence.
- More than 4 million women experience physical assault and rape by their partners.
- Men experience interpersonal violence that ranges up to 3,000,000 a year in personal relationships
- In 2 out of 3 female homicide cases, females are killed by a family member or intimate partner.
- Most coercive incidents happen between 6 pm and 6 am.
- More than 60% occur in the place of residence.
- Relational violence is the third leading cause of homelessness among families, according to the U.S. Department of Housing and Urban Development.

What Are the Effects of Domestic Violence on Mental Health?

- Domestic violence victims face high rates of depression, sleep disturbances, anxiety, flashbacks, and other emotional distress.
- Domestic violence contributes to poor health for many survivors including chronic conditions such as heart disease or gastrointestinal disorders.
  Most women brought to emergency rooms due to domestic violence were socially isolated and had few social and financial resources.

(Safe Horizon, retrieved from http://www.safehorizon.org/page/domestic-violence-statistics--facts-52.html)

that they could recognize the signs if their child was experiencing dating abuse, a majority of parents (58%) could not correctly identify all the warning signs of abuse ("Women's Health," 2004).

Researchers have revealed the link between verbal aggression and physical violence. For example, Vissing, Straus, Gelles, and Harrop (1991) have demonstrated that the psychosocial problems of children are more directly related to parental verbal aggression than to physical aggression. In this chapter, different types of abuse are discussed.

Conflict Tactics and Types of Abuse

What are common signs of abuse? Table 11.2 presents a common script for recognizing abuse warning signs adapted from the American Psychological Association. For the last 25 years, the Conflict Tactics Scale is the most widely used instrument to measure family and interpersonal violence (e.g., Straus, 2007; Straus & Douglas, 2004). In fact, it has been used in over 31 countries documenting abuse in dating and marital relationships (e.g., Straus, 2001, 2005, 2007; Signorelli, Arcidiacono, Musumeci, Di, & Aguglia, 2014). It has been used in the National Violence against Women Survey (Tjaden & Thoennes, 2000), and the National Survey of Child and Adolescent Well-Being. By 2005, over 600 research papers and at least ten books reporting results based on the CTS were published. The Conflict Tactics Scales measures victimization and perpetration of three tactics that are often used in conflicts between dating and marital partners: physical assault, psychological aggression (taunting, name calling, teasing, ridicule, sarcasm), and negotiation in which outside parties may be brought in for intervention. Furthermore, there are scales that measure injury and sexual exploitation by a partner. Straus (1990a, 1990b) discusses physical aggression in terms of differences between minor and severe assault. Examples of severe assault include punching, kicking, choking, stabbing, and shooting. Examples of minor assault include slapping, pushing, shoving, and biting.

Table 11.2. Scripts for warning signs of abuse.

Often, abuse in relationships does not come out of nowhere. This is a warning sign script indicating the potential for violence. To help determine if you are in an abusive relationship, check these warning signs…

You may be headed for danger if you date someone who:

- Tries to isolate you from friends and family.
- Does not want you to spend time with anybody else.
- Hits, punches, kicks, or shoves you. Or, threatens to hurt you in any way.
- Is extremely jealous.
- Gets mad when you talk to other people.
- Is possessive. Treats you like a belonging and does not want you to share your time with other people. Tracks what you are doing and who you spend time with.
- Is controlling. Insists that you call to "check in" or ask permission to do things.
- Checks your e-mail or cell-phone records.
- Tries to control what you wear, what you do, and how you act.
- Scares you. Makes you worry about reactions to things you say or do.
- Behaves violently. Owns weapons and threatens to use them.
- Has a history of fighting, loses temper quickly, and has hurt animals or other people.
- Is emotionally abusive. Puts you down, calls you names, and tells you are nothing without him/her.
- Makes many decisions in the relationship. Does not care about your thoughts and feelings.
- Abuses alcohol or drugs or pressures you to take them.
- Hypersensitive to perceived weaknesses in oneself.
- Won't accept breaking up. Threatens to hurt you, or himself/herself if you break up.
- Stalks you after you've tried to break if off.
- Blames other for temper tantrums.

Adapted from: American Psychiatric Association (2005). Retrieved 2008, February 23, from http://healthyminds.org/factsheets/LTF-DomesticViolence.pdf and http://www.takecareonline.org/warning_signs.htm

The Conflict Tactics Scale measures three types of abuse; physical, sexual, and psychological/emotional. *Physical abuse* includes the use of the body or weapons to threaten, punish, dominate, restrain, control, or injure another person. *Sexual abuse* is the use of forced sexual behaviors that may dominate, manipulate, threaten, injure, or corrupt another person. The idea is control and subjugation of the victim. *Social abuse* involves other forms of abuse to dominate, manipulate, or control another person's social relationships.

Emotional abuse is the use of mental strategies or mind games. According to Straus (1979), psychological/emotional abuse has been variously characterized as "the use of verbal and nonverbal acts which symbolically hurt the other or the use of threats to hurt the other" (p. 77). This would include such things as anger, aggression, humiliation, intimidation, stalking, fear, power, and control. The goal is to inflict emotional damage on the other person. Yet, there is no physical force.

A special type of emotional abuse is *social isolation*. According to Mouradian (2007), there is the to focus on interfering with and destroying or impairing the victim's support network and making the victim entirely or largely dependent on the abusive partner for information, social interaction, and satisfying emotional needs. Social abuse involves isolating the victim increases the abuser's power over the victim, but it also protects the abuser. If the victim does not have contact with other people, the perpetrator will not be as likely to have to deal with legal or social consequences for his behavior and the victim will not be as likely to get help, including help that may lead to an end to the relationship.

Sexual abuse includes behaviors that fall under legal definitions of rape, plus physical assaults to the sexual parts of a person's body, and making sexual demands with which one's partner is uncomfortable (Sheperd & Campbell, 1992). It has been defined as including "...sex without consent, sexual assault, rape, sexual control of reproductive rights, and all forms of sexual manipulation carried out by the perpetrator with the intention or perceived intention to cause emotional, sexual, and physical degradation to another person" (Abraham, 1999, p. 592). An example of a severe sexual coercion item from the Straus (1990a) Conflict Tactics Scale is forcing a partner to have sex without their consent ranging from never happening to more than 20 times in the past year.

Marshall (1994) distinguishes physical and psychological abuse. Physical abuse includes violent acts ranging from minor offenses such as grabbing and slapping to intense behaviors such as choking or burning. Psychological abuse is often a precursor to physical abuse and includes isolation, limiting food/sleep, threats of using violence, humiliation, and name calling. Walker (1986) discusses how most of these behaviors occur under the emotion of anger and expressed through withdrawal, yelling, and contempt as noted in sarcastic voice tones. From this perspective, Marshall (1994) states that a psychological abuser "would be a person who effectively undermined a partner's sense of self" (p. 298). However, she also indicates that while the purpose is often to cause harm, it can reflect love and caring to help oneself become happier.

Some researchers discuss *economic abuse*. This could be considered a subcategory of emotional abuse since it serves many of the same functions as emotional abuse and has some of the same emotional effects on victims (Mouradian, 2007). However, it can be distinguished by its focus on preventing victims from possessing or maintaining any type of financial self-sufficiency and enforcing material dependence of the victim on the abusive partner including providing basic material needs like food, clothing, and shelter or to supply the means to obtain them. The desire to isolate the victim from other people can be one of the motives for economic abuse as well.

A final type of abuse is *elder abuse*. All states have laws against elder abuse even though each state has its own definition of elder abuse. According to the National Center on Elder Abuse, definitions usually include physical and sexual abuse, financial exploitation, neglect, and self-neglect. Neglect is the refusal or failure by those responsible to provide food, shelter, health care, or protection for a vulnerable elder. Self-neglect is characterized as the behavior of an elderly person that threatens his/her own health or safety. Institutional abuse refers to any of the forms of abuse that occur in residential facilities for older persons (e.g., retirement centers, nursing homes, and board and care facilities). In addition, there is abandonment which is the desertion of a vulnerable elder by anyone who has assumed the responsibility for care or custody of that person. Some of these forms of abuse are used in combination along with emotional abuse, threats, coercion, and isolation.

Cycle of Abuse

According to this theory, domestic violence is characterized by a sequence of actions that follow each other in a cycle, increasing in severity and frequency each time it is played out (Walker, 1984). The first stage is referred to as the *tension building stage*. Here tension related to unexpressed anger and unresolved conflict builds within the abuser. This stage is characterized by psychologically abusive behavioral including criticism and complaints, intimidation, threats, and controlling behavior where the abuser begins to undermine the victim's self-confidence and attempts to exercise control over her activities. Furthermore, Walker (1984) indicates that in this stage the victim may be compliant trying to show "good" behavior and minimizes problems. The victim represses feelings of anger while the batterer takes control as the victim withdraws.

As tension increases, the cycle enters the *explosion stage* where the act(s) of abuse occur. This may involve verbal, physical, or sexual attacks on the victim. Furthermore, Walker (1984) indicates that there may be slapping, pushing, hitting, biting, kicking, or shoving. There may be threats or the use of a weapon, sexual abuse, or even murder. The *honeymoon period* follows the explosion stage in which the abuser appears to seek forgiveness, promises never to repeat the actions, and may act as if courting the victim. There may be a honeymoon-like euphoria while the couple "makes up" with presents, flowers, and romantic dinners out. According to Walker (1984), the victim may hope that the batterer is genuinely remorseful, and chooses to believe that the violence will not happen again. However, as tension begins to rebuild in the abuser the cycle is repeated.

The duration of each phase varies and changes over time. For example, the Honeymoon phases may become shorter, as the abuser begins to threaten even worse harm if the victim tries to leave. Yet, the tension-building phase may quickly absorb "honeymoon time" and often completely replaces it. The couple moves through the cycle more quickly as the abuse becomes more frequent and severe (Walker, 1984). Most abusive relationships begin with verbal abuse, and then move into violence, which escalates and becomes more deadly the longer the couple is together.

If a person leaves an abusive relationship, the abuser may face the realization that usual methods of control do not work. At this stage the victim is at risk of suffering repeated unwanted attention (stalking) from the former partner as attempts to "win" the victim back are made (Walker, 1991). Indeed, a number of studies have revealed an association between post-relationship stalking and various forms of violence within an intimate relationship (Davis, Ace, & Andra, 2000; Douglas & Dutton, 2001; Mechanic, Weaver, & Resick, 2000; Spitzberg & Rhea, 1999; Walker, 1991; Walker & Meloy, 1998). Stalking is discussed next.

Stalking

Research shows that partner stalking is a relatively common form of violence against women, and to a lesser degree men with partner stalking being the most common (Logan & Walker, 2010). Two-thirds of women who have been stalked reported that it was by a current or former intimate partner in their lifetime while approximately 40% of male stalking victims reported that they had been stalked by an intimate partner in their lifetime (Black et al., 2010).

Approximately 1 in 6 women (16.2%) in the United States has experienced stalking at some point in her lifetime, according to the CDC's 2010 National Intimate Partner and Sexual Violence Survey.

Spitzberg (2002) reviews over 100 studies dealing with stalking involving over 70,000 participants. He reports that 23.5% for women and 10.5% of men were stalked lasting for an average of 2 years. The average proportion of female victims across studies was 75%, and 77% of stalking emerged from some form of prior acquaintance, with 49% originating from romantic relationships. It is interesting that a summary of 32 studies of restraining orders indicated that they are violated an average of 40% of the time and are perceived as followed by worse events almost 21% of the time. As noted in the social media darkside chapter, cyber stalking is relatively common and shares some characteristics with real-life stalking in terms of pursuit or contacting others in an unsolicited fashion initially. Cyberstalking can intensify in chat rooms where stalkers systematically flood their target's inbox with obscene, hateful, or threatening messages and images. Identity theft can occur as a cyberstalker may assume the identity of his or her victim by posting information (fictitious or not) and soliciting responses from social media. Cyberstalkers may use information acquired online to further intimidate, harass, and threaten their victim via courier mail, phone calls, and physically appearing at a residence or workplace.

Spitzberg and Cupach (2007) distinguish legal definitions of stalking from social science definitions. Although there are numerous conceptions of stalking based on differences in power, control, personality abnormalities, a basic definition provided by Spitzberg is: "Stalking occurs when a person is pursued or harassed in an intentional, ongoing, unwanted, and fear-inducing manner" (p. 262). Although legal definitions of stalking vary from state to state and across different countries, "most States define stalking as the willful, malicious, and repeated following and harassing of another person" (US Department of Justice, 1998, p. 5).

Motives for stalking have not been investigated as much, but the available research reviewed by Spitzberg and Cupach (2007) appears to include issues involving desire to control a partner, jealousy, revenge, alcohol/drug usage, inability to accept the end of intimacy, and infatuation/obsession. A common characteristic of stalkers is an insecure, inadequate attachment style where there is a fear of abandonment (Kienlen, 1998; Lewis, Fremouw, Del Ben, & Farr, 2001). This may result in a variety of outcomes such as lack of trust, approach/avoidant behaviors, and ambivalence regarding commitment.

Spitzberg and Cupach (2007) discuss five primary tactics of stalking: hyperintimacy, pursuit and proximity, invasion, intimidation, and violence. Briefly, *hyperintimacy* reflect those actions aimed at romancing the object of affection. These tactics might be considered romantic under ordinary circumstances, but are viewed

Table 11.3. Common stalking behavior script.

- Making repeated phone calls with call blocking, sometimes with hang-ups.
- Calling you at work.
- Waiting outside your place or work.
- Following and tracking the victim (possibly even with a global positioning device).
- Sending unwanted e-mails, packages, cards, gifts, or letters.
- Monitoring the victim's phone calls or computer use.
- Watching the victim with hidden cameras.
- Complains that it is your fault for ruining their life.
- Leaving notes on windshield or place of residence.
- Contacting friends, family, coworkers, or neighbors for information about the victim.
- Using public records, online searching, or third parties to spy on you.
- Threatening to hurt you, family, friends, or pets.
- Going through the victim's possessions or garbage.
- Damaging the victim's home, car, or other property.
- Physically violent toward you.
- Making threats.

as excessive and inappropriate in the context of these relationships (Spitzberg & Cupach, 2007). *Pursuit and proximity* reflect a desire to increase and enhance attraction and communication with the target. *Invasion* tactics represent an escalation of surveillance both in covertness and stealth as well as in the planning and violation of personal privacy. *Intimidation* reflects the recognition of rejection by the object of affection, requiring an escalation of coercion in technique. Finally, *violence* tactics represent techniques of last resort or merely reactions of rage when rejection is made blatant. Spitzberg and Cupach (2007) note that there may be a sequencing of these tactics in which aggressive strategies are used after hyperintimacy strategies.

Stalking is seen as a subset of obsessive relational intrusion (ORI) which is an unwanted invasion of your privacy by another person who desires or presumes an intimate relationship (Cupach & Spitzberg, 1998). Based on Cupach and Spitzberg's (1998) description of unwanted relational intrusions of which stalking is a component, Table 11.3 contains a common script of behaviors that stalkers have demonstrated across numerous studies.

Gender Differences in Relational Abuse

Numerous studies report distinct gender differences in the type and severity of abuse that is used. For example, the National Family Violence Survey and the National Crime Victimization Survey estimate that at least 2 million women are beaten by their partners each year (Bachman & Saltzman, 1995; Straus & Gelles, 1990). Although the incidence of lethal perpetration is greater for men, data from the 1975 and the 1985 National Family Violence Surveys indicate that women assault their partners at least as often as men (Stets & Straus, 1990; Straus, Gelles, & Steinmetz, 1980). However, parity between intimate partners may end with the similarity in occurrence of aggressive acts. The studies by Straus and associates (1980) found that assaulted women were several times more likely than men to require medical care after severe assaults and were significantly more likely than assaulted husbands to experience psychological injuries related to their abuse (Stets & Straus, 1990). However, Straus (2005) also reviews numerous studies indicating that women initiate physical assaults on their male partners as frequently as men assault women and the injuries and fatalities resulting from the violence.

Many researchers claim that women use milder forms of coercion including slapping. For example, Thompson (1990) reports that women are twice as likely as men to slap their partners. A study in Canada revealed that while women used just as many physically coercive acts, they were 15 times more likely to slap their partners revealing less severe forms of coercion (Stets & Henderson, 1991). Longitudinal research by Straus, Kaufman, and Moore (1994) compared surveys in terms of norms approving of marital violence that were conducted over a 26-year time period with large samples, 1968 <n=1,176>, 1985 <n=6,002>, 1992 <n=1,970>, and 1994 <n=524>, with regard to the approval of facial slapping by a spouse. Approval of slapping by husbands decreased from 21% in 1968 to 13% in 1985, to 12% in 1992, to 10% in 1994. The approval of slapping by wives was 22% in 1968 and has not declined over the years.

Other research reveals that over time as a conflict escalates, women may recommend more aggressive, retaliatory actions. Honeycutt, Sheldon, Pence, and Hatcher (2015) examined how people judge the probability and advisability of aggressive (e.g., hitting) versus conciliatory actions (e.g., discussing disagreements rationally) in an unfolding dispute within a married couple, and if imagined interactions were seen as a desirable form of communication for the conflict-engaging couple. Individuals participated in a study employing two videotaped scenarios depicting martial conflict. One situation involved male-initiated while another one illustrated female-initiated conflict. Viewers were presented with a list of possible reactions, ranging from highly conciliatory actions (apologize, ask for forgiveness, discuss the issue calmly) to physical violence or aggression (push, grab, shove partner; slap partner; throw, smash, hit or kick something; hit or try to hit partner with something). A separate study revealed that the videos were highly believable. They predicted that the husband would be more likely to be conciliatory than the wife, and the wife would be more aggressive than her husband. Additionally, they found that the male was more likely to have retroactive imagined interactions (see

Chapter 3) and replay the conflict in his mind. Hence, they may feel catharsis by imagining discrepant scenarios that relieve tension or anxiety. Participants in the study advised the husband to replay the arguments in his mind before the next scene. We speculate that having retroactive IIs would help to relieve tension from the conflict in a previous scene, and potentially resolve the conflict.

Signal Detection Theory and the Ability to Notice Escalating Conflict

The research by Honeycutt and his associates is based on game theory and signal detection theory which is very important because of the importance of victimization in noticing verbal and nonverbal cues that an argument is escalating. When viewers watch an escalating conflict, game theory posits that people's cultural scripts for conflict resolution involve a "tit for tat" strategy. This game strategy is also referred to as "quid-pro-quo" and reflects equivalent retaliation (Rapoport, 1966). A person using this strategy initially cooperates and responds in kind to a competitor's prior action. If the competitor previously was cooperative, the person is cooperative as well as the inverse; if the competitor defects, then the player will defect as well.

According to Axelrod (1997) "tit for tat" is effective because it is nice and forgiving. A forgiving strategy is one which reciprocates cooperation if one's opponent does so; unforgiving strategies produce isolation and end cooperative encounters. In general, people believe that forgiveness is good, and retaliation is bad (McCullough, 2008). However, the implicit script of how the conflict will unfold does not meet people's expectations of rationalized argument. Indeed, the act of matching the partner's aggression is no longer reflective of the conflict itself, but of the anger and intensity of said conflict. Ito, Miller, and Pollock (1996) suggest that people respond in a "tit for tat" fashion because of a cognitive belief in eye-for-an-eye. Yet, does a trained police detective sense forgiving moves as conflict escalates? Research by Shergill, Bays, Frith, and Wolpert (2003) used tit-for-tat experiments in which pairs of subjects were told to give as good as they got when being rapped on the fingers. The study revealed that violence escalated rapidly, with subjects increasing the force they used by 38% on each turn.

Honeycutt and Eldredge (2015) provide the results of a case study in which a trained police detective was able to note cues for conflict escalation after only 12 seconds had passed in a conversation. The detective reported a total 13 signals which can be subsumed into four underlying cues. Three of these signals involved verbal cues including paralanguage in the form of sarcasm. The first signal was the sarcasm of wife's voice which occurred 12 seconds into the video. One of the main differences between the analysis of the detective and the analyses of laypeople is that the detective noticed this early sarcasm as the almost immediate initiation of conflict while the laypeople assessed conflict as beginning later in the video. Simultaneous to the vocal cue was a nonverbal signal in terms of exhalation. The conflict initiator when she sees him on the couch with eyes glanced upward.

The second cue that was reported occurred 36 seconds later in which there was sneering about how long it took. Essentially, this sneering reflects verbal contempt (Gottman, Gottman, & DeClaire, 2006). Verbal characteristics include attacking your partner's self-concept with the desire to insult or verbally abuse him/her, hostile humor, mockery or ridicule. Nonverbal cues are seen in body language and voice tone through sneering, rolling your eyes and curling your upper lip (Gottman et al., 2006). The third cue involves raised eyebrows and hostile voice tone at 1:02 seconds in the conflict. Her facial expression reveals anger and frustration. This cue also reflects contempt.

The fourth cue is criticism. Gottman (2013) notes how criticisms are productive in conflict while complaints should be avoided. A criticism is focused while a complaint is an attack on a person's personality or character traits. Indeed, complaining about one's spouse is normal. Yet the way that we express these complaints is very important. The detective's observations reflect Gottman et al. (2006) and Gottman's (2013) notion of the four horsemen of the apocalypse which are corrosive behaviors resulting in divorce or the ending of close, personal relationships. The behaviors are criticism, contempt, defensiveness, and withdrawal. These behaviors create a cascading sequence of reactions in which one partner expresses criticism and the other partner responds with defensiveness, causing the first partner to react to the defensiveness with contempt, sarcasm, and/ or hostility with their partner, eventually withdrawing from, or stonewalling, the conversation.

Straus (2001) reports on dating aggression from 31 universities in 16 countries worldwide. The sample contained 8,666 students including 5,919 women and 2,747 men. Results reveal that overall 25% of men and 28% of women assaulted their dating partner in the past year. A larger percentage of women than men assaulted their dating partner at 21 of the 31 universities studied. Moreover, in terms of severe assaults a higher rate of perpetration by women occurred in a majority (18 of the 31) of the sites. Five years later, Straus (2006) reports in a study of over 13,000 students at 68 universities in 32 countries that 33% of students assaulted their dating partners during the previous 12 months. In terms of initiation, mutual aggression accounted for 68.6% of physical violence, while women initiated violence 21.4% of the time and men initiated violence 9.9% of the time.

Over 30 studies examining differences in physical coercion found approximately equal rates of violence (in both frequency and severity of attacks) by the women. For example, Shook, Gerrity, Jurich, and Segrist (2000) report in a study of college dating students using 395 women and 177 men that significantly more women than men, 23.5% versus 13.0%, admitted using physical force against a dating partner. These findings may seem counterintuitive because of the cultural image of women as less violent than men, which in turn is bolstered by women's much lower rate of violent crime outside of the family. As a result, aggression by wives has been studied less than that of husbands, and findings of equal rates of violence by wives (Stets & Straus, 1990; Straus et al., 1980) have been regarded as controversial and have been challenged by some feminist scholars (Dobash, Dobash, Wilson, & Daly, 1992; Pleck, Pleck, Grossman, & Bart, 1978). However, White and Kowalski (1994) deconstruct the myth of nonaggressive women by offering explanations for this including the idea that female aggression is labeled differently. For example, a number of studies reveal that men but not women underreport their own aggression, both sexes underreport their own aggression, and men underreport their victimization (review Archer, 1999).

The motives for using physical violence during courtship differ slightly as a function of gender. Makepeace (1986) reports self-defense as the number one motive for women while uncontrollable anger was number one for men and number two for women. Intimidation was the second most common motive for men. Interestingly, both men and women commonly cited self-defense and retaliation. Since then, other studies have replicated this pattern of findings (Foshee, 1996; Kaiser & Powers, 2006).

Miller and Simpson (1991) reported that men and women perceive sanction risk and severity differently. Men are surer of informal and formal sanctions against violence while both sexes trivialized female violence against males, while male violence against females was viewed as more serious. This study also found that women were significantly more likely to seek formal or informal intervention and to end abusive relationships compared to men. However, women whose parents were violent were more likely to stay in the relationship compared to women whose parents were nonviolent.

It has been argued that physical violence by husbands and wives cannot be equated because of the greater potential for physical injury by husbands given their greater size and strength; women are six times more likely to require medical care for injuries sustained in family violence (Kantor & Straus, 1987; Stets & Straus, 1990). Culture and religiously scripted messages may influence the organization of traditional gender roles in families, and family integrity may be valued more than the cost of enduring abuse. For example, the only grounds for divorce in covenant marriage are physical or sexual abuse, a felony with jail time, and adultery.

Verbal Aggression, Arguing, and Physical Coercion

Infante and Wigley (1986) defined verbal aggression as a personality disposition that "predisposes persons to attack the self-concepts of other people instead of, or in addition to, their positions on topics of communication" (p. 61). Verbally aggressive messages degrade another's personality, skills, and physical appearance. It includes teasing, sarcasm, and profanity. Although the effort to put down the other is often verbal, it may also be nonverbal, involving "facial expressions, gestures, and eye behaviors that attack his or her self-concept" (Sabourin, Infante, & Rudd, 1993, p. 247). Conversely, argumentativeness is defined as the presentation and defense of one's positions on controversial issues while attacking the positions taken by others on issues. The locus of attack is the message, not the other person. This is contrary to other definitions of arguing that involve yelling, taunting, and anger. Hence, argumentativeness is constructive while verbal aggression is destructive (Infante & Rancer, 1995). Numerous studies find that arguing often precedes family violence (e.g., Roscoe, Goodwin, & Kennedy, 1987; Straus & Gelles, 1990; Straus et al., 1980). Arguing has been found to be a predictor of violence against wives (Hoffman, Demo, & Edwards, 1994; Stets, 1991). However, the definition of arguing in these studies reflects verbal provocation and aversive comments and is different from the concept of argumentativeness. It actually reflects verbal aggression in the form of attack on another's person's character.

In this regard, verbal aggression is associated with lower marital satisfaction while argumentativeness is positively correlated with higher marital satisfaction (Payne & Sabouarin, 1990; Sabourin et al., 1993). Moreover, Infante, Chandler, and Rudd (1989) found comparing a clinical sample of 60 abused wives from a battered shelter and 53 abusive husbands undergoing group therapy for wife abuse to a nonclinical sample of 80 males and 83 females that husbands and wives in violent marriages were lower in self-reported argumentativeness while being higher in verbal aggression than the nonviolent sample. Even though argumentativeness was slightly associated with verbal aggression, the magnitude of the correlation was low ($r = .24$). Furthermore, Infante and Wigley (1986) reported a correlation of .32 between physical assault and verbal aggression. Additionally, stress is linked with verbal aggression in various ways (Bodenmann, Meuwly, Bradbury, Gmelch, & Ledermann, 2010). Individuals who use maladaptive capacities for managing stress (e.g., consumption of substances, denial, focusing on negative emotions) use more verbal aggression when stress levels are low. Yet, when stress is higher, individuals who vary in their coping strategies reported similar levels of verbal aggression. We have all the heard cliché, "I've had enough and the straw that broke the camel's back." Stress increasingly occurs when demands outweigh the resources.

As rage mounts, verbal aggression intensifies, possibly culminating in physical violence. If a person experiences heightened arousal but stops short of physical violence, the result can be suppressed rage. Addressing the idea of increased arousal leading to violence, Zillmann (1983, 2003) discusses the notion of excitation transfer. According to this idea, a verbally aggressive act produces negative emotional reaction, such as anger, and a covert verbal response, which facilitates recall of the emotional experience at a later date. From this description, it seems likely that imagined interactions (IIs) facilitate the recollection process (Honeycutt, 2010). Recall from Chapter 3 that imagined interactions are a type of daydreaming in which we imagine talking to important people in our lives. They help maintain relationships with the relational partner. A proactive II occurs before an anticipated conversation as a person rehearses or plans what he/she will say while retroactive IIs occur after actual encounters, as a person replays the event in his or her mind.

Zillmann (2003) suggests that the trace of negative affect left behind (perhaps revisited through the use of IIs) can combine additively with subsequent verbally aggressive acts. "Basically, residues of excitation from previous verbally aggressive acts, if not dissipated, intensify intentions to behave aggressively toward the origin of the verbal aggression" (Infante et al., 1989, p. 165).

According to imagined interaction conflict-linkage theory, a factor that serves to perpetuate residual excitation is the proactive and retroactive imagined interaction. Theorem 1 of II conflict-management theory (Honeycutt, 2003, 2004) states that recurring conflict is maintained through retro- and proactive IIs. Individuals relive old arguments while simultaneously preparing for new ones. Hence, conversations are linked together as individuals replay fights in memory as well as sometimes anticipating what he/she will say at the next encounter. Aside from dwelling on past grievances, individuals unfortunately manage conflict through dysfunctional means because of an inability to effectively argue their points of view and how they are feeling.

Theorem 4 of II conflict-management theory states that suppressed rage is the result of the lack of opportunity or inability to articulate arguments with the target of conflict and reflect argumentative skill deficiency (Honeycutt, 2003, 2004, 2010). Research by Infante and his associates (1989) supports the notion that an inability to state arguments with a target of conflict causes increased levels of arousal as the individual becomes frustrated. Infante and Rancer (1995) argue (no pun intended) that verbal aggressiveness is a catalyst to physical violence, whereas argumentativeness may prevent it. Moreover, verbal aggression and lack of arguing extend to other aggressive interpersonal behavior including date rape.

Research reveals that acceptance of date rape myths is positively correlated with verbal aggression and negatively associated with argumentativeness (see Swift & Honeycutt, 2006).

Infante et al. (1989) discuss communication skills deficiency in terms of the inability to devise rational and coherent arguments that deal with the area of conflict, rather than personally or verbally attacking the person with whom one is in conflict. This research has found that an inability to articulate arguments with a target of conflict causes increased levels of arousal. As rage mounts, verbal aggression intensifies, possibly culminating in physical violence. If a person experiences heightened arousal but stops short of physical violence, the result can be suppressed rage. Additionally, a study reporting husband-to-wife violence contrasted three types of couples based on their scores on a marital quality survey and whether they physically assaulted their partner in the past year reveals that violent and nonviolent/low quality couples were more likely than nonviolent/high quality were less likely to reach agreement or make a decision when discussing relationship problems (Rehman, Holtzworth-Munroe, Herron, & Clements, 2009). Thus, distressed couples who are deadlocked when trying to resolve issues face more stress and lack the communication skills necessary to negotiate solutions. Moreover, this study was done in a laboratory where the couple was instructed to reach a solution and the experimenter even knocked on the door to remind the couple to decide on a solution. If the violent and unhappy couples were unable to perform in a lab where problem-solving was encouraged, "it seems unlikely that they are effectively solving problems in the real world" (Rehman et al., 2009, p. 486).

Prior studies of imagined interaction support that idea that some individuals have cannot forgive or forget. They ruminate about past transgressions. Self-focused rumination occurs when people repetitively focus on themselves and on the cause and implications of negative feelings (Lyubomirsky, Tucker, Caldwell, & Berg, 1999). Rumination enhances negative thinking and poor problem solving (Nolen-Hoeksema, 1991). Other research on rumination has revealed that people who seek revenge against offenders report more rumination and are more likely to retaliate following threats to their self-esteem (Collins & Bell, 1997; Stuckless & Goranson, 1992).

Imagined Interactions and Verbal Aggression in Predicting Physical Coercion

In a prior study, I ran a path analysis predicting physical coercion that contained the following characteristics of IIs: valence, frequency, proactivity, specificity, discrepancy, and self-dominance (Honeycutt, 2003). Table 11.4 predicts two sample imagined interactions from that data that reflect the difference between criticizing and complaining. Criticizing is bad while complaining is good. The first imagined interaction comes from a married 42-year-old female who complains about her husband's mental temperament. This is an example of Gottman et al.'s (2006) notion of criticism as distinguished from complaints. Criticisms are global statements using negative words (e.g., putdowns, taunts, ridicule) about a partner's personality while complaints address the specific area at which the partner failed. Criticizing is destructive while complaints are constructive.

The second imagined interaction comes from a 21-year-old male who is in an exclusive romance. He is criticizing his girlfriend's drinking. It is important to notice how his imagined interaction is more specific and devoid of personal attacks compared to the other imagined interaction. He also imagines that her responses are more positive and less defensive.

Table 11.4. Sample imagined interaction distinguishing criticism from complaints.

Imagined Interaction 1: Criticism

   Participant: Married, 42-year-old female

      Self: You have the absolute worst temper I've ever seen. You're always angry over the smallest thing.

      Partner: Why do you have to lecture me when I'm angry? You're bitchy.

      Self: I'm not lecturing you. I just don't understand, I mean who gets mad and throws a fit because they don't get their way?

      Partner: Listen, I don't need your comments when I'm angry.

      Self: I'm sorry, I just can't sit here and watch you get angry and then you turn on me. I think I'll just leave until you can cool off and think about things.

Imagined Interaction 2: Complaint

   Participant: Dating, 21-year-old male

      Self: How come, every time you drink, you get so drunk, you don't know how to walk or even resort to vomiting?

      Partner: I just like to have fun, when I drink. I'm not hurting anyone. You act like I do it all the time.

      Self: I feel like you cannot watch your limit. I worry about you. I believe you may have a drinking problem.

      Partner: I appreciate your concern.

Three functions of IIs were tested in the model: catharsis, self-understanding, and conflict-management. I sampled people in long-term relationships who were either dating or married. The participants consisted of 126 individuals containing 58 males and 68 females. The mean age of the sample was 23.95 and ranged from 18 to 52. Persons knew their partners an average of 6 years (Range: 4 months to 36 years, SD = 93.17) and averaged 4 years, 7 months exclusively seeing them. The data revealed that in the context of measuring verbal and physical aggression, activity, proactivity, and specificity best reflect the characteristics of IIs that are important in predicting verbal aggression. Catharsis and self-understanding were the most important functions of IIs in predicting verbal aggression.

Persuasive arguing was reflected by items indicating a tendency to either approach arguments (e.g., Arguing over controversial issues improves my intelligence. I am energetic and enthusiastic when I argue. I have the ability to do well in an argument" or items indicating a tendency to avoid arguments (e.g., I enjoy avoiding arguments (Infante & Rancer, 1982). Arguing with a person creates more problems than it solves. I find myself unable to think of effective points during an argument.). As expected, the best indicator of persuasive arguing was approaching arguments.

Verbal aggression was measured using Infante and Wigley's (1986) verbal aggression measure consisting of 10 items (e.g., When individuals are very stubborn, I use insults to soften the stubbornness. When individuals insult me, I get a lot of pleasure out of really telling them off. When nothing seems to work in trying to influence others, I yell and scream in order to get some movement from them.) Another 10 items reflected avoiding verbal aggression (e.g., I am extremely careful to avoid attacking individuals' intelligence when I attack their ideas. When people criticize my shortcomings, I take it in good humor and do not try to get back at them. When an argument shifts to personal attacks, I try very hard to change the subject.).

Physical coercion was measured using the Straus (1990) Conflict Tactics Scale (CTS) as earlier discussed. Recall that his scale measures reasoning, verbal aggression, and physical coercion as methods of dealing with relational conflict. For reasoning tactics, people are asked how often during the past year, they discussed issues calmly, got information to back up their position or tried to bring in someone to help settle things. Verbal aggression is measured by reports of insults or swearing, sulking or refusing to talk about an issue, leaving the room, spiting the partner, and threatening to hit or throw something. The use of insults or swearing and spiting the partner is reflected in Infante and Wigley's (1986) verbal aggression measure. Physical coercion represents actually throwing something, pushing, grabbing, shoving, slapping, kicking, biting, hitting, choking, threatening to use a gun or knife, and actually using a gun or knife.

II characteristics of frequency, proactivity, and specificity predicted verbal aggression. However, the II characteristics did not predict persuasive arguments. A possible explanation for that was the slight path from II functions to verbal aggression. The path analysis reflects how catharsis and self-understanding reflect II functions that predict verbal aggression. Perhaps, individuals who imagine being verbally aggressive as opposed to thinking about rational arguments let off steam (catharsis) while also believing that they understand their rage better (Honeycutt, 2003). The path analysis also supported Infante and Wigley's (1986) contention of a direct link between verbal aggression and physical coercion.

A limitation of that analysis was that imagined interactions were never tested as mediating the direct link between verbal aggression and physical violence. We gathered additional data (N = 216) in which imagined interactions were tested as a mediator between verbal aggression and physical coercion. Previously, withdrawal has been cited as an example of psychological aggression (Straus, Hamby, Boney-McCoy, & Sugarman, 1996). An example of withdrawal is in the first imagined interaction of Table 11.3 where the married woman wants to leave after criticizing her husband about his mental temperament. However, in the current analysis we eliminated withdrawal from the new model because it represents stomping out of the room, refusing to talk about an issue, saying something to spite the partner, or trying to bring someone in to help. Figures 11.1 and 11.2 contain two contrasting path models. In both models, the context of verbal aggression, imagined interaction was best represented by how frequent they occur (B = .83), occurring before the encounter (Proactivity B = .58) as well as having specific imagery about the scene of the encounter (Specificity B = .75). In addition, imagined interactions were indicated by slight feelings of catharsis (B = .26) as well as thinking and ruminating about conflicts with the relational partner (conflict linkage B = .63).

Figure 11.1 reveals the direct link verbal aggression and physical abuse (B = .59) which is quite strong. The ovals represent unmeasured variables not actually measured. For example, the concept of imagined interactions is measured by the indices represented in the boxes. Thus, the frequency of having IIs is a good indicator of the theoretical concept of imagined interactions. The higher the number, the more the variable predicts the theoretical construct in a positive or negative direction. The model contains standardized regression coefficients that take into account error associated with measurement. Notice that there is a slight path leading from imagined interactions to physical abuse (B = .17) even the association is small. The path between persuasive arguing and physical abuse is small, yet

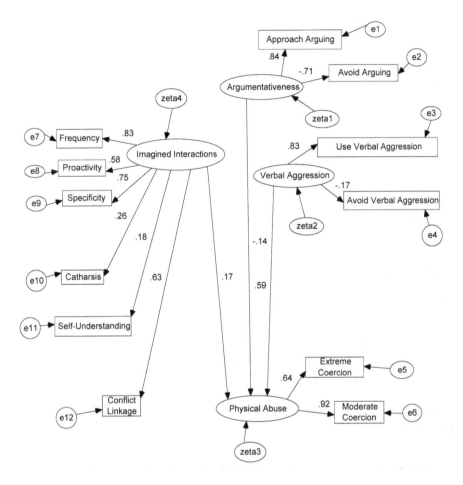

Figure 11.1. Standardized path model of argumentativeness, verbal aggression, and imagined interactions leading to physical abuse.

negative. ($B = -.14$). Hence, at first glance, it appears that persuasive argumentativeness is negatively associated with abuse. However, goodness of fit measures revealed that this model does not fit the data well despite a few good paths.

Alternative models were tested. A good-fitting model contains direct effects of verbal aggression on physical abuse as well as imagined interactions leading to abuse as they partially mediate the direct effect of verbal aggression on physical abuse. In this model, argumentativeness was eliminated from the analysis because of earlier poor fits. Indeed, the goodness of fit indices for the mediation model revealed a better fit of the data. Figure 11.2 reveals that imagined interactions mediate the link between verbal aggression and physical coercion. The

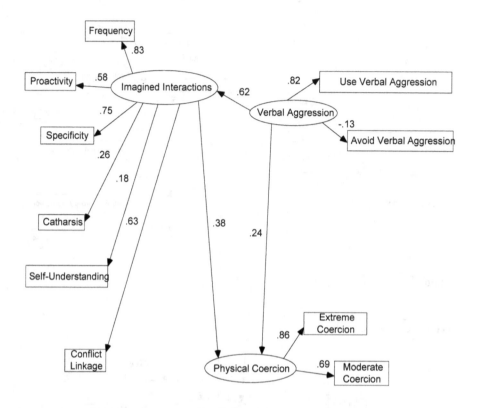

Figure 11.2. Standardized mediational model of imagined interactions, verbal aggression, and physical coercion.

meditational model reveals that imagined interactions intervene in the direct link between verbal aggression and physical coercion by reducing it to .12. Verbal aggression also leads to imagined interactions (B = .62) which in turn, lead to physical abuse (B = .38). The direct effect of verbal aggression is reduced from .59 in the first model to .24 in the meditational model. The bottom line is that some abusers have imagined interactions before striking out. The abuse appears to be planned and associated with ruminating about past grievances and conflicts. The abuse is *not* associated with argumentativeness in which individuals see arguing as intellectual exchanges of ideas and information such as in forensic debates.

Pit-Bull and Cobra Batterers

The meditational model can be interpreted as providing support for Gottman and Levenson (1999) profile of the pit-bull batterer. The majority of batterers fit this profile. There is a slow build up of anger. Hence, the conflict slowly escalates giving these batterers time to ruminate and plan their strike. Conversely, cobra batterers strike quickly with no forewarning. They use more severe types of violence including weapons and beatings with closed fists. While 62% of Pit-Bulls reported using closed fists, 91% of Cobras did this. Their heart-rates actually decrease as verbal aggression increases. Pit-bulls have unrelenting contempt for women and yet are very dependent on them. They fear abandonment while the Cobras do not.

The wives are less intimidated in Pit-Bull marriages and are likely to argue back. They are angrier, less fearful, and more constantly controlled compared to the wives of Cobras. Furthermore, half of pit-bull marriages dissolve within two years while 25% of Cobra wives left after a five-year follow-up (Gottman & Levenson, 1999). Finally, the Cobras are more likely to have a history of "antisocial personality disorder" including childhood episodes of lying, stealing, arson, and cruelty to animals as well as being chemically dependent on drugs or alcohol. Gottman and Levenson (1999) criticize the apparent futility of traditional psychotherapy programs in dealing with abuse. They found that 54% of male volunteers showed decreases in violence during the second of the 2 follow-up years. Yet, this decrease in violence may be misleading because once control is established over a needy partner; it may be maintained by continued emotional abuse with intermittent battering used as a terrifying reminder of what is possible.

Most treatment programs focus on how men's domination causes violence. Yet, the culture does not provide men behavioral scripts to regulate their negative emotions and sustain trust, compassion, or love. Gottman and Levenson (1999) provide examples of how society provides cultural scripts for women to have an emotional vocabulary that has nothing to do with educational level. When girls cry, they are rewarded for communicating fear or vulnerability (also see Shields, 1987). When little boys express emotion, he may be called a "sissy." Hence, boys are socialized and taught cultural scripts in which they keep vulnerable emotions submerged without developing an emotional vocabulary. If you cannot tell sadness from loneliness from disappointment from rejection for being devalued, bad feelings get overloaded easily.

As indicated in Chapter 2, the strongest emotion is anger. Historically, men have only been allowed to vent anger and this has often been done through constructive channeling such as athletic competition. Yet, communicating too much anger results in anger-management classes. Other basic emotions including surprise, fear, happiness, and sadness have not been socialized for communicating by boys. Indeed, a boy who expresses too many of these emotions may be called an "emotional sissy."

Rumination enhances negative thinking and poor problem solving (Nolen-Hoeksema, 1991). People who seek revenge against offenders report more rumination and are more likely to retaliate following threats to their self-esteem

(Collins & Bell, 1997; Stuckless & Goranson, 1992). This profile complements the imagined interaction mediation model.

We believe that the potential for rehabilitation may lie in our discovery that imagined interactions mediate the direct link between verbal aggression and physical violence. Hence, they are ruminating and thinking about their conflict. Therefore, communication interventionists may attempt to create communication skills for more effective arguing and listening. A number of intervention programs have been tried including empathy instruction (Warner, Parker, & Calhoun, 1984), problem-solving (Markman, Renick, Floyd, Stanley, & Clements, 1993), and training in creating persuasive arguments (Rancer, Kosberg, & Baukus, 1992). The final chapter presents a constructive communication script for effective arguing and listening in interpersonal relationships.

Finally, Gottman and Levenson (1999) discuss the merits of psychotropic drug intervention. For example, the antidepressant, Paxil has been used to increase serotonin levels. Yet, there is the stereotype that men are more likely to illicit drugs or alcohol to mask depression, anxiety, or stress instead of prescribed psychotropic medicines (Moore & Stuart, 2004). A lack of serotonin may lead to anger or depression which results in abuse (Maestripieri et al., 2006).

Summary

The research on abuse is replete with intercultural studies. Abuse is not constrained by economic differences, educational status, or gender. Indeed, the research by Murray Straus indicates few gender differences in abuse. Both men and women abuse; however, the severity of men's actions tend to be more serious. The highest levels of abuse in personal relationships emerge when both partners are initiators (Sabourin et al., 1993).

There are numerous causes of interpersonal violence including control, jealousy, chemical dependency, and financial problems (Stets & Henderson, 1991). Violence in courtship is often a precursor of violence in marriage (Lloyd, 1991). There are different types of abuse including physical, emotional, social, psychological, economic, and elder abuse. There is a definitive cycle of abuse including tension building which is followed by explosion and a honeymoon period; whereupon the cycle often repeats.

The research by Spitzberg and Cupach (2003) reveals how common stalking is. It is associated with an insecure, inadequate attachment style along with a fear of abandonment. Consequently, there is a lack of trust, approach/avoidant behaviors, and ambivalence about commitment. There are different tactics for stalking including hyperintimacy, pursuit, invasion, intimidation, and violence. Both sexes stalk even though more females report being the victims of more severe tactics including violence.

Finally, the link between imagined interactions and abuse was discussed. Some batterers including the pit-bull ruminate about past grievances and arguments and have a slow-burn in which they mentally envision their violent actions. Conversely, cobra batterers strike with no forewarning. It is counter-intuitive that their heart rates actually decrease when striking. Preliminary research suggests that different types of intervention including communication skills training and psychotropic medicines may help in some cases of abuse.

Discussion Questions

11.1. Define the different types of abuse. Is it possible to rank order the different types of abuse in terms of short-term and long-term severity?

11.2. What are the warning signs that someone is an abuser? Is abuse equally likely to occur among men or women? Why or why not?

11.3. Do you believe that abusers have a chemical imbalance in terms of serotonin or testosterone levels? Should abusers be treated with drugs, communication skills training or something else?

11.4. Are introverts or quiet people who desire to avoid arguing more likely to abuse? Why or why not? Are extraverts or out-going people who like to argue more likely to abuse?

Applications

11.1. Interview 2 men and 2 women and ask them their opinion if they believe the internet or media portrays violence and abuse in relationships in terms of jealousy, personality flaws, or communication skills deficiency.

11.2. Copy and access the following clip on YouTube that discusses tips for getting out of an abusive relationship. Would these tips apply to a pit-bull or cobra abuser? Are the tips feasible? http://www.youtube.com/watch?v=Exf4Xi7KW84.

References

Abraham, M. (1999). Sexual abuse in South Asian immigrant marriages. *Violence against Women,* 5, 591–618. doi:10.1177/10778019922181392

Archer, J. (1999). Assessment of the reliability of the conflict tactics scale. *Journal of Interpersonal Violence, 14*, 1263–1289. doi:10.1177/088626099014012003

Axelrod, R. (1997). *The complexity of cooperation: Agent-based models of competition and collaboration.* Princeton, NJ: Princeton University.

Bachman, R., & Saltzman, L. (1995). *Violence against women: Estimates from the redesigned survey.* Rockville, MD: US Dept. of Justice Bureau. Retrieved 2008, June 7, from http://www.ncjrs.gov/App/Publications/abstract.aspx?ID=154348

Black, M. C., Basile, K. C., Breiding, M. J., Smith, S. G., Walters, M. L., Merrick, M. T., ... Stevens, M. R. (2010). *The National intimate partner and sexual violence survey (NISVS): 2010 summary report.* Atlanta, GA: National Center for Injury Prevention and Control, Centers for Disease Control and Prevention.

Bodenmann, G., Meuwly, N., Bradbury, T. N., Gmelch, S., & Ledermann, T. (2010). Stress, anger, and verbal aggression in intimate relationships: Moderating effects of individual and dyadic coping. *Journal of Social and Personal Relationships, 27*, 408–424. doi:10.1177/0265407510361616

Collins, K., & Bell, R. (1997). Personality and aggression: The dissipation-rumination scale. *Personality and Individual Differences, 22*, 751–755. doi:10.1016/S0191-8869(96)00248-6

Cupach, W. R., & Spitzberg, B. H. (1998). Obsessive relational intrusion and stalking. In B. H. Spitzberg & W. R. Cupach (Eds.), *The dark side of close relationships* (pp. 233–263). Hillsdale, NJ: Lawrence Erlbaum.

Davis, K. E., Ace, A., & Andra, M. (2000). Stalking perpetrators and psychological maltreatment of partners. *Violence and Victims, 15*, 407–427.

Dobash, R. P., Dobash, E. D., Wilson, M., & Daly, M. (1992). The myth of sexual symmetry in marital violence. *Social Problems, 39*, 71–91. doi:10.2307/3096914

Douglas, K. S., & Dutton, D. G. (2001). Assessing the link between stalking and domestic violence. *Aggression and Violent Behavior, 6*, 519–546. doi:10.1016/S1359-1789(00)00018-5

Foshee, V. A. (1996). Gender differences in adolescent dating abuse prevalence, types and injuries. *Health Education Research, 11*, 275–286. doi:10.1093/her/11.3.275

Gottman, J. M. (2013). *The four horsemen: The antidotes.* Retrieved from https://www.gottman.com/blog/the-four-horsemen-the-antidotes/

Gottman, J. M., Gottman, J. S., & DeClaire, J. (2006). *Ten lessons to transform your marriage.* New York, NY: Crowne.

Gottman, J. M., & Levenson, R. W. (1999). What predicts change in marital interaction over time? A study of alternative models. *Family Process, 38*, 143–158. doi:10.1111/j.1545-5300.1999.00143.x

Hoffman, K. L., Demo, D. H., & Edwards, J. N. (1994). Physical wife abuse in an non-Western society: An integrated theoretical approach. *Journal of Marriage and the Family, 56*, 131–146. doi:10.2307/352709

Honeycutt, J. M. (2003). *Imagined interaction: Daydreaming about communication.* Cresskill, NJ: Hampton.

Honeycutt, J. M. (2004). Imagined interaction conflict-linkage theory: Explaining the persistence and resolution of interpersonal conflict in everyday life. *Imagination, Cognition, and Personality, 23*, 3–25. doi:10.2190/240J-1VPK-K86D-1JL8

Honeycutt, J. M. (2010). Forgive but don't forget: Correlates of rumination about conflict. In J. M. Honeycutt (Ed.), *Imagine that: Studies in imagined interaction* (pp. 17–29). Cresskill, NJ: Hampton.

Honeycutt, J. M., & Eldredge, J. H. (2015). Applying game theory and signal detection theory to conflict escalation: A case study of a police investigator viewing a domestic argument. In K. Chapman (Ed.), *Decision and game theory: Perspectives, applications and challenges.* New York, NY: Nova Science.

Honeycutt, J. M., Sheldon, P., Pence, M. E., & Hatcher, L. C. (2015). Predicting aggression, conciliation, and concurrent rumination in escalating conflict. *Journal of Interpersonal Violence, 30*, 133–151. doi:10.1177/0886260514532717

Infante, D. A., Chandler, T. A., & Rudd, J. E. (1989). Test of an argumentative skill deficiency model of interpersonal violence. *Communication Monographs, 56*, 163–177. doi:10.1080/03637758909390257

Infante, D. A., & Rancer, A. S. (1982). A conceptualization and measure of argumentativeness. *Journal of Personality Assessment, 46*, 72–80. doi:10.1207/s15327752jpa4601_13

Infante, D. A., & Rancer, A. S. (1995). Argumentativeness and verbal aggressiveness: A review of recent theory and research. *Annals of the International Communication Association, 19*, 319–352. doi:10.1080/23808985.1996.11678934

Infante, D. A., & Wigley, C. J. (1986). Verbal aggressiveness: An interpersonal model and measure. *Communication Monographs, 53*, 61–69. doi:10.1080/03637758609376126

Ito, T. A., Miller, N., & Pollock, V. E. (1996). A meta-analysis on the moderating effects of inhibitory cues, triggering events, and self-focused attention. *Psychological Bulletin, 120*, 60–82. doi:10.1037/0033-2909.120.1.60

Kaiser, H., & Powers, S. (2006). Testosterone and conflict tactics within late-adolescent couples: A dyadic predictive model. *Journal of Social and Personal Relationships, 23*, 231–248. doi:10.1177/0265407506062473

Kantor, G. K., & Straus, M. A. (1987). The "drunken bum" theory of wife beating. *Social Problems, 34*, 213–230. doi:10.2307/800763

Kienlen, K. K. (1998). Developmental antecedents of stalking. In J. R. Meloy (Ed.), *The psychology of stalking: Clinical and forensic perspectives* (pp. 139–161). San Diego, CA: Academic Press.

Lewis, S., Fremouw, W. J., Del Ben, K., & Farr, C. (2001). An investigation of the psychological characteristics of stalkers: Empathy, problem-solving, attachment and borderline personality features. *Journal of Forensic Sciences, 46*, 80–84. doi:10.1520/JFS14915J

Lloyd, S. A. (1991). The darkside of courtship: Violence and sexual exploitation. *Family Relations, 40*, 14–20. doi:10.2307/585653

Logan, T., & Walker, R. (2010). Toward a deeper understanding of the harms caused by partner stalking. *Violence and Victims, 25*, 440–455.

Lyubomirsky, S., Tucker, K. L., Caldwell, N. D., Berg, K. (1999). Why ruminators are poor problem solvers: Clues from the phenomenology of dysphoric rumination. *Journal of Personality and Social Psychology, 77*, 1041–1060. doi:10.1037/0022-3514.77.5.1041

Maestripieri, D., Higley, J. D., Lindell, S. G., Newman, T. K., McCormack, K., & Sanchez, M. M. (2006). Early maternal rejection affects the development of monoaminergic systems and adult abusive parenting in rhesus macaques. *Behavioral Neuroscience, 120,* 1017–1024. doi:10.1037/0735-7044.120.5.1017

Makepeace, J. M. (1986). Gender differences in courtship violence victimization. *Family Relations, 35,* 383–388.

Markman, H. J., Renick, M. J., Floyd, F. J., Stanley, S. M., & Clements, M. (1993). Preventing marital distress through communication and conflict management training: A 4- and 5-year follow-up. *Journal of Consulting and Clinical Psychology, 61,* 70–77. doi:10.1037/0022-006X.61.1.70

Marshall, L. L. (1994). Physical and psychological abuse. In B. H. Spitzberg & W. Cupach (Eds.), *The darkside of interpersonal communication* (pp. 283–311). Hillsdale, NJ: Lawrence Erlbaum.

McCullough, M. E. (2008). *Beyond revenge: The evolution of the forgiveness instinct.* San Francisco, CA: Jossey-Bass.

Mechanic, M. B., Weaver, T. L., & Resick, P. A. (2000). Intimate partner violence and stalking behavior: Exploration of patterns and correlates in a sample of acutely battered women. *Violence and Victims, 15,* 55–72.

Miller, S. L., & Simpson, S. S. (1991). Courtship violence and social control: Does gender matter? *Law and Society Review, 25,* 335–365. doi:10.2307/3053802

Moore, T. M., & Stuart, G. L. (2004). Illicit substance use and intimate partner violence among men in batterers' intervention. *Psychology of Addictive Behaviors, 18,* 385–389.

Mouradian, V. E. (2007). *Abuse in intimate relationships: Defining the multiple dimensions and terms.* Retrieved 2007, July 3, from http://www.musc.edu/vawprevention/research/defining.shtml

Nolen-Hoeksema, S. (1991). Responses to depression and their effects on the duration of depressive episodes. *Journal of Abnormal Psychology, 110,* 569–582.

Payne, M. J., & Sabourin, T. C. (1990). Argumentative skill deficiency and its relationship to quality of marriage. *Communication Research Reports, 7,* 121–124. doi:10.1080/08824099009359865

Pleck, E., Pleck, J. H., Grossman, M., & Bart, P. B. (1978). The battered data syndrome: A comment on Steinmetz' article. *Victimology, 2,* 680–683.

Rancer, A. S., Kosberg, R. L., & Baukus, R A. (1992). Beliefs about arguing as predictors of trait argumentativeness: Implications for training in argument and conflict management. *Communication Education, 41,* 375–387. doi:10.1080/03634529209378899

Rapoport, A. (1966). *Two-person game theory: The essential ideas.* Ann Arbor, MI: University of Michigan Press.

Rehman, U. S., Holtzworth-Munroe, A., Herron, K., & Clements, K. (2009). "My way or no way": Anarchic power, relationship satisfaction, and violence. *Personal Relationships, 16,* 475–488. doi:10.1111/j.1475-6811.2009.01235.x

Roscoe, B., Goodwin, M. P., & Kennedy, D. (1987). Sibling violence and agonistic interaction experienced by early adolescents. *Journal of Family Violence, 2,* 121–137. doi:10.1007/BF00977037

Sabourin, T. C., Infante, D. A., & Rudd, J. E. (1993). Verbal aggression in marriages: A comparison of violent, distressed but nonviolent, and nondistressed couples. *Human Communication Research, 20,* 245–267. doi:10.1111/j.1468-2958.1993.tb00323.x

Shepard, M. F., & Campbell, J. A. (1992). The Abusive Behavior Inventory: A measure of psychological and physical abuse. *Journal of Interpersonal Violence, 7*, 291-305. doi:10.1177/088626092007003001

Shergill, S. S., Bays, P. M., Frith, C. D., & Wolpert, D. M. (2003). Two eyes for an eye: The neuroscience of force escalation. *Science (New York, N.Y.), 301*(5630), 187.

Shields, S. A. (1987). Women, men, and the dilemma of emotion. In P. Shaver & C. Hendrick (Eds.), *Sex and gender*. Beverly Hills, CA: Sage.

Shook, N. J., Gerrity, D. A., Jurich, J., & Segrist, A. E. (2000). Courtship violence among college students: A comparison of verbally and physically abusive couples. *Journal of Family Violence, 15*, 1–22. doi:10.1023/A:1007532718917

Signorelli, M. S., Arcidiacono, E., Musumeci, G., Di, N. S., & Aguglia, E. (2014). Detecting domestic violence: Italian validation of revised conflict tactics scale (CTS-2). *Journal of Family Violence, 29*(4), 361–369. doi:10.1007/s10896-014-9594-5

Spitzberg, B. H. (2002). The tactical topography of stalking victimization and management. *Trauma, Violence, & Abuse, 3*, 261–288. doi:10.1177/1524838002237330

Spitzberg, B. H., & Cupach, W. R. (2003). What mad pursuit? Obsessive relational intrusion and stalking related phenomenon. *Aggression and Violent Behavior, 8*, 345–375. doi:10.1016/S1359-1789(02)00068-X

Spitzberg, B., & Cupach, W. (2007). The state of the art stalking: Taking stock of the emerging literature. *Aggression and Violent Behavior, 12*, 64–86. doi:10.1016/j.avb.2006.05.001

Spitzberg, B. H., & Rhea, J. (1999). Obsessive relational intrusion and sexual coercion victimization. *Journal of Interpersonal Violence, 14*(1), 3–20. doi:10.1177/088626099014001001

Stets, J. E. (1991). Psychological aggression in dating relationships: The role of interpersonal control. *Journal of Family Violence, 6*, 97–114. doi:10.1007/BF00978528

Stets, J. E., & Henderson, D. A. (1991). Contextual factors surrounding conflict resolution while dating: Results from a national study. *Family Relations, 40*, 29–36. doi:10.2307/585655

Stets, J. E., & Straus, M. (1990). Gender differences in reporting marital violence and its medical and psychological consequences. In M. A. Straus & R. J. Gelles (Eds.), *Physical violence in American families: Risk factors and adaptations to violence in 18,145 families* (pp. 151–165). New Brunswick, NJ: Transaction Books.

Straus, M. A. (1979). Measuring intrafamily conflict and violence: The Conflict Tactics Scales. *Journal of Marriage and the Family, 41*, 75–88. doi:10.2307/351733

Straus, M. A. (1990a). Measuring intrafamily conflict: The conflict tactics (CTS) scales. In M. Straus & R. J. Gelles (Eds.), *Physical violence in American families: Risk factors and adaptations to violence in 8,145 families* (pp. 29–45). New Brunswick, NJ: Transaction Books.

Straus, M. A. (1990b). The Conflict Tactics Scales and its critics: An evaluation and new data on validity and reliability. In M. A. Straus & R. J. Gelles (Eds.), *Physical violence in American families: Risk factors and adaptations to violence in 8,145 families* (pp. 49–73). New Brunswick, NJ: Transaction.

Straus, M. A. (2001). Prevalence of violence against dating partners by male and female university students worldwide. *Violence against Women, 10*, 790–811. doi:10.1177/1077801204265552

Straus, M. A. (2005). Women's violence toward men is a serious social problem. In D. R. Loseke, R. J. Gelles, & M. M. Cavanaugh (Eds.), *Current controversies on family violence* (2nd ed., pp. 55–77). Thousand Oaks, CA: Sage.

Straus, M. A. (2006, May). *Dominance and symmetry in partner violence by male and female university students in 32 nations.* Paper presented on Trends in Intimate Violence Intervention, sponsored by University of Haifa and New York University.

Straus, M. A. (2007). Conflict tactics scales. In N. A. Jackson (Ed.), *Encyclopedia of domestic violence* (pp. 195). New York, NY: Routledge.

Straus, M. A., & Douglas, E. M. (2004). A short form of the revised Conflict Tactics Scales, and typologies for severity and mutuality. *Violence and Victims, 19,* 507–520. doi:10.1891/088667004780927800

Straus, M. A., & Gelles, R. J. (1990). How violent are American families? Estimates from the National Family Violence Resurvey and other studies. In M. Straus & R. Gelles (Eds.), *Physical violence in American families: Risk factors and adaptations to violence in 8,145 families* (pp. 95–112). New Brunswick, NJ: Transaction.

Straus, M. A., Gelles, R. J., & Steinmetz, S. K. (1980). *Behind closed doors: Violence in the American family.* Garden City, NY: Anchor/Doubleday.

Straus, M. A., Hamby, S. L., Boney-McCoy, S., & Sugarman, D. B. (1996). The revised conflict tactics scales (CTS2). *Journal of Family Issues, 17,* 283–316. doi:10.1177/019251396017003001

Straus, M. A., Kaufman, G. K., & Moore, D. W. (1994, August). *Change in cultural norms approving marital violence from 1968 to 1994.* Paper presented at the American Sociological Association, Los Angeles, CA.

Stuckless, N., & Goranson, R. (1992). The vengeance scale: Development of a measure of attitudes toward revenge. *Journal of Social Behavior and Personality, 7,* 25–42.

Swift, C. L., & Honeycutt, J. M. (2006, November). *Emotional responses and acceptance of rape myths by college students.* Paper presented at the annual National Communication Association Convention, San Antonio, CA.

Thompson, E. H., Jr. (1990). Courtship violence and the male role. *Men's Studies Review, 7,* 4–13.

Tjaden, P., & Thoennes, N. (2000). Extent, nature, and consequences of intimate partner violence. *National Institute of Justice.* Retrieved 2016, July 9, from https://www.ncjrs.gov/pdffiles1/nij/181867.pdf

U.S. Department of Justice. (1998). *Violence by intimates: Analysis of data on crimes by current or former spouses, boyfriends, and girlfriends.* Retrieved from http://bjs.gov/content/pub/pdf/vi.pdf

Violence Against Women. (2015). Retrieved from the World Health Organization. Retrieved from http://www.who.int/mediacentre/factsheets/fs239/en/

Vissing, Y. M., Straus, M. A., Gelles, R., & Harrop, J. W. (1991). Verbal aggression by parents and psychosocial problems of children. *Child Abuse and Neglect: The International Journal, 15,* 223–238. doi:10.1016/0145-2134(91)90067-N

Walker, L. E. (1984). *The battered woman syndrome.* New York, NY: Springer-Verlag.

Walker, L. E. (1986). Psychological causes of family violence. In M. Lystad (Ed.), *Violence in the home: Interdisciplinary perspectives* (pp. 71–91). New York, NY: Brunner/Mazel.

Walker, L. E. (1991). Post-traumatic stress disorder in women: Diagnosis and treatment of battered women syndrome. *Psychotherapy, 28*, 21–29. doi:10.1037/0033-3204.28.1.21

Walker, L. E., & Meloy, J. R. (1998). Stalking and domestic violence. In J. R. Meloy (Ed.), *The psychology of stalking: Clinical and forensic perspectives* (pp. 139–161). San Diego, CA: Academic.

Warner, M. H., Parker, J. B., & Calhoun, J. E. (1984). Inducing person perception change in a spouse-abuse situation. *Family Therapy, 11*, 123–138.

White, J. W., & Kowalski, R. M. (1994). Deconstructing the myth of the nonaggressive woman: A feminist analysis. *Psychology of Women Quarterly, 18*, 487–508. doi:10.1111/j.1471-6402.1994.tb01045.x

Women's Health. (2004). Family violence prevention fund and advocates for youth. Retrieved from http://www.med.umich.edu/whp/newsletters/summer04/p03-dating.html

Zillmann, D. (1983). Transfer of excitation in emotional behavior. In J. T. Cacioppo & R. E. Petty (Eds.), *Social psychology: A sourcebook* (pp. 215–240). New York, NY: Guilford.

Zillmann, D. (2003). Theory of affective dynamics: Communication and emotion. In J. Bryant, D. R. Roskos-Ewoldsen, & J. Cantor (Eds.), *Essays in honor of Dolf Zillmann* (pp. 553–567). New York, NY: Guilford.

CHAPTER TWELVE

The Dark Side of Social Media Communication

Social media differ from traditional media such as newspapers, radio, and television, as they are less expensive and more accessible. They allow every consumer of a media product to be a producer as well. The most significant difference is the absence of a gatekeeper. While there are many positive benefits of social media, news headlines remind us daily that social media can negatively affect our lives. This chapter discusses the dark side of social media, including a shorter attention span and social media addiction, selective self-presentation and narcissism, the declining quality of interpersonal relationships, issues of privacy and security, cyberstalking, cyberbullying, misinformation and online deception.

Mechanization, Attention Deficit, and Addiction

In his book *Digital Pandemic*, Hicks (2010) argues that digital technologies have made us very passive. We shop, play games, and socialize while sitting at home. Mechanization, he argues, is impairing our critical thinking and communication. The Pew Research Center (2012) survey of 1,021 technology stakeholders revealed concern for the Millennial generation (people born between 1980 and 2000, also known as Generation Y), predicting that they would lack patience, settle for quick choices, and thirst for instant gratification. Lack of patience is related to a dropping attention span. An attention span is defined as the amount of time concentrated on a task without becoming distracted. According to the National Center for Biotechnology Information (NCBI) at the U.S. National Library of Medicine, the average attention span of a human being has dropped from 12 seconds in 2000 to 8 seconds in 2013 (NCBI, 2014). This deficit has negative consequences on an individual's ability to focus in school, at work, and even when meeting friends in restaurants. People text during meetings and tweet while watching television, falsely believing that they can multitask. In his book *Obsession with Technology and Overcoming Its Hold on Us*, Rosen (2012) reports that, on average, 13-to-18 year olds use more than six types of media simultaneously when not at school.

DeWeese (2014) surveyed students and teachers at affluent public school in San Francisco Bay area to find out if adding technology at school is allowing students to be more connected, and how that technology affects their brains, as well as their social and emotional well-being. Many of the teachers interviewed agreed that there is an epidemic of anxiety and depression as well as an addiction to texting. Students were also less connected to their peers because of technology. When asked about multitasking 90% said they use various technologies at the same time. Only 10% said that they do one thing at a time. Many feel the fear of missing out, meaning that if they are not connected digitally they are not a part of what is going on. Digital natives switch their attention at the first sign of boredom (DeWeese, 2014).

Another problem related to overuse of social media is an addiction. According to Griffiths (2000), an Internet user is considered addicted if he or she scores highly on the following criteria: salience (when the activity becomes the most important thing in an individual's life), mood change, tolerance (the process of requiring continually higher doses of the activity to achieve the original sensation), withdrawal symptoms (negative feelings that accompany not being able to perform the online activity), and conflict (interpersonal conflict with family or partner due to online activity). Despite existing research, a precise estimate of the prevalence of Internet addiction does not exist. In 2006, a group of researchers (Aboujaoude, Koran, Gamel, Large, & Serpe, 2006) at the Stanford University School of Medicine found that one out of eight Americans exhibited at least one possible sign of problematic Internet use. This problem has become more noticeable with the widespread adoption of social network sites such as Instagram, Facebook, and Second Life. For example, Gilbert, Murphy, and McNally (2011) looked at the 3D virtual world of Second Life. They found that approximately one-third of the participants met the criterion for Internet addiction. That rate was several times higher than determined in a previous study (Bakken, Wenzel, Gotestam, Johansson, & Oren, 2003).

Hormes, Kearns, and Alix Timko (2014) explained why someone could be addicted to social media. First, social media possess a number of characteristics that encourage users to recheck the sites frequently. Social media content is stimulating. When somebody comments on our posts, we get a notification. New material is constantly posted online. Second, for some individuals, social media are a way to escape from reality, or to cope with stress and depression.

There is also a biological explanation for addiction. Beard (2005) argued that individuals who are more likely to get addicted are those with an insufficient amount of serotonin/dopamine. Serotonin is responsible for maintaining mood balance (medicinenet.com, 2014), while dopamine is a chemical that controls arousal and motivation. It is released in the brain as a result of rewarding experiences (e.g., food and sex) (Arias-Carrión & Pöppel, 2007). Playing social media games or receiving "likes" on Instagram can be rewarding, resulting in an increase in dopamine.

Some researchers have suggested that there might be a chemical explanation for social media addiction. Simply logging onto a site such as Facebook can give people an adrenaline rush. "Liking" a status can feel rewarding and therefore increases the levels of dopamine (Horn, 2012). Other researchers (Liu & Potenza, 2007; Schaffer, Hall, & Bilt, 2000) have also questioned the possibility that a preoccupation with the Internet might be another way to gratify other addictions. Thus, Gilbert et al. (2011) found a moderate positive correlation between addiction to Second Life and various compulsions in real life such as shopping, sex, gambling, drug, and alcohol addictions. For example, compulsive shoppers might be attracted to Second Life because they have more purchasing power. Second Life also allows the users to create another world where all of their problems disappear. This creates a false sense of security (Gilbert et al., 2011).

A number of personality traits have been found to predict Internet addiction. These include low self-esteem, shyness, introversion, neuroticism, and a high degree of loneliness and depression (Andreassen, Pallesen, & Griffiths, 2017; Cao & Su, 2006; Griffiths & Dancaster, 1995; Smahel, Brown, & Blinka, 2012). For people with low self-esteem, social media has become a safe haven to interact. Andreassen et al. (2017) examined addictive social media use in over 23,500 Norwegians (M_{age} = 35.8 years) and found that addictive use of social media was related to lower self-esteem and higher narcissism. Social media applications are ideal social arenas for individuals who are attracted to ego-enhancing activities (Wang, Jackson, Zhang, & Su, 2012) as those platforms may fulfill their need for affiliation and confirm the sense of an idealized self. Andreassen et al. (2017) found that social media addiction was also being associated with being young, female, and single. For single people, social media like Tinder represent ground for meeting potential partners (Andreassen et al., 2017).

Hong, Huang, Lin, and Chiu (2014) found that university students who are more depressed tend to be addicted to Facebook. They defined this addiction as Facebook Addiction Disorder, which refers to an individual's inability to control one's own actions on Facebook. In their study, the more time that students spent on Facebook, the more likely they were addicted to the site. Individuals not in relationships are also more likely to develop addiction to technology (Kuss, Griffiths, Karila, & Billieux, 2014).

Research has demonstrated sex differences when it comes to addiction to technology. Men are more likely to become addicted to online video games, pornography, and online gambling, while women tend to develop addictive use of social media and online shopping (Andreassen et al., 2017; Chiu, Hong, & Chiu, 2013; Davenport, Houston, & Griffiths, 2012; Durkee et al., 2012; Ferguson, Coulson, & Barnett, 2011; Kuss et al., 2014). Women have been taught to be more expressive and open in their communication and therefore they tend to involve in social interaction more than men, while men often engage in solitary activities that feature aggressive and competitive content (online games) (Andreassen et al., 2013; Kuss & Griffiths, 2015; Kuss et al., 2014).

College students around the world experience a similar addiction to social media. Researchers from the University of Maryland's International Center for Media and the Public Agenda (ICMPA) and the Salzburg Global Seminar's Salzburg Academy on Media and Global Change conducted a study (Moeller, 2011), on twelve campuses across ten countries asking young adults (ages 17–23) to give up mobile phones, the Internet, social media, and television for twenty-four hours while keeping a diary of their thoughts during this time. Their study found that students' addiction to technology was similar to a drug addiction. Four in five students experienced significant mental and physical distress, panic, and confusion. Many students felt sad, lonely, depressed, and bored. Other studies conducted in China, South Korea, and the Netherlands reported similar findings; 8.1% of 17,599 Chinese adolescents experienced problematic Internet use (Cao, Sun, Wan, Hao, & Tao, 2011), and 10.7% in a study of 903 middle and high school students in South Korea were classified as being addicted (Park, Kim, & Cho, 2008). In the Netherlands, 3.7% of adolescents were classified as being addicted to the Internet (Kuss, van Rooij, Shorter, Griffiths, & van de Mheen, 2013).

Durkee et al. (2012) investigated the prevalence of pathological internet use (PIU) and maladaptive internet use (MIU) among adolescents in 11 European countries in relation to demographic, social factors, and internet accessibility. Using the Young Diagnostic Questionnaire for Internet Addiction they found a prevalence of PIU among 4.4% adolescents, especially those lacking emotional and psychological support. Overall, the prevalence of PIU among males and females was highest in Israel, while the lowest was found in Italy. In addition, adolescents living in metropolitan areas had an increased risk of both MIU and PIU. Adolescents living without a biological parent, low parental involvement, and parental unemployment were the most influential factors in determining MIU and PIU. Durkee et al. (2012) argued that adolescents with a lack of familiar support use Internet as a virtual substitute to cope. This increases their risk for pathological behavior.

Internet addiction has a variety of detrimental outcomes. Among others, those include poor academic performance among college age students (Tsitsika et al., 2011) and a low quality of interpersonal relationships (Milani, Osualdella, & Di Blasio, 2009). Internet addiction in adolescence also has a negative impact on identity formation (Kim et al., 2012). For example, Stefanone, Lackaff, and Rosen (2011) found that college women use social network sites as a platform to compete with others through photo sharing. Social network sites have a number of features that might encourage social comparisons and reassurance seeking. For example, Sheldon and Newman (2016) found that Instagram might be a fruitful environment for depressed preteens. In their study, excessive reassurance-seeking could explain why teens use Instagram to become popular, to escape from reality, and for creative purposes. Individuals who suffer from excessive reassurance-seeking are insecure and needy and are overly dependent on others (Joiner, 1999). Because they are insecure, they use Instagram to get positive feedback—"likes"—to validate their sense of self. Reassurance-seeking is a form of depression-related social behavior (Joiner & Metalsky, 2001). Toronto (2009) also found that Generation Z youth (born after 2000; also called post-Millennial generation) may be using technology in order to avoid struggles in their offline lives or to find belongings, by using escapism and fantasy to fill emotional voids. Sheldon and Newman (2016) also found a relationship between interpersonal rejection and using Instagram to escape from reality and to avoid loneliness. Again, those teens use social media to compensate for the lack of social contacts that they have with others face-to-face.

Overall, it has been generally accepted that any kind of addiction is caused by a combination of biological, social, and psychological factors (Griffiths, 2005). When it comes to social skills, people who prefer virtual over face-to-face communication have inadequate self-presentational skills (Griffiths, 2013). They are addicted to social media because they can present themselves in any way they want. In the short run, this leads to a higher life satisfaction; however, in the long run, it has adverse work and academic consequences.

Selective Self-Presentation and Narcissism

Social media offer a "nonymous" online setting that provides an ideal environment for the expression of the "hoped-for possible self" or, rather, a socially desirable identity that an individual wants to establish (Mehdizadeh, 2010; Zhao, Grasmuck, & Martin, 2008). Adolescents often experiment with their online identities, pretending to be someone else or just realizing aspects of themselves that are limited in their offline lives (Manago, Graham, Greenfield, & Salimkhan, 2008). Walther (2007) used the term "selective self-presentation" to describe how, in the absence of nonverbal cues, more emphasis is placed on linguistic cues. Reduced cues and asynchronous computer-mediated communication (CMC) contribute to selective self-presentation (Smock, 2010; Walther, 2007). Selective self-presentation includes revealing attitudes and aspects of the self in a controlled and socially desirable fashion (Walther, 2007).

Pempek, Yermolayeva, and Calvert (2009) found that self-presentation is one of the main reasons college students use Facebook. For example, on Facebook, individuals can carefully select photos they want to share with "friends." With the privacy settings, users can also limit who can tag a photo of them on Facebook and thus prevent an embarrassing photo from showing up on their timeline.

When it comes to self-expression, news media express concerns about "sexting" and "sexual selfies" (Bazelon, 2013; Berry, 2013). People post sexual selfies to get more attention and to attract the opposite sex. According to Festinger's social comparison theory (1954), humans are naturally driven to compare themselves to others. The direction of comparison can be upward, downward, or lateral. An upward comparison is a comparison to someone who looks better than us. On the other hand, lateral comparison is a comparison to peer groups (Sohn, 2010). While most studies have focused on upward comparisons through media images, in several studies (e.g., Cash, Cash, & Butters, 1983; Sheldon, 2010), comparisons to peers have resulted in greater body dissatisfaction than comparisons to attractive models on television. Krones, Stice, Batres, and Orjada (2005) speculated that these may occur because it is easier to attain an attractive body of a peer, rather than a model on television. In addition, most people have everyday interactions with peers, and not media figures, and may consider peers to be more relevant for self-evaluation (Wasilenko, Kulik, & Wanic, 2007). It is then likely that social media can contribute to lateral comparison. Gabriel (2014) writes that social media demand that young people actively think about and negotiate their own visibility on social network sites, even if they lack the maturity to choose what is better for them. Steinberg's (2008) research revealed that, during adolescence, the brain's socioemotional systems mature faster than the cognitive-control systems. Teenagers, therefore, are often not aware of how their posts can harm them in the long run.

Research shows that social media appealing to narcissists. Narcissism is a personality trait reflecting an inflated self-concept (Buffardi & Campbell, 2008), a need for admiration, and an exaggerated sense of self-importance (Oltmanns,

Emery, & Taylor, 2006). Many have argued that narcissists prefer online communities consisting of shallow relationships as they have complete control over their self-presentation (Buffardi & Campbell, 2008; Leung, 2013; Mehdizadeh, 2010). Narcissists generally think that they are better than others, unique, and special (Leung, 2013). The most important indicators of narcissism on Facebook are the main profile photo and the number of social contacts (Buffardi & Campbell, 2008). Narcissists are highly motivated to choose profile photos that emphasize their attractiveness (Kapidzic, 2013). Those who score higher on narcissism update their Facebook statuses more often, and also self-disclose more (Winter et al., 2014). Self-disclosure is their strategy to increase attention to themselves.

Sheldon (2016a) found that college students who score higher on narcissism are liking, commenting, and uploading their own photos on Facebook more often than those who score lower on narcissism. For narcissists these activities might be a way of self-presentation. When a person "likes" or responds on somebody else's photos, the friends of the person who liked them will get the newsfeed notification of the activity. As Greenwood (2013) argued, one of the psychological needs individuals have includes the need to be "seen."

Sheldon and Bryant (2016) studied the use of Instagram among college students and found a positive relationship between narcissism and using Instagram for surveillance and popularity purposes. In addition, narcissism was positively and significantly related to the amount of time that participants spend editing photos before posting them on Instagram. Sheldon and Newman (2016) did a study with middle school students (12–17 years old) and found that of all the variables included in their study, narcissism was the most important predictor of Instagram use. Among teens, "selfies," or photographs that users take of themselves with a smartphone, are very popular on Instagram. Selfies have been described as a symptom of social media-driven narcissism (Weiser, 2015). Research (Twenge, Konrath, Foster, Campbell, & Bushman, 2008) has also shown that narcissism scores are significantly higher among young adults in the 2000s than they were in the 1980s and 1990s.

Declining Quality of Interpersonal Relationships

The idea of the Internet contributing to the declining quality of interpersonal relationships is not new. In 1998, Kraut et al. revealed the increased Internet use led to decreased social involvement, feelings of loneliness and depression, as well as a decrease in communication among family members. However, few research studies have been conducted to explore how social media influence family relationships today.

In her book *Alone Together: Why We Expect More from Technology and Less from Each Other,* Turkle (2011) discusses how people act differently online, confusing social media usage with authentic communication. Turkle mentions people who prefer texting over face-to-face communication. This is especially true for the younger generation. In the TIME mobility poll (2012), 32% of all respondents said that they would rather communicate by text than phone, even with people they know very well. While texting is fun, easy, and convenient, from the developmental psychology standpoint, its excessive use inhibits young adults' proper interpersonal skills development (Wolak, Mitchell, & Finkelhor, 2002). Brown (2011) explains the techno brush-off, or breaking up with a significant other via e-mail or text message. It is much easier to break up with another person when nonverbal cues are missing.

Social network sites can also negatively affect romantic relationships, causing jealousy, partner surveillance, and conflict due to different perceptions of privacy rules (Drouin, Miller, & Dibble, 2014; Utz & Beukeboom, 2011). Fox, Osborn, and Warber (2014) employed Baxter and Montgomery's (1996) relational dialectics theory (RDT) to explore Facebook's role in the emerging adults' romantic relationships. According to RDT, relationships are not linear, and relational life is characterized by change. People in the relationships continue to feel the push and pull of conflicting desires. Those desires include both autonomy and connection, openness and protection, and novelty and predictability (West & Turner, 2010). Social media research shows that of three relational dialectics, participants experienced the most problems with openness and protection. Different individuals have different privacy practices, so a conflict arises if a couple does not agree about those rules. In Fox et al. (2014) study, all 47 participants agreed that they would be better off without Facebook in their romantic relationships.

Another problem may arise when partners have different views about the status of the relationship or the willingness to disclose it to other people. For example, "going Facebook official" represents a significant turning point in a relationship (Fox & Warber, 2013) as other people start perceiving the couple as being serious. The existence of Facebook also makes it easier to connect with ex-partners or even meet romantic alternatives. According to social exchange theory (Thibaut & Kelley, 1959), "every individual voluntarily enters and stays in any relationship only as long as it is adequately satisfactory in terms of his or her rewards and costs" (p. 37). Social exchange theory is applicable to CMC. When costs (e.g., stress, time, energy, attention) start exceeding the rewards (e.g., fun, loyalty, attention), individuals either terminate the relationship or look for the alternative.

Facebook usage has been related to physical and emotional cheating, breakups, and divorce (Clayton, Nagurney, & Smith, 2013). The evidence of a widespread problem is the website devoted to stories about partners cheating on each other through Facebook (www.facebookcheating.com). A Valenzuela, Halpern, and Katz (2014) survey of married individuals shows that using social network sites is negatively correlated with marriage quality and happiness, and positively correlated with experiencing a troubled relationship and thinking about divorce. Individuals in unhappy marriages use social network sites more often because it proves beneficial to them by providing emotional support (Valenzuela et al., 2014).

Privacy and Security

With rapid technological advancement, things that were once private knowledge have now become public. Social network sites usually encourage users to disclose a great deal of information about themselves (Antheunis, Valkenburg, & Peter, 2010), including private information such as relationship status, political views, and sexual preferences. This could be problematic if one's social network includes supervisors, strangers, and even friends who do not have good intentions. There have been multiple reported cases of employees being dismissed due to their Facebook posts, comments, photos, and the types of groups that they were linked with. One was Caitlin Davis, an 18-year-old cheerleader with the New England Patriots, who was fired over photos she posted on Facebook.

In a study looking at college students' opinions about employers checking their social media profiles, 68% of students who took the survey did not believe it was unethical for employers to look at their social network sites (Clark & Roberts, 2010). This high percentage might indicate a generational shift in what is accepted use of social media. Using social media to make employment decisions can create confusion because of a lack of clarity about whether content posted to social media sites is public or private (Aase, 2010). Employers can use information found on social media sites as part of their hiring process because publicly searchable information is not considered private (Brown & Vaughn, 2011).

Another negative aspect of social media use includes high school and college students making drug and alcohol references for the public—and future employers—to see. Egan and Moreno (2011) conducted a study examining alcohol references on undergrad males' Facebook profiles. The study found that students who were of legal drinking age referenced alcohol 4.5 times more than underage students. Out of all the profiles, 85.3% contained alcohol references. Egan and Moreno argued that such depiction of alcohol-related events could be damaging to personal and professional reputations.

Recently, communication privacy management theory (Petronio, 2002) has been used to explain the "privacy paradox," or why users disclose personal information on social network sites while at the same time expressing concerns about privacy. According to Boyd (2010), "a conversation you might have in the hallway is *private by default, public through effort*," but on the Facebook wall "the conversation is *public by default, private through effort*." In other words, information shared face-to-face is something people easily forget, whereas information shared online is stored and archived and is easily replicated.

Professors and educators deal with privacy dialectics on a daily basis when trying to decide which information to reveal to their students on social network profiles and which to conceal. According to the American Association of University Professors' (AAUP) ethical principles and standards, college personnel should "avoid dual relationships with students where one individual serves in multiple roles that create conflicting responsibilities, role confusion, and unclear expectations that may involve incompatible roles and conflicting responsibilities" (ACPA Ethics Code, 2006).

Sheldon (2016b) conducted a study to examine what motivates professors to add students as Facebook friends. Of 117 participants, almost half (n = 55) said that they are currently a Facebook friend with one or more students. When asked who initiated the Facebook friendship, 41 participants said "my students," and 13 said "both." No faculty chose the category "I." In fact, many faculty members mentioned that they would add a student as a friend after he or she graduates but only if the student initiated the relationship. The fact that not a single faculty member surveyed in this study admitted that they had initiated a Facebook friendship with a student is evidence of the privacy concerns that many still fear. Responses to an open-ended question ("What is the main reason that you are a Facebook friend with your student(s)?") revealed that there are three major reasons: (a) it is a social obligation (49%), (b) for alumna tracking (39%), and (c) for class content discussions (12%). Results showed that most participants added students because they felt than an *obligation* to do so, but they also felt the students were mature and responsible.

Cyberbullying

Social media also provide new ways to hurt victims over and over again. Cyberbullying and cyberstalking are other concerns for parents. Cyberbullying is defined as use of the Internet, cell phones, or other technology to send or post text or images intended to hurt or embarrass another person (Levinson, 2013). A variety of definitions of cyberbullying exist, but researchers tend to agree about 3 things that occur when bullied: (1) intent to harm, (2) imbalance of power, and (3) a repeated action with a specific target (National Science Foundation, 2011). Like traditional bullying, cyberbullying can result in physical and psychological harm, and has been related to emotional distress, losing confidence and self-esteem, depression, and problematic use of alcohol and cigarettes (Patchin & Hinduja, 2006; Raskauskas & Stoltz, 2007; Shariff & Hoff, 2007; Sourander et al., 2010; Wang, Nansel, & Iannotti, 2011). Cyberbullying presents itself in multiple forms, from the dissemination of derogatory comments, offensive and embarrassing pictures and videos, to rumors spread by social media, SMS (texting), e-mail, or chat (Ybarra & Mitchell, 2004).

Cyberbullying often coexists with traditional bullying (Patchin & Hinduja, 2006; Raskauskas & Stoltz, 2007), but due to the ability of the bully to remain anonymous it can be more dangerous than traditional bullying. Unlike traditional bullying that often happens in the school environment, cyberbullying can take place at any time of the day (Carter & Wilson, 2015). Furthermore, Juvonen and Gross (2008) argued that the absence of adult supervision in online environment creates an environment where bullies feel safe and distant. This distance between victim and bully leads to a reduced empathic response (Williard, 2005), with adolescents often not recognizing that they have caused harm to another person.

Frequent technology use increases an adolescent's risk of being bullied online (Machmutow, Perren, Sticca, & Alsaker, 2012; Mishna, Cook, Gadalla, Daciuk, & Solomon, 2010). Patchin and Hinduja (2006) conducted an Internet-based study of 571 respondents between the ages of 12 and 20 to learn about their experience with various types of cyberbullying. Almost 60% of their participants self-reported living in the United States, and the majority were Caucasian females younger than 18 years. The researchers found that almost 30% of the minor-age respondents reported being victims of online bullying, 11% reported being the bully, and almost half reported witnessing this aggression. The majority of participants (57%) said that they have disclosed online bullying to their friends, but they were reluctant to report it to an adult. Other studies (Kowalski & Limber, 2007; Mishna et al., 2010) have noted that adolescents fear losing technology privileges if they disclose cyberbullying to their parents and teachers. The most common strategies (Hamm et al., 2015) reported by adolescents to cope with cyberbullying are passive, such as blocking the sender, ignoring or avoiding messages, and protecting personal information. Active coping strategies such as confronting the bully or fighting back are less common.

Carter and Wilson (2015) examined bullying and cyberbullying practices among 367 adolescents 10 to 18 years of age who were attending school in the Midwest United States. Results showed that one third of participants had been bullied during school, and 17% had been cyberbullied, mostly through social networking sites. There were no significant differences in bullying or cyberbullying based on location (urban or suburban) or demographic characteristics. Similarly,

Wang et al. (2011) found that 21.2% of youth who participated in a national survey (N = 7,313) reported an experience with physical bullying and 13.8% with cyberbullying.

Although most research has focused on peer-to-peer bullying, the victim and the perpetrator might not always know each other. Pyzalski (2012) created a taxonomy to examine the relationships between the cyberbullying victim and the perpetrator. This taxonomy includes six categories: cyber aggression against peers; cyber aggression against the vulnerable (i.e., the homeless, alcoholics); random cyber aggression (i.e., the victim is anonymous to the perpetrator); cyber aggression against groups (i.e., an ethnic or religious group); cyber aggression against celebrities; and cyber aggression against school staff. Peers are still the most common perpetrators of cyberbullying, and online aggressive comments direct toward them are perceived most negatively (Whittaker & Kowalski, 2015). In addition, those who cyberbully others are at a higher risk for their own cybervictimization (Meter & Bauman, 2015).

Bullies like to see themselves on YouTube, so they post videos online. A recent event included a fifteen year old girl who was assaulted by multiple young men after getting drunk. After photographs were posted online, the teen committed suicide. Recently, researchers (Kowalski & Limber, 2007; Patchin & Hinduja, 2006; Ybarra & Mitchell, 2004) have tried to determine the relationship between cyberbullying and gender. While Ybarra and Mitchell (2004) and Patchin and Hinduja (2006) found no significant differences between the incidence of cyberbullying in young people, Kowalski and Limber (2007) found that females outnumbered males in engaging in cyberbullying, arguing that as previous studies show, women are more likely to participate in indirect forms of aggression.

In terms of social networking use, studies of young adults have found that the more time they spent on Facebook and the more friends they have, the greater the likelihood that they will experience cyberbullying victimization (Faucher, Jackson, & Cassidy, 2014; Kokkinos, Antoniadou, & Markos, 2014; Whittaker & Kowalski, 2015). Peluchette, Karl, Wood, and Williams (2015) examined the impact of risky social network site practices and individual differences in self-disclosure and personality on the likelihood of cyberbullying victimization among young adult Facebook users. Results from 572 participants show that posting indiscreet content, having Facebook friends who post such content, and number of Facebook friends were all strong predictors of cyberbullying victimization. In addition, extroversion and openness were significant predictors of cyberbullying victimization, as those characteristic may contribute to being perceived as an easy target (Festl & Quandt, 2013). Hamm et al.'s (2015) meta-analysis of 36 studies that evaluated the use of a social media tool in the context of cyberbullying revealed that name-calling or insults, spreading gossip and rumors, and virally sharing pictures were listed as common forms of cyberbullying. The main motivation behind cyberbullying, as reported by bullies and the victims, included a lack of confidence, a desire for control, entertainment, and retaliation.

Wegge, Vandebosch, Eggermont, and Walrave (2015) surveyed 1,458 eighth-grade students to find out how young people's connections on social network sites are related to their risk of being involved in cyber harassment. Their results showed that victimization and perpetration are linked to the composition of one's network of online connections. The presence of many connections with fellow students ("weak ties") who are not friends elevates the risk of cyber harassment and cyberbullying.

Cyberstalking

Cyberstalking is another form of cyber abuse. It is defined as persistent, unwanted online monitoring or contact with a target, to the point of obsession (Levinson, 2013). Cyberbullying and cyberstalking started with instant messaging and in chat rooms where the perpetrator could stay anonymous. Later they migrated to social media. E-mail, Facebook, Instagram, and Twitter all allow cyberstalkers to easily track someone's personal life. Most studies actually suggest that the Internet provides stalkers with an additional means to exert control over victims (Welsh & Lavoie, 2012). A cyberstalker can pursue a victim despite the geographic or temporal separation. Most victims who are stalked online have been stalked by the same people offline (Sheridan & Grant, 2007). Welsh and Lavoie (2012) examined the relationship between the sharing of personal information on social network sites and the risk for cyberstalking. In a sample of 321 female undergraduate students, they found that increasing the amount of time spent engaging with online social networking, as well as high levels of online disclosure of personal information, contribute to increased risks for cyberstalking.

Who are the cyberstalkers? Some studies suggests that online environment attracts people who would not harass others outside the virtual world (Dreβing, Bailer, Anders, Wagner, & Gallas, 2014). According to a number of studies (Alexy, Burgesss, Baker, & Smoyak, 2005; Maple, Short, & Brown, 2011; Sheridan & Grant, 2007), ex-partners are the most frequent category of cyberstalkers. Dreβing et al. (2014) did a study with 6,000 users of German social network StudiVZ. In their study, the prevalence rate of cyberstalking was estimated at 6.3%. They, however, included a narrow definition of cyberstalking and thus excluded all occurrence where "stalking" did not cause the fear, such as "Facebook stalking," or gathering information about people on social network sites. Most cyberstalkers are men, although 28% of the victims report a female cyberstalkers (Dreβing et al., 2014). In one-third of cases, cyberstalking was the ex-partner. A high number of female cyberstalkers might be due to the online environment, which provides women with less direct way to contact the victim. Other studies (Sinclair & Frieze, 2000) have also suggested that women use indirect stalking behaviors.

Spitzberg, Marshall, and Cupach (2001) have identified other forms of cyberstalking including hyperintimacy and threats. Hyperintimacy includes repeated efforts at cybercommunication with the victims including sending exaggerated messages of affection or pornographic images. A threat is an online invasion of privacy and may include intimidating e-mails and Facebook messages. Another form of digital harm is self-harassment or self-cyberbullying, which includes teens anonymously posting mean questions to themselves and then answering them. This is a very effective mechanism for getting attention, according to Boyd (2010). Sometimes teens do it because they need their parents to notice them ("a cry for help"), and other times teens want to look cool and interesting to their peers. In 2013, media outlets reported a story about Hannah Smith, a 14-year-old from England who committed suicide after receiving hateful messages on ask.fm. Executives at ask.fm carried out an investigation into abusive posts and then discovered that most of them were sent from a computer with the same IP address as Smith's, concluding then that she had sent most of the vile messages to herself.

Misinformation and Deception on Social Media

Another dark side of social media is that misinformation can spread quickly. With the absence of gatekeepers, citizen journalists can publish erroneous information that is spread to a global audience in seconds. The problem is when the mainstream media share the unverified information from citizen journalists. A recent example includes the April 2013 Boston bombings. After the bombings, social media users engaged in an attempt to identify the bombers from photos of the scene and incorrectly speculated that a missing student was one of the bombers. Misinformation on social media still represents a challenge for those seeking to use social media during crises (Stabird, Maddock, Orand, Achterman, & Mason, 2014).

As social media continues to advance so does the possibility of online deception. Online deception is defined as a broad set of malicious practices that use the Internet as a medium to intentionally give a target an incorrect mental representation of the circumstances of a social exchange (Grazioli & Jarvenpaa, 2003).

When making choices about what information to include, what to leave out, and whether to engage in deception many people take advantage of the properties of CMC (Toma, Hancock, & Ellison, 2008). Among the places where deception can occur are online dating sites. The uncertainty of being accepted by potential partners increases the likelihood that daters will resort to deception to appear more appealing.

In his book *The Presentation of Self in Everyday Life*, Erving Goffman (1959) described social life by using theatrical metaphors. According to the metaphors, we are all performers who take on unique roles in different situations. He distinguished between the signals that we "give" intentionally and those we "give off" unintentionally. Intentional signals are used to convey a particular impression to others. CMC allows us to present ourselves more selectively than is possible face-to-face. In an online dating context, for example, users try to present themselves as attractive as possible (Fiore, Shaw Taylor, Mendelsohn, & Hearst, 2008). In Hancock, Toma, and Ellison's (2007) study, 81% of online dating users lied about their age, weight, or height. Ellison, Heino, and Gibbs (2006) argued that such deceptions are not always intentional, as users might subconsciously describe their "ideal self." According to Walther's theory of hyperpersonal interaction, asynchronous messages and reduced communication cues contribute to selective self-presentation in CMC settings. Not only do users have more time for message construction, but they also have more control over what cues are sent (Walther, 1996).

Due to the increase in the amount of online deception, a new phenomenon known as "Catfishing" has emerged. "Catfishing" is defined by most people as the phenomenon of Internet scammers who fabricate online identities and entire social circles to trick people into romantic relationships (Peterson, 2013). A deceiver creates a fake profile on a social network site with the motive to trick people into thinking that they are someone else. Though online deception has always been a part of social media, only recently has the topic of "catfishing" been so prominent in the media.

Summary

This chapter discussed the dark side of CMC, primarily focusing on social media and social network sites. Reduced nonverbal cues are responsible for selective self-presentation, which helps narcissists choose the identity that they wish to portray online. Facebook can be addictive because it provides an opportunity to escape from real life. Social media can also fulfill a number of needs not fulfilled elsewhere.

This includes attention from others in the form of likes, comments, and shares. For some, social media are another place to flirt with an ex-partner. This can be negative and destroy marriages and families. Information shared through social media can be stored and archived, and, unlike face-to-face conversation, never forgotten. This can get people in trouble if their privacy settings are not adjusted. Cyberstalkers and cyberbulliers are using the advantages of social network sites as well, as they allow them to easily track someone's personal life—thus giving them more control over victim. Overall, social media can help us or harm us, depending on how we use it.

Discussion Questions

12.1. Discuss your own social media use. Do you know anyone who has been addicted to Internet or social network sites? What were their symptoms?

12.2. Do you engage in social comparisons online?

12.3. Do you think that people should get fired for social media mistakes? Do you know anybody who has lost their job because of social media?

12.4. Do you prefer texting over face-to-face communication? Discuss your answers.

Applications

12.1. Interview two women and two men who are addicted to social media. Report what their symptoms are. Compare the men's responses with the women's responses. Does one group experience more or less addiction?

12.2. Ask a mixed-gender group what their daily life would be like if they did not have cell phones and social media. How would they talk to each other?

References

Aase, S. (2010). Toward e-professionalism: Thinking through the implications of navigating the digital world. *Journal of the American Dietetic Association, 110*(10), 1442, 1444, 1446–1447. doi:10.1016/j.jada.2010.08.020.

Aboujaoude, E., Koran, L. M., Gamel, N., Large, M., & Serpe, R. (2006). Potential markers for problematic Internet use: A telephone survey of 2,513 adults. *CNS Spectrums, 11*(10), 750–755.

ACPA Ethics Code. (2006). *Statement of ethical principles and standards*. Retrieved from http://www.myacpa.org/au/documents/EthicsStatement.pdf

Alexy, E. M., Burgess, A. W., Baker, T., & Smoyak, S. A. (2005). Perceptions of cyberstalking among college students. *Brief treatment and crisis Intervention, 5*(3), 279–289. doi:10.1093/brief-treatment/mhi020

Andreassen, C. S., Griffiths, M. D., Gjertsen, S. R., Krossbakken, E., Kvam, S., & Pallesen, S. (2013). The relationships between behavioral addictions and the five-factor model of personality. *Journal of Behavioral Addictions, 2*, 90–99. Retrieved from http://dx.doi.org/10.1556/JBA.2.2013.003

Andreassen, C. S., Pallesen, S., & Griffiths, M. D. (2017). The relationship between addictive use of social media, narcissism, and self-esteem: Findings from a large national survey. *Addictive Behaviors, 64*, 287-293. doi:10.1016/j.addbeh.2016.03.006

Antheunis, M. L., Valkenburg, P. M., & Peter, J. (2010). Getting acquainted through social network sites: Testing a model of online uncertainty reduction and social attraction. *Computers in Human Behavior, 26*, 100–109. doi:10.1016/j.chb.2009.07.005

Arias-Carrión, Ó., & Pöppel, E. (2007). Dopamine, learning, and reward-seeking behavior. *Acta Neurobiologiae Experimentalis, 67*(4), 481–488.

Bakken, I., Wenzel, H., Gotestam, C., Johansson, A., & Oren, A. (2003). Internet addiction among Norwegian adults: A stratified probability sample study. *Scandinavian Journal of Psychology, 50*, 121–127.

Baxter, L. A., & Montgomery, B. M. (1996). *Relating: Dialogues and dialectics*. New York, NY: Guilford Press.

Bazelon, E. (2013, April 16). Another teen tragedy proves sexting is more than bullying. *The Age*. Retrieved from www.theage.com.au/technology/technology-news/another-teen-tragedy-proves-sextingis-more-than-bullying-20130416-2hqv.html

Beard, K. W. (2005). Internet addiction: A review of current assessment techniques and potential assessment questions. *CyberPsychology & Behavior, 8*, 7–14. doi:10.1089/cpb.2005.8.7

Berry, S. (2013, July 15). The sexual selfie. *The Age*. Retrieved from www.theage.com.au/lifestyle/life/thesexual-selfie-20130715-2pyrp.html

Boyd, D. (2010). *Digital self-harm and other acts of self-harassment*. Retrieved from http://dmlcentral.net/blog/danah-boyd/digital-self-harm-and-other-acts-self-harassment

Brown, A. (2011). Relationships, community, and identity in the new virtual society. *Futurist, 45*(2), 29.

Brown, V. R., & Vaughn, E. D. (2011). The writing on the (Facebook) wall: The use of social networking sites in hiring decisions. *Journal of Business Psychology, 26*(2), 219–225. doi:10.1007/s10869-011-9221-x

Buffardi, L. E., & Campbell, W. K. (2008). Narcissism and social networking web sites. *Personality and Social Psychology Bulletin, 34*, 1303–1314. doi:10.1177/0146167208320061

Cao, F., & Su, L. (2006). Internet addiction among Chinese adolescents: Prevalence and psychological features. *Child: Care, Health & Development, 33*(3), 275–281. doi:10.1111/j.1365-2214.2006.00715.x

Cao, H., Sun, Y., Wan, Y., Hao, J., & Tao, F. (2011). Problematic Internet use in Chinese adolescents and its relation to psychosomatic symptoms and life satisfaction. *BMC Public Health, 11*(1), 802–809. doi:10.1186/1471-2458-11-802

Carter, J. M., & Wilson, F. L. (2015). Cyberbullying: A 21st century health care phenomenon. *Pediatric Nursing, 41*(3), 115–125.

Cash, T. F., Cash, D. W., & Butters, J. W. (1983). 'Mirror, mirror, on the wall?': Contrast effects and self-evaluations of physical attractiveness. *Personality and Social Psychology Bulletin, 9*, 351–358. doi:10.1177/0146167283093004

Chiu, S.-I., Hong, F.-Y., & Chiu, S.-L. (2013). An analysis on the correlation and gender difference between college students' Internet addiction and mobile phone addiction in Taiwan. *ISRN Addiction, 2013*, 360607. Retrieved from http://dx.doi.org/10.1155/2013/360607

Clark, L. A., & Roberts, S. J. (2010). Employer's use of social networking sites: A socially irresponsible practice. *Journal of Business Ethics, 95*(4), 507–525. doi:10.1007/s10551-010-0436-y

Clayton, R. B., Nagurney, A., & Smith, J. R. (2013). Cheating, breakup, and divorce: Is Facebook use to blame? *Cyberpsychology, Behavior and Social Networking, 16*, 717–720. doi:10.1089/cyber.2012.0424

Davenport, K., Houston, J. E., & Griffiths, M. D. (2012). Excessive eating and compulsive buying behaviors in women: An empirical pilot study examining reward sensitivity, anxiety, impulsivity, self-esteem and social desirability. *International Journal of Mental Health and Addiction, 10*, 474–489. Retrieved from http://dx.doi.org/10.1007/s11469-011-9332-7

DeWeese, K. L. (2014, May 1). *Screen time, how much is too much? The social and emotional costs of technology on the adolescent brain.* Master's thesis. Dominican University of California.

Dreßing, H., Bailer, J., Anders, A., Wagner, H., & Gallas, C. (2014). Cyberstalking in a large sample of social network users: Prevalence, characteristics, and impact upon victims. *Cyberpsychology, Behavior & Social Networking, 17*(2), 61–67. doi:10.1089/cyber.2012.0231

Drouin, M., Miller, D. A., & Dibble, J. L. (2014). Ignore your partners' current Facebook friends; beware the ones they add! *Computers in Human Behavior, 35*, 483–488. doi:10.1016/j.chb.2014.02.032

Durkee, T., Kaess, M., Carli, V., Parzer, P., Wasserman, C., Floderus, B., ... Wasserman, D. (2012). Prevalence of pathological internet use among adolescents in Europe: Demographic and social factors. *Addiction, 107*, 2210–2222. doi:10.1111/j.1360-0443.2012.03946.x

Egan, K., & Moreno, M. (2011). Alcohol references on undergraduate males' Facebook profiles. *American Journal of Men's Health, 5*, 413–420. doi:10.1177/1557988310394341

Ellison, N., Heino, R., & Gibbs, J. (2006). Managing impressions online: Self-presentation processes in the online dating environment. *Journal of Computer-Mediated Communication, 11*, 415–441. doi:10.1111/j.1083-6101.2006.00020

Faucher, C., Jackson, M., & Cassidy, W. (2014). Cyberbullying among university students: Gendered experiences, impacts, and perspectives. *Education Research International*, 1–10. doi:10.1155/2014/698545

Ferguson, C. J., Coulson, M., & Barnett, J. (2011). A meta-analysis of pathological gaming prevalence and comorbidity with mental health, academic and social problems. *Journal of Psychiatric Research, 45,* 1573–1578. doi:10.1016/j.jpsychires.2011.09.005

Festinger, L. (1954). A theory of social comparison processes. *Human Relations, 7,* 117–140. doi:10.1177/001872675400700202

Festl, R., & Quandt, T. (2013). Social relations and cyberbullying: The influence of individual and structural attributes on victimization and perpetration via the internet. *Human Communication Research, 39,* 101–126. doi:10.111/j.1468-2958.2012.01442.x

Fiore, A. T., Shaw Taylor, L., Mendelsohn, G. A., & Hearst, M. A. (2008). Assessing attractiveness in online dating profiles. *Proceedings of ACM computer-human interaction,* Florence, Italy.

Fox, J., Osborn, J. L., & Warber, K. M. (2014). Relational dialectics and social networking sites: The role of Facebook in romantic relationship escalation, maintenance, conflict, and dissolution. *Computers in Human Behavior, 35,* 527–534. doi:10.1016/j.chb.2014.02.031

Fox, J., & Warber, K. M. (2013). Romantic relationship development in the age of Facebook: An exploratory study of emerging adults' perceptions, motives, and behaviors. *CyberPsychology, Behavior, & Social Networking, 16,* 3–7. doi:10.1089/cyber.2012.0288

Gabriel, F. (2014). Sexting, selfies and self-harm: Young people, social media and the performance of self-development. *Media International Australia, 151,* 104–113.

Gilbert, R., Murphy, N., & McNally, T. (2011). Addiction to the 3-dimesional internet: Estimated prevalence and relationship to real world addictions. *Addiction Research & Theory, 19,* 380–390. doi:10.3109/16066359.2010.530714

Goffman, E. (1959). *The presentation of self in everyday life.* New York, NY: Anchor.

Grazioli, S., & Jarvenpaa, S. L. (2003). Consumer and business deception on the Internet: Content analysis of documentary evidence. *International Journal of Electronic Commerce, 7,* 93–118.

Greenwood, D. N. (2013). Fame, Facebook, and Twitter: How attitudes about fame predict frequency and nature of social media use. *Psychology of Popular Media Culture, 2,* 222–236. doi:10.1037/ppm0000013

Griffiths, M. (2000). Does Internet and computer 'addiction' exist? Some case study evidence. *CyberPsychology & Behavior, 3,* 211–218. doi:10.1089/109493100316067

Griffiths, M. (2005). A "components" model of addiction within a biopsychosocial framework. *Journal of Substance Use, 10,* 191-197. doi:10.1080/14659890500114359

Griffiths, M. (2013). Social networking addiction: Emerging themes and issues. *Addiction: Research & Therapy, 4.* doi: 10.4172/2155-6105.1000e11. Retrieved from http://omicsonline.org/social-networking-addiction-emerging-themes-and-issues-2155-6105.1000e118.pdf

Griffiths, M. D., & Dancaster, I. (1995). The effect of type A personality on physiological arousal while playing computer games. *Addictive Behaviors, 20,* 543–548. doi:10.1016/0306-4603(95)00001-S

Hamm, M. P., Newton, A. S., Chisholm, A., Shulhan, J., Milne, A., Sundar, P., & ... Hartling, L. (2015). Prevalence and effect of cyberbullying on children and young people: A scoping review of social media studies. *JAMA Pediatrics, 169*(8), 770–777. doi:10.1001/jamapediatrics.2015.0944

Hancock, J. T., Toma, C., & Ellison, N. (2007). The truth about lying in online dating profiles. *Proceedings of the SIGCHI Conference on Human factors in computing systems* (pp. 449–452). Ipswich, MA: ACM.

Hicks, M. R. (2010). *The digital pandemic. Reestablishing face-to-face contact in the electronic Age.* Far Hills, NJ: New Horizon Press.

Hong, F., Huang, D., Lin, H., & Chiu, S. (2014). Analysis of the psychological traits, Facebook usage, and Facebook addiction model of Taiwanese university students. *Telematics and Informatics, 31*, 597–606. doi:10.1016/j.tele.2014.01.001

Hormes, J. M., Kearns, B., & Alix Timko, C. (2014). Craving Facebook? Behavioral addiction to online social networking and its association with emotion regulation deficits. *Addiction, 109*, 2079–2088. doi:10.1111/add.12713

Horn, L. (2012). Study finds chemical reason behind Facebook 'addiction.' *PC Magazine*, 1.

Joiner, T. E., Jr. (1999). A test of the interpersonal theory of depression in youth psychiatric inpatients. *Journal of Abnormal Child Psychology, 27*, 77–85. doi:10.1023/A:1022666424731

Joiner, T. E., Jr., & Metalsky, G. I. (2001). Excessive reassurance seeking: Delineating a risk factor involved in the development of depressive symptoms. *Psychological Science, 5*, 371–378. doi:10.1111/1467-9280.00369

Juvonen, J., & Gross, E. F. (2008). Extending the school grounds? Bullying experiences in cyberspace. *Journal of School Health, 78*(9), 496–505. doi:10.1111/j.1746-1561.2008.00335.x

Kapidzic, S. (2013). Narcissism as a predictor of motivations behind Facebook profile picture selection. *Cyberpsychology, Behavior, and Social Networking, 16*, 14–19. doi:10.1089/cyber.2012.0143

Kim, Y., Son, J., Lee, S., Shin, C., Kim, S., Ju, G., & … Ha, T. (2012). Abnormal brain activation of adolescent internet addict in a ball-throwing animation task: Possible neural correlates of disembodiment revealed by fMRI. *Progress in Neuro-Psychopharmacology & Biological Psychiatry, 39*(1), 88–95. doi:10.1016/j.pnpbp.2012.05.013

Kokkinos, C., Antoniadou, N., & Markos, A. (2014). Cyberbullying: An investigation of the psychological profile of university student participants. *Journal of Applied Developmental Psychology, 35*, 204–214. doi:10.1016/j.appdev.2014.04.001

Kowalski, R. M., & Limber, S. P. (2007). Electronic bullying among middle school students. *Journal of Adolescent Health, 41*, 22–30. doi:10.1016/j.jadohealth.2007.08.017

Kraut, R., Patterson, M., Lundmark, V., Kiesler, S., Mukopadhyay, T., & Scherlis, W. (1998). Internet paradox: A social technology that reduces social involvement and psychological well-being? *American Psychologist, 53*, 1017–1031. doi:10.1037/0003-066X.53.9.1017

Krones, P., Stice, E., Batres, C., & Orjada, K. (2005). In vivo social comparison to a thin-ideal peer promotes body dissatisfaction: A randomized experiment. *International Journal of Eating Disorders, 38*, 134–142. doi:10.1002/eat.20171 Kuss, D. J., & Griffiths, M. D. (2015). *Internet addiction in psychotherapy.* London, England: Palgrave.

Kuss, D. J., Griffiths, M. D., Karila, L., & Billieux, J. (2014). Internet addiction: A systematic review of epidemiological research for the last decade. *Current Pharmaceutical Design, 20*, 4026–4052. doi:10.2174/13816128113199990617

Kuss, D. J., van Rooij, A. J., Shorter, G. W., Griffiths, M. D., & van de Mheen, D. D. (2013). Internet addiction in adolescents: Prevalence and risk factors. *Computers in Human Behavior, 29*(5), 1987–1996. doi:10.1016/j.chb.2013.04.002

Leung, L. (2013). Generational differences in content generation in social media: The roles of the gratifications sought and of narcissism. *Computers in Human Behavior, 29*, 997–1006. doi:10.1016/j.chb.2012.12.028

Levinson, P. (2013). *New new media* (2nd ed.). New York, NY: Penguin Academics.

Liu, T., & Potenza, M. (2007). Problematic Internet use: Clinical implications. *CNS Spectrums, 12*, 453–466. doi:10.1017/S1092852900015339

Machmutow, K., Perren, S., Sticca, F., & Alsaker, F. D. (2012). Peer victimisation and depressive symptoms: Can specific coping strategies buffer the negative impact of cybervictimisation? *Emotional & Behavioral Difficulties, 17*(3/4), 403–420. doi:10.1080/13632752.2012.7043 10

Manago, A. M., Graham, M. B., Greenfield, P. M., & Salimkhan, G. (2008). Self-presentation and gender on MySpace. *Journal of Applied Developmental Psychology, 29*(6), 446–458. doi:10.1016/j.appdev.2008.07.001

Maple, C., Short, E., & Brown, K. (2011). *Cyberstalking in the United Kingdom: An analysis of the ECHO pilot.* National Center for Cyberstalking Research, University of Bedfordshire, Luton, England.

Medicinenet.com. (2014). *Definition of serotonin.* Retrieved from http://www.medicinenet.com/script/main/art.asp?articlekey=5468

Mehdizadeh, S. (2010). Self-presentation 2.0: Narcissism and self-esteem on Facebook. *Cyberpsychology, Behavior, & Social Networking, 13*, 357–364. doi:10.1089/cyber.2009.0257

Meter, D. J., & Bauman, S. (2015). When sharing is a bad idea: The effects of online social network engagement and sharing passwords with friends on cyberbullying involvement. *Cyberpsychology, Behavior, and Social Networking, 18*(8), 437–442. doi:10.1089/cyber.2015.0081

Milani, L., Osualdella, D., & Di Blasio, P. (2009). Quality of interpersonal relationships and problematic Internet use in adolescence. *Cyberpsychology & Behavior, 12*(6), 681–684. doi:10.1089/cpb.2009.0071

Mishna, F., Cook, C., Gadalla, T., Daciuk, J., & Solomon, S. (2010). Cyber bullying behaviors among middle and high school students. *American Journal of Orthopsychiatry, 80*(3), 362–374. doi:10.1111/j.1939-0025.2010.01040.x

Moeller, S. (2010). *The world unplugged.* Retrieved from http://theworldunplugged.wordpress.com/, http://theworldunplugged.wordpress.com/addictions/

National Center for Biotechnology Information. (2014). *Attention span statistics.* Retrieved from http://www.statisticbrain.com/attention-span-statistics/

National Science Foundation. (2011, November 8). *Defining a cyberbully.* Retrieved from http://www.nsf.gov/discoveries/disc_summ.jsp?cntn_id=121847&org=NSF

Oltmanns, F. T., Emery, E. R., & Taylor, S. (2006). *Abnormal psychology.* Toronto: Pearson Education Canada.

Park, S., Kim, J., & Cho, C. (2008). Prevalence of Internet addiction and correlations with family factors among South Korean adolescents. *Adolescence, 43*(172), 895–909.

Patchin, J. W., & Hinduja, S. (2006). Bullies move beyond the schoolyard: A preliminary look at cyberbullying. *Youth Violence and Juvenile Justice, 4*(2), 148–169. doi:10.1177/15412040062862

Peluchette, J. V., Karl, K., Wood, C., & Williams, J. (2015). Cyberbullying victimization: Do victims' personality and risky social network behaviors contribute to the problem? *Computers-n Human Behavior, 52*, 424–435. doi:10.1016/j.chb.2015.06.028

Pempek, T. A., Yermolayeva, Y. A., & Calvert, S. L. (2009). College students' social networking experiences on Facebook. *Journal of Applied Developmental Psychology, 30*(3), 227–238. doi:10.1016/j.appdev.2008.12.010

Peterson, H. (2013). 'Catfishing': The phenomenon of Internet scammers who fabricate online identities and entire social circles to trick people into romantic relationships. *Mail Online*. Retrieved from http://www.dailymail.co.uk/news/article-2264053/Catfishing-The-phenomenon-Internet-scammers-fabricate-online-identities-entire-social-circles-trick-people-romantic-relationships.html

Petronio, S. (2002). *Boundaries of privacy: Dialectics of disclosure*. New York, NY: State University of New York Press.

Pew Research Center. (2012). *Millennials will benefit and suffer due to their hyperconnected lives*. Retrieved from http://www.pewinternet.org/files/old-media//Files/Reports/2012/PIP_Future_of_Internet_2012_Young_brains_PDF.pdf

Pyzalski, J. (2012). From cyberbullying to electronic aggression: Typology of the phenomenon. *Emotional & Behavioral Difficulties, 17*, 305–317. doi:10.1080/13632752.2012.704319

Raskauskas, J., & Stoltz, A. D. (2007). Involvement in traditional and electronic bullying among adolescents. *Developmental Psychology, 43*(3), 564–575. doi:10.1037/0012-1649.43.3.564

Rosen, L. D. (2012). *iDisorders: Understanding our obsession with technology and overcoming its hold on us*. New York, NY: Palgrave Macmillan.

Schaffer, H., Hall, M., & Bilt, J. V. (2000). Computer addiction: A critical consideration. *American Journal of Orthopsychiatry, 70*, 162–168. doi:10.1037/h0087741

Shariff, S., & Hoff, D. L. (2007). Cyber bullying: Clarifying legal boundaries for school supervision in cyberspace. *International Journal of Cyber Criminology, 1*(1), 76–118. Retrieved from http://www.cybercrimejournal.com/shaheenhoff.pdf

Sheldon, P. (2010). Pressure to be perfect: Influences on college students' body esteem. *Southern Communication Journal, 75*(3), 277–298. doi:10.1080/10417940903026543

Sheldon, P. (2016a). Self-monitoring, covert narcissism, and sex as predictors of self-presentational activities on Facebook. *The Journal of Social Media in Society, 5*, 70-91.

Sheldon, P. (2016b). Facebook friend request: Applying the theory of reasoned action to student-teacher relationships on Facebook. *Journal of Broadcasting and Electronic Media, 60*, 269–285. doi:10.1080/08838151.2016.1164167

Sheldon, P., & Bryant, K. (2016). Instagram: Motives for its use and relationship to narcissism and contextual age. *Computers in Human Behavior, 58*, 89–97. doi:10.1016/j.chb.2015.12.059

Sheldon, P., & Newman, M. (2016). *Instagram and American teens: Understanding motives for its use and relationship to depression and narcissism*. Presented at the National Communication Association annual meeting, Philadelphia, PA.

Sheridan, L. P., & Grant, T. (2007). Is cyberstalking different? *Psychology, Crime, & Law, 13*, 627–640. doi:10.1080/10683160701340528

Sinclair, H. C., & Frieze, I. H. (2000. Initial courtship behavior and stalking: How should we draw the line? *Violence and Victims, 5*(1), 23-40.

Smahel, D., Brown, B. B., & Blinka, L. (2012). Associations between online friendship and internet addiction among adolescents and emerging adults. *Developmental Psychology, 48*, 381–388. doi:10.1037/a0027025

Smock, A. (2010). *Self-presentation on Facebook: Managing content created by the user and others.* Paper presented at the annual conference of the International Communication Association, Singapore.

Sohn, S. H. (2010). Sex differences in social comparison and comparison motives in body image process. *North American Journal of Psychology, 12*, 481–500.

Sourander, A., Brunstein Klomek, A., Ikonen, M., Lindroos, J., Luntamo, T., Koskelainen, M., … Helenius, H. (2010). Psychosocial risk factors associated with cyberbullying among adolescents: A population-based study. *Archives of General Psychiatry, 67*(7), 720–728.

Spitzberg, B. H., Marshall, L., & Cupach, W. R. (2001). Obsessive relational intrusion, coping, and sexual coercion victimization. *Communication Reports, 14*, 19–30. doi:10.1080/08934210109367733

Stabird, K., Maddock, J., Orand, M., Achterman, P., & Mason, R. M. (2014). *Rumors, false flags, and digital vigilantes: Misinformation on Twitter after the 2013 Boston Marathon bombing.* Retrieved from http://faculty.washington.edu/kstarbi/Starbird_iConference2014-final.pdf

Stefanone, M. A., Lackaff, D., &Rosen, D. (2011). Contingencies of self-worth and social-networking-site behavior. *Cyberpsychology, Behavior and Social Networking, 14*, 41–49. doi:10.1089/cyber.2010.0049

Steinberg, L. (2008). A social neuroscience perspective on adolescent risk-taking. *Developmental Review, 28*, 78–106. doi:10.1016/j.dr.2007.08.002

Thibaut, J., & Kelley, H. (1959). *The social psychology of groups.* New York, NY: Wiley.

Toma, C. L., Hancock, J. T., & Ellison, N. B. (2008). Separating fact from fiction: An examination of deceptive self-presentation in online dating profiles. *Personality and Social Psychology Bulletin, 34*, 1023–1036. doi:10.1177/0146167208318067

Toronto, E. (2009). Time out of mind: Dissociation in the virtual world. *Psychoanalytic Psychology, 26*(2), 117–133. doi:10.1037/a0015485

Tsitsika, A., Critselis, E., Louizou, A., Janikian, M., Freskou, A., Marangou, E., … Kafetzis, D. (2011). Determinants of Internet addiction among adolescents: A case-control study. *The Scientific World Journal, 11*, 866–874.

Turkle, S. (2011). *Alone together: Why we expect more from technology and less from each other.* New York, NY: Basic Books.

Twenge, J., Konrath, S., Foster, J., Campbell, W., & Bushman, B. (2008). Egos inflating over time: a cross-temporal meta-analysis of the Narcissistic Personality Inventory. *Journal of Personality, 76*(4), 875-928. doi: 10.1111/j.1467-6494.2008.00507.x

Utz, S., & Beukeboom, C. J. (2011). The role of social network sites in romantic relationships: Effects on jealousy and relationship happiness. *Journal of Computer-Mediated Communication, 16*, 511–527. doi:10.1111/j.1083-6101.2011.01552.x

Valenzuela, S., Halpern, D., & Katz, J. E. (2014). Social network sites, marriage well-being and divorce: Survey and state-level evidence from the United States. *Computers in Human Behavior, 36*, 94–101. doi:10.1016/j.chb.2014.03.034

Walther, J. B. (1996). Computer-mediated communication: Impersonal, interpersonal, and hyperpersonal interaction. *Communication Research, 23*, 3–43. doi:10.1177/009365096023001001

Walther, J. B. (2007). Selective self-presentation in computer-mediated communication: Hyperpersonal dimensions of technology language, and cognition. *Computers in Human Behavior, 23*, 2538–2557. doi:10.1016/j.chb.2006.05.002

Wang, J., Nansel, T. R., & Iannotti, R. J. (2011). Cyber and traditional bullying: Differential association with depression. *Journal of Adolescent Health, 48*(4), 415–417. doi:10.1016/j.jadohealth.2010.07.012

Wang, J. L., Jackson, L. A., Zhang, D. J., & Su, Z. Q. (2012). The relationships among Big Five personality factors, self-esteem, narcissism, and sensation-seeking to Chinese University students' uses of social networking sites (SNSs). *Computers in Human Behavior, 28*, 2313–2319. doi:10.1016/j.chb.2012.07.001

Wasilenko, K. A., Kulik, J. A., & Wanic, R. A. (2007). Effects of social comparison with peers on women's body satisfaction and exercise behavior. *International Journal of Eating Disorders, 40*, 740–745. doi:10.1002/eat.20433

Wegge, D., Vandebosch, H., Eggermont, S., & Walrave, M. (2015). The strong, the weak, and the unbalanced: The link between tie strength and cyberaggression on a social network site. *Social Science Computer Review, 33*(3), 315–342. doi:10.1177/0894439314546729

Weiser, E. B. (2015). #Me: Narcissism and its facets as predictors of selfie-posting frequency. *Personality and Individual Differences, 86*, 477–481. doi:10.1016/j.paid.2015.07.007

Welsh, A., & Lavoie, J. A. A. (2012). Risky eBusiness: An examination of risk-taking, online disclosiveness, and cyberstalking victimization. *Cyberpsychology: Journal of Psychosocial Research on Cyberspace, 6*(1), article 4. doi:10.5817/CP2012-1-4

West, R., & Turner, L. H. (2010). *Introducing communication theory: Analysis and application* (4th ed.). Boston, MA: McGraw-Hill Higher Education.

Whittaker, E., & Kowalski, R. (2015). Cyberbullying via social media. *Journal of School Violence, 14*(1), 11–29. doi:10.1080/15388220.2014.949377

Williard, N. (2005). *Educator's guide to cyberbullying and cyberthreats: Responding to the challenge of online social aggression, threats, and distress.* Center for Safe and Responsible Internet Use. Retrieved from http://www.accem.org/pdf/cbcteducator.pdf

Winter, S., Neubaum, G., Eimler, S. C., Gordon, V., Theil, J., Herrmann, J., … Krämer, N. C. (2014). Another brick in the Facebook wall—How personality traits relate to the content of status updates. *Computers in Human Behavior, 34*, 194–202. doi:10.1016/j.chb.2014.01.048

Wolak, J., Mitchell, K. J., & Finkelhor, D. (2002). Close online relationships in a national sample of adolescents. *Adolescence, 37*, 441–455.

Ybarra, M., & Mitchell, K. J. (2004). Online aggressor/targets, aggressors, and targets: A comparison of associated youth characteristics. *Journal of Child Psychology and Psychiatry, 45*(7), 1308–1316.

Your Wireless Life: Results of TIME's Mobility Poll. (2012). Retrieved from http://content.time.com/time/interactive/0,31813,2122187,00.html

Zhao, S., Grasmuck, S., & Martin, J. (2008). Identity construction on Facebook: Digital empowerment in anchored relationships. *Computers in Human Behavior, 24*, 1816–1836. doi:10.1016/j.chb.2008.02.012

CHAPTER THIRTEEN

Scripts for Constructive Communication

Can constructive communication be taught or is it inborn? Indeed, there has been an ongoing debate on the utility of the effectiveness of teaching communication skills versus the idea that communication behaviors are innate, hardwired, and a matter of genes and hormones (Beatty, Heisel, Hall, Levine, & La France, 2002; McCroskey & Beatty, 2000). We believe that communication skills can be refined. However, in some cases, biological factors appear to be strong. For example, as noted in the previous chapter, serotonin is lacking in abusers.

Advice for enhancing constructive communication is everywhere, including blogs, web sites, assertive training and self-help books, and commercials encouraging people to communicate with loved ones. Unfortunately, most of this advice is anecdotal and based on personal opinion without the merit of social science research based on laboratory and home observation of thousands of couples. For example, Honeycutt (1996) researched the types of lay, popular advice given and found that a majority reported that the information seemed like "common sense" or intuitive rather than containing surprising information. A useful function of self-help books on relationships may be to remind readers what they already presume to know. A common reason for reading about popular literature on relationships was not for advice or information, but for entertainment purposes.

In this chapter, we will provide a series of working scripts for constructive communication in interpersonal relationships based on conclusions from social science studies. From our interaction laboratory, we have amassed a videotape collection of couples who are having productive and dysfunctional conversations about problems in their relationships and discussion of daily events as well as positive and humorous conversations. The lab is conducive to communication because it is set up as a contemporary living room with comfortable seating (e.g., leather couch and wingback chair), coffee table, landscape paintings, plants, mirrors, and lamps. The lab contains nonverbal artifacts in the form of magazines and trinkets to distract someone if he/she wants to avoid communicating about a topic. Hence, they have the opportunity to relieve anxiety by picking up selected artifacts. The couple is observed through a one-way mirror and the interaction is videotaped through an unobtrusive, digital camera. We gather physiological data and measure heart rate variability, beats per minutes, blood pressure, and somatic activity by wearing a comfortable wrist monitor. We manipulate background variables such as background music in terms of music therapy. For example, the Mozart effect has been shown to help ease the tension and anxiety of arguing couples. This effect holds even if they report disliking classical music. Hence, some of our advice emanates from clinical observation of over 300 couples from over a 20-year period as well as compiling results from other studies.

First, we define communication competence, and then we discuss four behaviors leading to breakup. Three types of conflict tactics are discussed followed by the LOVE acronym for enhancing effective communication as well as an intriguing linguistic cue that reflects relational quality. The chapter ends with some sample tests of grievances designed to reflect decision-making and conflict-resolution behaviors.

Communication Competence

An early definition of communication competence was "the ability to interact well with others" (Spitzberg, 1988, p. 68). "The term 'well' refers to accuracy, clarity, comprehensibility, coherence, expertise, effectiveness, and appropriateness" (p. 68). A much more complete operationalization is provided by Friedrich, Hair, Wiemann, and Wiemann (1997), who suggested that communication competence is best understood as "a situational ability to set realistic and appropriate goals and to maximize their achievement by using knowledge of self, other, context, and communication theory to generate adaptive communication performances." Canary, Cody, and Manusov (2003) provide six criteria for assessing competence which include, but are not limited to, perceived appropriateness and effectiveness. The criteria include adaptability, conversational involvement, conversational management, empathy, effectiveness, and appropriateness.

One of the most eloquent definitions of effective communication that we have seen comes from Gottman (1982) in which he reviews studies on the escalation of conflict among happy and unhappily married couples. Effective communication is defined as low discrepancy between the intent behind a sender's message (e.g., positive affect, negative affect, ridicule, sarcasm, praise, admiration, etc.) and the impact of the message on a receiver (e.g., the message was perceived accordingly). Hence, if a relational partner wanted to signal ridicule or contempt by being sarcastic, using mockery, and using nonverbal cues such as eye-rolls, raising the upper lip, or nose wrinkle and the partner interprets this as ridicule, that would be good communication because there is agreement between the sender and receiver in terms of the meaning behind the intent and the received impact of the message.

This definition of communication effectiveness says nothing about how positive or negative the message is. Instead, the critical component is accuracy of interpretation. Good communication is defined as agreement between intent and impact, while bad communication is viewed as disagreement between intent and impact. For example, arguing does not predict divorce. In this regard, Gottman (1994) reviewed a number of studies indicating that happily married couples were distinguished from unhappily married couples by their ability to accurately interpret verbal and nonverbal messages. Moreover, nonverbal cues (e.g., smiling/laughter, voice tone, facial expressions, eye movements, less sarcasm) were more characteristic of happy couples than unhappy couples than verbal statements including topics and percentage of agreements/disagreements. Indeed, the two groups did not differ on the frequency with which they expressed their feelings, but unhappy couples were more likely to express emotions with negative affect (also see Gottman, Markman, & Notarius, 1977).

Communication Behaviors Leading to Breakup or Divorce

The vast research of Gottman and his associates over the years has clearly revealed that happy and unhappy couples both argue. Yet, it is how the arguing is done that discriminates between the couples. Unhappy couples tend to argue with negative emotions and use a variety of dysfunctional tactics. Indeed, Gottman (1994) and Gottman and Silver (2015) say that there are four major communication signs indicating if a couple is headed toward divorce. While these can occur in any order and frequency, the prototypical ordering is: criticisms, contempt, defensiveness, and withdrawal.

As noted earlier, complaining is good, while criticisms are bad. Recall from the previous chapter that criticisms are personal attacks on the partner's character and include statements that directly impact an individual's self-esteem. Indeed, unhappy couples are likely to enter into a repetitive cycle of cross-complaints while happy couples have validation sequences. Imagine an unhappy partner coming home and she complains about the rough day she had at the office. He responds with, "So did I. In fact, my day was even worse than yours." A complaint is responded to with a countercomplaint. Conversely, in a validation sequence, his response would be, "I am sorry about that. I understand. You may feel some stress. What can I do?" His response is nonjudgmental and has validated what she is feeling without causing her to become defensive.

The second dysfunctional communication behavior is contempt. As indicated from the previous chapter, it signals disgust and ridicule. Common contempt behaviors are sarcasm, eye rolls, and facial expressions with tightened cheeks. Contempt often leads to the escalation of conflict rather than reconciliation. Ironically, Gottman (1994) reports a correlation of .51 between a wife's facial expressions of disgust with the number of months that the couple will be separated in the next 4 years. Also, her facial expressions of disgust are a good predictor of the wife's physical illness 4 years later.

The third dysfunctional behavior is defensiveness. The person feels picked on by their partner. It is an attempt to protect one's self-esteem and deflect criticism. Typically, there is a denial of responsibility, counterblame, or a whine (Gottman, 1994). Mindreading statements occur in the form of "You always" or "You never" statements. It is quite common in exclusive relationships, but if it is done with negative emotion, the effects are devastating because the listener feels that they are being blamed and accused of negative behaviors. Conversely, if it is delivered with positive feelings, the listener feels validated or supported.

Another sign of defensiveness is "whining." The whiner feels that unfair accusations are being made and they are being picked on. Behind the whining lies the nonverbal message that the listener wants pity. Whining is often done with a nasal pitch that is irritating to the listener. It may be a substitute for crying and is related to sadness (Gottman, 1994).

The final dysfunctional behavior leading to divorce is withdrawal or stonewalling. The majority of stonewallers are male (85% reported in Gottman, 1994). When wives stonewall, the marriage is over. Numerous studies point to women initiating discussion about relational grievances while the men are more likely to withhold comments (Denton & Burleson, 2007; Kelly, Fincham, & Beach, 2003; Sagrestano, Heavey, & Christensen, 2006).

Conflict Tactics

Communication competence affects how an individual approaches conflict. Integrative strategies, which are perceived as more positive approaches to conflict, have been positively linked to competence (Spitzberg & Cupach, 1984). Distributive and avoidant strategies, which are perceived as negative approaches to conflict, are negatively associated with communication competence. Researchers indicate that competence in most conflicts requires integrative rather than avoidant or distributive tactics (Canary & Spitzberg, 1989; Sillars, 1998). Because using appropriate communication is equated with trying to meet the goals of both partners, integrative strategies are seen as competent.

Conflict can be a foundation for social and personal change (Lulofs, 1994). Managing conflict includes two particular dimensions of communication: affect and engagement (Sillars, Weisberg, Burggraf, & Wilson, 1987). As noted from Chapter 2, affect refers to messages that convey either positive or negative emotions for the other. Engagement describes how likely one is to confront or to avoid conflict. In interpersonal relationships, the challenge is to manage a conflict so that the positive consequences outweigh the negative ones (Roloff & Soule, 2002).

There is research on the effectiveness of conflict tactics (Canary & Spitzberg, 1987). Table 13.1 summarizes these tactics. A classic typology comes from Sillars, Coletti, Parry and Rogers (1982) as well as Canary and Cupach (1988) who identified three types of conflict tactics. Happily married couples use more integrative tactics in which there is cooperation (Meeks, Hendrick, & Hendrick, 1998). The problems are mutually defined and areas of agreement are noted. There are supportive comments. A negative conflict tactic is distributive conflict which is competitive and belligerent. The individual is selfish and individually focused rather than relationally focused. Characteristics include threats, ridicule, contempt, intimidation, and coercion. A third type of conflict tactic that is also negative is avoidance in which the individual withdraws from communication hoping to keep tensions buried. Characteristics include denial that a conflict exists, withholding a criticism or complaint when communication is viewed as too costly, making irrelevant remarks to divert communication from conflict to a nonthreatening topic, leaving the scene. Hence, since integrative tactics are associated with more quality relationships, they are encouraged.

Table 13.1. Three types of conflict tactics.

---

1. Integrative—There is cooperation. It is direct and nice. The problems are mutually defined and areas of commonality and agreement are noted. There are supportive comments and listening in a supportive manner through using "pseudo agreements." Compromise is used to "split the difference." This is a win–win strategy for both parties.
2. Distributive—It is competitive and belligerent. The individual is selfish and individually focused rather than being focused on another's needs.

    Characteristics include: Threats, demands, coercion, intimidation, hostility, personal criticisms, ridicule, put-downs, defensiveness, hit-and-run tactics, sarcasm, and contempt
3. Avoidance—There is a withdrawal and the idea is to keep tensions buried. Avoidance can be cooperative or competitive, agreeable or disagreeable.

    Characteristics include: Verbally denying that there's a conflict, withholding a complaint when confrontation is deemed to be too costly, making irrelevant remarks to divert communication from conflict to a nonthreatening topic, giving into the demands of another, leaving the scene, not voicing complaints for fear of retaliation: "the chilling effect."

Rules for Arguing

Aside from the aforementioned studies on conflict tactics, we have produced a list of four composite rules for effective arguing. In terms of rules, we distinguish prescriptive rules (What you should do) from restrictive rules (What to avoid). For example, the negative conflict tactics of avoidance and distributive strategies are restrictive in that they should be avoided in order to facilitate effective communication. Honeycutt, Woods, and Fontenot (1993) conducted a factor analysis of rules that engaged and married couples reported were important to follow while arguing. They also asked the couples how often they followed the rules and whether or not it occurred in public and private settings. The initial list of rules was identified by Jones and Gallois (1989) based on interviews with couples who watched themselves on videotape as they discussed a grievance in their relationship (e.g., household tasks, lack of expression of feelings, finances, in-laws, demonstration of affection, use of leisure time, morals/values). Four types of rules for arguing were discovered. Table 13.2 presents the four rules and a list of examples.

The first set of rules is "positive understanding" and reflected being able to say sorry to the other, resolving the problem for a happy outcome, giving praise to the other, listening to the other, acknowledging the other, and being honest. The second set of rules was labeled "rationality." Examples are being calm and not raising the voice or avoiding anger. The third set of rules reflects "conciseness" and refers to getting to the point quickly and being specific about the issue. The final set of

Table 13.2. Primary factor loadings for rules about arguing.

Rules

Positive Understanding
Should be able to say you are sorry (.81)
Resolve problem so both are happy (.79)
Support and praise your partner where due (.69)
Listen to your partner (.67)
See your partner's viewpoint (.64)
Be honest and say what is on your mind (.63)
Should look at each other (.57)
Explore alternatives (.55)
Make joint decisions (.55)
Don't dismiss your partner's issue as unimportant (.55)

Rationality
Don't get angry (.85)
Shouldn't argue (.75)
Don't raise voice (.72)
Avoid combative issues (.60)
Don't lose your temper or be aggressive (.58)
Try to remain calm and not get upset (.52)

Conciseness
Be specific, don't generalize (.68)
Be consistent (.66)
Keep to the main point (.63)
Clarify the problem (.59)

Consideration
Don't talk too much (.69)
Don't make your partner feel guilty (.66)
Don't push your view as the only one (.65)
Don't mimic or be sarcastic to your partner (.62)
Understand other's faults and don't be judgmental (.62)
Don't talk down to your partner (.55)

Note: All of the sample rules had a primary factor loading above .55.

rules is "consideration." Examples include not pushing your point of view as the only point of view and not talking too much.

Engaged couples endorsed all of the rules more than married couples. A reason for this is that they are still in a "honeymoon" or euphoric state and cynicism may not have grown since they have not been in their joint, marital roles. In addition, couples who reported that they shared a lot of activities and joint time endorsed the rules compared to couples who were more likely to freely engage in arguments. All of the rules were seen as characterizing happy couples rather than unhappy couples as well as applying equally in public and private settings. Hence, these four factors provide an easy list of how to argue with a relational partner. Further analysis reveals that positive understanding is most related to having a happy relationship (Honeycutt et al., 1993). Despite the continuing research on arguing, this list of rules is intuitive and compelling.

An Acronym for Effective Communication Tips: Listen Observe (or Oxytocin) Verify (or Validate) Express

Over the years, the senior author has conducted communication workshops for engaged couples. An effective mnemonic device that facilitates reflective listening and effective communication with a partner is Listen Observe Verify Express. Table 13.3 presents a summary of guidelines for resolving conflict in personal relationships. It is important to note that these general guidelines are not a panacea. Unfortunately, we are emotional and irrational creatures, but we can try to control emotions while arguing.

1. The L stands for Listen. Listen to your partner. This means avoiding interruptions and simultaneous talk. Avoid quick, impetuous prejudgments. We have found that happily married couples use a communicator style that signals attentiveness (Honeycutt, Wilson, & Parker, 1982). Head nods, eye gaze while listening, and use of timed pseudo-agreements facilitate the appearance that you are interested in what your partner is saying. A major point is to signal attentiveness even if you could care less about what your partner is saying.

2. The O stands for Observation. Observe what your partner is nonverbally communicating through facial expressions, tone of voice, body posture, or rigidity. Recall that contempt is often signaled by eye rolls. There is vast amount of research on nonverbal immediacy cues and signaling interest (Andersen, 1985; Coker & Burgoon, 1987; Jones, 2004). Hence, you should observe how they appear to be feeling in addition to what they are actually saying. The classic Mehrabian (1981) formula says that the total impact of a message on a partner is primarily conveyed through nonverbal means with 55% of the meaning of a message being based on facial expressions, 38% being based on voice qualities (tone, volume, pitch, nasality),

and only 7% of the meaning being based on the content of the message in terms of what is actually said.

The O can also stand for the bonding hormone Oxytocin which was discussed in the physiology Chapter 4. Oxtyocin is also with willingness to disclose emotions (Lane et al., 2013) as well as trust (Cardoso, Ellenbogen, Serravalle, & Linnen, 2013).

3. The V stands for Verify or Validate. You should verify your interpretation of what you feel your partner is saying and feeling. One way to do this is to summarize other's (Gottman, 1994) statements, which further signals attentiveness and interest. Unhappy couples tend to be forced to use summarizing self-statements in which they constantly repeat what they want because they feel that their partner is not listening and "doesn't get it" (Gottman, 1994; Gottman, Markman, & Notarius, 1977). You want to validate your partner even if you disagree with their claims.

Recall from the preceding chapter how the deterioration of marital interactions is affected by stress, and examples of stressful communication are criticism, contempt, and belligerence which reflects Gottman and Gottman's (2012) four horsemen of the apocalypse that predict divorce with 85% accuracy. Positive behaviors are validation, stating problem solutions, paraphrasing, active listening.

An interesting thing that happens in terms of validation is the non-acknowledgment of news of success or discussion of daily events. Yet, communication skills training can facilitate gratitude. Supportive communication is enhanced through regularly sharing positive experiences and showing enthusiasm for another's success. In fact, relational partners may take it as an insult if they are the "last to know of a partner's achievement" which sometimes happens because of the rapidity of universal disclosure through Twitter and Instagram. Yet, American culture through its emphasis on individualism, self-reliance, and narcissism has been criticized by sometimes being silent when others share success because of a sense of self-entitlement for oneself that one has been recognized (Honeycutt, Pence, & Gearhart, 2013). This is satirical because it is often mathematically impossible (cf., ties are often eliminated) for everyone to be number one. Research reveals that couples who are trained to communicate more active-constructive responses when their partners share good news report higher relationship satisfaction and reciprocal gratitude (Woods, Lambert, Brown, Fincham, & May, 2015).

4. The E stands for Expression. Express in a rational, calm manner what you are feeling. Do not be belligerent since this will arouse defensiveness and

even contempt in the partner. Simple guidelines for effective expression based on compiling research of arguing in couples include the following: be descriptive rather than evaluative, equal rather than superior, cooperative rather than competitive, provisional rather than certain.

Table 13.3. Guidelines for resolving conflict.

Acronym for Effective Listening and Communication

L—Listen
O—Observe (Oxytocin)
V—Verify (Validate)
E—Express

Features of Constructive Conflict

---

1. Avoid reciprocating negative affect—An "eye for an eye" doesn't work because aggression that is met with aggression is seen as socially inept, both in terms of work and play.
2. Flee the scene of violence before it occurs—Use avoidance rather than distributive conflict as discussed above.
3. Free the avenues of exchange between the parties—Listen to the other party and ask them what they fear. Why do they have this fear? What can be done about overcoming the fear? Given the other party the opportunity to present views.
4. Adopt a nonviolent stance—Once a person uses coercion, force, or violence, she or he loses the ability to listen.
5. If necessary, agree to disagree with the understanding the both parties' points of views are legitimate.

Respond Proactively to Anger

---

1. One has the right to become angry at intentional wrongdoing and at unintended misdeeds—if those misdeeds are due to negligence.
2. Direct anger at objects or people who are responsible for the actions.
3. Do not vent anger on innocent third parties "nor should it be directed at the target for reasons other than the instigation."
4. The objective is to correct the problem and restore fairness, not fear in the other person.
5. One's response to anger should match the instigation; it should not exceed what is necessary to correct the situation or prevent the instigation from happening again.
6. One's expression of anger should follow the provoking event as soon as possible rather than later.
7. One's expression of anger should involve a commitment to solve the problem, including any necessary follow-through.

Guidelines for Effective Arguing

1. Use rules of arguing reflecting positive understanding, rationality, conciseness, and consideration.
2. Complain but don't blame.
3. Use "I" or "We" statements instead of "You"—(We can work this out. I would like if you'd listen to me instead of "You aren't listening to me.").
4. Be specific rather than general or vague.
5. Avoid name calling and obscenities.
6. Avoid absolutes such as "never" and "always."
7. Discuss one issue at a time; don't store things up ready to unleash your recriminations.

Biofeedback to Reduce Stress

Recall that Chapter 4 discusses the physiology of relationships. Heart rate variability is associated with better health, security, and stable relationships according to the poly-vagal theory of Porges (2011). The Institute of HeartMath (www.heartmath.org) has conducted decades of research on how and why positive emotions improve health and performance. Emotions have a powerful impact on the human body. Positive emotions like appreciation, care, and love not only feel good, they are good for you. They help your body's systems synchronize and work better, like a well-tuned car.

Figure 13.1 reveals that heart rhythms associated with positive emotions, such as appreciation, are clearly more coherent—organized as a stable pattern of repeating sine waves—than those generated during a negative emotional experience involving frustration or anger. The heart rhythm pattern shown in the top graph, characterized by its erratic, irregular pattern (incoherence), is typical of negative emotions such as anger or frustration. So in the heat of battle with someone, there is fluctuating, asymmetrical heart rate variability. The bottom graph shows an example of the coherent heart rhythm pattern that is typically observed when an individual is experiencing sustained, modulated positive emotions, in this case appreciation. The association between positive emotional experience and this distinctive physiological pattern is evident in studies conducted in both laboratory and natural settings, and for both spontaneous emotions and intentionally generated feelings (McCraty, Atkinson, Tiller, Rein, & Watkins, 1995).

The Institute of HeartMath's (www.hearthmath.com) research has shown that when you intentionally shift to a positive emotion, heart rhythms immediately change. This shift in heart rhythms creates a favorable cascade of neural, hormonal, and biochemical events that benefit the entire body. The effects are

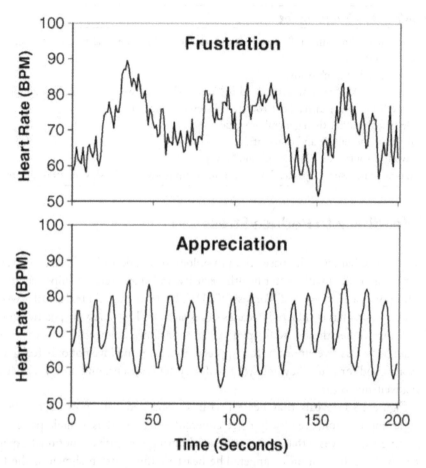

Figure 13.1. Heart rate rhythms of a negative and positive emotion.

Note: BPM refers to beats per minute. Adapted from *The Coherent Heart: Heart-Brain Interactions, Psychophysiological Coherence, and the Emergence of System-Wide Order* by R. McCraty, M. Atkinson, D. Tomasino, and R. T. Bradley. Copyright 2006 by Institute of HeartMath, Reprinted with permission.

both immediate and long lasting. As a result, they advocate a three-step procedure called the "Quick Coherence Technique" for stress reduction and improving relational communication.

The Quick Coherence Technique

1) Heart Focus: Focus your attention in the area around your heart. You can place your hand over your heart to help.

2) Heart Breathing: The second step is to pretend you are breathing through your heart area. Breathe slowly, deeply, and gently (to a count of 5 or 6) until your breathing feels smooth and balanced. Do this for about one minute and notice the changes.

3) Heart Feeling: The third step involves positive feeling and attitudes. Continue to breathe through the area of your heart and find a positive feeling, like appreciation for someone or something. You can recall a time when you felt appreciation or care and reexperience that feeling. It can be a positive retroactive imagined interaction in which you relive a positive encounter with your relational partner. It could be for a pet, a special place in nature, or an activity that was fun. Once you have found a positive feeling—sustain this feeling by continuing heat focus, heart breathing, and heart feeling. Meditation or prayer also works for some people.

The Quick Coherence tool is a simple way to interrupt the stress response and bring your system into coherence. Practice this tool 4–5 times a day, every day for a minimum of 3 weeks. Use this tool prior to or during events or situations that provide emotional challenges. Good times to practice are first thing in the morning, before going to sleep at night, break time in the middle of the day, or anytime you want to rebalance or get an energy boost. Once you have completed the steps, ask yourself, "How could I handle this in a better way?" With practice, you'll find you have more intuitive choices or options for what you might do next—even in the middle of a challenging or high-pressure situation.

Linguistic Cues Signifying a Happy Relationship

Over the years in our communication interaction lab, we have observed a subliminal, linguistic cue that happy couples use. Note how many of your friends do this. Happy couples in conversations about how their day went as well as discussing grievances often use the plural "We," while unhappy couples use the singular "I" and second person "You." For example, a happy couple is more likely to say "We need to spend more time together" as opposed to "You spend too much time surfing the internet while I'm always the one cleaning the house." "We-ness" signals affiliation, closeness, and bonding while the use of "I" and "You" signal distance. Honeycutt (1999) found that both husbands' and wives' marital happiness was predicted by the use of "we-ness" by both partners. "We-ness" reflects interdependence and sharing even though most couples are unaware of these linguistic codes.

Knapp, Vangelisti, and Caughlin (2014) discuss the differentiation stage of decaying relationships in which partners' conversation is often characterized by what distinguishes them. Differences are concentrated on personality, attitudes, friends, interest, or even sexual needs. The use of "I" and "You" may reflect subliminal differences that reflect core, underlying values (e.g., helping others versus selfishness).

An intriguing study involved videotaping marital couples discussing a marital grievance (e.g., lack of communication, disagreement about household tasks) at their homes or in a research laboratory. The videotapes were coded for content themes that revealed differences among couples (Sillars et al., 1987). Happy couples' conversations reflected more communal themes where their relationship is seen as the product of joint qualities (e.g., "We enjoy the same things" "We enjoy doing chores together" "We work together"). Unhappy couples' conversations reflect more individual themes where their relationship is viewed as a product of separate identities and roles. Typical examples of individual themes include the following: "You have your friends and I have mine." "I need to be left alone sometimes." "You bitch all the time." "I've never been a person to do a lot of touching." "You have your things to do and I have my things to do." "I'm not good at communicating." "I get mad when you don't get something done."

Another study found that couples who endorsed an ideology of marriage involving sharing and companionship compared to couples who endorsed more independence or avoided open conflict (separates) used more plural "we-ness" in their conversations, while the independents and separates used more of the singular "I" (Fitzpatrick, 1988). However, it has been found that in terms of text messaging on smartphones, happy couples do not use more "we-ness" (Slatcher, Vazire, & Pennebaker, 2008).

Tests of Grievances and Arguing Behaviors

Following are two sample techniques that we use in our interaction to encourage discussions. The first technique is to have partners simply discuss how their days went followed by a discussion of grievances. They can use the list to determine how many of the guidelines for effective arguing are being followed. Table 13.4 presents a list of common grievances that are easily used in decision-making and conflict-resolution tasks in interpersonal relationships (Honeycutt, 2001). Individuals rate how satisfied they are with or how often they have discussed each of the topics. They then choose the topic(s) that they are most pleased or displeased with and are instructed to discuss the topic with their partner for 5 minutes and attempt to explain their point of view. Many couples have told us how they have had repetitive conversations over many of the topics.

Table 13.4. Satisfaction with relational topics instrument.

In the following items, indicate the degree of satisfaction you feel for each of these aspects of your relationship.

		Extremely dissatisfied		Average				Extremely satisfied
1.	Moral and religious beliefs	1	2	3	4	5	6	7
2.	Self or partner's job	1	2	3	4	5	6	7
3.	How we communicate		2	3	4	5	6	
4.	My partner's attitudes about children	1	2	3	4	5	6	7
5.	How the house is kept	1	2	3	4	5	6	7
6.	The amount of influence I have over the decisions we make	1	2	3	4	5	6	7
7.	Our social life	1	2	3	4	5	6	7
8.	How open my partner is in communicating with me	1	2	3	4	5	6	7
9.	Amount of money coming in	1	2	3	4	5	6	7
10.	How we express affection for each other	1	2	3	4	5	6	7
11.	How we discipline children	1	2	3	4	5	6	7
12.	How we manage our finances	1	2	3	4	5	6	7
13.	Our sex life	1	2	3	4	5	6	7
14.	How we fight	1	2	3	4	5	6	7
15.	Our shared goals or interests	1	2	3	4	5	6	7
16.	Our sexual compatibility	1	2	3	4	5	6	7
17.	My partner's faithfulness		2	3	4	5	6	
18.	The fun or excitement in our relationship	1	2	3	4	5	6	7
19.	How my partner treats drugs or alcohol	1	2	3	4	5	6	7
20.	Issues of equality	1	2	3	4	5	6	7
21.	How family members are treated	1	2	3	4	5	6	7
22.	Activities and time spent together	1	2	3	4	5	6	7
23.	How often we talk about daily events	1	2	3	4	5	6	7
24.	How much time we spend on the social media	1	2	3	4	5	6	7
25.	Amount of time my partner listens to me	1	2	3	4	5	6	7
26.	Remembering errands	1	2	3	4	5	6	7
27.	Information about people in the news	1	2	3	4	5	6	7

The topic(s) that I am most pleased with are _____ (Write the item number of the topics that you are most satisfied with in preceding space in the order of the most serious).

The topic(s) that I am most concerned about and displeased with are _____ (Write the item number of the topics that most concern you in preceding space in the order of the most serious).

For the next 5 minutes, discuss the most (pleasing/displeasing) topic with your partner.

Some of the underlying dimensions that are represented in the instrument include: communication (e.g., Topics 3, 8, 14, 25), interpersonal sharing (e.g., Topic 6, 15, 20), repetitive activities (e.g., Topics 5, 22, 23, 24), financial management (e.g., Topics 2, 9, 12), sexual compatibility (e.g., Topics 10, 13, 16), and fidelity/ chemical dependency (e.g., Topics 13, 17, 19). It is interesting that in a sample of 636 individuals comprising 33% separated/divorced individuals and 67% intact, married couples we found that infidelity correlates very highly with the use of alcohol and drugs by a partner, $r = .55$, $p < .001$ and is loaded on one factor.

Another instrument to reflect how well you argue and engage in decision making is found in Table 13.5. This instrument comes from the Inventory of Marital Conflicts (Olson & Ryder, 1970). Couples are given a series of vignettes and instructed to role-play attempting to persuade their partner to their viewpoint. Sample vignettes include husband or wife having incompatible views about the visitation of a partner's friend, satisfaction during sex, partner leaving clothes around the home, conflict regarding partner's party behavior, partner's conversations with men/women at parties, spending too much time on work, and watching too much televised sports. Because there are computing goals, the task is excellent at reflecting how often you use some of our guidelines for effective arguing.

Table 13.5. Induced Conflict-Resolution Vignettes—Role-Playing.

Following are ten scenarios that you can use to reflect decision making and resolve disagreements among relational partners. Choose any of the topics and partner roles and discuss it for 5–10 minutes following the instructions for each partner. The different relational partners are simply designated by "Partner A" or "Partner B." How would you resolve the hypothetical disagreement?

1. **Topic: Sharing Events of the Day**
   Partner A's Instructions: "A" is excited about sharing with "B" something he/she experienced during the day.
   Partner B's Instructions: "B" is feeling harassed and is looking forward to some privacy and time alone.

2. **Topic: Money**
   A's Instructions: Both partners are told that they have been on a tight budget because they have been saving for a major purchase. "A" has been feeling pretty short of pocket money because of the budget and wants to let his partner know he/she needs more money.
   B's Instructions: "B" has been feeling deprived and has managed to save some food money to purchase something small but special for him/herself. He/she likes the purchase very much and is looking forward to sharing it with his/her partner.

3. **Topic: Sex**
   A's Instructions: "A" very much wants to complete some activity of his/her choosing "this evening" without being disrupted.
   B's Instructions: "B" wants to be close and to make love.

4. **Topic: Relatives**
   A's Instructions: "A" wants to visit his/her family for 4 days during Christmas and is looking forward to enjoying the special holiday festivities.
   B's Instructions: "B" is reluctant to visit the parents of his/her partner because of specific grievances with them.

5. **Topic: Decision to Have Children**
   A's Instructions: "A" is opposed to having children at this time for various reasons.
   B's Instructions: "B" wants to have children and wants a decision to be made about this.

6. **Topic: Discipline of Children**
   A's Instructions: "A" advocates spontaneity and permissiveness as important for children.
   B's Instructions: "B" feels that the children need firmer discipline.

7. **Topic: Job Transfer**
   A's Instructions: "A" has a wonderful relationship with "B." However, "A" has been approached about his/her interest in a promising, career-enhancing job in another town that would require him/her to move. "A" is unhappy in his/her current job and is considering the other job.
   B's Instructions: "B" has a wonderful relationship with "A." "B" has a great job in his/her current town that they love. It is difficult, if not impossible to find a parallel job in another city. "B" does not want to sacrifice his/her job stability but still loves "A."

8. **Topic: Watching too much sports on TV**
   A's Instructions: "A" wants to watch the Game Day college football show on ESPN on Saturday morning to see how his/her university is portrayed by the announcers. "A" watches college football games all day.
   B's Instructions: "B" believes that "A" is addicted to watching football games on TV and wants to do something active such as go bicycling on a beautiful park trail as well as having a picnic at the park.

9: **Topic: Partner's conversations with others at parties**
   A's Instructions: "A" likes to socialize and talk with friends at a party.
   B's Instructions: "B" feels ignored by his/her partner and left alone at parties. Indeed, they feel that their partner flirts with other people at parties while ignoring them.

10: **Topic: Household cleanliness**
    A's Instruction: "A" always likes the house tidy and clean. "A" gets tired of picking up after his/her partner.
    B's Instructions: "B" likes to relax at the home and leaves things around because he/she knows where they are and that they are easily retrievable.

Summary

There is considerable debate about the utility of enhancing communication skills for conflict resolution. If you want to maintain your relationship, you can attempt to avoid the four behaviors that predict divorce and breakups: constant criticisms, contempt, defensiveness, withdrawal. A positive conflict tactic is cooperation while avoidance and belligerent strategies are negative. Rules for arguing were discussed.

These include positive understanding, rationality, consideration, and conciseness. An effective acronym for effective communication is LOVE: Listen Observe (or Oxytocin for the bonding hormone discussed in the physiology Chapter 4). Verify (Can also be expressed as Validation) Express. An intriguing linguistic cue signifying relational bonding and sharing is the use of "We" while the constant use of "I" and "You" reflect distance, differentiation. Finally, a series of sample tests of grievances are demonstrated so that you can determine which guidelines of effective communication you are using.

Discussion Questions

13.1. Using Table 13.4, identify some of the topics that you are most pleased and displeased with in the most important relationship in your life. Which of the topics do you discuss most? Why?

13.2. Consider examples of the LOVE acronym in the most recent argument you had with someone. What was your relationship with them? How important is the relationship to each of you?

13.3. Discuss integrative, distributive, and avoidant conflict strategies. Think of two people who you think are the most effective communicators that you know. Which of the conflict strategies do they tend to use? Which of the following rules for arguing (e.g., positive understanding, rationality, conciseness, consideration) do they seem to follow?

Application

13.1. From Table 13.5, role-play with one of your classmates' one of the vignettes. How did you feel about the conflict-resolution scenario? Were you frustrated? Which of the conflict styles did you use?

References

Andersen, P. A. (1985). Nonverbal immediacy in interpersonal communication. In A. W. Siegman & S. Feldstein (Eds.), *Multichannel integrations of nonverbal behavior* (pp. 1–36). Hillsdale, NJ: Lawrence Erlbaum.

Beatty, M. J., Heisel, A. D., Hall, A. E., Levine, T. R., & La France, B. H. (2002). What can we learn from the study of twins about genetic and environmental influences on interpersonal affiliation, aggressiveness, and social anxiety? A meta-analytic study. *Communication Monographs, 69*, 1–18. doi:10.1080/03637750216534

Canary, D. J., Cody, M. J., & Manusov, V. M. (2003). *Interpersonal communication: A goals-based approach* (3rd ed.). New York, NY: Bedford/St. Martin's.

Canary, D. J., & Cupach, W. R. (1988). Relational and episodic characteristics associated with conflict tactics. *Journal of Social and Personal Relationships, 5*, 305–325. doi:10.1177/0265407588053003

Canary, D. J., & Spitzberg, B. H. (1987). Appropriateness and effectiveness perceptions of conflict strategies. *Human Communication Research, 14*, 93–120. doi:10.1111/j.1468-2958.1987.tb00123.x

Canary, D. J., & Spitzberg, B. H. (1989), A model of the perceived competence of conflict strategies. *Human Communication Research, 15*, 630–649. doi:10.1111/j.1468-2958.1989.tb00202.x

Cardoso, C., Ellenbogen, M. A., Serravalle, L., & Linnen, A. M. (2013). Stress-induced negative mood moderates the relation between oxytocin administration and trust: Evidence for the tend-and-befriend response to stress? *Psychoneuroendocrinology, 38*, 2800–2804. doi:10.1016/j.psyneuen.2013.05.006

Coker, D. A., & Burgoon, J. K. (1987). The nature of conversational involvement and nonverbal encoding patterns. *Human Communication Research, 13*, 463–494. doi:10.1111/j.1468-2958.1987.tb00115.x

Denton, W. H., & Burleson, B. R. (2007). The initiator style questionnaire: A scale to assess initiator tendency in couples. *Personal Relationships, 14*, 245–268. doi:10.1111/j.1475-6811.2007.00153.x

Fitzpatrick, M. A. (1988). A typological approach to marital interaction. In P. Noller & M. A. Fitzpatrick (Eds.), *Perspectives on marital interaction* (Vol. 1): *Monographs in the social psychology of language* (pp. 98–120). Clevedon and Philadelphia: Multilingual Matters.

Friedrich, G. O., Hair, H. D., Wiemann, J., & Wiemann, M. (1997). *Human communication: A communication competency approach* (2nd ed.). New York, NY: St. Martin's Press.

Gottman, J. M. (1982). Emotional responsiveness in marital conversations. *Journal of Communication, 32*, 108–120. doi:10.1111/j.1460-2466.1982.tb02504.x

Gottman, J. M. (1994). *What predicts divorce?* Mahwah, NJ: Lawrence Erlbaum.

Gottman, J. M., & Gottman, J, S. (2012). Bridging the couple chasm: Gottman couples therapy: A research-based approach. Seattle, WA: The Gottman Institute.

Gottman, J. M., Markman, H. J., & Notarius, C. (1977). The topography of marital conflict: A study of verbal and nonverbal behavior. *Journal of Marriage and the Family, 39*, 461–477.

Gottman, J. M., & Silver, N. (2015). *The seven principles for making marriage work.* New York, NY: Harmony.

Honeycutt, J. M. (1996). How 'helpful' are self-help relational books? Common sense or counterintuitive information. *Personal Relationship Issues, 3*, 1–4.

Honeycutt, J. M. (1999). Typological differences in predicting marital happiness from oral history behaviors and imagined interactions. *Communication Monographs, 66*, 275–291. doi:10.1080/03637759909376478

Honeycutt, J. M. (2001). Satisfaction with marital issues and topics scale (SMI). In J. Touliatos, B. F. Perlmutter, & M. A. Straus (Eds.), *Handbook of family measurement techniques* (Vol. 1, p. 92). Thousand Oaks, CA: Sage.

Honeycutt, J. M., Pence, M. E., & Gearhart, C. C. (2013). Using Imagined Interactions to predict covert narcissism. *Communication Reports, 26,* 26-38. doi:10.1080/08934215.2013.773051

Honeycutt, J. M., Wilson, C., & Parker, C. (1982). Effects of sex and degrees of happiness on perceived styles of communicating in and out of the marital relationship. *Journal of Marriage and the Family, 44,* 395–406. doi:10.2307/351548

Honeycutt, J. M., Woods, B. L., & Fontenot, K. (1993). The endorsement of communication conflict rules as a function of engagement, marriage, and marital ideology. *Journal of Social and Personal Relationships, 10,* 285–304. doi:10.1177/026540759301000208

Jones, S. (2004). Putting the person into person-centered and immediate emotional support. *Communication Research, 31,* 338–360. doi:10.1177/0093650204263436

Jones, E., & Gallois, C. (1989). Spouses' impressions of rules for communication in public and private marital conflicts. *Journal of Marriage and the Family, 5,* 957–967. doi:10.2307/353208

Kelly, A. B., Fincham, F. D., & Beach, S. R. H. (2003). Communication skills in couples: A review and discussion of emerging perspectives. In J. O. Greene & B. R. Burleson (Eds.), *Handbook of communication and social interaction skills* (pp. 723–752). Mahwah, NJ: Lawrence Erlbaum.

Knapp, M. L., Vangelisti, A. L., & Caughlin, J. P. (2014). *Interpersonal communication and human relationships* (7th ed.). New York, NY: Pearson.

Lane, A., Luminet, O., Rimé, B., Gross, J. J., de Timary, P., & Mikolajczak, M. (2013). Oxytocin increases willingness to socially share one's emotions. *International Journal of Psychology, 48,* 676–681. doi:10.1080/00207594.2012.677540

Lulofs, R. S. (1994). *Conflict: From theory to action.* Scottsdale, AZ: Gorsuch Scarisbrick.

McCraty, R., Atkinson, M., Tiller, W. A., Rein, G., & Watkins, A. D. (1995). The effects of emotions on short-term power spectrum analysis of heart rate variability. *American Journal of Cardiology, 76,* 1089–1093.

McCraty, R., Atkinson, M., Tomasino, D., & Bradley, R. T. (2006). *The coherent heart: Heart-brain interactions, psychophysiological coherence, and the emergence of system-wide order.* Available from http://store.heartmath.org/store/e-books/coherent-heart

McCroskey, J. C., & Beatty, M. J. (2000). The communibiological perspective: Implications for communication instruction. *Communication Education, 49,* 1–6. doi:10.1080/03634520009379187

Meeks, B. S., Hendrick, S. S., & Hendrick, C. (1998). Communication, love, and relationship satisfaction. *Journal of Social and Personal Relationships, 15,* 755–773. doi:10.1177/0265407598156003

Mehrabian, A. (1981). *Silent messages: Implicit communication of emotions and attitudes* (2nd ed.). Belmont, CA: Wadsworth.

Olson, D. H., & Ryder, R. G. (1970). Inventory of marital conflicts (IMC): An experimental interaction procedure. *Journal of Marriage and the Family, 32,* 443–448. doi:10.2307/350110

Porges, S. W. (2011). *The polyvagal theory Neurophysiological foundations of emotions, attachment, communication, and self-regulation.* New York: W.W. Norton.

Roloff, M. E., & Soule, K. P. (2002). Interpersonal conflict: A review. In M. L. Knapp & J. A. Daly (Eds.), *Handbook of interpersonal communication* (pp. 475–528). Thousand Oaks, CA: Sage.

Sagrestano, L. M., Heavey, C. L., & Christensen, A. C. (2006). Individual differences versus social structural approaches to explaining demand-withdraw and social influence behaviors. In K. Dindia & D. J. Canary (Eds.), *Sex differences and similarities in communication* (pp. 379–396). Mahwah, NJ: Lawrence Erlbaum.

Sillars, A. L. (1998). (Mis)Understanding. In B. H. Spitzberg & W. R. Cupach (Eds.), *The dark side of close relationships* (pp. 73–102). Mahwah, NJ: Lawrence Erlbaum.

Sillars, A. L., Coletti, S. F., Parry, D., & Rogers, M. A. (1982). Coding verbal conflict tactics: Nonverbal and perceptual correlates of the "avoidance-distributive-integrative" distinction. *Human Communication Research, 9*, 83–95. doi:10.1111/j.1468-2958.1982.tb00685.x

Sillars, A. L., Weisberg, J., Burggraf, C. S., & Wilson, E. A. (1987). Content themes in marital conversations. *Human Communication Research, 13*, 496–528. doi:10.1111/j.1468-2958.1987. tb00116.x

Slatcher, R. B., Vazire, S., & Pennebaker, J. W. (2008). Am "I" more important than "we"? Couples' word use in instant messages. *Personal Relationships, 15*, 407–424. doi:10.1111/ j.1475-6811.2008.00207.x

Spitzberg, B. H. (1988). Communication competence: Measures of perceived effectiveness. In C. H. Tardy (Ed.), *A handbook for the study of human communication* (pp. 67–105). Norwood, NJ: Ablex.

Spitzberg, B. H., & Cupach, W. R. (1984). *Interpersonal communication competence.* Beverly Hills, CA: Sage.

Woods, S., Lambert, N., Brown, P., Fincham, F., & May, R. (2015). "I'm so excited for you!" How an enthusiastic responding intervention enhances close relationships. *Journal of Social and Personal Relationships, 32*, 24–40. doi:10.1177/0265407514523545

Author Index

A

Aase, S., 306, 313
Abelson, R. P., 122, 142, 146
Aboujaoude, E., 299, 313
Abraham, M., 272, 291
Acar, A., 230, 239
Acedevo, W., 3, 18
Achterman, P., 311, 320
Acitelli, L. K., 66, 68–9, 75
Ackard, D. M., 246, 262
ACPA Ethics Code, 307, 314
Acquisti, A., 228, 241
Adams, S. K. R., 257, 264
Adelman, P. K., 13, 22
Adolphs, R., 81, 108
Afifi, W. A., 185, 207
Agnew, C. R., 199, 210
Aguglia, E., 271, 295
Aguinis, H., 248, 263
Ainsworth, M. D. S., 16, 18, 88, 108
Alessi, G., 40, 48

Alexy, E. M., 310, 314
Alix Timko, C., 300, 317
Allen, M., 202, 208
Allen, T., 185, 209, 212, 222
Allen, T. H., 54, 75
Aloia, L. S., 81, 108
Aloni, M., 162, 167
Alsaker, F. D., 308, 318
Altman, I., 153, 155, 157, 168, 171, 228, 239
Anders, A., 310, 315
Andersen, P. A., 29, 34–5,
47, 49, 118, 142, 161, 168, 330, 340
Anderson, C. I., 246–7, 252, 262
Anderson, C. J., 251, 262
Anderson, N. B., 85, 108
Anderson, P. E., 85, 108
Anderson, T. L., 237, 239
Anderson, W. A., 44, 48
Andreassen, C. S., 300–1, 314
Andrews-Hanna, J. R., 56, 75
Anokhin, A. P., 13, 18
Antheunis, M. L., 227–8, 239, 306, 314
Antoniadou, N., 309, 317

Archer, J., 280, 292
Arcidiacono, E., 271, 295
Ard, B. N., 132, 142
Argyle, M., 27, 47, 217, 221
Arias-Carrión, Ó., 300, 314
Ariely, D., 12, 20
Arliss, L. P., 165, 168
Aron, A., 61, 76, 149, 171
Askham, J., 153, 168
Atkins, L., 132, 145
Atkinson, M., 333–4, 342
Austen, J., 2, 18
Axelrod, R., 278, 292

B

Bachman, G., 185, 207
Bachman, R., 277, 292
Bachrach, Y., 44, 51
Backer-Fulghum, L. M., 25, 50
Baer, R. A., 93, 108
Bagwell, C. L., 232, 239
Bahrami, B., 85, 112
Bailer, J., 310, 315
Baker, T., 310, 314
Bakken, I., 299, 314
Bala, H., 43, 50
Baldwin, M. W., 15, 18, 35–8, 48, 116, 142
Balsavage, L., 11, 21
Bane, C., 90, 111
Banerjee, A., 3, 18
Bannon, B., 84, 110
Barber, B. L., 44, 47, 234, 240
Barelds, D. P. H., 14, 18
Barge, J. K., 138, 142
Bargh, J., 236, 242
Barker, V., 45, 47, 234, 239
Barnes, H. L., 166, 170
Barnett, J., 301, 316
Barr, A., 117, 142
Barron, S., 216, 222
Bart, P. B., 280, 294
Barta, W., 33, 47

Bartzokis, T., 93, 110
Basile, K. C., 274, 292
Basow, S., 132, 142
Batres, C., 303, 317
Batson, C. D., 31, 47
Baucom, D. H., 39, 48
Baukus, R A., 290, 294
Bauman, S., 309, 318
Baumeister, R. F., 2, 19, 56, 75, 93, 108, 132, 141, 142–3
Baxter, L. A., 152–3, 157, 159, 168, 182–4, 186, 207, 213, 222, 305, 314
Bayer, J., 45, 51
Bays, P. M., 278, 295
Bazarova, N. N., 229, 241
Bazelon, E., 303, 314
Beach, S. R. H., 327, 342
Beard, K. W., 300, 314
Beatty, M. J., 79, 81, 108, 112, 323, 340, 342
Beavin, J., 158, 171
Becker, T., 44, 50
Bell, E., 137–138, 143
Bell, R., 283, 290, 292
Ben-Artzi, E., 236, 241
Berg, J., 236, 239
Berg, K., 283, 293
Berger, C. R., 152, 160–1, 168, 204, 207, 227, 239
Berkos, K. M., 64, 75
Bermann, U., 27, 50
Bernieri, F. J., 162, 167
Berry, D. S., 15, 21
Berry, S., 303, 314
Berscheid, E., 147, 169, 229, 243
Bertona, M., 87, 109
Beukeboom, C. J., 305, 321
Bevan, J. L., 185, 207
Bianchi, M., 87, 109
Billieux, J., 301, 317
Bilt, J. V., 300, 319
Bilton, N., 233, 240
Birmingham, W., 84, 110
Birnbaum, D. A., 30, 47
Biswas-Diener, R., 26, 48

Black, J. B., 122, 124, 143, 179, 182, 195, 207
Black, M. C., 274, 292
Blease, C. R., 44, 47
Blinka, L., 300, 320
Blomfield Neira, C. J., 44, 47, 234, 240
Bodenmann, G., 281, 292
Bogle, K. A., 135, 143
Boltwood, M., 93, 110
Bonebrake, K., 235, 240
Bonetti, L., 45, 47, 234, 240
Boneva, B., 235–6, 241
Boney-McCoy, S., 286, 296
Boon, S. D., 188, 210
Booth-Butterfield, M., 151, 169
Boothroyd, L. G., 14, 22
Boren, J. P., 81, 109
Boska, C. R., 25, 50
Bower, G. H., 40, 49, 122, 124, 143, 179, 182, 195, 207
Bowlby, J., 16, 19, 30, 47, 88, 109
Boyatzis, R., 32, 48
Bozeman, B., 250, 262
Bradbury, T. N., 281, 292
Bradac, J. J., 152, 168
Bradley, R. T., 334, 342
Braithwaite, D. O., 211, 222
Braver, S., 103, 109
Breiding, M. J., 274, 292
Brickman, P., 27, 48
Broetzmann, S., 127, 144, 161, 169
Brogan, S., 138, 145
Brooks, R. C., 12, 19
Broughton, S., 9, 19
Brown, V. R., 306, 314
Brown, A., 305, 314
Brown, B., 157, 168
Brown, B. B., 300, 320
Brown, K., 310, 318
Brown, L. L., 61, 76
Brown, P., 331, 343
Brown, R., 72, 77
Browne, K. R., 255–6, 258, 262
Bruckman, A., 231, 240

Bruno, D., 4, 19, 73, 75
Brunstein Klomek, A., 308, 320
Bryan, A., 117, 118, 142, 145
Bryan, S. P., 73, 75
Bryant, E. M., 230–1, 240
Bryant, K., 136–7, 143, 232–3, 237, 240, 304, 319
Buchel, C., 81, 111
Buckner, R. L., 56, 75
Buehler, C., 62, 75
Buffardi, L. E., 303–4, 314
Bukowski, W. M., 232, 239
Bullis, C., 182, 207
Burger, J., 236, 240
Burgess, A. W., 310, 314
Burggraf, C. S., 70, 78, 327, 343
Burgoon, J. K., 124–5, 143, 330, 341
Burke, K., 121–2, 143
Burleson, B. R., 103, 109, 190, 208, 327, 341
Burnett, R., 102, 109, 176, 200, 202–3, 207, 220, 222
Burr, W. R., 154, 169
Busby, D. M., 11, 21
Buss, D. M., 38, 48, 51, 116, 132, 143–4, 163, 168
Butler, E. J., 138, 143
Butters, J. W., 303, 315
Buunk, B. P., 8, 19
Buxmann, P., 43, 49
Byrne, D., 248, 264

C

Cacioppo, J. T., 92–3, 111
Calabrese, R. J., 227, 239
Calder, A. J., 81, 111
Caldwell, N. D., 283, 293
Calhoun, J. E., 290, 297
Calvert, S. L., 303, 319
Cameron, K. S., 6, 19
Campbell, D., 247, 262
Campbell, L., 200, 208
Campbell, M. A., 45, 47, 234, 240

Campbell, M. E., 123, 143
Campbell, W. K., 303–4, 314
Canary, D. J., 203, 210, 326–7, 331
Cantrill, J. G., 165, 169, 177, 185, 202, 2019, 212, 222
Cao, F., 300, 314
Cao, H., 301, 315
Capaldi, D. M., 103, 111
Caplan, R. D., 83, 109
Cardoso, C., 331, 341
Carey, C. M., 116, 145
Carli, V., 301–2, 315
Carlston, D. E., 186, 207
Carmona, J., 136, 145
Carnelley, K. B., 16, 19
Carrere, S., 91, 109
Carroll, J. S., 11, 21
Carter, J. M., 308, 315
Cash, D. W., 303, 315
Cash, T. F., 303, 315
Casillas, A., 15, 21
Cassidy, W., 309, 315
Cate, K. L., 132, 143
Cate, R. M., 132, 144
Caughey, J. L., 62, 75
Caughlin, J. P., 125, 144, 150, 169, 182, 185, 207, 209, 335, 342
Cavanaugh, A. M., 62, 75
Chamberlain, L. J., 255, 262
Chandler, T. A., 281, 293
Chang, Y., 232, 244
Chanowitz, B., 126, 143
Charlesworth, S., 255, 263
Chatterjee, N., 149, 171
Chen, E., 80, 111
Cheshire, C., 12, 21
Chesney, M., 93, 110
Childre, D., 93, 109
Chisholm, A., 308–9, 316
Chiu, S., 301, 317
Chiu, S.-I., 301, 315
Chiu, S.-L., 301, 315
Cho, C., 301, 318
Choi, H., 190, 207
Christensen, A., 147, 155, 169

Christensen, A. C., 327, 343
Christoff, K., 56, 76
Clark, L. A., 306, 315
Clark, R. D., 132, 143
Clarke, L., 255–6, 262
Clayton, R. B., 305, 315
Clements, K., 283, 294
Clements, M., 290, 294
Clinebell, S., 249, 262
Clore, G., 31, 49
Clore, G. L., 30–31, 48
Coan, J., 91, 102, 105, 109
Coates, D., 27, 48
Cody, M., 199, 208, 211, 213, 222
Cody, M. J., 230, 241, 324, 341
Cohn, D., 5, 19
Coker, D. A, 330, 341
Coleman, M., 200, 208
Coletti, S. F., 327, 343
Collins, K., 283, 290, 292
Collins, N. L., 228, 240
Collins, N. W., 250, 262
Collins, W. A., 28, 51
Connolly, J. F., 63, 75
Consumer-rankings, 2, 19
Contractor, N. S., 248, 263
Conville, R. L., 156, 159, 168
Conway, M., 31, 48
Cook, C., 308, 318
Cools, C. A., 127, 143
Cooney, P., 11, 21
Cooper, A., 231, 240
Cornelius, T. L., 40, 48
Corty, E., 64, 78
Cotten, S. R., 44, 48
Couch, D., 137, 143, 232, 240
Coulson, M., 301, 316
Cox, E., 44, 50
Crawford, A., 236, 241
Crawford, M., 72, 75
Critselis, E., 302, 320
Croghan, J. M., 65, 75
Croghan, T. L., 65, 75
Croll, W. L., 30, 47
Crosby, L., 103, 111

Crowley, M., 255, 262
Cruz, M. A., 30, 48
Culnan, M. J., 225, 240
Cummings, J., 43, 50, 236, 241
Cupach, C. R., 217–8, 222
Cupach, W., 275–276, 295
Cupach, W. R., 276, 290, 292, 295, 311, 320, 327, 341, 343
Curtis, P., 234, 240

D

D'Addario, K. P., 226, 244
Daciuk, J., 308, 318
Daft, R. L., 226, 240
Dahl, K. A., 85, 112
Daly, J. A., 127, 146
Daly, M., 280, 292
Dancaster, I., 300, 316
Davenport, K., 301, 315
Davidson, M. J., 249–51, 263
Davis, K. E., 274, 292
Davis, S., 162, 168
de Sales French, R., 236, 241
de Timary, P., 331, 342
De, I., 29, 49
Deaux, K., 166, 168
Deci, E. L., 1, 19
DeClaire, J., 279, 292
Del Ben, K., 275, 293
Delongis, A., 80, 111
Demo, D. H., 281, 292
Dennis, C., 93, 110
Denton, W. H., 103, 109, 190, 208, 327, 341
Derlega, V. L., 236, 240
Deters, F. G., 43, 48
Deutsch, M., 1, 22
DeWeese, K. L., 299, 315
Di Blasio, P., 302, 318
Di Malta, G., 85, 112
Di, N. S., 271, 295
Diamond, L. M., 92, 109
Dibble, J. L., 305, 315

Dickinson, S. L., 90, 111
Diener, E., 26, 48
Dienes, B., 31, 48
Dijkstra, P., 8, 14, 18, 19
Dillard, J. P., 30, 48, 248, 252, 262
Dindia, K., 202, 208
DiVerniero, R. A., 238, 240
Dobash, E. D., 280, 292
Dobash, R. P., 280, 292
Dobosz, B., 39, 49
Dolan, R. J., 81, 85, 111–2
Domschke, T. J., 185, 210
Donohoe, M. L., 12, 19
Dougan, W. I., 247, 264
Douglas, E. M., 270, 296
Douglas, K. S., 274, 292
Douglas, W., 127, 143
Dov, C., 97, 109
Dreßing, H., 310–11, 315
Drouin, M., 305, 315
Dubrovsky, V., 226, 243
Duck, S., 15, 19
Duflo, E., 3, 18
Duggan, M., 237, 243
Dunleavy, K. N., 151, 169
Durkee, T., 301–2, 315
Dutton, D. G., 274, 292

E

Eden, J., 71, 77
Edwards, J. N., 281, 293
Edwards, R., 54–5, 51, 63, 67–8, 71, 73, 76
Egan, K., 306, 315
Egan, K. G., 44, 50
Eggermont, S., 310, 321
Eidenmuller, M. E., 93, 110
Eimler, S. C., 304, 321
Eisenberg, M. E., 246, 262
Eisenberger, N. I., 80, 110
Eldredge, J. H., 278, 293
Ellamil, M., 56, 76
Ellenbogen, M. A., 331, 341

Ellison, N., 312, 315, 317
Ellison, N. B., 230, 240, 243, 312, 320
Emanuele, E., 87, 109
Emery, E. R., 304, 318
Epermanis, K., 259, 264
Epstein, N., 39, 48
Escobar, S., 233, 241
Esterly, E., 200, 208

F

Farley, S., 2, 20
Farr, C., 275, 293
Farris, C., 163, 169
Fauber, R. L.
Faucher, C., 132, 145
Feeney, M., 250, 262
Fehr, B., 35–8, 48
Feinberg, D. R., 2, 21
Felmlee, D. H., 6, 7, 19
Fennel, A., 247, 265
Ferguson, C. J., 301, 316
Festinger, L., 303, 316
Festl, R., 309, 316
Fetchenhaur, D., 8, 19
Field, C. J., 123, 143
Filosa, C., 247, 265
Fincham, F., 2, 20, 331, 343
Fincham, F. D., 135–36, 145, 327, 342
Finkelhor, D., 305, 321
Finley, K. N., 238, 242Fore, A. T., 12, 21, 312, 316
Fisher, C., 251, 262
Fisher, H., 4, 19, 61, 71, 76, 116, 143, 148–50, 169
Fisher, H. E., 86–8, 109
Fiske, S. T., 15, 21, 122, 143
Fitness, J., 28, 32, 34–5, 37, 40, 48, 115, 117, 119, 144
Fitzgerald, N. M., 132, 144
Fitzpatrick, M. A., 70–1, 76, 336, 341
Flannagan, D., 118, 144
Flannery, R., 69, 76, 166, 169

Fletcher, G., 200, 208
Fletcher, G. J. O., 32, 327, 48, 115, 117, 119, 144
Floderus, B., 301–02, 315
Floyd, F., 42, 50
Floyd, F. J., 42–43, 49, 290, 294
Floyd, K., 84, 109, 228, 234–5, 252
Foa, E. B., 191, 208
Foa, U. G., 191, 208
Foley, S., 248, 252–54, 263–4
Fontenot, K., 219, 222, 328, 342
Forgas, J. P., 38–43, 49
Foshee, V. A., 280, 292
Foster D. A., 83, 109
Foster, J., 304, 320
Fox, J., 305, 316
Fox, K. C., 56, 76
Franiuk, R., 97, 109
Frazier, P. A., 200, 208
Fremouw, W. J., 275, 293
Freskou, A., 302, 320
Friedrich, G. O., 324, 341
Frieze, I. H., 311, 320
Frink, D. D., 259, 264
Friston, K. J., 81, 111
Frith, C. D., 81, 85, 111, 278, 295
Fry, R., 5, 19
Fuhrman, R., 118, 144
Fuhrman, R. W., 68, 78, 118, 146
Fujita, F., 31, 48
Furnham, A., 12, 14, 21

G

Gable, S. L., 236, 241
Gabriel, F., 303, 316
Gadalla, T., 308, 318
Gadlin, H., 5, 19
Gagne', F. M., 185, 208
Gagnon, J. H., 131, 144
Gallas, C., 310, 315
Gallois, C., 217–9, 222, 328, 342
Galvin, K. S., 211, 222

Gamel, N., 299, 313
Gangestad, S. W., 116, 146
Gannon, K. E., 44, 50
Ganong, L., 200, 208
Garnick, N. N., 211, 222
Gayle, B. M., 190, 208
Gearhart, C. C., 58, 77, 331, 342
Gee, J., 11, 20
Gelles, R., 270, 296
Gelles, R. J., 132, 144, 277, 281, 296
Gergen, K. J., 212, 222
Gergen, M. M., 212, 222
Geroldi, D., 87, 109
Gerrity, D. A., 280, 295
Ghatak, M., 3, 18
Gibbs, J., 312, 315
Gilbert, R., 299–300, 316
Gilmore, L., 45, 47, 234, 240
Ginsburg, G. P., 126, 140, 144
Gjertsen, S. R., 301, 324
Glaser, R., 90, 92–3, 111
Gleason, M. E. J., 87, 111, 236, 242
Gleiberman, L., 37, 49
Gmelch, S., 281, 292
Godwin, D. D., 188, 209
Goffman, E., 312, 316
Goldberg, J. G., 7, 19
Golding, J., 91, 111
Golfetti, R., 85, 112
Gomes, G. M., 246, 262
Goodwin, I., 231, 242
Goodwin, M. P., 281, 295
Goodwin, R., 184, 208
Goranson, R., 283, 290, 296
Gordon, E. A., 132, 145
Gordon, V., 304, 321
Gotestam, C., 299, 314
Gottman, J. M., 9, 11, 20, 28, 32, 41, 49,
    51, 68, 71, 76, 84, 89–91, 93–4, 98,
    102–3, 105, 109, 139, 144, 184–5, 190,
    208, 215–6, 222, 279, 284, 288–90, 292,
    325–6, 331, 341
Gottman, J. S., 279, 292, 331, 341
Grace, A. J., 25, 50

Graem, P., 178, 209Graham, M. B., 303,
    318
Grandin, T., 216, 222
Grant, T., 310, 320
Grasmuck, S., 303, 322
Gray, W. D., 178, 209
Grazioli, S., 311, 316
Greene, R. W., 165, 169, 177, 209
Greenfield, P. M., 303, 318
Greenwood, D. N., 304, 316
Greicius, M. D., 56, 76
Greitemeyer, T., 229, 241
Grice, H. P., 178, 208
Griffith, K. A., 254, 263
Griffiths, M., 299, 302, 316
Griffiths, M. D., 299–301, 314–8
Gross, E. F., 236, 241, 308, 317
Gross, J. J., 34, 49, 331, 342
Gross, R., 228, 241
Grossman, M., 280, 294
Guerrero, L., 29, 35, 47, 185, 207
Guerrero, L. K., 34, 49, 185, 207
Guldner, G. T., 59, 76

H

Ha, T., 302, 317
Haig, J., 14, 21
Hair, H. D., 324, 341
Halberstadt, J., 30, 49
Hall, A. E., 333, 340
Hall, J. A., 83, 111, 230, 241
Hall, M., 300, 319
Halpern, D., 306, 321
Hamburger, Y. A., 236, 241
Hamby, S. L., 286, 296
Hamm, M. P., 308–9, 316
Hample, D., 58, 78, 190, 209
Hancock, J. T., 229–30, 241, 243, 312, 317,
    320
Hanzal, A., 185, 210
Hao, J., 301, 315
Harburg, E., 37, 49

Harrop, J. W., 270, 298
Hartling, L., 308–9, 316
Hartup, W. W., 230, 241
Harvey, J. H., 69, 76, 147, 166, 169, 211, 214, 222
Harvey, S. M., 209, 210
Haselton, M. G., 116, 144
Hastings, P. D., 29, 49
Hatcher, L. C., 36, 49, 84, 110, 190, 209, 277, 293
Hatfield, E., 132, 143
Haubner, T., 14, 21
Hayes, A., 237, 242
Haynes, M. T., 84, 109
Hays, R. B., 156–7, 169
Hearst, M. A., 312, 316
Heavey, C. L., 327, 343
Heim, M., 235, 242
Heimberg, R. G., 132, 145
Heino, R., 312, 315
Heisel, A. D., 79, 81, 108, 110, 112, 323, 340
Helenius, H., 308, 320
Henderson, D. A., 38, 51, 277, 290
Henderson, M., 217, 221
Hendrick, C., 327, 342
Hendrick, S. S., 327, 342
Henningsen, D. D., 116, 144
Herman, M. R., 123, 143
Herold, E. S., 132, 144
Heron, J., 91, 111
Herrmann, J., 304, 321
Herron, K., 283, 294
Hesse, C., 84, 109
Hicks, A. M., 92–3, 109
Hicks, M. R., 298, 317
Hicks, R. A., 228, 242
Higley, J. D., 290, 303
Hill, C. T., 68, 76, 165, 170, 185, 200, 208–9, 220, 222
Hill, W. 87, 112
Hinduja, S., 308–9, 319
Hodson, R., 255, 262
Hoff, D. L., 308, 319

Hoffman, K. L., 281, 292
Hoffman, L., 249, 262
Hofstede, G., 216, 222, 260, 262
Hofstede, G. J., 216, 222, 260, 262
Holman, T. B., 11, 21, 154, 169
Holmberg, D., 68, 78, 127, 144, 203–4, 209
Holmes, J., 32, 49
Holt-Lunstad, J., 84, 110
Holtzworth-Munroe, A., 283, 294
Honeycutt, J. M., 9, 16, 20, 36, 49, 52–5, 57–63, 66–7, 69–73, 75–8, 80–1, 83–4, 93–4, 99, 102–3, 110, 123–4, 144–5, 148, 152, 161–2, 165, 169–70, 176–7, 179, 185–90, 192–6, 199–200, 202–4, 208–9, 212–13, 219, 222, 226–7, 243, 277–8, 282–4, 286, 292–93, 296, 323, 328, 330–31, 335–36, 341–42
Hong, F., 301, 317
Hong, F.-Y., 301, 315
Hong, J., 13, 20
Horgan, T. G., 83, 111
Hormes, J. M., 300, 317
Horn, L., 300, 317
Horowitz, L., 235–6, 241, 244
Hosek, A. M., 238, 240
Houston, J. E., 301, 315
Howe, G. W., 83, 109
Huang, D., 301, 317
Hughes, S., 2, 20
Hunsaker, P. L., 246–7, 252, 262
Huston, T. L., 14, 20, 132, 144, 147, 179
Huszti, H. C., 211, 221
Hutton, F., 231, 242

I

Iannotti, R. J., 308, 321
Ikonen, M., 308, 320
Inagaki, T. K., 80, 110
Infante, D. A., 281–3, 285–6, 293
Ironson, G., 93, 110
Issacowitz, D. M., 26, 49
Ito, T. A., 278, 293

J

Jackson, D. D., 158, 171
Jackson, L. A., 300, 321
Jackson, M., 309, 315
Jagsi, R., 254, 263
Janikian, M., 302, 320
Jankowiak, W., 148, 169
Janoff-Bulman, R., 16, 19
Janoff-Bulman, R. J., 27, 48
Jarvenpaa, S. L., 311, 316
Jelenchick, L. A., 44, 50
Jiang, L. C., 229, 241
Johansson, A., 299, 314
Johnson, D. M., 178, 209
Johnson, E., 85, 112
Johnson, K. L., 58, 190, 209
Johnson, S. M., 90, 111
Joiner, T. E., Jr., 234, 241, 302, 317
Joinson, A., 236, 241
Jones, E., 218–9, 222, 328, 342
Jones, B. Q., 84, 110
Jones, G., 252, 263
Jones, R., 254, 263
Jones, S., 330, 342
Jose, P. E., 30, 50
Ju, G., 302, 317
Julius, M., 37, 49
Jurich, J., 280, 295
Juvonen, J., 236, 241, 308, 317

K

Kaciroti, N., 37, 49
Kaess, M., 301–2, 315
Kaiser, H., 280, 293
Kalbfleisch, P., 250, 263
Kantor, G. K., 280, 293
Kapidzic, S., 304, 317
Kaplan, S. J., 1, 22
Karila, L., 301, 317
Karl, A. A., 254, 263

Karl, K., 309, 319
Karlsen, M., 204, 209
Karnery, B. R., 14, 20
Katz, J. E., 306, 321
Kaufman, G. K., 277, 296
Kearns, B., 300, 317
Keaton, S. A., 58, 77, 149, 169, 190, 209
Kellermann, K., 127, 144, 161, 169, 204, 207
Kelley, H., 305, 320
Kelley, H. H., 147, 169
Kelly, A. B., 327, 342
Kelly, P., 202, 209
Kennedy, D., 281, 294
Kenrick, D. T., 8, 19, 117, 142
Kiecolt-Glaser, J. K., 90, 92–3, 111–2
Kienlen, K. K., 275, 293
Kiesler, S., 225–6, 241, 243, 304, 317
Kilpatrick, J., 249, 262
Kim, H. K., 103, 111
Kim, J., 301, 318
Kim, S., 227, 244, 302, 317
Kim, Y., 302, 317
Kimberley, T., 33, 50
Kimuna, S. R., 123, 143
King, C. E., 155, 169
Kinney, T. A., 30, 48
Kitao, K., 127, 144, 161, 169
Klinger, E., 53, 63, 77
Klohnen, E. C., 15, 21
Knapp, M. L., 83, 111, 125, 144, 150–3, 155, 159, 169, 182, 193, 198–9, 205, 209, 335, 342
Knight, K., 61, 77
Koch, E., 140, 144
Kohn, P. M., 132, 145
Kokkinos, C., 309, 317
Komarovsky. M., 92, 111
Koran, L. M., 299, 313
Kosberg, R. L., 290, 294
Koskelainen, M., 308, 320
Kowalski, R., 309, 321
Kowalski, R. M., 280, 297, 308–9, 317
Kram, K. E., 250, 263
Krämer, N. C., 304, 321

Krantz, S., 40, 49
Krasnova, H., 43, 45, 49
Krasnow, B., 56, 76
Kraut, R., 235–6, 241, 304, 317
Kreibig, S. D., 34, 49
Krones, P., 303, 317
Kross, E., 45, 51
Krossbakken, E., 301, 314
Kulik, J. A., 303, 321
Kunz, I., 229, 241
Kuperberg, A., 134–5, 144
Kuppens, P., 37, 50
Kuss, D. J., 301, 317–8
Kvam, S., 301, 314

L

La France, B. H., 116, 154, 323, 340
Lackaff, D., 302, 320
Lafortune, J., 3, 18
LaManca, J. J., 85, 112
Lambert, N., 331, 343
Lambert, N. M., 2, 20
Lambkin, D., 202, 209
Lampe, C., 230, 240
Lane, A., 331, 342
Lang, F. R., 57, 77
Langer, E., 124–6, 143, 145
Langer, E. J., 124–5, 143
Large, M., 299, 313
Larsen, A. S., 166, 170
Lavoie, J. A. A., 310, 321
Lawson, H., 232, 241
Lazarus, R. S., 30, 51
Lea, M., 159, 169
Leary, M. R., 56, 75
Leck, K., 232, 241
Ledermann, T., 281, 292
LeDoux, J., 32, 49
Lee, D. S., 45, 51
Lee, G. R., 26, 50
Lee, L., 13, 20
Lee, S., 302, 317

Lees, P. L., 247, 264
Lehmiller, J. L., 247, 263
Leigh, G. K., 154, 169
Lemeshow, S., 90, 111
Lengel, R. H., 226, 240
Lenton, A., 118, 145
LePoire, B. A., 264
Lerman, M., 116, 146
Letcher, A., 136, 145
Leung, L., 235, 242, 304, 318
Levenson, R. W., 89, 109, 288–90, 292
Levine, D., 231, 241
Levine, T. R., 323, 340
Levinger, G., 147, 153–4, 169–70
Levinson, P., 307, 310, 318
Lewandowski, G. W., 11, 20
Lewis, R. A., 8, 20, 155, 170
Lewis, S., 275, 293
Li, H., 61, 76
Liamputtong, P., 137, 143, 232, 240
Libby, P. L., 8–9, 21
Likowski, K. U., 89, 112
Lim, T. S., 127, 144
Limber, S. P., 308–9, 317
Lin, H., 301, 317
Lindell, S. G., 290, 293
Lindroos, J., 308, 320
Linnen, A. M., 331, 341
Liu, T., 300, 318
Lloyd, S. A., 290, 293
Locke, H. J., 92, 111
Loewenstein, G. F., 12, 20
Logan, T., 274, 293
Losee, S., 249, 263
Louizou, A., 302, 320
Loving, T. J., 87, 90, 111
Lulofs, R. S., 327, 342
Luminet, O., 331, 342
Lundmark, V., 235, 241, 304, 317
Luntamo, T., 308, 320
Lydon, J. E., 185, 208
Lykken, D., 27, 50
Lyons, A. C., 231, 242
Lyubomirsky, S., 283, 293

M

Ma, M., 235, 242
MacCallum, R. C., 93, 111
Machmutow, K., 308, 318
MacKenzie, S., 127, 144
Mackey, S., 149, 171
MacLean, B., 93, 111
Madathil, J., 3, 21
Maddock, J., 311, 320
Maestripieri, D., 290, 293
Mainiero, L. A., 246, 248, 252–3, 260, 263
Makepeace, J. M., 280, 294
Malarkey, W. B., 90, 92, 111, 112
Malis, R. S., 190, 209
Manago, A. M., 303, 318
Manczak, E. M., 80, 111
Mandler, G., 27–8, 30, 40, 50
Mano, R., 260, 263
Manthos, M., 135, 145
Manusov, V. M., 324, 341
Maple, C., 310, 318
Marangou, E., 302, 320
Margolin, G., 89, 112
Markey, C. N., 11, 20
Markey, P. M., 11, 20
Markman, H. J., 9, 21, 42, 50, 290, 294, 325, 331, 341
Markos, A., 309, 317
Marks, N. F., 190, 207
Markus, H., 27, 51
Markus, M. L., 225, 240
Marmo, J., 230–1, 240
Marsh, D., 118, 144
Marshall, L., 311, 320
Marshall, L. L., 272–3, 294
Martin, J., 303, 322
Mashek, D., 61, 76
Mason, R. M., 311, 320
Matook, S., 43, 50
May, R., 331, 343
McAuley, J. W., 238, 242
McBride, M., 211, 22
McCain, T. A., 11, 20

McCann, R. M., 55, 77
McClanahan, A. M., 138, 145
McClintock, E., 169, 170
McCormack, K., 290, 293
McCraty, R., 93, 109, 333–4, 342
McCroskey, J. C., 11, 20, 81, 108, 111, 323, 342
McCubbin, H. I., 166, 170
McCullough, B. M., 44, 48
McCullough, M. E., 278, 294
McDonald, P., 255, 263
McFall, R. M., 163, 169
McGuire, T. W., 226, 241, 243
McKee, A., 32, 48
McKenna, K., 234, 236, 242
McKenna, K. Y. A., 236, 242
McKinney, K., 131, 146
McManus, B., 237, 242
McManus, S., 250, 263
McNally, T., 299, 316
McNulty, J. K., 14, 20
Mechanic, M. B., 274, 294
Medicinenet.com, 300, 318
Medved, C. E., 138, 145
Meeks, B. S., 327, 342
Mehdizadeh, S., 303–4, 318
Mehl, M. R., 43, 48
Mehrabian, A., 330, 342
Meloy, J. R., 274, 297
Mendelsohn, G. A., 12, 21, 312, 316
Menon, V., 56, 76
Mercer, G. W., 132, 145
Merluzzi, T. V., 128–31, 145, 179, 195, 209
Merolla, A. J., 58, 78
Merrick, M. T., 274, 292
Mervis, C. B., 178, 209
Metalsky, G. I., 234, 241, 302, 317
Meter, D. J., 309, 318
Metts, S., 217–8, 222, 236, 240
Metzger, A. H., 238, 242
Meuwly, N., 281, 292
Mewhinney, D. K., 132, 144
Meyer, C., 54, 78
Meyer, J. R., 71, 77

Meyers-Winton, S., 228, 242
Michalski, R. L., 34, 51
Miell, D., 123, 143
Mikolajczak, M., 331, 342
Milani, L., 302, 318
Miller, D. A., 305, 315
Miller, K. I., 252, 262
Miller, L., 117, 145
Miller, L. C., 228, 240
Miller, N., 278, 303
Miller, P. J. E., 14, 20
Miller, S. L., 280, 294
Milne, A., 308–9, 316
Minieri, A., 132, 142
Minkov, M., 216, 222
Minoretti, P., 87, 109
Mishna, F., 308, 318
Mitchell, K. J., 305, 308–9, 321–2
Moeller, S., 301, 318
Monge, P. R., 248, 263
Mongeau, P. A., 61, 77, 116, 145
Montesi, J. L., 132, 145,
Montgomery, B. M., 159, 168, 305, 314
Moore, C. H., 258, 265
Moore, D. W., 277, 296
Moore, T. M., 290, 294
Morahan-Martin, J., 235–6, 238, 242
Moreno, M., 306, 315
Moreno, M. A., 44, 50
Morgan, J. F., 246, 262
Morgan, L. M., 249–51, 263
Morgan, M., 69, 76, 166, 169
Morris, J. F., 138, 145
Morris, J. S., 81, 111
Morry, M. M., 11, 20
Moss, D., 93, 111
Mouradian, V. E., 272–3, 294
Mühlberger, A., 89, 112
Mukopadhyay, T., 235, 241, 304, 317
Mulder, S., 2, 20
Murphy, N., 299, 316
Murphy, S. T., 13, 22
Murstein, B. I., 2, 20, 147, 153–4, 170
Musumeci, G., 271, 295

Muxen, M. J., 166, 170
Myers, J. E., 3, 21
Myers, K. A., 230, 244

N

Nagurney, A., 305, 315
Nansel, T. R., 308, 321
Natelson, B. H., 85, 112
National Center for Biotechnology
    Information, 299, 318
National Science Foundation, 307, 318
Neff, L. A., 14, 20
Neubaum, G., 304, 321
Neumark-Sztainer, D., 246, 262
Newcomb, A. F., 232, 239
Newman, M., 45, 51, 234, 243, 302, 304,
    319
Newman, T. K., 290, 293
Newton, A. S., 308–9, 316
Newton, T., 93, 111
Newton, T. L., 90, 111
Neyer, F. J., 57, 77
Nezlek, J. B., 37, 50
Nichols, N. B., 25, 50
Niedenthal, P., 30, 49
Niedenthal, P. M., 13, 22
Niehuis, S., 14, 20
Niland, P., 231, 242
Nisbett, R. E., 66, 78, 162, 170
Nolen-Hoeksema, S., 283, 294
Noller, P., 43, 50
Norwood, K. M., 157, 168
Nosanchuck, T. A., 30, 47
Notarius, C., 325, 331, 341
Nus, S. E., 15, 21

O

O'Connor, J. M., 2, 21
O'Connor, T. G., 91, 111

Oates, A., 116, 144
Olen, H., 249, 263
Oleson, K. C., 31, 47
Olson, A. M., 231, 242
Olson, D. H., 166, 170, 338, 342
Oltmanns, F. T., 303, 318
Omar, A., 250, 264
Orand, M., 311, 320
Orbuch, T. L., 211, 222
Oren, A., 299, 314
Orjada, K., 303, 317
Ortony, A., 31, 48
Orvell, A., 45, 51
Osborn, J. L., 305, 316
Osualdella, D., 302, 318
Otter-Henderson, K., 92, 109
Overall, N., 248, 263
Overall, N. C., 200, 208
Owen, J., 135–6, 145
Owens, J. M., 246, 262

P

Padgett, J. E., 134–5, 144
Palazzo, V., 11, 21
Pallesen, S., 300–1, 314
Park, J., 45, 51
Park, N., 27, 50, 230, 241
Park, S., 301, 318
Parke, S., 149, 171
Parker, C., 330, 342
Parker, J. B., 290, 297
Parks, A. C., 84, 112
Parks, M. R., 228, 242
Parry, D., 327, 343
Parzer, P., 301–2, 315
Patchin, J. W., 308–9, 319
Patterson, J., 69, 77
Patterson, M., 235, 241, 304, 317
Paul, E. L., 237, 242
Pawlowski, B., 14, 22
Payne, M. J., 281, 294

Pearson, J. C., 166, 170
Pecchioni, L., 227–9, 243
Peckerman, A., 85, 112
Pellegrini, R. J., 228, 242
Peluchette, J. V., 309, 319
Pempek, T. A., 303, 319
Pence, M. E., 36, 49, 58, 77, 79, 81, 108, 112, 277, 293, 331, 342
Pennebaker, J. W., 336, 343
Peplau, L., 68, 76, 185, 208, 220, 222, 236, 239
Peplau, L. A., 165, 170, 200, 209, 235, 242
Perren, S., 308, 318
Perumalswami, C. R., 254, 263
Peter, J., 227, 239
Peterson, C., 27, 50
Peterson, D. R., 147, 169
Peterson, H., 312, 319
Petronio, S., 236, 240, 306, 319
Pew Research Center, 298, 319
Piaget, J., 40, 50
Pierce, C. A., 248–9, 256–8, 263–4
Planalp, S., 28–9, 35, 41, 50, 125, 145, 152, 170, 188, 209
Pleck, E., 280, 294
Pleck, J. H., 280, 294
Poerio, G. L., 56, 78
Politi, P., 87, 109
Pollock, V. E., 278, 293
Pomerantz, E. M., 97, 109
Pope, M. T., 87, 111
Pöppel, E., 300, 314
Porges, S. W., 83, 91, 105, 112, 333, 342
Porter, M. A., 56–7, 78
Potenza, M., 300, 318
Poulsen, F. O., 11, 21
Powell, G., 254, 262
Powell, G. N., 252–3, 264
Powers, S., 280, 293
Preiss, R. W., 190, 208
Prentice, D., 15, 21
Pryor, J. B., 128–31, 145, 179, 195, 209
Pyzalski, J., 309, 319

Q

Qiu, L., 226, 244
Quandt, T., 309, 316
Quinn, R. E., 6, 19, 246–8, 252–4, 264
Qureishi, B., 85, 112

R

Raichle, M. E., 56, 78
Rancer, A. S., 281–2, 285, 290, 293–4
Rapoport, A., 278, 294
Raskauskas, J., 308, 319
Re, D. E., 2, 21
Read, S. J., 117, 145
Rees, G., 85, 112
Regan, P. C., 132, 145
Rehman, U. S., 283, 294
Rein, G., 333, 342
Reinhart, A., 79, 112
Reis, H. A., 2, 21
Reisman, J. M., 231, 242
Reiss, A. L., 56, 76
Renick, M. J., 290, 294
Resick, P. A., 274, 294
Resnick, M. D., 246, 262
Revina, N. E., 84, 112
Rhea, J., 274, 295
Rhodes, B., 2, 20
Riach, K., 247, 251–2, 264
Rimé, B., 331, 342
Roberts, S. J., 306, 315
Robinson, R. K., 259, 264
Robles, T. F., 92, 112
Roese, N. J., 29, 50
Rogers, M. A., 327, 343
Roggensack, K. E., 216, 222
Roloff, M. E., 58, 77, 161, 168, 190, 209, 327, 342
Rosch, E. R., 178, 209
Roscoe, B., 281, 294
Roseman, I. J., 30, 50

Rosen, D., 302, 320
Rosen, L. D., 299, 302, 319
Rosenblatt, P. C., 54, 78
Rosenfeld, L., 8, 21
Ross, L., 66, 78, 162, 170, 213, 222
Ross, M., 68, 78, 203–4, 209
Rotenberg, K. J., 33, 50
Rowell, L. B., 84, 112
Roy, D., 247, 264
Rubin, Z., 68, 76, 154, 165, 170, 185, 200, 202, 208–9, 220, 222
Ruch, W., 27, 50
Rudd, J. E., 281, 290, 293–4
Rusbult, C. E., 184, 210
Russell, D., 235–6, 242
Rutherford, D. K., 188, 209
Ryan, R. M., 1, 19
Ryan, T., 235, 242
Ryder, R. G., 338, 342

S

Sabatelli, R. M., 161–2, 170
Sabourin, T. C., 281, 290, 294
Saffrey, C., 29, 50
Sagrestano, L. M., 327, 343
Salimkhan, G., 303, 318
Saltzman, L., 277, 292
Samson, A. C., 34, 49
Sanchez, M. M., 290, 293
Sanford, K., 25, 50
Sawyer, C. R., 148, 169
Saxbe, D. E., 89, 112
Schacter, D. L., 56, 75
Schacter, S., 27, 50
Schaefer, C. M., 258, 264
Schaffer, H., 300, 319
Schank, R. C., 117, 121–2, 146
Scherlis, W., 235, 241, 304, 317
Schlueter, D. W., 138, 142
Schmidt, M. E., 232, 239
Schmitt, D. P., 34, 51, 132, 143
Schork, M. A., 37, 49

Schouten, A. P., 236, 242
Schumacher, P., 235–6, 238, 242
Schutz, W. C., 158, 166, 170
Schwartz, N., 31, 48, 50
Scott, C. K., 68, 78, 118, 146
Seccombe, K., 26, 50
Segall, G. M., 93, 110
Segrin, C., 185, 210
Segrist, A. E., 280, 295
Seibt, B., 89, 112
Seligman, M. E. P., 26–7, 49–50, 84, 112
Serewicz, M. C. M., 116, 145
Serpe, R., 299, 313
Serravalle, L., 331, 341
Shablack, H., 45, 51
Shackelford, T., K., 34, 51
Shaffer, V. A., 92, 112
Shannon, K., 11, 21
Shapiro, A. F., 41, 51
Shariff, S., 308, 319
Shaw Taylor, L., 312, 316
Shaw, C., 61, 77
Shaw, C. M., 116, 144
Shaw, L. L., 31, 47
Shaw, T. L., 12, 21
Sheets, V. I., 4, 21
Shehan, C. L., 26, 50
Sheldon, P., 36, 44–5, 49, 51, 136–7, 143,
    126–8, 232–5, 237–8, 240, 242–3, 277,
    293, 302–4, 307, 319
Shepherd, G. J., 138, 145
Shergill, S. S., 278, 295
Sheridan, L. P., 310, 320
Sherman, S. J., 64, 78
Shewchuk, V. A., 33, 50
Shields, S. A., 29, 51, 289, 295
Shimek, C., 179, 209
Shin, C., 302, 317
Shook, N. J., 280, 295
Shorey, R. C., 40, 48
Short, E., 310, 318
Shorter, G. W., 301, 318
Shulhan, J., 308–9, 316
Sibley, C., 248, 263

Siegel, J., 225–6, 241, 243
Signorelli, M. S., 271, 295
Sillars, A., 217, 222
Sillars, A. L., 70, 78, 327, 336, 343
Silver, N., 11, 20, 91, 94, 109, 184, 190, 208,
    325, 341
Simon, W., 131, 144
Simpson, J. A., 28, 51, 116, 146, 200, 208
Simpson, S. S., 280, 294
Sinclair, H. C., 311, 320
Singer, J., 27, 50
Singer, J. L., 53, 63, 78
Slatcher, R. B., 336, 343
Smahel, D., 300, 320
Smallwood, J., 56, 78
Smith, A., 237, 243
Smith, C. W., 30, 51
Smith, J. R., 305, 315
Smith, S. G., 274, 292
Smith, S. W., 138, 143
Smock, A., 303, 320
Smoyak, S. A., 310, 314
Snyder, M., 229, 243
Sohn, S. H., 303, 320
Solomon, D. H., 81, 108, 255, 258, 264
Solomon, S., 308, 318
Son, J., 302, 317
Song, H., 230, 241
Soule, K. P., 327, 342
Sourander, A., 308, 320
Spanier, G. B., 6, 20, 69, 78
Spindel, M. S., 30, 50
Spitzberg, B., 275–6, 295
Spitzberg, B. H., 274–6, 290, 292, 295, 311,
    320, 324, 327, 341, 343
Sportolari, L., 231, 240
Sprecher, S., 2, 21, 131, 146
Spreng, R. N., 56, 76
Stabird, K., 311, 320
Stafford, L., 58, 78, 127, 146, 190, 203, 210
Staines, G. L., 8–9, 21
Stanley, S. M., 290, 294
Steen, T., 84, 112
Stefanone, M. A., 302, 320

Steinberg, L., 303, 320
Steinfield, C., 230, 240
Steinmetz, S. K., 277, 296
Stephen, T., 6, 9–10, 21, 123, 146, 154, 159–60, 170
Stets, J. E., 38, 51, 277, 280–1, 290, 295
Stevens, M. R., 274, 292
Stewart, A., 254, 263
Stewart, G., 232–3, 243
Stewart, S., 8, 21
Sticca, F., 308, 318
Stice, E., 303, 317
Stieger, S., 14, 21
Stillwell, A. M., 132, 143
Stinnett, H., 8, 21
Stoltz, A. D., 308, 319
Stowell, J. R., 90, 111
Straus, M., 38, 51, 271, 277, 280, 295
Straus, M. A., 123, 143, 269–72, 277, 279, 280–1, 286, 290, 293, 295–6
Strong, G., 61, 76
Strongman, K. T., 28, 48
Stuart, G. L., 290, 294
Stuckless, N., 283, 290, 296
Su, L., 300, 314
Su, Z. Q., 300, 321
Sugarman, D. B., 286, 296
Summerville, A., 29, 50
Sun, Y., 301, 315
Sundar, P., 308–9, 316
Surra, C. A., 132, 144, 147, 171
Sutton, C. L., 254, 263
Swami, V., 12, 14, 21
Swann, W. B., Jr., 15–6, 21
Swanson, C., 91, 109
Swift, C. L., 283, 296

T

Tan, K., 199, 210
Tang, J., 228, 243
Tanke, E. D., 229, 243
Tannen, D., 93, 112
Tao, F., 301, 315

Taylor, C. B., 93, 110
Taylor, D., 228, 239
Taylor, D. A., 155, 157, 168, 171
Taylor, J., 237, 243
Taylor, S., 303, 318
Taylor, S. E., 122, 143
Tellegen, A., 27, 50
Tennov, D., 148, 171
Theil, J., 304, 321
Therrien, L. F., 116, 145
Thibaut, J., 305, 320
Thoennes, N., 271, 296
Thompson, E. H., Jr., 277, 296
Tian, Y., 79, 112
Tidwell, L. C., 226, 229, 243–4
Tiller, W. A., 333, 342
Timmons, A. C., 89, 112
Tingle, L. R., 3, 21
Tjaden, P., 271, 296
Todd-Manchillas, W., 166, 170
Todorov, A., 15, 21
Toma, C., 312, 317
Toma, C. L., 230, 243, 312, 320
Tomasino, D., 334, 342
Tong, S. T., 227, 229, 243–4
Tope, D., 255, 262
Toronto, E., 302, 320
Tourigny, L., 247, 264
Tracey, T. J. G., 234–5, 244
Træen, B., 204, 209
Tranel, D., 81, 108
Treat, T. A., 163, 169
Tsitsika, A., 302, 320
Tucker, K. L., 283, 293
Tudor, T. R., 258, 264
Turkle, S., 305, 320
Turner, L. H., 166, 170, 305, 321
Turner, T. J., 122, 143, 179, 207

U

U.S. Department of Justice, 275, 296
Ubel, P., 254, 263
Udeh, I., 250, 264

Ulbrich, T. R., 238, 242
United States Department of Labor, 251, 264
United States Equal Employment Opportunity Commission, 255, 265
Utz, S., 305, 321

V

Valenzuela, S., 306, 321
Valkenburg, P. M., 227, 236, 239, 242, 306, 314
Valliant, G. E., 26, 49
Van Acker, E., 9, 19
van de Mheen, D. D., 301, 318
Van Der Heide, B., 227, 244
Van Kelegom, M. J., 54, 78
van Rooij, A. J., 301, 318
Vandebosch, H., 310, 321
VanderDrift, L. E., 199, 210
Vangelisti, A. L., 125, 144, 150, 169, 182, 185, 207, 209, 335, 342
VanLear, C. A., 158, 171
Vaughn, E. D., 306, 314
Vazire, S., 336, 343
Veksler, A. E., 81, 109
Verduyn, P., 45, 51
Vijayasiri, G., 255, 265
Viken, R. J., 163, 169
Vinacke, W. E., 11, 21
Vinsel, A., 157, 168
Vissing, Y. M., 270, 296
Vitkus, J., 235, 244
Volkova, S., 44, 51
von Hippel, W., 12, 19
Voracek, M., 14, 21, 34, 51

W

Wagner, H., 310–1, 315
Wagner, J., 57, 77
Walker, L. E., 272–4, 296, 297
Walker, R., 274, 293

Wallenfelsz, K. P., 58, 78
Walrave, M., 310, 321
Walters, M. L., 274, 302
Walther, J., 227, 244
Walther, J. B., 225–9, 232, 243–4, 303, 312, 321
Wan, Y, 301, 315
Wang, C., 228, 232, 243–4
Wang, J., 308–9, 321
Wang, J. L., 300, 321
Wang, W., 226, 244
Wanic, R. A., 303, 321
Warber, K. M., 305, 316
Ward, C. C., 234–5, 244
Warner, M. H., 290, 297
Wasilenko, K. A., 303, 321
Wasserman, C., 301–2, 315
Wasserman, D., 301–2, 315
Watkins, A. D., 333, 342
Watkins, S. J., 188, 210
Watson, D., 9, 15, 21
Watzlawick, P., 158, 171
Weaver, T. L., 274, 294
Weber, A. L., 211, 222
Weekes-Shackelford, V. A., 34, 51
Wegge, D., 310, 321
Wegner, D. M., 203, 210
Weisberg, J., 70, 78, 327, 343
Weiser, E. B., 304, 321
Weiss, R. L., 39–40, 51
Welsh, A., 310, 321
Wenninger, H., 43, 49
Wenzel, H., 299, 314
West, R., 305, 321
Westerman, D., 227, 244
Westmyer, S. A., 230, 244
Weyers, P., 89, 112
White, J. W., 280, 297
White, R. C., 179, 209
Whittaker, E., 309, 321
Widjaja, T., 43, 49
Wiemann, J., 324, 341
Wiemann, J. M., 70–2, 77
Wiemann, M., 324, 341
Wigley, C. J., 281, 285–6, 293

Williams, J., 61, 77, 309, 319
Williams, M. L. M., 116, 145
Williard, N., 308, 321
Wilmot, W., 152, 168
Wilson, C., 87, 112, 330, 342
Wilson, E. A., 70, 78, 327, 343
Wilson, F., 247, 251–2, 264
Wilson, F. L., 308, 315
Wilson, M., 280, 292
Wilson, R. J., 247, 265
Winter, S., 304, 321
Wish, M., 1, 7, 22
Wiszewska, A., 14, 22
Witteman, H., 248, 262
Wolak, J., 305, 321
Wolpert, D. M., 278, 295
Women's Health., 270, 297
Wood, C., 309, 319
Woods, B., 219, 222
Woods, B. L., 328, 342
Woods, J. T., 93, 112
Woods, S., 331, 343
Wotman, S. R., 132, 143
Wright, C. N., 54, 78
Wright, N. D., 85, 112
Wright, P. H., 201, 208, 230, 244
Wrzus, C., 57, 77
Wuensch, K. L., 258, 265
Wyer, R. S., 68, 78, 118, 146

X

Xenos, S., 235, 242

Y

Yamamoto, Y., 85, 112
Ybarra, M., 308–9, 322
Yermolayeva, Y. A., 303, 319
Yiannis, G., 260, 263
Young, A. W., 81, 111
Young, H., 44, 50

Young, J., 12, 20
Younger, J., 149, 171
Your wireless life: Results of TIME's
    Mobility Poll., 305, 322

Z

Zagacki, K. S., 54–5, 63, 71, 73, 76–8, 102,
    110
Zahn, G. L., 248, 265
Zajonc, R. B., 13, 22, 27, 51
Zhang, D. J., 300, 321
Zhao, S., 303, 322
Zhao, Y., 226, 244
Zhu, Y., 226, 244
Zillmann, D., 282, 297

Subject Index

A

Abandonment (elder abuse), 273
Accommodation, 6–7, 31, 40
ACTH (adrenocorticotropic hormone), 86–87, 92
Active uncertainty strategy, 227
Activities. *See* Behavioral activities
Adaptability, 8, 42, 325
Adaptors, 83
Addiction, Internet, 299–302
Additive scale for relationship development, 155
Adolescents. *See* Teens
Adrenocorticotropic hormone (ACTH), 86–87
Affect
    cognitive theories of emotion and representation of, 27–28
    conflict management and, 327
    defined, 28, 31

    emotional scripts for relationships and, 38–39
    imagined interactions (IIs) and, 63–64
Affection, 5, 6, 84, 216
Agape love, 200
Age
    cyber dating motives and, 237
    mate preference and, 9
    relational maintenance and, 57
    response to emotional *vs.* sexual infidelity and, 34
Agenda initiation, 102–103, 105
Aggrandized traits, 148
Aggression. *See also* Physical aggression
    communibiology assumptions regarding, 79–80
    conciliatory actions in marital conflict *vs.*, 277
    cyber, 309
    dating, 269–270, 279–280
    gender differences in response to anger and, 38

psychological, 271
scripts for escalation of anger leading
    to, 36
verbal. *See* Verbal aggression
Agrarian societies, 4, 5
American cultural script, 3
American Heart Association, 84
American National Aeronautics Space
    Administration, 134
American Psychological Association, 270
Anger
    causes of, 37–38
    gender differences and, 29–30, 38
    physiological reactions associated with,
        37
    pit-bull batterer, 288–289
    proactive response to, 332
    prototypes of, 35–36
    psychological abuse and, 272–273
    script for escalation of, 36
    scripts for, 37–38
    similarities among love, hate, jealousy,
        and, 32–35
    types of, 36–37
Antidepressants, 88
Anxious attachment style, 92–93
Anxious-preoccupied attachment style, 88
Appraisal theories of emotion, 30
Arguing, 281
    communication skill deficiency and, 81
    gender differences and, 92
    guidelines for effective, 333
    heart rate and, 106
    imagined interactions (IIs) and, 71,
        99–102
    long-term effects of, 190
    memory structures and, 176, 178
    persuasive, 285, 286
    recalling, 203
    relationship decay and, 189–190
    relationship development and, 152
    in romantic scripts, 178
    rules for, 328–330
    serial, 58, 190
    verbal aggression. *See* Verbal aggression

Argumentativeness, 281–282, 287–288
Argumentative skill deficiency, 282
Arranged marriages, 3
Asian American/White unions, 123
Assimilation, 31, 39–40
Association, friendship of, 231
Attachment, oxytocin, 89
Attachment styles
    abusive tendencies and, 92–93
    anxious-preoccupied, 88
    avoidant, 88, 92–93
    dismissive, 88
    interpersonal attraction and, 11
    rehearsal function of imagined
        interactions and, 71
    secure, 88
    stalking and, 290
Attention span, 298–299
Attraction, fatal, 6–9
Attraction-similarity model, 12
Attractors, three most common types of, 6
Attributional bias, 185, 212–213
Attributional conflict, 183–184
Attribution theory, 66, 212–213
Austen, Jane, 2
Autonomic nervous system, 32, 83
Aversive communication, 181, 184, 199
Avoidance (negative conflict tactic), 327,
    328
Avoidance attachment, 92–93
Avoidant attachment style, 88, 92–93
Avoiding stage of relationship development,
    151
Avoiding the other, 194, 199, 219

B

BBC World Service Love series, 86
Behavioral activities
    de-escalating, 181–184
    escalating, 180, 182
    inferences *vs.*, 180
    rating typicality and necessity of,
        186–189

Behavioral confirmation, 229–230
Behavioral-de-escalation strategy, 199
Beta coefficients, 102, 187, 189, 190
"Big 3," 12
Bilateral awareness, 153
Biofeedback, 90, 93, 97–98, 333–335
Biological explanation for addiction, 300
"Birds of a feather flock together," 11
Black/White unions, 123
Blood glucose, 84
Blood pressure
    diffuse physiological arousal and, 90
    flooding and, 94
    marital satisfaction and, 84
    study on impact of IIs and arguing
      among couples on heart rate, 99, 101,
      102
    systolic vs. diastolic, 85
Bodily attractiveness, 14
Boredom, 25, 185
Brain and brain chemistry. See also
    Physiology/physiological arousal
    biological love and, 81
    classifying images into "hot or not"
      categories, 13
    Default Mode Network (DMN), 56
    emotional memories, 32
    falling in love/infatuation and, 4
    human primordial mating system, 4, 149
    infatuation and, 148–149
    kissing and, 87
    love as hardwired into the, 81, 86
    romantic attraction and, 89
    social media addiction and, 300
    socioemotional processing, 55–56
    stages of love, 86–88, 148–149
Bullying, online, 307–310
Burke's five-part model of communication,
    121–122

C

Cardiovascular disease, 93
Cardiovascular system, 90, 106

Card-sorting experiment, 192–193
Catfishing, 312
Catharsis, 285–286
    function of imagined interactions (IIs),
      54–55, 59, 61, 65–67, 73, 277–278,
      285–286
    self-disclosure and, 229
Celebrities, imagined interactions (IIs) with,
    62, 74
Certainty, mindlessness and, 125
Chance, happy marriages as a result of, 2
Chat rooms, 225
Children, imaginary playmate (IP)
    relationships among, 62–63
Chocolate, 86
Circumscribing stage of relationship
    development, 150
Civil Rights Act (1964), Title VII, 255, 259
Clinginess, 88
Clusters, de-escalating, 193–195
Cobra batterers, 289
Cocoa, 86
Cognition
    role in emotion, 39
    role in establishing beliefs about
      behavior in relationships, 200
    social, 161–162
    working with emotion in conversations,
      41
Cognitive accommodation, 6–7
Cognitive editing, 71
Cognitive theories of emotion, 27–28
Cold (organizational) climate, 260
Colonial period (18th century), 4–5
Commissions, 211–212
Communibiology, 79–80, 97
Communication
    about sexual encounters, 132
    behaviors leading to breakup or divorce,
      325–326
    challenges with intercultural couples, 127
    expectations on first date, 133–134
    gender differences in approaches to, 68
    genetic and neurobiological foundation
      of, 79–80

imagined interactions (IIs)
compensating for lack of real, 54
most discussed topics among couples,
69–70
role in eliciting emotion, 35
sentiment-override hypothesis and, 41,
42–43
stage models of relationship
development and, 159–160
verbal aggression and deficiency in, 283
Communication apprehension, 80–81
Communication competence. *See also*
Constructive communication
conflict tactics for, 327–328
criteria for assessing, 324–325
definition, 324
Communication effectiveness. *See*
Constructive communication
Communication privacy management
theory, 306–307
Communication skills deficiency, 81, 283
Companionate love, 33, 256, 257
Comparison alternatives, 60, 190, 199, 212
Comparisons, social media images and, 303
Compensation function of imagined
interactions (IIs), 58–59
Complaining/complaints, 7, 91–92, 190,
215, 279, 284, 326
Computational thinking, 54
Computer-mediated communication. *See
also* Online relationships; Social media;
Social network sites
behavioral confirmation in, 229–230
decreasing uncertainty with, 227–228
emoticons and, 226
explained, 225
face-to-face communication *vs.*,
225–226
online deception and, 311–312
relationship development and, 229
self-disclosure and, 228–229
Conciseness (rule for arguing), 328, 329
Conflict. *See also* Relational decay
biological link to, 80–81

cues for escalation of, 278–279
emotional intensity and, 63–64
escalation of anger and, 35–36
features of constructive, 332
imagined interactions (IIs) conflict-
linkage theory, 80–81
kept alive through imagined
interactions, 64–65
strategies for managing, 327–328
three types of emotion during, 25
Conflict-avoiders, 11
Conflict-engagers, 11
Conflict-linkage, imagined interactions and,
57, 61, 72
Conflict-linkage theory, 57, 80–81, 282
Conflict Tactics Scale (CTS), 270–272, 285
Connotative characteristics of scripts, 38
Consideration (rule for arguing), 328–329
Constructive communication
advice for enhancing, 323
clinical observation on, 324
definition of communication
effectiveness, 325
definitions of communication
competence/effectiveness, 324–325
guidelines for resolving conflict,
332–333
linguistic cues for, 335–336
Listen Observe Verify Express
guidelines for, 330–332
role playing with conflict-resolution
vignettes, 338–340
rules for arguing, 328–330
satisfaction with relational topics
instrument, 336–338
Contempt, 29, 35, 91, 215, 326
Content analysis of escalating and de-
escalating romantic scripts, 179–185
Contentment, 149
Context, sexual scripts influenced by, 132
Conversation(s)
imagined interactions as similar to real,
55
in initial interactions, 127

linking prior conversations to anticipated, 64–66

Cooperative/friendly *versus* competitive/hostile relationships, 1

Cortisol, 81, 84, 86–87, 92

Cost escalation, 184

Counseling, imagined interactions (IIs) used for, 54, 55

Couples. *See also* Marriage/married couples; Romantic relationships
 diffuse physiological arousal in, 89–93
 engaged. *See* Engaged couples
 impact of imagined interactions (IIs) on heart rate of, 99–102
 intercultural, 127
 long-distance, 58–60, 73
 most discussed topics among, 69–70
 physiological impact on discussion of pleasing and displeasing topics by, 102–106
 unhappy. *See* Unhappy couples

Courtship
 agrarian society, 5
 biological drive for procreation and, 4
 initial impressions and, 2
 through computer contact, 4

Covert narcissism, 58

Criticizing/criticisms, 91, 190, 215, 216, 217, 279, 284, 326

Cross-complaints, 326

Cues-filtered out theories, 226

Cultivation, 250

Cultivation (mentoring relationship), 250

Cultural influences
 dating scripts, 128, 131
 infatuation and, 150
 initial interaction scripts and, 127
 organizational climate and workplace romances, 259–260
 predictors of happiness and, 27
 workplace romantic relationships and, 259–260

Cultural scripts, 3, 5, 137–138, 141, 278, 289

Cyberbullying, 307–310

Cyber dating. *See* Online dating

Cyberstalking, 275, 310–311

D

Dark chocolate, 86

Date rape, 132–134, 282–283

Date rape myths, 283

Dating. *See also* Online dating
 changes relationships and, 140
 expectations for infidelity, 189
 hooking up and, 134–135
 infidelity and, 188–189
 office. *See* Workplace romantic relationships
 physical assault in, 269
 post-college, 135–136
 relationship development and, 150, 152, 193, 197
 relationship recalibration and, 158
 rule violation in relationships, 217

Dating aggression/abuse
 initiated by women *vs.* men, 279–280
 parents recognizing signs of, 269–270
 warning signs, 271

Dating experts, 129

Dating scripts, 117, 121
 expectations about sexual intercourse and, 133–134
 first dates, 128, 129, 130–131
 getting a date, 128, 129–130
 grouping of sequences in, 130–131
 post-college, 135–136
 sequence of behaviors, 129–130
 sexual contact in, 131–134
 variations within, 128–129

Dating websites. *See* Online dating

Daydreaming, 53, 56

Decision rule, 182, 198

Declarative knowledge, 115–116

Declining quality of interpersonal relationships, 304–306

De-escalating clusters, 193–195

De-escalating memory structures, 178

De-escalating scripts/actions
  card-sorting experiment for, 192–193
  clusters of, 193–195
  script expectations, 180, 181–182
  story-segmentation analysis, 197,
    198–200
  strategies, 183–185

De-escalation stages in relationship
  development, 150–151

Default Mode Network (DMN), 56

Defensiveness, 91–92, 215, 279, 326,
  331–332

Demand/withdraw patterns, 190

Depression, 29, 44–45, 190, 234, 290, 299,
  300

Detachment, 148, 149

Developmental models
  communication behavior model,
    150–151
  criticisms of, 153–157
  differentiating stage, 152
  five-stage dissolution model, 155
  helpful uses of, 152–153
  movement through stages, 151–152,
    155, 159
  physiology model, 148–150
  post-termination awareness of
    ex-partner, 151
  relational dialectic models, 157–161
  script approach, 161–162
  stages of decay, 150–151, 155–156
  stimulus-value-role (SVR) model,
    154–155
  stories of relationship events and, 153
  three-stage awareness model, 153–154

Diagnostic and Statistical Manual (DSM),
  44–45

Dialectic model of relationship
  development, 157–161

Diastolic blood pressure, 85, 99, 108n1

Dichotomization, mindlessness and, 125

Differentiating stage of relationship
  development, 150, 152, 335–336

Diffuse physiological arousal (DPA), 89–90

Digital Pandemic (Hicks), 298

Direct strategies for ending a relationship,
  183–184

Discrepant imagined interactions (IIs), 70,
  71, 73, 102, 106, 278

Disengagement, 91, 159

Dismissive attachment style, 88

Distributive conflict, 327, 328, 332

Divorce
  causes, 6
  communication behaviors leading to,
    215
  4 horsemen and, 91
  gender differences in filing for, 103
  grounds for, in covenant marriage, 280
  occurring around the 4th year of
    marriage, 149
  physiological, cascade model of, 93–94

Domestic violence
  cycle of, 273–274
  effects on mental health, 270
  pit-bull and cobra batterers, 288–289
  statistics, 270

Dopamine, 89, 300

Downward comparisons, 303

Dual-memory model of impression
  formation, 186

Dysfunctional behavior
  communication behaviors, 325–327
  imagined interactions (IIs) and, 55,
    61–63

Dysfunctional relational scripts, 15. See also
  Relational abuse

E

Economic abuse, 273

Education level
  marriage rates and, 5
  mate preferences and, 9

Effective communication. See
  Communication competence;
  Constructive communication

Ego (motive), 253, 256–257, 300

E-harmony, 2
Elder abuse, 273
Electrodermal analysis, 84
Electroencephalogram (EEG), 84
Elite Single, 2
E-mail(s), 225, 232, 305, 308, 310, 311
Embarrassment, 29
Emoticons, 226
Emotion(s). *See also* Affect
    affecting recall of events, 40
    cultural scripts about, 289
    defining, 29–31
    as evaluative when describing romantic
        partners, 25
    expectations for, in relationships, 28
    facial scripts for communicating, 33–34
    with infatuation, 148
    influence on interpretation of behaviors,
        40–41
    moods *vs.*, 31–32
    perceptions of feelings and, 27–28
    physiological arousal and, 89
    socialization of males communicating,
        94
    social media relationships and, 43–45
    suppressing, 37
    working with cognition in conversation,
        41
Emotional abuse, 272, 273
Emotional inferences. *See* Inferences
Emotional infidelity, 33, 34
Emotional intensity, evaluation of, 63–64
Emotional scripts for relationships, 38–39
Endogenous opioids, 86
Endorcrine system, 106
Endorphins, 85, 149
Engaged couples
    imagined interactions (IIs) and,
        70– 72
    rules of conflict and, 329
    sample marriage schema of, 119–120
    symbolic interdependence, 10
Epinephrine, 32, 89
Equal *versus* unequal relationships, 1
Error-management theory, 116

Escalating memory structure actions,
    182–183
Escalating scripts/actions
    behavioral expectations, 180
    card-sorting experiment for, 192–193
    gender differences in processing,
        200–205
Excitation transfer, 282
Exit-Voice-Loyalty-Neglect Model of
    Relational Dissatisfaction, 184–185
Ex-partners
    cyberstalking by, 310–311
    Facebook and, 305
    imagined interactions (IIs) and, 53,
        60–61
    post-termination awareness of, 151
    social media and flirting with, 313
Expectations, relational, 15–16, 123. *See also*
    Knowledge structures
    emotional responses influenced by, 28
    imagined interactions and, 53, 71
    interactive scripts and, 139–140
    journal entries on, 163–166
    partner selection, 8
    relational dialectic models and, 160–161
    relationship development, 8–9, 115
    relationship satisfaction and, 10
    sample marriage schema, 119–120
    scripts for escalating relationships, 180
    scripts in de-escalating relationships,
        181–182
Experts, dating, 129
Explosion stage (cycle of abuse), 274
Expression (communication guideline),
    331–332
Extroversion, 26, 39, 58, 205, 236, 309
"Eye for an eye," 332
Eye gazing, 103
Eye rolling, 330

F

Facebook
    addiction to, 301

changing nature of relationships, 4
college professors as friends of students on, 307
cyberbullying and, 309
cyberstalking and, 310
damage from passive usage of, 45
depression and, 44
"friends" on, 73, 230–232
lacking visual social cues, 226
narcissism and, 304
passive uncertainty strategy and, 227
reasons for using, 234
relationship between social loneliness and self-disclosure on, 44
selective self-presentation on, 303
self-disclosure and, 228–229
students and professors adding each other as friends on, 238
Tinder and, 233
Facebook Addiction Disorder, 301
Face-to-face communication, 45, 59, 225–226, 229, 231–232, 234–235, 302, 307
Facial attractiveness, 14
Facial expressions, 28, 30, 279, 326. *See also* Nonverbal cues
Facial mimicry, 13–14, 89
Facial muscles, 14, 33
Facial slapping, 277
Fair Employment Practices, 258
Fait-accompli-actions, 183
False positives/negatives, 116
Familial aggression, 81
Fatal attraction, 6–9
Fearful avoidant attachments. *See* Avoidant attachment style
Filters, 148
First Date script, 128–131
Fisher, Helen, 86
Five-part model of communication (Burke), 121–122
Five-stage model of relationship development, 154
"Flat" emotion, 25
Flirting

gender differences in interpreting signs of, 116–117
head canting and, 116
mentorships and, 250
on social media with an ex-partner, 313
Flooding, 94, 97
Flow, as predictor of happiness, 26
FMRI studies, 56
Foster, Jodi, 62
Four horsemen of the apocalypse, 91–92, 98, 331
Fox, Anne-Liese Juge, 98
Friends/friendships
definition, 230
dialectic behaviors in development of, 158
friends with benefits and, 61
gender differences in same-gender, 201
imagined interactions (IIs) with, 55
rules for, 217
scripts for, 204–205
Friends with benefits (FWBs), 61, 136, 151, 179, 204–205, 246
Functional relational scripts, 15
Fundamental attribution error, 66, 213

G

Galvanic skin conductance, 84
Game theory, 278
Gay men
dating sites for, 233
verbal harassment of, 255
Gay relationships, office romances and, 252
Gender differences
addiction to technology and, 301
agenda initiation and, 102–103
attributes for long-term *vs.* short-term romantic partners, 8
avoidant attachment and, 92–93
on being influenced by physical attractiveness, 12–13
causes of anger and, 38

cyberbullying and, 309
in effects of hooking up, 135
in emotions, 29
in enduring relational abuse, 280
in expression of emotions, 289
filing for divorce and, 103
in formation of online relationships, 234
in interpreting flirtatious signs, 116
in intimate-relationship scripts, 162–166
marital dissolution and, 92
marital satisfaction and, 9
in omissions and commissions, 219–220
in partners' reactions to expressions of
   anger, 38
in physiological effects of marital
   conflict, 89
in predicting developmental beliefs, 187
in redundancy in romantic scripts,
   176–178
in relational abuse, 276–278
in responses to being angered, 38
romantic expectations and, 9
sexual initiatives and, 132
Gender-role stereotypes, 203
Gender scripts, in office romances, 251–252
Generation Z youth, 302
Genetics
   communication apprehension and,
      80–81
   as predictor of happiness, 26, 27
Getting a Date script, 128–131
Glycohemoglobin, 84
Gottman's four horsemen of the apocalypse,
   91–92, 98, 331
Grice's maxim of non-redundancy, 178–179
Gridlock, 91
Guilt, 29

H

Habits, mindlessness and, 125–126
Happiness, predictors of, 26–27
Happy couples

arguing rules and, 330
linguistic cues use and, 335–336
mutual understanding and, 160
nonverbal cues and, 325
rules for arguing and, 330
validation among, 326
"Hard" emotion, 25
Hate, 32–35
Head canting, 116
HeartMath Institute, 32, 85, 90, 93
Heart rate
   ability to calm down and, 90–91
   communicating emotion and, 34
   diffuse physiological arousal and, 90
   discussion of pleasant and unpleasant
      topics and, 104–105
   emotions and, 34
   flooding and, 94
   remaining elevated after an argument,
      32
   resiliency of negative emotions on, 93
   resting, 84
   study of the impact of IIs and arguing
      among couples on, 99–102
Heart rate interbeat intervals (IBI), 83–84,
   103, 106, 108n2
Heart rate variability, 81, 91–93, 103–104,
   190, 324, 333
Heart rhythms, biofeedback and, 93,
   333–334
Heat beats, interbeat intervals and, 83–84
Hierarchy, organizational, 252–255
High-level interruptions, 28
Hinckley, John, 62
Holman v. Indiana, 159
Honeymoon period (cycle of abuse), 274
Hooking up, 134–137, 151, 232, 236–237
Hostile work environment, 255, 257
Hot (organizational) climate, 260
HOTorNOT.com, 12
Human primordial mating system, 4, 149
Humor, 72, 74
Hyperintimacy, 275–276, 290, 311
Hyperpersonal interaction, theory of, 312

Hyperpersonal perspective, 229–230

I

IBI. *See* Heart rate interbeat intervals (IBI)
Idealization of partners, 58
Idioms, 151
"I love you," 125, 155, 183
Imaginary playmate (IPs), 1, 62–63
Imagined interactions (IIs), 16
   affect and, 63–64
   catharsis function of, 54–55, 59, 61,
     65–67
   characteristics of, 283–284
   comparisons between friends and friends
     with benefits (FWBs), 61
   compensation function of, 58–59
   conflict linkage function, 61, 72
   conflict-linkage theory, 57, 80–81, 282
   creating relationship scripts through,
     52–53
   daydreaming, 53–54
   with ex-partners, 60–61
   explained, 52
   gender differences in use of, 67–69
   imaginary playmates and, 62–63
   long-distance relationships, 58–60
   main features of, 53–56
   marital conflict and, 277–278
   in marriage, 69–72
   parasocial relationships and, 61–62
   rehearsal function of, 53, 59, 65, 71–72
   relational maintenance function of,
     57–59
   self-understanding function, 54, 61, 66,
     73, 285–286
   study on impact on heart rate, 99–102
   third-party, 56–57
   used to connect prior conversations
     together, 64–66
   verbal aggression and, 282, 283–290,
     285–290
   in virtual relationships, 72–73

Imagined interactions (IIs) conflict-linkage
   theory, 80–81
Implicit benefit-of-the-doubt, 214–216
Income, of husbands *vs.* wives, 5
Independents (marital type), 70–71
India, arranged marriages in, 3
Indirect strategies for ending a relationship,
   184
Industrial Revolution, 3–4
Industrial society, 3
Infants, 4-year cycle of marriage and, 4–5
Infatuation, 148–149
Inferences, 25
   associated with relationship decay,
     185–186
   behavioral activities *vs.*, 180
   with commissions and omissions, 219,
     220, 221n1
   stimulus-value-role (SVR) model and,
     154
Infidelity, 2, 33, 39, 188–189, 253
Information theory, 176
Initial impressions, 2, 6–7, 15, 41, 126
Initial interaction scripts, 126–127
Initiation (mentoring relationship), 250
Initiation, agenda, 102–103
Instagram, 226, 299, 331
   cyberstalking and, 310
   depression and, 45, 302
   "friending" on, 4, 231
   narcissism and, 304
   passive uncertainty strategy and, 227
   reassurance-seeking and, 234, 302
   selective self-presentation and, 230
   social media addiction and, 300
   uncertainty reduction and, 227
Institute of HeartMath, 90, 333–334
Institutional abuse, 273
Integrative conflict tactics, 327, 328
Intense *versus* superficial relationships, 1
Interactive scripts
   changes in, 138, 140
   expectations and, 139, 140
   memorable messages, 138, 139

misunderstandings in, 139
uncommunicated, 140
Interactive uncertainty strategy, 227–228
Interbeat intervals. *See* Heart rate interbeat
intervals (IBI)
Intercultural couples, initial interaction
scripts and, 127
Internal dialogues. *See* Imagined interactions
(IIs)
Internal locus of control, 26
International Center for Media and the
Public Agenda (ICMPA), 301
Internet. *See also* Social media
addiction, 299–302
online relationship scripts, 136–137
social contact among older adults and, 44
Internet groups, 121
Interpersonal attraction, 11–15
Interpersonal communication theories,
227–230
Interpersonal needs theory, 158–159, 166
Interpersonal resource theory, 191
Interracial relationships, 123
Intimacy
colonial period, 5
continuum of, 1
ending a relationship by withdrawal of,
184
in friends with benefits, 61
history of concept of, 3
journal entries on expectations for,
163–165
relationship commitment dependent
on, 5
social penetration model of relational
development and, 157
stage models of relationship
development and, 147–148, 159
Intimate relationship scripts, gender
differences in, 162–166
Intimidation, 276, 290
Introversion, 236–237, 300
Intrusive thinking, 36, 71, 74, 148
Invasion tactics, 276

Inventory of Marital Conflict, 338
"I" statements, 333, 335–336, 340
Item-total correlation, 221n1

J

Japanese, imagined interactions (IIs) and, 55
Jealousy, 29, 32–35, 40, 182, 275, 305
Jokes/joke-telling, 72, 74, 126
Journal entries
on expectations form intimacy and
relationships, 163–166
imagined interaction about an
ex-girlfriend, 60–61
imagined interaction about seeing a
long-distance lover, 59–60
imagined interaction account of a man
encountering a woman after a long
absence, 66–67

K

Kin resemblance, 14
Kissing, 86–87, 183
Kissing compatibility theory, 87
Knowledge structures, 16, 33–34, 115–116,
117. *See also* Schemata

L

Lateral comparisons, 303
Linear assumption, 155, 156
Linked imagined interactions (IIs), 64–67
Listening (communication guideline), 330
Listen Observe Verify Express guidelines,
330–332
Lock-and-key view of relationship
development, 159–160
Loneliness
imagined interactions (IIs) and, 62

Internet addiction and, 300
Internet groups and, 121
Internet use and, 235–236
online relationships and, 234–235
social media and, 43–45, 302
Long-distance couples, imagined
interactions (IIs) and, 58–60, 73
Long-term attachment, 88
Long-term relationships, 8–10, 57. *See also*
Engaged couples; Marriage/married
couples
Louisiana, 269
Louisiana State University (LSU), 82–83,
99, 192, 195
Love. *See also* Romantic love
brain chemistry and, 81
disengagement and, 159
physiology of, 85–89
romantic *vs.* obsessive, 4
similarities among hate, anger, jealousy
and, 32–35
as a social emotion, 29
women's distinctions between liking and,
201
workplace romances and, 256, 257
LOVE acronym, 324, 330–331, 340
Love and commitment *versus* unlove and
instability dimension of romance, 38–39
"The love is blind bias," 14
Love map, 150
Low-level interruptions, 28
Loyalty, 184–185
Lust, 85–86, 89

M

Magazines, learning about relationships in,
124
Maladaptive Internet use (MIU), 301–302
Males. *See also* Gender differences
initiating dating violence, 279–280
initiative in asking for a date, 128
marrying up, 5

matching hypothesis and, 12
negative emotions and, 29
physical attraction and, 12
sequences of dating behavior and, 129
stalking of, 275
withdrawal by, 94
Marital conflict. *See also* Conflict; Relational
decay
aggressive *vs.* conciliatory actions in,
277–278
physiological arousal and, 89–93
positive imagined interactions (IIs) and,
65–66
Marital satisfaction. *See also* Happy couples;
Marital conflict; Unhappy couples
argumentativeness and, 281
arranged marriages, 3
blood pressure and, 84
communication effectiveness
influencing, 188
gender differences in, 9
negative affect and, 28
relationship awareness and, 68–69
in study on discussion of pleasant and
displeasing topics, 103
verbal aggression and, 281
withdrawal and, 185
Marital types, 70
Marriage/married couples
4-year cycle of, 4–5
affection and, 6
collecting an oral history of, 68
economic gains from, 5
imagined interactions among, 69–72
workplace romantic relationships
resulting in, 246–248
Marriage rates, decline in, 5
Marriage script
interracial marriage, 123
wedding and, 137–138
Matchbox Interaction Lab, Louisiana State
University (LSU), 99
Match.com, 2, 4
Matching hypothesis, 10,–12, 123

Mateen, Justin, 233
Mean arterial pressure (MAP), 85, 99, 101, 102, 108n1
Media richness theory, 226
Mehrabian formula, 330
Memorable messages, 138–139
Memory(ies). *See also* Knowledge structures; Schemata
  expectations for relationships and, 115
  gender differences in, 67–68, 203
  influencing relational scripts, 16
  knowledge structures and, 117
  relationship development and, 159
  scripts accessed from, 124
  sentiment-override hypothesis and, 40
Memory organization packet, 121
Memory structures, 17
  actions, 182–183
  card-sorting experiment, 192
  limitations, 191
  redundancy of romantic scripts and, 176–179
  scenes and, 124
  story-segmentation analysis, 195–200
Men. *See* Males
Mental health, domestic violence and, 270
Mental templates, 150
Mentoring scripts, 249–251
Metamemory organization packets, 121
Meta-talk, 71
Military dating sites, 233
Miller v. Department of Corrections (2005), 257
Mindfulness, 124
Mindlessness, 124–126
Mindreading statements, 326
Minor assaults, 271
Misinformation on social media, 311
Mobile dating apps, 136–137, 226, 230, 232–233
Monogamy, 149
Moods
  emotion *vs.*, 31–32

sentiment-override hypothesis and, 41–42
Morry's attraction-similarity model, 12
Motion, in relationships, 15, 152–153
Mozart effect, 324
Murstein, B. I., 2
Muscle movements, 84
Mutual awareness, 153
Mutuality, 39
Mutual understanding, 160
Mutual user relationships, 256–257

N

Nagging, 92, 190
Names, friending on Facebook and, 229
Narcissism, 58, 300, 303–304
National Center for Biotechnology Information (NCBI), 299
National Center on Elder Abuse, 273
National Crime Victimization Survey, 277–278
National Family Violence Survey, 276–277
National Intimate Partner and Sexual Violence Survey, 275
National Survey of Child and Adolescent Well-Being, 271
National Violence against Women Survey, 271
Necessity ratings, 187–189
Negative affect, marital satisfaction and, 28
Negative conflict tactics, 327–328
Negative emotions
  anxious avoidant attachment and, 93
  appraisal theories on, 30
  cited in gender differences in emotions study, 29
  expressed on Twitter, 44
  heart rate and, 93
  heart rhythms and, 333–334
Negative imagined interactions (IIs), 57
Negative loyalty, 185
Negotiated farewell strategy, 184

Neuroticism, 205, 300
Neurotransmitters, 81, 149
Neurotrophin nerve growth factor, 87
Newlyweds
    idealizing each other, 14
    stress hormones in, 92
Niche dating sites, 233
Nonverbal cues, 281, 325, 330–331. *See also*
    Facial expressions; Voice qualities
Norepinephrine, 32, 89
Novices, dating, 129
Null behaviors, 213–214, 216–217

O

Observation (communication guideline),
    330
*Obsession with Technology and Overcoming Its
    Hold on Us* (Rosen), 299
Obsessive compulsive disorder (OCD),
    87–88
Obsessive love, 4
Obsessive relational intrusion (ORI), 276
Office romances. *See* Workplace romantic
    relationships
Omissions, 211–212
Oncale-v-Sundowner Offshore Serv., Inc., 259
One-sided relationships, imagined
    interactions (IIs) and, 61–63
Online dating, 2–4, 226
    age and motives for, 237
    attitudes toward, 237
    dating sites, 232–233
    deception and, 312
    for "hook up" reasons, 237
    hyperpersonal perspective applied to,
        230
    importance of physical attractiveness
        and, 12–13
    matching hypothesis and, 12
    motives for, 136–137
Online deception, 311–312

Online games, relationships with characters
    on, 1
Online relationships, 1. *See also* Social media
    attitudes toward, 237–238
    characteristics of people who form,
        234–237
    friendships, 230–232
    imagined interactions in, 72–73
    romantic relationships, 232–233
    scripts, 136–137
    self-disclosure and, 228–229
"Opposites attract," 11
Optimism, 26, 44, 71, 84, 190
Oral History Interview, 93–97
Organizational climate, 260
Organizational culture, 258, 260
Organizational romances. *See* Workplace
    romantic relationships
Organizations, imagined interactions (IIs)
    in, 65
Our Time, 2
Oxytocin, 85–86, 89, 94, 331

P

Parasocial relationships, 1, 53, 61–62, 73–74
Parasympathetic nervous system (PNS),
    83–84, 90–91
Parental verbal aggression, 280
Parents. *See also* Attachment styles
    abusive relationships and violence by,
        280
    cyberbullying and, 308, 311
    influence of empathy and support from,
        79–80
    learning about relationships through,
        165, 166
    life satisfaction influenced by conflict in
        marriages of, 26
    mate selection based on potential for, 5
    memorable moments and, 138
    recognizing signs of dating abuse,
        269–270

relationship scripts based on interactions with, 16
Partial correlations, 219–220
Particularistic resources, 191
Passionate love, 256
Passive uncertainty strategy, 227, 233
Pathological Internet use (PIU), 301–302
PEA (phenylethylamine), 85–86
Perceived social isolation, Internet use and, 44
Personal scenes, 121, 122
Perspiration, diffuse physiological arousal and, 90
Persuasive arguing, 285–287
Pessimists, 84
Pets, relationships with, 1
Phases, 148
Phenolics, 86
Physical abuse
    explained, 272
    link between verbal aggression and, 286–288
    psychological abuse vs., 272
Physical affection, 115, 150, 159, 162, 180, 182–183, 192–193, 197
Physical aggression, 281, 282. See also Physical abuse
    escalation of anger resulting in, 35–36
    gender differences in, 38
    imagined interactions and the link between verbal aggression and, 283–290
    minor assaults, 271
    severe assault, 271
Physical appearance/attractiveness
    Facebook friends and, 229
    friending on Facebook and, 229
    judging personality impressions of strangers based on, 2
    ratings on importance of, 8, 12–13, 14–15
    relationship formation and, 11
    selective self-presentation with online communication and, 230, 302–303

sexual harassment cases and, 257–258
    similarities in (matching hypothesis) and, 12–13
Physical assault, 271
Physical attraction
    age and facial vs. bodily attractiveness, 14
    as dimension of interpersonal attraction, 12
    gender differences in intimate-relationship scripts and, 162
    hormones and, 85
Physical coercion, 285–286
Physical scenes, 121–122
Physical violence. See Physical aggression
Physiological signs of flooding, 94
Physiology/physiological arousal
    anger and, 37
    common measures of, 83–85
    discussing pleasing and displeasing topics and, 102–106
    impact of imagined interactions and arguing on heart rate, 99–102
    physiological, cascade model of divorce, 93–94
    physiological development of love, 85–89
    reasons for studying relationships and, 82–83
    satirical wedding vows and, 97, 98
    script for relational decay, 89–93
Pick-up lines, 124
Pit-bull batterer, 288–289
Pluralistic society, 6
PNS. See Parasympathetic nervous system (PNS)
Pollyanna Principle, 41
Polyvagal theory, 91
Pornography, 137, 138
Positive emotions
    appraisal theories on, 30
    cited in gender differences in emotions study, 29
    in emotional people, 29

heart rhythms and, 333–334
imagined interactions (IIs) and, 59, 63
impact on the body, 33
power of, in relationships, 90
Quick Coherence technique and, 335
suppressing emotions and decrease in, 37
Positive imagined interactions (IIs), 65–66
Positive understanding (rule for arguing), 328–329
Post-Millennial generation, 302
Post-termination awareness, 60, 151, 199
Predictive romantic expectations, 8–9
Premature cognitive commitment, 126
Prescriptive rules, 217, 219, 328
The Presentation of Self in Everyday Life (Goffman), 312
Privacy issues, social media and, 306–307
"Privacy paradox," 306–307
Proactive imagined interactions (IIs), 53–54, 55, 58, 64, 106, 282
Proactive responses to anger, 332
Proactivity (imagined interactions), 286
Procedural knowledge, 116
Procreation, biological drives for, 4
Protégé, 223, 249–251
Prototypical de-escalating scripts, 194
Prototypical escalating scripts, 195–196
Proximity theory, 248–249
Prozac, 88
Pseudo-agreements, 328, 330
Pseudo de-escalation, 184
Psychological abuse, 272–273
Psychological aggression, 271, 286
Pulse, 83, 90. *See also* Heart rate
Pursuit and proximity (stalking), 276

Q

Quick Coherence tool, 334–334
"Quid-pro-quo," 278
Quid pro quo sexual harassment, 255

R

Racial homogamy, 123
Rad, Sean, 233
Rage, 35–36, 282, 283
Rape, 272. *See also* Date rape
Rape myths, 132, 283
Rationality (rule for arguing), 328, 329
Reagan, Ronald, 62
Reassurance-seeking, 234, 302
Recalibration, relationship, 158
Receptivity, friendship of, 231
Reciprocity, friendship of, 231
Reciprocity of disclosure, 158
Redefinition (mentoring relationship), 250
Redundancy coefficient, 179
Redundancy in romantic scripts, 176–179, 219
Regret, 29
Regulation of interaction, 218
Rehearsal function of imagined interactions (IIs), 59, 65, 71
Rehearsing messages, 102
Relational abuse. *See also* Domestic violence; Verbal aggression
    Conflict Tactics Scale for measuring, 270–272
    cues to escalating conflict, 278–279
    dating aggression, 279–280
    gender differences in, 276–278, 280
    scripts for warning signs of, 270–271
    stalking, 274–276
    statistics on, 269–270, 276–277
    types of, 272–273
Relational cognitive approach, 160
Relational cohesion, 217–218
Relational conflict. *See* Conflict
Relational decay. *See also* Conflict; De-escalating scripts/actions; Marital conflict
    blame for breakups, 183–184, 211
    communication behaviors leading to, 325–327
    inferences associated with, 185–186

influence of expectations about relationships on, 161–162

linguist codes of omission and commission, 211–212

physiological script for, 93–98

predicting beliefs about, 189–190

reasons for breakups, 217–218

reversal hypothesis for, 159

semantic codes of action, 212–220

underlying dimensions, 191–200

Relational deterioration. *See* Relational decay

Relational development. *See* Developmental models; Relationship development

Relational dialectics, 157–161, 190

Relational expectations. *See* Expectations, relational

Relational investment model, 199

Relational maintenance function of imagined interactions, 57–59

Relational roles, 217–218

Relational satisfaction. *See also* Marital satisfaction

imagined interactions (IIs) and, 72

observer ratings of partners' physical attractiveness and, 14

use of idioms and, 151

Relational schema, 10, 15, 118–120, 152, 176

Relational scripts. *See also* Romantic scripts; Scripts

created through imagined interactions (IIs), 52–53

fatal attraction, 6–9

function of, 123

interracial relationships and, 123

introduction to, 15–17

learned from magazines, 124

Relationship awareness, marital quality and, 68–69

Relationship development. *See also* Developmental models

computer-mediated communication and, 226

expectations of, 8–9

linear assumption, 155

online relationships, 226–230

script approach, 161–162

turning points and, 182–183

typicality *vs.* necessity in predicting beliefs about, 186–189

underlying dimensions of, 191–200

Relationship diversity, 1

Relationships. *See also* Romantic relationships; Workplace romantic relationships

classified among four bipolar dimensions, 1–2

developing. *See* Relationship development

exchange of resources in, 191

expectations for. *See* Expectations, relational

mental templates for, 150

predictive of life satisfaction, 26

recalling past history of, 94–97

symbolic interdependence in, 9–10

turning points in, 182–183

Relationship satisfaction. *See also* Marital satisfaction

rating of physical attractiveness and, 14

recalling past history of relationships and, 94–97

Relationship worldview, 9–10, 160

Relationship Worldview Inventory, 9–10

Relations Station Lab, 102

Representation of affect, 27–28

Reproductive strategy, 4–5, 149

Respiration, 84

Restless leg movement, 83

Restrictive rules, 217–218, 328

Retroactive imagined interactions (IIs), 53–54, 55, 58, 60, 64, 277–278, 282, 335

Rich-get-richer hypothesis, 236

Ritualism, 125–126

Romantic attraction, as second stage of love, 86–89

Romantic love

attachment stage of, 149
characteristics of, 33
detachment stage of, 149
infatuation stage of, 148–149
percentage of relationships as, 148
remaining steady, 4
as a universal experience, 86
Romantic relationships. *See also* Online
dating; Workplace romantic relationships
emotional scripts for, 38–39
expectations on development of, 8–9
intercultural differences, 259–260
long-term commitment *vs.* short-term, 8
mentoring relationships and, 249–250
online, 232–233
reading magazines to learn about, 124
Romantic scripts, 175
card-sorting for escalating and
de-escalating actions in, 192–193
content, 179–183
de-escalating scripts, 183–185, 193–195
gender differences in generating and
processing escalating, 200–205
redundancy and the complexity of,
176–179
sequential ordering of expected actions
in, 191
story-segmentation analysis, 195–200
Roommate relationships, gender
differences in using imagined interactions
to maintain, 69
Rules-based approach, 216–219
Rules for arguing, 328–330
Rules for conflict resolution, 218–219
Rules for disclosure, 216–217
Rumination, 283, 289–290

S

Sadness, 29
Saliva, kissing and, 87
Salivary control studies, 81
Salzburg Academy on Media and Global
Change, 301

Same-gender friendships, 201
Same-sex sexual harassment, 258–260
Sarcasm, 81, 184, 189–190, 278–279, 325,
326
Scenes, 121–122, 124, 197
Schemata, 15, 118–120, 123, 126, 131
Scripts. *See also* Relational scripts; Romantic
scripts
accessing from memory, 124
for anger, 37–38
changes in, 3
changes in interactive, 138, 140
for constructive communication. *See*
Constructive communication
cultural performances for sex, 137–138
dating, 117, 121, 128–131
de-escalating. *See* De-escalating scripts/
actions
defined, 122
development of. *See* Developmental
models
escalation. *See* Escalating scripts/actions
for escalation of anger leading to
aggression, 36
for friendship *vs.* friends with benefits
(FWBs), 204–205
function of, 124
gender differences in intimate-
relationship, 162–166
initial interaction, 126–127
interactive. *See* Interactive scripts
memorable messages and, 138–139
mentoring, 249–251
as mindless, 122–123
mindlessness and, 124–126
online relationship, 136–137
pair bonding rituals, 2
primary function of, 117–118
reflecting escalation of anger, 35–36
relationship development and, 161–162
for romantic relationships, 38–39
scenes, 121–122, 124
sexual, 131–136
sexual harassment, 254–258
stalking behavior, 276

uncommunicated interactive, 140
  for warning signs of abuse, 271
Second Life, 299–300
Secure attachment style, 71, 88
Selective self-presentation, 230, 302–303
Self-adaptors, 83
Self-disclosure
  expectation for relationship
    development, 180, 182
  on Facebook, 44
  in friends with benefits, 61
  gender differences in, 202–203
  online relationships and, 227–229, 235
  rating typicality *vs.* necessity of, 188
  relational development and, 150, 152,
    158, 197
Self-esteem
  anger and, 35
  attachment type and, 88
  criticisms and, 326
  cyberbullying and, 308
  cyber dating and, 136, 236–237
  emotion regulation and, 37
  Internet addiction and, 300
  jealousy and, 33
  as predictor of happiness, 26
  preference for relational partners and,
    15–16
  self-disclosure on Facebook and, 231
  social media and, 300
  social networking use and, 234
Self-expansion model, 4
"Selfies," 304
Self-understanding, 54, 61, 66, 73, 285, 286
Semantic code referencing, 211–220
  attributional explanations, 212–213
  gender differences in omissions and
    commissions, 219–220
  implicit benefit-of-the-doubt
    explanation, 214–216
  linguistic codes of omission and
    commissions, 211, 212
  null language codes, 214
  rules-based explanation, 216–219
Senior dating sites, 233

Sense of humor, 3, 8, 12–13, 72
Sentiment-override hypothesis, 39–43
Separates (marital type), 70
Separation (mentoring relationship), 250
Sequences of dating behavior, 129–130
Serial conflict/arguing, 58
Serotonin, 86, 88–89, 290, 300, 323
Severe assaults, 271
Sex
  gender differences in interpreting
    flirtatious signs and, 116
  lustful, 86
Sex differences. *See* Gender differences
Sex hormones, 85
Sex role stereotypes, 162
"Sexting," 303
Sexual abuse, 272
Sexual favoritism, 257
Sexual harassment scripts, 128, 254–259
Sexual infidelity, 33–34
Sexual intercourse/encounters
  cyber dating and, 137
  date rape, 133–134
  as escalating activity, 182, 192
  friends with benefits, 136, 204–205
  hooking up, 134–136
  men rating necessity of for intimacy, 203
  mentoring relationships and, 250–251
  pornography and, 137–138
  relational development and, 151, 175,
    197–198
  with robots or androids, 134
  "sleeping together," 197–198
  wedding and, 137–138
Sexual peak, beliefs about gender differences
  in, 117
Sexual schema, 116
Sexual scripts, 131–136, 204
"Sexual selfies," 303
Shyness, 234–235, 300
Signal detection theory, 278–279
Simulation heuristic, 64
Skin conductance, 84
Skype, 226
Slapping, 277

"Sleeping together," 197–198
Smiling, 129
Social abuse, 272
Social attraction, 11
Social cognition, 161–162
Social comparison theory, 303
Social compensation hypotheses, 236
Social emotions, 29
Social homogamy, 9
Social information processing theory, 226, 232
Social isolation, 272. *See also* Loneliness
Social loneliness. *See* Loneliness
Social media, 1
    addiction to, 299–302
    attention span impacted by, 298–299
    cyberbullying and, 307–310
    cyberstalking, 310–311
    declining quality of interpersonal
        relationships and, 304–306
    drug and alcohol references on, 306
    emotions and, 43–45
    employment decision and, 306
    imagined interactions and, 72–73
    loneliness and, 43–44
    misinformation and, 311
    narcissism and, 303–304
    online deception and, 311–312
    relationship development through,
        226–230
    selective self-presentation with, 302–303
    traditional media *vs.*, 298
Social network sites, 225, 226. *See also*
    Facebook; Instagram
    changing the nature of friendship,
        230–232
    cyberstalking and disclosing personal
        information on, 310
    Internet addiction and, 299
    privacy issues, 306–307
    reassurance-seeking and, 302
    teen use of, 234
Social-penetration escalating stages model,
    155, 157, 193, 198, 199, 205

Social penetration theory, 228–229
Societal scene, 121–122
Society for Human Resource Management,
    247–248
Socioeconomic status, dating scripts and,
    128
Socioemotional/informal *versus*
    task-oriented/formal relationships, 1
"Soft" emotion, 25
Soldiers, deployed, 59
Somatic activity, 83
"Soulmate" script, 97
Specificity, 67, 156, 177, 283, 285–286
Speed dating, 13, 15
Spreading activation, 41–42, 195
Stage of relationship development. *See*
    Developmental models
Stages of relationship decay, 150–151,
    155–156
Stagnating stage of relationship
    development, 151
Stalking, 272, 274–276, 290
Stalking script, 128
Standard of living, level of happiness and, 27
State-of-the-relationship talk strategy, 183
Stimulus-value-role (SVR) theory, 2–3,
    154–155
Stonewalling, 92, 94, 215, 279, 326–327
Story-reading procedure, 193
Story-segmentation analysis, 195–200
Stress
    biofeedback for reducing, 333–335
    cortisol and, 86–87
    verbal aggression and, 281
Stress hormones, 92
Stress reactivity, conflict intensity and, 81
StudiVZ, 310–311
Subliminal imitations of facial expressions,
    13–14
Subliminal linguistic cues, 335
Suppressed rage, 282
Survey of Relational Issues, 69–70
SVR theory, 154–155, 203
Sweating, 94

Symbolic interdependence, 9–10
Sympathetic nervous system (SNS), 32, 80, 91
Systems theory, 191
Systolic blood pressure, 84, 85, 99, 108n1

T

Taiwanese bloggers, 228
Task attraction, 11–12
Taxi Driver (film), 62
Teens
    cyberbullying and, 308–309
    Internet addiction and, 301–302
    self-cyberbullying by, 311
    social media and depression among, 44–45
    social media-driven narcissism and, 304
    social media use and comparisons by, 303
    use of social networking sites, 234
Temperate (organizational) climate, 260
Tension building stage (cycle of abuse), 273–274
Termination stage of relationship development, 151
Testosterone, 85
Text-messaging, 59, 182, 186, 192, 225, 299, 305, 308
Thai, imagined interactions (IIs) and, 55
Theorem 1 of II conflict-management theory, 282
Theorem 4 of II conflict-management theory, 282
The punctuation problem, 158
"Thin slices," 2
Third-party imagined interactions (TPIIs), 56–57
Threats, 311
Three-stage awareness model, 153–154
Tinder, 4, 137, 226, 233, 300
"Tit for tat" strategy, 278

Title VII. *See* Civil Rights Act (1964), Title VII
Topic avoidance, 185
Traditionals (marital type), 70–72
Turning points, 182–183
Twin studies, 27
Twitter, 44, 226, 310, 331, 333
Typicality ratings/beliefs, 187, 189, 190

U

Uncertainty
    imagined interactions (IIs) and, 54–56, 102
    mindlessness and, 125
    omissions, 216
    relationship decay and, 185
Uncertainty reduction theory, 227–228
Unhappy couples
    arguing with negative emotions, 325
    cycle of cross-complaints among, 326
    expression of emotions by, 325
    negativity in communication by, 216
    physiological arousal and, 90
    reactivity exhibited in, 92
    validation and, 331
Unilateral awareness, 153
Universalistic resources, 191
University of Maryland, 301
Upward comparisons, 303
Urban society, 3
Utah, 269
Utilitarian relationships, 247, 252, 256, 257

V

Valence, 31, 283
Validation, 326, 331, 340
Vasopressin, 86, 89
Vegetarians, dating sites for, 233
Verbal aggression
    argumentativeness and, 281

biological link to, 80–81
communication skills deficiency and, 283
date rape and, 282–283
defined, 281
physical violence and, 270, 282–290
stress and, 281
Verbal imagery, 52–53
Verify (communication guideline), 331
Violence. See Domestic violence; Physical aggression; Relational abuse
Violence (stalking), 276
Virtual relationships. See Online relationships
Visual imagery, 53
Voice qualities, 2–3, 101, 279, 325, 330–331

W

Weddings, 96, 137–138, 141
Wedding vows, satirical, research-based, 97–98
"We" orientation/"we-ness," 95, 97, 182, 333, 335–336, 340
Wet measures of physiological activity, 84
Whining, 91–92, 215, 326
Withdrawal, 32–33, 92. See also Stonewalling
    diffuse physiological arousal and, 90, 91
    ending a relationship with, 213
    in imagined interaction, 286
    marital satisfaction and, 185
    serial arguing and, 190
Women. See also Gender differences
    abuse of. See Relational abuse
    cyberstalking by, 311
    initiating dating violence, 279–280
    initiation of conflict by, 102–103
    "losing" in office romances, 251–252
    marrying up, 5
    matching hypothesis and, 12
    selecting partners looking like their father, 14

sexual scripts and, 132
stalking, 275–276
stonewalling by, 326–327
in the workforce, 251
Working out of the home, 3–4
"Work-it-out" relational script, 97
Workplace romantic relationships
    coworkers and, 246–247
    definitions, 246
    difficulties resulting from, 247–248
    gender scripts in, 251–252
    hierarchy differences in, 252–255
    intercultural differences and, 259–260
    mentoring scripts and, 249–251
    prevalence of, 246–247, 251
    proximity theory and, 248–249
    results of, 246
    sexual harassment as a result of ending of, 256–257
    typologies of, 247
    unwarranted gossip about, 245
Workplace sexual harassment, 254–259
World Health Organization, 269
Wrist movement, 83, 101, 104–105

Y

Young Diagnostic Questionnaire for Internet Addiction, 301
"You" statements, 333, 335–336, 340
YouTube, 309

Z

Zoosk, 2
Z test of correlation differences, 219–220
Zuckerberg, Mark, 73